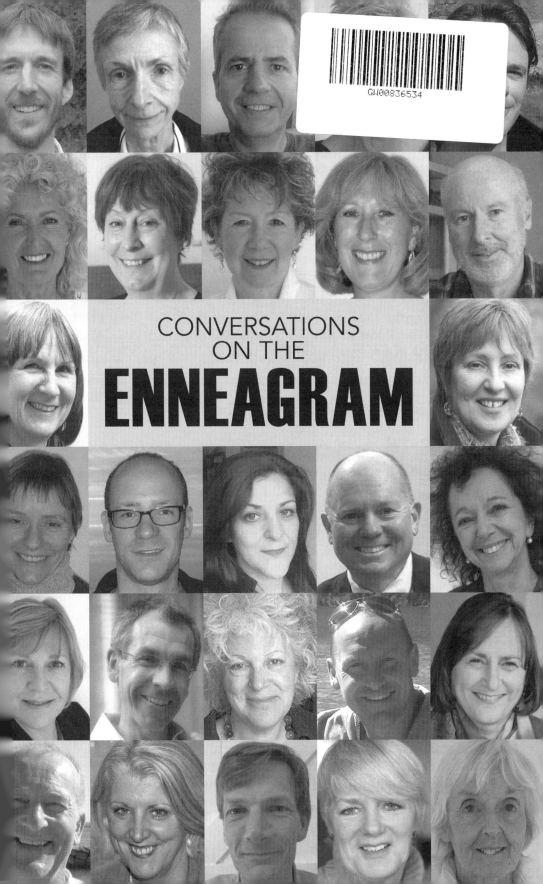

CONVERSATIONS ON THE
ENNEAGRAM

Conversations on the Enneagram first published in 2015 in Great Britain by Cherry Red Books (a division of Cherry Red Records), Power Road Studios, 114 Power Road, London W4 5PY.

Copyright © concious.tv 2015

ISBN: 978 1 909454 34 7

Design Dave Johnson
Cover by Kilian Gilbert
Printed and bound by Ashford Colour Press, UK

Conversations on the Enneagram

A collection of interviews and panels

Edited by Eleonora Gilbert

TABLE OF CONTENTS

Introductions

Eleonora Gilbert
The transformative role of the Enneagram in my life 6
Iain and Renate McNay
Our journey with the Enneagram 10

Interviews and Panels

Sandra Maitri
Introduction to the Enneagram 15
Panel: *Type One* 27
Panel: *Type Two* 42
Panel: *Type Three* 54
Panel: *Type Four* 69
Panel: *Type Five* 84
Panel: *Type Six* 99
Panel: *Type Seven* 114
Panel: *Type Eight* 129
Panel: *Type Nine* 144
Tom Condon
Living the Dynamic Enneagram 158
Tom Condon
The Enneagram and relationships 173
Helen Palmer
Relationships matter: The Enneagram tells us how 188
Ginger Lapid-Bogda
The Enneagram in business 204
Sandra Maitri
Passions and Virtues 221
Helen Palmer
The Enneagram: Gateway to spiritual liberation 234
Faisal Muqaddam
The Essential Enneagram as a spiritual path to awakening 250
Claudio Naranjo
Seeker After Truth 265

Notes

Bibliography and Websites 279
conscious.tv – Information 280
conscious.tv – The idea 281
Acknowledgements 284

The transformative role of the Enneagram in my life

Eleonora Gilbert

It all started in 1997 when I first joined the Diamond Heart Approach in California. This became my spiritual path for over thirteen years, and here is where I heard the word 'Enneagram' for the first time.

What the Enneagram provided for spiritual seekers such as myself seemed rather mysterious. This was exacerbated by the fact that our group teachers, despite having done personal work with the Enneagram in relation to their own work in the Diamond Heart process, did not include the Enneagram principles in their teachings. There was so much hype amongst us students about the possibility the Enneagram held for understanding our personality at a deeper level, that I was left with no alternative but to seek Enneagram teachers back in the UK.

The prospect of at long last finding something that would shed light on all the darkest recesses of my mind only filled me with curiosity, hope, and great expectation. I had no fear in exploring my psyche. I had gone through years of therapy, trained as a psychosynthesis therapist, participated in self-developmental workshops for decades, and attended numerous trainings. What other stones could possibly have been left unturned in what I considered an already healthy psyche? My motivation for exploring what the Enneagram offered was to be as unencumbered as possible by personality obstacles, to better absorb and integrate the Diamond Approach teachings. I think you can see already, in my enthusiasm and desire for the Holy Grail called 'enlightenment', that the delusional process was very much alive and running the show. Still, it is all about the journey and not arriving at the destination, and the Enneagram journey whilst not being exactly 'fun' was very intense and illuminating. Did I find unturned stones? You bet!

In parallel with the spiritual path into the Diamond Heart Approach, I had also asked my then-husband for a divorce. This long-term relationship and the process of divorcing took a number of years to unravel, during which we both sought the help of various spiritual and psychological practices, including the Enneagram. I know without a doubt that we were both able to untangle ourselves in a very honourable, loving, and respectful way, with our children's well-being a priority, thanks to what we had learnt about ourselves. Understanding our personalities through the Enneagram, and those of our children and important members of both our families, was a fantastic support over the years following the divorce. The Enneagram helped us all to understand what had brought us to this painful place in our lives and how we had not met each other in the marriage. It helped us to work with the pain that follows the breaking up of a family, to let go of what 'could have been' and to move on with love and dignity.

Focusing again on the Enneagram journey, it started at Emmaus House in Clifton near Bristol. This was a week-long introduction, and I came out of that week confused as to what personality type I was. I remember feeling frantic in my desire to want to belong to a type and obviously to at least one of the groups that had been forming over that week. I couldn't possibly be the only odd one out who did not know who she was! I left that workshop with more questions than answers.

The next step was a three-day workshop with Sandra Maitri in London. Sandra happens to be a Diamond Heart Approach teacher as well, and one of the very few who includes the Enneagram in her retreats. So I was very excited about the prospect of deepening my limited knowledge of the Enneagram, with the added bonus of Sandra combining the Enneagram with the spiritual language of the Diamond Heart Approach. My journey in search of my personality type was far from being over. I was still unsure of what type I was, but played with the possibility of being a Type Three. Looking back, it is really funny to see how dedicated I was to finding my personality type so that I could understand it, dismantle it through spiritual work, and eventually be my True Self. Whatever that mythical 'True Self' is.

Years went by. I was deeply engaged in my spiritual work, and my former husband, who by then was very much enamoured of the Enneagram and embraced being a Type Four, organised an introductory weekend in London run by Don Riso and Russ Hudson of the Enneagram Institute in the USA. This was their very first workshop in the UK. I participated and loved their take on the Enneagram. Don and Russ were also Diamond Heart Approach students, so we shared a common language and a desire for transformation, not just working on our personality but focusing also on experiencing the potential of our Ennea-type.

The outcome of this initial visit to the UK was the suggestion by my former husband that I might want to take this on and organise workshops on their behalf. After contacting the Enneagram Institute offering my help, they put me in touch with Peter Field who, independently, had also expressed an interest in bringing them over on a regular basis. So Peter and I were introduced, we felt we could work together, and within a short time we started a company offering just that. For the next four years Don and Russ came to the UK twice a year, training students in the richness and complexity of the Enneagram.

In 2006, my spiritual journey unfolded between the Diamond Heart Approach and the Enneagram. After spending a few years looking at the world from the perspective of a Type Three, and attending many workshops and retreats on the complexity of each Enneagram type, I swung my perspective and allegiance from Type Three to Type Seven. You may wonder 'Is it so hard to find one's type, or is this woman particularly confused?' In my experience, some types are absolutely obvious and there is no confusion about identifying their true Ennea-type. It fits just like a glove. Other types have more difficulties in identifying themselves. The recognition of the characteristics of a type can be so disturbing that what arises is a rejection of that type. This in itself can be a clue. In my case I did not dislike the types I confused myself with; I had done so much therapy before this juncture that I could recognise myself in both of them. Types Seven and Three are considered look-alike types because they are energetic, active, and task-oriented, and they both have the tendency to avoid negative feelings. The inner debate between these two types that I lived with for a number of years was very helpful in eventually unearthing my actual type: Type Three. The original wounding of this personality type is that of needing to do to be loved. My sense of worth depends on what I can do for others and not for 'what' I am. Recognising the automatic patterns of doing life at the expense of Being opened up a whole world of choice and change for me. With self-awareness, first one can see, and then one has a choice to either go with the usual automatic, unconscious reactivity, or change the habitualness of the response.

The next part of my Enneagram journey brought me to conscious.tv. Having met both Iain and Renate McNay (a Type Six and Two respectively) on the Eurostar train on our way to a retreat in Holland via Belgium, we immediately struck up a friendship which continues to this day. They started conscious.tv in 2007, and I joined them a year later when the demands of running this TV channel became too much for just two people.

Here I am in 2015 putting together this book of transcripts of interviews with well-known Enneagram teachers and transcripts of nine panels representing each type. These interviews span from 2011 to 2014. I drew from my list of contacts, friends, and acquaintances to enlist the participation of each type. It was a bit of a journey in itself putting this project together. The panels would not have happened without the willingness of all participants to put themselves 'on the spot' as it were and talk about their personality type strengths and weakness. Once a programme is recorded, there is no post-production editing.

In addition to the panels, we have included two interviews with Sandra Maitri in which she gives an overview of each type, plus their 'virtues' and 'passions'. An interview with Ginger Lapid-Bogda covers the on-going influence the Enneagram has in the business world. And the interview with Claudio Naranjo gives an autobiographical narrative of one of the most influential people responsible for spreading the principles of the Enneagram in the West.

More recently we conducted two interviews with Tom Condon on the Dynamic Enneagram and on the Enneagram and relationships. We also twice had the pleasure of interviewing Helen Palmer, an intuitive and one of the most respected and long-standing Enneagram teachers. One of our last interviews on this topic was with Faisal Muqaddam, who offers a spiritual interpretation of each type.

The aim of this book is to give the reader a taste of what the Enneagram has to offer. Finding your particular type is a journey on its own, which offers liberation and profound compassion not only for oneself but for all we come into contact with. It is an invitation to pay attention to one's body and possible reactivity when reading how each type uniquely expresses itself. There are many, many excellent books on the market which give detailed descriptions of each type, should one wish to pursue exploring one's personality. These explorations call forth what holds us back, as well as the gifts we have to offer that go way beyond the limitations of our personality.

I am going to conclude with a quote by Byron Katie:
Personalities don't love.
They want something.
Perhaps through studying the Enneagram we can learn to wear our personalities lightly and express the love that we intrinsically are.

Eleonora Gilbert, Editor
Berkshire, UK 2015

Our journey with the Enneagram

Iain and Renate McNay

Iain…

When I was much younger, I was often puzzled by how different people appeared to be. I knew how I felt in various situations and found it strange that most others often felt and reacted in entirely dissimilar ways. It sometimes led me to feel quite isolated; there didn't seem to be many kindred souls around. I was often nervous and anxious and sometimes struggled to deal with situations that I was confronted with. I just didn't always understand people. To be blunt, I couldn't work them out at all at times.

This and other factors took me on a journey that started with Transcendental Meditation, then to the Rajneesh movement, and eventually to the Ridhwan School. I was as committed as I could be in everything I was involved with. I wasn't one for half measures. That seemed a bit pointless. I made many mistakes but also learned a lot, about myself and the world, and of course about other people. In time I got to the point that I could accept that people were very different without necessarily always understanding why.

Shortly after joining the Ridhwan School in 1993, I was introduced to the Enneagram as part of their teachings. I had never heard of it before. I duly ordered one of Helen Palmer's books and put it on a growing pile that I was intending to read. It stayed there for a time until my wife Renate became interested and started reading it.

One morning she announced excitedly, "You're a Type Six, listen to this!" and she read me a very accurate description of myself. It was actually a big relief to hear that there was a reason I was the way I was and that approximately one-ninth of the world's population had a personality similar to mine. It then became a bit of a party trick for Renate and myself to see if we could work out the Enneagram type of the people we knew.

As I studied it more and started to understand the character of the other types, the Enneagram became very useful in all areas of my life. I had always found certain people very difficult to handle and they turned out to be mainly Type Eights. When I realised how they functioned and how they saw reality, it changed my relationship with them.

The more I studied and understood the Enneagram, the more I saw its potential in so many different ways. The books of Sandra Maitri and A.H. Almaas on this subject took my understanding to another level in terms of our potential as human beings or, if looked at from a higher level, how being a human being is an expression of something much, much more.

We are all on a journey whether we realise it or not. And every journey can take a myriad of different paths. The more we can integrate our understanding of life along the way, the richer we become.

So, enjoy this book. The main feature is the nine panels of the different types. We recorded the interviews over a period of four years or so, in three different TV studios in London (you can find the actual interviews at www.conscious.tv). Reading these transcripts should give you a good feel for what it is like to be each type.

If you don't know your type yet, these chapters should help you spot it. Then you might begin to understand how it impacts your life and find tools to progress the journey of discovering who you really are. Can anything else in life be more fascinating? I think not.

Iain McNay
Oxfordshire, UK 2015

Renate...
I was sitting in the garden of our house in Oxfordshire holding an Enneagram book by Helen Palmer in my hands and was just about to unknowingly embark on a journey to the bottom of the most hidden parts of myself. Iain had come back a few days earlier from his first Diamond Heart Retreat (the spiritual school created by A.H. Almaas) in Germany where he had heard about the Enneagram. He had told me briefly about it and I was immediately intrigued.

I opened the book randomly wondering what Iain's type might be... Type Six it said on one of the pages, 'The Loyalist'. I became curious and started reading. After studying some pages this all sounded very familiar; a picture emerged which seemed to point to my husband! I got really excited and exclaimed to him, "I think I've found you! Listen to this..." He was indeed surprised by the accuracy of the description of himself.

'OK now let's see what type I am' I thought to myself. I looked at the index and started reading through the chapters... Type Two 'The Helper'. 'Ah that sounds like me!' I thought, feeling rather proud of myself. After reading the first pages I noticed an uncomfortable feeling in my stomach arising, a feeling of anxiousness, something I had never experienced before and the more I went on reading the worse it became. Sheer embarrassment followed; I closed the book as it became too painful to continue reading. I looked over the fields adjoining our garden wondering what to do. Everything I had ever tried to hide, not only from my friends and family but also from myself, was written in here. The perfect mirror of my so many unconscious patterns in detail. 'Oh my God, what a disaster, everybody out there knows what I am really like' I thought despairingly.

I really wanted to disappear. Slowly a feeling of sadness arose as I realised how far away I was from myself when I slipped into the role of being the Helper. Tirelessly I would help everybody around me even when they had not asked for it because that was the only way I thought that I could be loved.

That's how my Enneagram journey started more than twenty years ago. I went to a workshop with Sandra Maitri who was, and still is, my teacher in the Diamond Approach. I tried to learn everything possible about myself, how I functioned, what made me think the way I did, my belief structures and identifications, and also why I became a 'Helper' in the first place. Once I got over my embarrassment, the Enneagram helped me on a very rich journey guiding me closer to finding my True Nature. It has been for me one of the most helpful tools on my ongoing spiritual journey. I slowly learned about each type, their neurotic side and also their more enlightened side. I started typing everybody in my family, and friends, and had fun with Iain seeing the world and its people through the eyes of the Enneagram. It became an incredibly useful tool for situations which were somewhat delicate. Knowing people's weaknesses and strengths helped me have a better understanding of them and I could thus navigate difficult times more easily. And it also helped me in understanding my children in a much deeper way.

Many years have passed now and during that time I have studied many Enneagram books and integrated their wisdom. I became aware more and more of how the 'True Helper' in me would come forward which meant I was 'serving' without an unconscious agenda.

And the delight today is when I read through an Enneagram book the pointers are mostly empty. Only occasionally do I still get hit over the head by being shown a structure that I haven't quite balanced yet. What an amazing journey of Wonder and Mystery!

Renate McNay
Oxfordshire, UK 2015

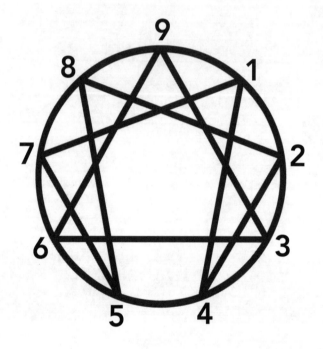

Sandra Maitri
Introduction to the Enneagram

Interview by Iain McNay

Iain: Today we have as our guest Sandra Maitri. Sandra has actually written two books on the Enneagram, and we will talk about these books in a little more detail towards the end. Sandra, I wanted to ask you first of all, before we get into the Enneagram itself, how did your spiritual adventure start? How old were you? What triggered it? Where did you take that adventure to start with?

Sandra: Well, probably the first spiritual experience I ever had was when I was about eight years old and I would sit in a chair and say my name over and over and over again to myself. Then I would find myself not understanding who I was any more and kind of leaving and merging with a higher consciousness. I didn't understand it as that at the time, but I do now. I told my mother about that experience and she got very freaked out and said, "I don't want to hear about this." So, I pretty much forgot, for a long time, that there was anything else [besides conventional reality -*SM*].

Iain: It's quite an evolved experience to have, at an early age, isn't it?

Sandra: Yes. I read a book by Suzanne Segal called *Collision with the Infinite* and she described the exact same experience. I was just shocked when I read it, because I had never heard of anyone else who had ever done anything like that, and I don't know where I got it from. I imagine it's from a past life, probably. After that, I would say that the doors of my perception opened as a teenager in Haight-Ashbury. We lived quite close to San Francisco, so I would skip out during school and go up there. I started to see another reality, another potentiality, and at a certain point I got really convinced that if it was really real, there had to be a way to access it directly without drugs.

Iain: When you say you saw another reality, what do you mean?

Sandra: I perceived it. My whole visual sense of reality changed. The way I was seeing other people was in a very altered way from conventional reality. I was basically seeing a sense of oneness.

Iain: The interconnectedness...

Sandra: Yes, and that had a really deep impact on me that I wasn't consciously seeking, I don't think. I was mostly consciously suffering and trying to get some help.

Iain: Was that hard to integrate into your life as you knew it at that time, that experience?

Sandra: Yes, it was impossible to integrate, although the culture around me was very supportive because I was living during the late sixties.

Iain: Flower power time, peace.

Sandra: Exactly.

Iain: LSD and dope and things. And the music was also very inclusive, wasn't it?

Sandra: Right, and the Beatles, of course, were a very strong influence, and in some ways the Beatles had a lot to do with my spiritual search.

Iain: Really?

Sandra: [*laughing*] Yes, I met them twice.

Iain: Really? Tell us about that. How did it come about?

Sandra: I was living in Bangkok – my dad was stationed over there – and there was a little tiny article in the *Bangkok Post* one day, and it said 'The Beatles are coming on their way to Australia'. I really didn't know anything about them, but my girlfriends knew all about them. Their father knew the Minister of Tourism in Bangkok, so we got press passes and we got to go out to the plane. We gave them flowers and we were on TV, and for a fifteen-year-old it was just incredible [*laughing*].

Then, one day after school, I was sitting around with my girlfriend and I said, "Well, if they went that way [to Australia] they are probably coming back that way too." So we started going out after school to the airport, every single day. Then finally [about two weeks after we had met them the first time -SM], the guy at British Air said one day, "If you don't tell anyone else and you are here tomorrow night at such-and-such time, they will be, too." So we went back to the airport the next day and we got to spend an hour with them.

Iain: Was that before they discovered the Maharishi, or after?

Sandra: It was before.

Iain: But they were moving that way, weren't they?

Sandra: I think they were tuned into a whole wave length that my generation picked up on and just kind of went with. So they were quite a strong formative force in my life really.

Iain: So you were having this feeling of oneness. And where did your journey go next?

Sandra: I was around twenty and I was in art school in Berkeley, in yet another terrible relationship. I was pretty miserable, I was looking for help, and my friend came over one night with a blurb about this guy named Claudio Naranjo. He was a very important figure in the human potential movement in the States, and he was the first person to begin integrating spirituality and psychology. He had worked with Fritz Perls at Esalen, he was a Gestalt practitioner, and he was starting a group. I was looking for a Gestalt group. That was the happening therapy of the time and he was offering a Gestalt therapy group that was also a spiritual group, and I said, "Well, great, that sounds fabulous."

I didn't really know what I was getting into at all, but I went over to his house. There was a group of about a dozen of us there and Hameed Ali – the founder of The Diamond Approach who writes under the name of A. H. Almaas – was one of the people there. Claudio did what he calls Trespasso, which is basically a transmission, looking into each person's eyes and transmitting Being, consciousness. He was just deeply in a state of presence, energetically communicating. That just knocked my socks off. It was unbelievable. I was sold and that was it. I signed up to the group and it was quite an adventure, quite a crazy adventure in many ways. He had just come back from working with Oscar Ichazo in Arica, Chile [Arica Institute], and Ichazo taught the system of the Enneagram, which is the system of nine different personality types. Claudio was just back from that whole training and that was part of what he was teaching us. So we learned it in the context of spiritual unfoldment and spiritual development.

Iain: And this group you were in, I think that was called SAT, which stands for Seekers After Truth?

Sandra: Right.

Iain: That sounds a fascinating title.

Sandra: Well, he borrowed it from Gurdjieff. It's the same name that Gurdjieff had for his band of followers. And there was a Gurdjieffian feel to the way that Claudio was leading the group.

Iain: It was Gurdjieff, I think, who first used the Enneagram, in a slightly different way. I don't know where he found it, but it's supposed to be five thousand years old. Do you want to tell us a little bit, as you know the history of the Enneagram, from Gurdjieff to Claudio?

Sandra: Just backing up a little bit, I don't think anyone knows where the Enneagram came from. What Gurdjieff said is that he had learned it from the Sarmoung Brotherhood, a secret brotherhood probably in what's currently Afghanistan, and Claudio always said he thought that probably Ichazo learned it there as well.

Iain: In Afghanistan?

Sandra: Yes, although he never really said. Later on Ichazo said that he channelled it, I think. I am not quite sure if that is the exact way he put it, but nobody knows for sure [where the Enneagram came from -SM]. The Gurdjieffian way of using the Enneagram was quite different; it has to do with understanding cycles in the universe, like the movement of the planets and the days of the week and the musical scale. So, different sets of cyclic processes were things that he used the Enneagram to chart. And Ichazo was really the first to use it to understand personal consciousness.

Iain: What was your response when you first heard about the Enneagram? What did it do for you in terms of the journey you had just started?

Sandra: It was a huge part of that journey. [In Claudio's group] we basically lived and breathed the Enneagram. None of us seemed to be working in those days, and we just spent all of our time processing and talking about our own experience, and really bringing the map to life within our own direct experience. So, it was a very, very powerful map for me and for my friends, my colleagues at SAT as well. It took a lot of the guesswork out of ourselves, out of some of the things about ourselves that maybe we wouldn't have wanted to see. Here it was in this map and it was kind of like 'Yes, that's right, this is how I am. These are parts of my personality'.

Iain: Did you discover what Enneagram type you were fairly early on?

Sandra: Yes, I was fairly sure that I was one of two of them, and there was one I would rather be and of course I was the other one. I went up to Claudio one day and asked him. He said, "What do you think?" and I said, "I think I am either this, or that," and he said, "You are that," and I said, "Okay, I got it, it makes sense."

Iain: And that helped you understand yourself more?

Sandra: Yes, and that was thirty-eight years ago, and I think I could say that there really hasn't been a day that has gone by since then that the Enneagram hasn't had some place in my understanding of myself and also of others. So for me, it's been a very powerful map.

Iain: The SAT group you were in lasted about four years, and you also learnt other forms of spiritual practise and psychological explorations. What were the other main influences in that group?

Sandra: [Claudio had worked with Idries Shah, the Sufi teacher, and so his teaching stories were a strong influence -SM]. Claudio dragged in every spiritual teacher that came through Berkeley at the time. So, I met Tarthang Tulku, who is a very well respected Tibetan Buddhist Lama. There was a Thai Theravada monk named Dhiravamsa who taught us. There were Hindu teachers, Sufi teachers… let's see, what other traditions am I leaving out? Even Scientology – we met a couple of renegade Scientologists at that time.

Iain: Right, so all in all, you had a really good picture of what was available, and you could see what worked for you and what was worth integrating and developing?

Sandra: Yes, exactly.

Iain: When you left that group, I think you then became involved in A. H. Almaas [work] in the Ridhwan School?

Sandra: Well, it wasn't as direct as that. Actually I came over here to the UK to meditate. The Thai monk that I mentioned, Dhiravamsa, had a meditation centre in a tiny village called Leverington [near Peterborough], and he invited me over to become trained as a teacher in meditation. So I came over and lived here for two years. I was in my late twenties.

It was a very sheltered existence at the meditation centre, and one day I was looking out the window thinking things over. And I really felt that if what Buddhism had to teach was real, it had to be something that one could use out in the world. I just felt a really strong calling to go back and to not live in a monastic [way] – we were not really monastic, we did not take orders, or take vows – but we were pretty, pretty isolated. So, I came back to the States and all my friends started telling me about this fabulous work that my old housemate actually, Hameed, had begun to develop, and I was of course green with envy for quite a while and wouldn't have anything to do with it, but I kept hearing how fabulous it was...

Iain: You were quite resistant at the time.

Sandra: Yes, a couple of years... and then a very close friend of mine, Karen Johnson, who I had been a roommate in Art school with, was visiting one day. I was going through some difficulty, personally. I was dealing with a hard space within myself and it was actually the space I had been stuck in from the period when I had been meditating. The meditation brought me deeper and deeper into myself and into a great deal of deficiency at the core of my personality structure. Karen said, "Could I work with you for a minute?" And I said, "Okay," and she just started asking me questions and before I knew it, within five minutes, I had completely gone through the stuck place I had been in for two years and I said, "Oh my god, I have to learn how to do this." So, I called Hameed up and said, "Hameed?" and he said, "Sandra?" and I said, "Yes, I'd like to come to your group," and he was very sweet, he said, "I'm deeply honoured," and that was, let's see... nineteen-eighty-one.

Iain: That's twenty-seven years ago.

Sandra: Yes, so I have been working with The Diamond Approach ever since and I am a teacher of it.

Iain: Coming back to the Enneagram, and for people who don't really know what the Enneagram is, let's give them a very brief overview. As we were saying earlier, there are nine different personality types. Now, I know, from my limited knowledge of it, that each type has a potential. Just run through and talk about, for maybe a minute or so, each personality type and what their potential is.

Sandra: Sure. I would look at it more the other way round. The way that I learned the Enneagram is that our ego structure, or personality structure, develops as a result of loss of contact with spiritual reality, Ground of Being, True Nature, whatever one wants to call it, the Divine. That loss happens in early childhood, usually in the first four years. Each of the nine types develops a core belief about the nature of reality and therefore the nature of oneself as a result of that loss. So each of the types is based on a fundamental distortion, or delusion, about reality, and this creates all sorts of suffering for each of the types, and very particular kinds of suffering.

Iain: So we have lost touch with who we really are.

Sandra: Exactly. So, the potential is reclaiming who we really are. Briefly, moving around the Enneagram beginning with point Nine which is considered the archetype, this central Ennea-type is like… if it were a white light and the others were refracted through a prism, they would be variations on the same theme. So the personality Type Nine is basically the principle of going to sleep on one's ultimate nature. So the whole style that develops is based on going to sleep on oneself. Turning away from oneself, getting preoccupied, getting busy with what is going on outside and not paying attention to oneself.

Iain: How would that manifest practically in someone's life? So if they are listening to you talking about these nine types and they are playing a little game trying to spot their type, what would be the major characteristic for them to look for?

Sandra: A sense of worthlessness.

Iain: So personally, they feel worthless.

Sandra: That other people are much more interesting, much more special, that other people have characteristics that are important, but that they [themselves] don't. They tend to be people who harmonise a lot. They can see other people's realities quite well and so they are very good mediators. The reality they don't encompass easily is their own. Part of it is that they like things to stay peaceful.

Iain: Yes, that's a quality… being able to mediate, isn't it?

Sandra: Yes, you can see where other people are coming from and you can kind of connect the dots between people. So they tend to be very gracious, very loving people, but very self-absenting: 'I'm not very important'.

The next type – moving around the wheel of the Enneagram: point One are the perfectionists of the Enneagram and they have lost contact with their inherent perfection, the inherent rightness or suchness, as they say in Zen Buddhism, of oneself and of how things are. Because of that, the fundamental belief is that something is wrong somewhere and their job is to fix it.

Iain: They feel things should be perfect and they see imperfection everywhere, is that right?

Sandra: Well, looking at it slightly differently, they assume that things are not perfect, so they need to fix them either in themselves, or in other people. They can be quite critical, quite judgemental, preachy and picky.

Iain: They have high standards for themselves and others?

Sandra: Very high standards yes, and they tend to identify themselves as good people, doing the right thing.

Twos are the dependents of the Enneagram. Their basic conviction is that they are not fundamentally loveable and that what they need to do is to become a very special indispensable person to someone very important, or a group of important people. So it is through the connection that they get a sense of value, and it is through the self-importance in relationship to others that they get a strong sense of self.

Iain: Right, they are also the helpers aren't they? They are going out and helping people a lot and through that they often lose their centre.

Sandra: Exactly. They are so busy anticipating other people's needs that they don't really tune into their own and basically the game is 'giving to get'. It's like the Christian maxim of do unto others as you would have them do unto you. So they do unto others and they hope that others will do unto them, in kind.

Iain: Doesn't always work though, does it?

Sandra: Doesn't always work that way and then they get very annoyed. That's one of the ways that one can distinguish if that's your Ennea-type.

Iain: Okay, we got Type Three next.

Sandra: Type Threes are the achievers and the quintessential image types of the Enneagram. Their core belief is that only the surface matters – only the presentation, the product, the result. How I get there, what it takes to get there, what kind of corners I have to cut, or however devious I need to be, it doesn't matter because it's the end achievement that matters. Their sense of self-worth comes from achieving a lot, being successful, and being recognised as such.

Iain: I think they are also quite hung up on image as well, aren't they? Their personal image is quite important to them.

Sandra: Yes, they tend to present the image of their culture, or their subculture. Whatever the ideal, the ego-ideal, essentially is, they attempt to become it. They kind of shape-shift in order to look like what's needed, what's wanted, what's the best.

Type Fours are the melancholics of the Enneagram, and their basic conviction is that they have lost contact with 'true nature', which if you are abiding in true nature, you know isn't possible. We are true nature. We might not be conscious of it, and so to feel that we have lost it, as Fours do, doesn't ultimately make any sense. This whole personality style is based on longing. Longing for some lost 'other' who is the beloved, the perfect beloved, and the personality style is one of being unique and special, sensitive. They very much pride themselves on their finely attuned sensitivities, which they are convinced are much more sensitive than other people's.

Iain: They are a bit more tragic/romantic about it, aren't they?

Sandra: Yes, exactly.

Iain: The thing that I always find with Fours is that they think the grass is greener the other side of the hill. That is the dissatisfaction you were talking about… if I lived over there, life would be better.

Sandra: Right, and that translates internally to a sense that whatever I have, or whatever is going on with me, isn't as good as what is happening with that other person. That is their suffering. It's a very painful Ennea-type.

Fives are convinced of their ultimate separation from other people, and so they tend to be hoarders. They hold onto what they have, because there is the sense that 'I am an island and who knows if another ship is going to show up or not, so I should preserve what I have here'. They tend to hide; they are self-contained.

Iain: Yes, they are quite secretive in a way, aren't they?

Sandra: Yes, and often what they hold on to and look to – as what will help them – is knowledge. If they can understand things well enough, then maybe they will feel safe.

Next: Sixes, as a result of being identified with the body, which we all become as we develop a personality structure, and because bodies are temporary, bodies get sick, bodies get hurt…

Iain: They don't always work very well, I find.

Sandra: Right, they don't always work very well [*laughing*], so there is a sense of fear that dominates this type, and the character structure is built around looking out for danger, what could possibly go wrong, and trying to ward it off, in some way…

Iain: Prepare for it.

Sandra: Prepare for it, yes.

Iain: As a Type Six, I find that is a big thing.

Sandra: Yes, so there is a conviction that something terrible is going to happen sometime…

Iain: [*laughing*] That's right.

Sandra: …and 'I just need to figure out when'.

Iain: Yes, figure out and prepare the best I can.

Sandra: So they are very vigilant, convinced that there is danger. On the other hand, if we really know that who and what we are is something that can't be destroyed, which is the truth of our nature – not so true for our body, but definitely true for our nature – then we have a potential for liberation from fear.

Point Seven is another fear type, in the fear corner of the Enneagram, which is a longer story… but Sevens have the reputation of being dilettantes, of being people who don't go deeply into things, but explore lots and lots of things on the surface and gain lots of information and collect it, but never dive too deeply into things. A lot of that is because they are afraid of pain.

They value being up, being happy, being okay, and they are phobic around pain. They tend to be gluttonous, it's like... I don't know if you have ice cream shops [in the UK] where they have many, many different flavours.

Iain: I think we do, but I have never been in one, like Ben and Jerry's?

Sandra: Yes, or like a sweet shop, they want one of everything, just to have a taste of it.

Iain: Have an adventurous quality, don't they? They want experience.

Sandra: Yes, they want to have a little bite of everything life has to offer and they want to make connections between things. They want to pull all of these disparate experiences together and have a sense of how things work – what the map is, what the plan is, and what the big picture is. Joseph Campbell was a great Seven in terms of unifying the mythology throughout human history and understanding the overall schemes. Another... well, it's disputed, but I think Ken Wilber is a Seven due to his vast charting of spiritual states of consciousness. Basically Sevens have lost contact with their connection with the big picture, so they try to figure it out.

Eights are the bullies of the Enneagram, the tough guys and girls, and they value very much being strong and not showing any of the vulnerable or soft human emotions. Being strong, being on top, and nothing happening to them that could be devastating, and so on is what they really value. They tend to be rather pragmatic, and whatever they can experience through the five senses is what's real and the rest is basically bullshit, as they would say.

Iain: Yes, they are kind of typical big company bosses a lot of the time, aren't they? Quite ruthless, very determined, very focused, but not very humanitarian.

Sandra: Right.

Iain: I know a few Eights. It's interesting – very briefly an aside – I did this Enneagram workshop with you a few years ago in Germany, and one of the exercises we did in this workshop was you divided us up into the various Enneagram types. Ones get together, Twos get together, etc., and the Eights corner was empty as there were no Type Eights in the workshop [*both laughing*], which for me it defined what Eights are like: 'I don't need this kind of stuff!'

Sandra: Right, [Eights would say] this is a lot of airy fairy expletive [*laughing*], but the interesting thing is – as you know, I lead a couple of groups here in the UK – I have quite a few Eights in those groups.

Iain: Okay, that's good. Maybe the British Eights are more open to that, than the continental ones.

Sandra: I don't know why... it is the same in the States: there are very few Eights in spiritual circles, although there have been a number of Eight teachers, like Gurdjieff for instance, Swami Muktananda, the infamous Madame Blavatsky who founded Theosophy...

Iain: If we take people in the news at the moment, would you know what their type is? What would Sarah Palin be? Do you know what her Enneagram is?

Sandra: Oh let's see, Sarah Palin… I am not really sure, she comes across a lot as a Three. I would say either a Three or a One. She has a lot of that fundamentalist doing what she considers to be the right thing and wanting to 'off' those who don't do the right thing, which is very One-ish. So that's a possibility, although she looks more like a Three.

Iain: Right. And McCain and Obama. How do you feel they would stack up in category?

Sandra: Well, I think Obama could be a Three, possibly. He has the same kind of charisma that John F Kennedy had who was a great Three, who really embodied the cultural current of the time, the cultural idealism, and expressed it, so that is a possibility. [In hindsight, it has become clear to me that Obama is a Five. He has had difficulty asserting himself and the criticism he gets is that he's aloof. -SM] McCain, I would say he is an Eight. He has quite a temper apparently, and that reputation of being a maverick.

Iain: And what's our own Gordon Brown here, do you think? Do you know much about him?

Sandra: He strikes me as being an Eight actually. Tony Blair was way slicker, much smoother. I think he probably was a Seven. He had a famous relationship with George Bush who I think is also a Seven, so there was a similarity there. I think there was an affinity in terms of their personality styles.

Iain: I also remember you saying at one point that countries can have Enneagram types as well, which I found very interesting. What, for instance, would the US be and the UK be?

Sandra: Let me just say, first of all, that much of my understanding of that comes from Claudio Naranjo, so it's not something that I originated. I like to really reference my sources. America is to me a very uneasy blend of One and Three. You all – England – got rid of the most puritan, the factions, and they went to America and there they are, with a lot of – how can I put it? – do-good mentality, trying to be good people, very upright people, and being very hateful towards those they don't consider to be good, or right, or moral. So that whole moral majority idea is very much a One-ish thing. And then there is the rugged individualism of America which is very Three-ish, doing whatever it takes to achieve. Achievements, making money, recognition, fame, all those things that America unfortunately is exporting to the rest of the planet as a cultural ideal, are very Three-ish.

Britain strikes me as a blend of One and Four. There's the stiff upper lip, and the putting on a good show of things [rigid posture], and yet suffering underneath, under the surface, which is very Four-ish. And the Victorian strain in British culture feels very One-ish to me, similar to the puritanical strain but not quite so moralistic. But it was much more surface here [in Britain], having more to do with appearances, rather than actually what was going on. A lot could be going on under the surface that nobody need know about, and may be so still to this day. I don't know the culture that well any more, but that's very Four-ish.

Iain: I want to move on to talk about the two books you have written. Maybe we could start first of all with *The Spiritual Dimension of the Enneagram,* and just give us a little more insight into what someone could learn from this book about themselves. It's not a basic book about the Enneagram, but it's a very deep book and brings in lots of different angles.

I still use the Enneagram, so if I could just briefly talk about myself. My experience of the Enneagram is that it's been so helpful to me; I learnt it in the Ridhwan School quite early on. It has helped me to understand myself better and be less hard on myself at times because I know it's a basic trait of my conditioning. The Enneagram shows me my potential. Also, I found it immensely useful in business. If there is someone I don't get on with and I have difficulties with, or I don't really understand, I do a bit of research into the books I have and try to see if I can work out, from what I know about them, their Enneagram type. And if I read about their type and understand it, then I can put myself in their shoes and try to understand them. It makes my relationship with them far easier because I understand them. I know that you take that understanding far deeper and it's a way of working – what I would call in my language – working back from the personality towards our ultimate potential. We don't have so long left, only a few minutes. I don't know if you want to just briefly talk us through how that is portrayed in your book and what people can learn from it.

Sandra: Well, to me it is a very simple book. There was a plethora of books on the Enneagram when I wrote that book and it was a wave that had already moved through the culture really, so I was quite lucky with [finding] my publisher. But the reason that I wrote the book was because what was being taught was simply the Enneagram of personalities: the nine Ennea-types and their characteristics, without any sense of what the spiritual root of the types was.

To me that's a rather hopeless way of looking at ourselves. It's all very well and good to understand how one's personality works, but what else is there to us? So that was why I wrote the book. I was trying to bring into the Enneagram world, and people's understanding of the Enneagram, the whole context in which I learned it [which is that of the work of reconnecting to true nature. That is what the map of the Enneagram is for -SM]. Also, I think what you have said, Iain, is [that it can give us] a sense of empathy, of understanding, how other people work. And instead of observing how people are behaving that may be problematic for oneself and feeling like they are doing something to us, or they have got it wrong – just understanding that this is simply another style, it's a whole other take on reality and on how to live, how to be, how to behave and…. People's patterns obey nine different styles. It's rather obvious once one knows the map.

Iain: Right. And your second book is *The Enneagram of Passions and Virtues*. Take us through that very briefly as well.

Sandra: The map of the Enneagram of passions and virtues helps us understand different inner orientations that support our personal development, or personal growth, personal unfoldment, becoming more conscious of ourselves. Basically, the Enneagram of passions and virtues helps us to look at the difficult emotions that we get into and what other possibilities [there] might be – different ways of relating to the world. In other words, we talked about envy in the Four Enneatype, and Fours are really racked with envy. It's a sense of 'Oh God, it's so much better over there than what I have here'. By understanding that it is a passion – a type of knee-jerk reactive pattern – and that an alternative to that is looking toward oneself and seeing the goodness within oneself, and accepting oneself, [a Four] can really change that quite painful orientation to reality.

Iain: In a way, it seems you are mapping out a process, you are mapping out a possibility for people to allow movement forward in themselves – I would use 'the way forward' – but you would probably say more like back into the 'real them'.

Sandra: Well, it's the same thing. I think that forward movement is a movement into what's true about us. Yes, that's a good way to put it. It is basically setting a context, so that we have in our minds what our potential is as human beings and to feel that we are not stuck.

Iain: We might feel like we are in a trap, but somewhere – we may not see the way out – there is a way out. The way out is in understanding [ourselves] and then the door starts to open and the trap starts to disentangle.

I know you do run some seminars in Wales, I think twice a year, that have been ongoing for a few years and they are part of the Ridhwan School founded by A. H. Almaas. I think those groups are closed at the moment, aren't they?

Sandra: Yes.

Iain: But maybe something opens in the future on that.

Sandra: Yes, I work with about… I guess it's around two hundred people who come from, actually, all over. One person flies from Kathmandu to come to the group. People come from South Africa, a lot of Norwegians. Interestingly enough it's the old Viking trade route, or the 'plunder' route, or however one wants to look at it.

Iain: Well, thank you very much for coming onto conscious.tv, and I hope we can meet you again next time you are over and talk in more detail about the Enneagram, which I think will be very interesting for people.

Sandra: That would be good.

To watch this interview please go to:
http://www.conscious.tv/consciousness/enneagram

CONVERSATIONS ON THE ENNEAGRAM

Enneagram Type One – The Perfectionist

Discussion with James, Anne and Carlos

Moderated by Iain McNay

Iain: Today we are talking about Type One, how it is to be this type, and the potential of being a Type One. I have with me in the studio today three Type Ones. We have Carlos, who has actually flown all the way from Spain to be here. We really appreciate that, Carlos. And we have Anne and James. Just to give us a starting point, I have to say that Type One has been the hardest programme to put together out of all the Enneagram types. Twice we have thought we had it all together and then people have pulled out. Someone else pulled out on Sunday night and Carlos jumped to the rescue, which is fantastic. I'm really happy we are all here and I am sure this shows something about Type One, but I guess that will come out in due course. Let's start with you, Carlos. Tell us a bit about the Enneagram and how it has affected your life.

Carlos: The theory behind the Enneagram is that at a very young age, [usually] between three and five years old, we have a contraction of energy and we disconnect from the oneness of the universe. There are nine different ways that this disconnection takes place, and we spend the rest of our lives expressing this loss through a different personality type. The particular type we are talking about here today, Type One, forms part of the 'instinctive triad': Types Eight, Nine, and One. Type One has been given the title of 'the reformer' [or 'the perfectionist'].

The reformer is a very apt name for it as we are constantly seeking to better what we have around us. Things are not right, they are not perfect, and we want to make them perfect, we want things to look good, we want to be good, and we want everybody around us to be good and to be on the same level that we are, or that we consider to be good. Things can start going wrong depending on how unhealthy or healthy you are [personality-wise] if things don't go your way. I first discovered the Enneagram about three years ago through conscious.tv. You interviewed Sandra Maitri and I got very interested. I bought her book, I read a few other books about it. I love to talk about the Enneagram and to express my feelings and share what I know with other people, which is another typical trait of Type One. We like to share what we learn and what comes our way. We like people to enjoy it the same way we do.

Iain: How did you feel when you found out you were Type One?

Carlos: I think I felt, in a way, relieved, and I felt freed as well because sometimes I think Ones can suffer from and become a little bit intense. We are aware of this intensity, and knowing how the inner forces within us work was a wake-up, an epiphany moment for me. It was wonderful, it was a complete relaxation, an understanding: 'Ah, I finally understand why I behave this way'.

Iain: That's a real relief, isn't it?

Carlos: It was a hell of a relief. I am constantly catching myself because now that I am self-aware, I am not working on auto-pilot. I am now conscious of my words and my actions. I often, when the inertia of my personality takes over, catch myself and pull myself back in again when I feel I am maybe going down the wrong road.

Iain: Has it given you insights into how your personality is functioning and manifesting in the world?

Carlos: Definitely. And it has also had an effect on the people around me. Everybody that knows me has said that I have gone through a tremendous transformation and the Enneagram is partly responsible for that, not exclusively, but certainly on the day-to-day basis it's responsible for that.

Iain: James, you [and Anne] were waiting to come in there, I think.

James: It's funny, I hadn't thought about the perfectionist bit before, but the thing that really made me laugh was when you were talking about making things better and getting it right. It made me think about loading the dishwasher. It's just a really mundane thing, but I have noticed since I have been aware of being a Type One and being a bit more aware of doing that, how it really annoys my wife. But I am really annoyed at her for not having loaded it properly because everything can clearly tessellate a lot better, and I can load it perfectly. So I will often come along and reload it and she will just watch me in despair, whereas I am despairing that it wasn't loaded properly in the first place because you would get a load more cups in and the forks could all be in the right place. It's like 'Why can't you just do it properly in the first place?' There is anger and resentment about not being able to do it properly. But it's been incredibly liberating and that is why I am smiling about realising that. You use the word 'relax', it's about relaxing. I can now be aware I am doing it and almost relax into it and I can still do it, because I perhaps enjoy doing it. I guess there is a kind of comfort in that vague obsessive nature, and being aware of it has just changed the energy around it on good days. On bad days, it's still there and all kinds of things come up as a result.

Iain: On a practical level, are you saying you are more understanding of your wife not doing the loading perfectly in your eyes?

James: Yes, on good days, absolutely.

Iain: [*laughing*] On good days…

James: I'm being straight. On the days I am not feeling very generous, or where I have been really criticising myself… because I think a lot of it comes from my inner criticism that I'm not good enough, or I need to do this right for some reason, or that there is a right way, so I have got to do it. I have got a standard I have to set which is my standard, which is the highest standard, the right standard. I have to live to that, so if I don't see someone else living to it, then I am kind of 'You should be living to that'. It's a real trap of my own standard that I am never going to live up to. It's been really nice to realise that I am just trapping myself in this prison, if I am not careful.

Anne: And it's very draining, isn't it? All that energy and being so cross with other people in the household because they haven't loaded [the dishwasher perfectly] could be put into something else.

James: Absolutely yes, it's physically… really draining. It is exhausting and then you realise 'What have I done?' I have got so exhausted over something really stupid.

Iain: Could we say, generally speaking, for Type Ones this issue of perfection is a very paramount issue, or is it just manifesting in different areas? Do you feel you want the same precision and perfection in other areas of your lives?

Anne: I wish I could say that. Actually, I think for me, yes there is a perfectionism about things, but sometimes I feel really important things, much deeper things… I am quite happy to just float away. For example, I can be quite hypocritical in that I am setting all these standards, but actually deep down I won't actually carry out those standards myself. I drop the standards for myself. It's not in every aspect of life, it's just in easier things to identify with.

Carlos: I think what James was saying about the perfectionist – the dishwasher story – I agree with you a hundred percent. I know exactly where you are coming from. The perfection thing with me is, I don't seek perfection, but imperfection seeks me. I'll give you an example. I am looking at those flowers there [*on table*], and I know they are very nice but for some reason I am drawn to the leaf on the side there that is not quite right, the one that is crooked. That is what I am noticing. I am aware that everything is beautiful, but for some reason it is pulling me there and I have…

Iain: [*smiling and leaning towards the flowers*] So which leaf is it? [*Iain and James pointing at leaves, group laughter*]

Carlos: I got to the point, more or less when I woke up in the morning and got out of bed to the moment I got back into bed, it was like going to court, being in court. I was the prosecutor, I was the judge, defendant, the executioner, the whole thing. It was a constant judgement going on in my mind. I would be driving down the road and the weeds on the side of the road were annoying me. I'd be thinking someone should be here and that should be cleaned up, or some litter or whatever. It didn't matter what it was about, it was that imperfection seeking me out. With the Enneagram, when I realised that, I thought 'You don't have to be perfect all the time, you don't have to...' I needed to free myself. It was liberating, as I said before, from the constraints of having to expect everything to be that way [perfect]. It's exhausting, you are absolutely right, I completely agree with you.

Anne: I think losing energy is so important, isn't it? That's been a real benefit to me with the Enneagram. Life is difficult as it is, and to be wasting energy in getting so angry about things… it's just pointless and plus it upsets other people.

Iain: One thing that's been said about Ones is that they are the policemen and policewomen of the Enneagram and they are a bit like a policeman saying [*writing on imaginary notepad*] 'Ere 'ere, what are you doing 'ere...?' Is that something that you would agree with, or connect with?

James: Yes, I can relate to the sense of 'checking-upness' and the idea of noticing things [*gesturing to flowers*] and needing to point it out that it could be done in a different way, a better way – checking out on anything, on anybody really, if I am not careful, and tending to notice what's not happening right, what's not being adhered to, rather than the fact that it's roughly right at all. We had our house decorated a while ago and we had one of these glass-paned doors with twenty panes of glass, and the paintwork had to be done between each of the glass panes. My wife was just pleased that it had all been done, someone had come and done it. We had three young kids and blah, blah, blah, but the first thing I do is, I walk in the hall and I notice that they have missed one of the strips, just a tiny bit about that long [*a finger length*]. I noticed it and I could not help myself but to say that, knowing full well that it would cause an argument and that I was not being grateful. Yes… so I almost had my clipboard [*in hand*] saying, "That's not right! [*pointing*] That's quality control, I can't be happy with what these people have done, we need to get them back." That's really to your [Anne] point about energy that is so sapping. I feel tense talking about it even now, so I don't want to be there. I am really glad that I don't have to be there, as much as I was trapped in it before.

Iain: I know this type is called the policeman of the Enneagram. Is that something that you [Carlos] feel you have in yourself?

Carlos: I think really, I may have been. I used to watch people and how they behaved and see if they'd meet my standards, which are pretty high, and I must say – we were talking about the people standards – Ones have an

CONVERSATIONS ON THE ENNEAGRAM

incredible ability to be ruthless with themselves as well, not just with other people. I know what you [Anne] said before about there could be an element of hypocrisy, but generally the court case isn't just about everything that's around us, it's about ourselves and where our mind is. Certainly it is with me, and I have taken myself to terrible places in my mind in the past where I wasn't aware. As you [Anne] say, it is such a waste of energy because you don't have to be angry and the clothes don't have to be folded perfectly over the chair and it doesn't matter if the boots aren't in a neat little corner. We can be very anal I think. Life is not about that, is it, at the end of the day?

Anne: Yes, I suppose the other thing too is that you can get so carried away it then trips you, you ignore the obvious, and I find that at work. I am a nurse and where I am with patients, they come and see me and are completely disorganised and I am thinking 'You know, I can't see a way through all this… it should be like this. This person should be presenting with a problem which is A, B, C, and D'. I get so worked up in trying to understand what the problem is, that I then go and completely overlook the obvious. And I think in doing that, then I do exude that tenseness and anger with the patient, and probably the outcome isn't terribly satisfactory because they have not really got what they need. I think that perfectionism can just blind one as to what actually is going on.

Iain: I have got some notes here of other indicators. For people who are watching this and who are not sure which type they are but feel they might be Type One, just tell me guys how you feel about this in terms of your own experiences: 'It's difficult to be spontaneous'. Would you say that's true sometimes?

Carlos: I think I probably need to prepare myself; I need to work myself up. I am not an off-the-cuff person. I like the rare occasions that I am, but generally I am not really like that, so I can probably relate to that.

Iain: But you were spontaneous flying over for this interview, weren't you? [*group laughter*] What about you guys [Anne and James]? Do you feel that you lack spontaneity sometimes?

James: Oh absolutely, yes, the need to plan and have an element of control over what is going to happen. So, the idea of what a weekend could look like, almost planning it by the hour and trapping myself in that plan. I have to follow the plan even if it clearly doesn't feel right, and it doesn't very often. Really it's quite miserable in that way. So I would say yes, it's a freedom when you can have that spontaneity, but it seems to trap me if I'm not careful. I said I was going to do this and then doggedly carry on.

Iain: And then [*reading*], 'often feel guilty about not getting enough accomplished'. Does that apply to you, Anne, at all?

Anne: Yes, absolutely. At the end of the day when I am going over things, a good day to me is when this was achieved and that was achieved. So if I haven't managed to do those things... I think it's this feeling of accomplishment which is very important.

James: Yes, list-making…

Iain: Are you into making lists?

James and Anne: Oh yes, yes.

James: I really try and free myself from lists because a day will always be judged by if I have done my list, irrespective of how hard it is, and of course it was always too hard. Then I would put that on other people, and if we have done loads of stuff and perhaps different things have happened in my paid work, or at home, but if we hadn't done the list, there was still a sense of 'It's not good enough'.

Iain: Something else on my list, talking about lists [*laughing*]. Something that came up earlier is 'incorrect grammar and spelling bothers me a lot', and you [James] mentioned this was something that bothers you sometimes.

James: It's something that I pick up absolutely, especially in what I see as important occasions. If you are doing a big presentation or something, I notice apostrophes or hyphens or units of measure. I have a scientific background and if the units of measure aren't in the right way, then I have found I am more relaxed about it but I still, in a more relaxed way, want to correct it. So yes, I can relate to that.

Iain: And you are 'idealistic and want to make the world a better place'. Is that right?

Carlos: Oh definitely, definitely, that's a never-ending story really, but that can become quite frustrating. In my case I have done a lot of research, I have read an awful lot of books about things, and I would like to go back to what you mentioned before about anger. Ones have an issue with anger. I think the only way you can take the benefits of the Enneagram is when you accept these terrible negative traits that we have, and I think for many years I was trying to lock up anger in a safe deposit and throw away the key. But it's like holding a ball under water, the ball will want to rise to the surface and if you take your hands off it, it will come up somewhere else, and I think people perceive this tension that we have. We are constantly keeping this ball under water and so, with things like trying to 'make the world a better place', this creates a lot of frustration. And certainly in my past, I have been frustrated about many things. I think Ones do a lot of civic [work], you know, they go into politics; we want to make things better so we have got to do our bit. Ones will tend to...

James: ...dutifulness, we have a sense of duty, I find, which can be quite trapping again in terms of the standards you set about how much you should be doing and about what a fair contribution is and what you choose to do as your work. I can relate to that in the paid work I have chosen. It is about, in theory, a lack of acceptance of what is in front of us. I work with environmental issues and ethical issues in the manufacturing industries, and if I am not careful, I hold that with a great deal of anger and resentment: 'Well it just shouldn't be like this!' Rather like when you [Anne] were telling the story about treating a patient, if that anxiety and anger is coming through, I am almost acting out the absolute opposite of what I am trying to work towards.

Iain: Isn't that interesting... You are 'acting out the opposite of what you are trying to work towards'.

James: Yes, if I am being unfair on others, or if I am being tyrannical.

Iain: When you see that, what kind of effect does that have on you?

James: Now it's really lovely to realise that. As I am saying that to you, I feel quite warm and happy in that because I can do something about that and I can talk about it, which in itself seems really helpful to other people. Just naming it seems to take such a lot of... I can feel it as I talk to you, the tension out of my jaw and my face and the anger goes because for a start, I have showed it to you. I have given this humility and vulnerability, which is the complete and utter opposite of the fear that I am not good enough. Just by putting it out there feels like 'Okay then, come on, if you are going to kick me... kick me'. But somehow trusting that having got to that place, I can put it out there, so that word 'liberation' comes back time and again when you realise these things are going on. Really helpful.

Iain: Another one that I was going to read out sort of ties in with this: 'you have a tendency to hang onto resentment for a long time'. But if you are naming it, coming out with it, that's beginning to break that trait, isn't it?

Anne: Yes, yes, and I was saying earlier I am like one of these bag ladies, I just pull along loads of resentment. All my life, I think I have resented, and I noticed just recently that is getting better. There was something that occurred recently and I felt I was getting very angry and resentful, but I was able to drop it actually and it felt just so much better. There was nothing that could be done, so there is no point in us getting so worked up about it. I still had to relate to this person, so the best thing now is just to leave it and start up anew. But I think that's a fairly recent step I have made in dealing with resentment. I almost feel that I have carried so many resentments in my life that every day I am going to have to make a real effort to just put these all to the back now.

Iain: You have all, in your own way, said that when you understood something in yourself and acknowledged it, that has been the start of a change, and in terms of that, it hasn't been so strong from there onward. So I think that's something very positive we can take from this with Type Ones – that once you do understand it, you have the intelligence and the integrity to then start to try and change things in yourself for the better. Would you agree with that?

Carlos: That word 'integrity' is something that all Ones look for, would you agree? [*group agreement*] And I think Ones are so passionate about the things they believe in, they have very strong convictions, you know. And when we transmit our ideas and beliefs to other people we become resentful when... we kind of know what is best for other people...

James: It's that righteousness, isn't it?

Carlos: Yes, definitely, and we become resentful when we feel we are not being listened to. I think deep down there are good intentions. Obviously, depending on how healthy you are [psychologically], there is resentment, and I feel that in myself sometimes.

James: That point about the good intention, and when you [Anne] were talking about the day-by-day accepting, those things really seem to come together for me because... isn't the point here behind the Oneness, being able to see the world as it is? As actually being quite perfect as it is? And so that active accepting – it's a relief because we are being able to see the world as it is. That's one of the transformational things it feels I am going to be able to work with. Having been able to name this a bit more and, in the examples I have been giving, I can sense that's happening. One of the things that Ones have is this ability to see the world as it is. So if we can get through that distortion of being really angry about how it is and seeking the reform, or the justice, or whatever, but saying 'Okay, it is how it is', now we can use our energy, our tenacity and integrity to do something with it. It feels incredibly energising, as opposed to that complete exhaustion and debilitation that comes with it. That's the sense I got from what both of you just said there, and pulling those things together. [*Anne nodding*]

Iain: Something else that's down on this list I have here. Don't worry it's not quite never-ending, we are almost there... is that 'you tend to worry a lot'.

James: Yes, we worry about things that haven't happened, may never happen, and planning scenarios. Certainly in my case, for things that may never happen, and that is also very exhausting. I remember on one particular day, I said to myself, "I am absolutely sick of myself and of listening to myself!" And funnily enough, when I said it, it was over. The other day I was doing something in the kitchen and I was lost in my mind and my wife said to me, "You are not having a very good day today, are you?" I looked at her and the words, just the question, were enough to pull me out of it.

Anne: Could it be that... I mean we do have an ability to be disinterested, we can sort of stand back and look at things objectively, and I just wondered if you were able to just step out of yourself for a period of time and just realise that this really isn't necessary, this is 'I'm me, I'm not all these worries'.

Iain: But what does that mean to you, 'I'm me but I am not all these worries'?

Anne: Well, I think that sometimes one can get so overwhelmed with these worries that you forget about yourself.

Iain: What I am getting at is... you see yourself as separate from your worries. Is that correct?

CONVERSATIONS ON THE ENNEAGRAM

Anne: Yes, I think Ones do have that ability to be fair and to look at things in proportion. And when they are with other people with competing demands, they can keep that all quite balanced. And it will be the same with ourselves that we can stand back and realise that there's all this concern, that I have this feeling that I have all this on my shoulders. Sorry, that probably sounds a bit confusing.

Iain: No, I'm interested. When you stand back, what do you see about yourself?

Anne: I think standing back is just being able to say 'I'm me' and 'I don't need to be right and perfect'. Unfortunately, Type Ones can slip into a feeling that we *have to be right,* to be *me,* but the idea is to accept that I don't need to be right all the time.

Iain: So you see that you don't have to be driven by this conditioning all the time?

Anne: Absolutely, yes, and that was the benefit for me when I learnt about the Enneagram. Going back to what you were saying – your personality developing at a very young age – you can then just be driven by these motives, or reasons for behaving in a particular way, and that can just take over the way you grow up, or relate to other people. For example, I can remember as a very young child people teasing me and saying, "Your nose is painted white because you think you are always right." I was very young, but I have kept that going in my mind. I think they were just friends; it's quite an early memory. I think I was only about five or six.

Iain: I have got a few books that I will show at the end, but one of them here, *The Wisdom of the Enneagram*, has a list of examples of some of the people in various types and I wrote down some Type Ones. I am going to read these people out as it's interesting partly for people watching who know them. Let's see what you guys feel in terms of a connection with them, or how you see these people. There's Gandhi. Now Gandhi was a very good person, but it seems he was a perfectionist, he knew what he wanted and he went for it. What's your feeling when I say that Gandhi was a Type One?

James: Righteousness.

Carlos: I think Ones want to do the right thing. We can be quite courageous and put a lot of things on the line and Gandhi is a perfect example of that. The truth for a One is so paramount, so important. The truth will be heard. I don't know if that is the case with you [Anne and James], but if we were to list our fundamental values, the truth is one of them, possibly above loyalty and other things. The truth is, certainly in my life, very, very important. So there is a perfect example, Gandhi and the truth.

Anne: And he was altruistic, he was very focused and he knew from a very early age. He started campaigning in South Africa didn't he? I think he was a lawyer, then he moved to India and he kept that focus through a lot of very bitter political situations.

Iain: Is this something you see as one of your qualities, in terms of… you are able to take something that is important to you, stay focused and keep going with it?

Anne: Yes.

James: Yes, doggedness.

Iain: I don't think it's necessarily always doggedness – we will come on to this later – but it's also [about] the potential of Type One. We are not talking about personality traits; we are talking more about who you really are from your essence and the potential of that in the world. And so [with] these people, we are not necessarily looking at their neurosis, but looking at it [potential] may include part of their neurosis and their qualities as well. I will go down the list and it might trigger more things for you guys. George Harrison was apparently a Type One.

Carlos: I can't say much about him apart from his music.

Iain: Okay, there is Al Gore, who obviously has been very determined, especially on the environmental front, to keep running with what he believes, which takes a lot of courage to do that, especially in America.

Anne: Gosh, I don't know enough about him to say anything.

James: There's something also, about how long he has been doing it. He started that a long time ago, twenty-eight or twenty-nine years ago.

Iain: Well, someone who is more in the front of things now is Hillary Clinton; she's apparently a Type One. There are no English people here unfortunately, Americans or from other countries, but she obviously is in the news a lot.

Anne: I suppose she is quite blunt, isn't she? I mean, she comes out with statements and points out faults in a take-it-or-leave-it…

Iain: Is that how you see yourself, quite blunt at times?

Anne: I think Ones can be, yes. They can be quite offensive in the way they say things. I mean she is a politician, I'm sure she knows how to do that, but I just wonder if that's a quality in her.

Carlos: I think Hillary Clinton has probably got a thicker skin, I would say she was probably an Eight. I think with Ones our conscience comes back to haunt us later after the misdeeds that we have done and said and offended people, you know. We are back in court again and I don't think she would be able to survive. I don't understand why she is on that list actually, and how she would be able to survive, particularly in politics.

Iain: Anyway we are not here to debate the list. I want to give you one more, a good British woman who has been in the news recently, Vanessa Redgrave, apparently a Type One, and I don't know if she portrays anything that triggers…

Carlos: There is a tension about her, isn't there, Vanessa Redgrave. You can feel it when she is acting and when she is giving interviews. I could probably relate to that one. I can see that, because when we met – you [Anne and James] met me just before the show started – I immediately recognised you [Anne], just by the way you were talking, that you were a Type One. With James, right up until you opened your mouth and started talking, I didn't quite pick it up. But certainly with Anne I did, so that's why I can probably say that.

Iain: One of the things that we have hinted on and started talking about is the potential – not the neurosis, not the conditioning. Where do you guys feel you are moving as a Type One, and where do you feel you are moving to? Otherwise there is no point in having all this information and then not integrating it, as you all obviously have, and then seeing where you can go. I am wondering how you have been finding that. You mentioned specific examples of things, but let's have a little chat about generally how you see your potential from Type One's [pattern], with examples from your life.

Anne: I feel that this coming to terms with – picking up on what you [James] said – the world isn't perfect, we can see flaws, but accepting how the world is, and just being more aware of things that one can do and things that one can't do… I am just thinking of that quote by, is it Niebuhr? 'God grant me the serenity to accept the things I cannot change; the courage to change the things I can; and the wisdom to know the difference'. I feel that's very helpful for a Type One to learn to just grow in wisdom and to see that actually there are a lot of things one just has to leave for other people.

James: Yes, that hit home, and to be really compassionate with myself when that happens. The act of accepting that I can't and don't need, and am probably not best placed to do, all those different things. And the wisdom about being able to discern it. I had this real sense as you [Anne] were speaking that relaxing into it, relaxing into all these challenges and perhaps just letting them be there for a while, the answer comes a bit more, in terms of choosing the right place. Whereas when I am holding the number of the challenges all together – this long list – it's very hard to do anything very well. But when I say 'Okay let's find out which one is the right one that I can do', that felt like a bit of a trap: 'the right one'. But now I tend to just be able to do that in a way that feels more helpful, and again the way of doing it seems to transmit more positively. As I am describing it, I feel a lot of the traps of Oneness about using the words like, 'better' and 'rightness'… There is a hell of a lot to work with in that area, but just the naming, and the accepting, is really helpful.

Iain: You see there is also another way to look at it. It's also possibly falling back more into who you really are; i.e., you leave the conditioning aside and then… what starts to be revealed? I don't know if that connects with any of you?

Carlos: Well, the word 'wisdom' has been used twice by both of you [Anne and James], and you [Iain] used a word before, 'integrity', and wisdom is one of the qualities I think that Ones aspire to. I think it is on our list of things to achieve in our life: to be wise people and to help others, and I think that Ones can also be quite playful. Once we learn to, and come to terms with who we are... I don't know about you, but I certainly like to have some fun and enjoy other people's company and enjoy sharing my things. But I have learnt not to get frustrated when things aren't seen the way that I expect them to be seen and that other people do have an opinion and a right to their own experiences. For many years, that wasn't the case with me. I just couldn't understand why people behaved the way they did until the Enneagram gave me that as a tool, knowing that there are nine different ways of seeing life through these eyes [pointing to eyes] not just this vision.

James: Actually the richness I found that comes with that, of accepting that the way someone else is doing something, or the way they are behaving – if I can watch it and see it through objectively, about its happening in front of me, and actually see it, rather than judge it as not how I would be doing it – I have found I have learnt and benefited from just watching that happen. Seeing that there is a different way of doing stuff and that I am not infallible and I don't need to be infallible, because it's not about fallibility or infallibility. It's about how things are and about how other people can do things, in different ways. Things can happen in a different way to the way in which I perhaps imagined it needed to happen, and of course it didn't. We used the word 'liberation' very early on; it just feels very strong in that way.

Carlos: You just used the word 'judgement', and I feel that when one frees themselves of judgement and everybody else, that's when the plant, flower, begins to flourish and we can grow. Answering your question [Iain], I think we have to come to terms with that first. I think we have to do that, and we have to accept the negative traits of our personality, which I think – when I compare them to the other personality types – are quite... we have used not very nice words to describe who we are... I think we have to come to terms with anger. I have come to terms with it anyway, and it's working for me.

Iain: Having been so fixed on perfection and wanted perfection as you see it on the outside, is it that once you start to loosen up, you start to find that the beginning of everything is actually quite perfect without your tweaking adjustments?

Carlos: Definitely.

Iain: That's a big realisation, isn't it?

James: And it's lovely. It means you can put somewhere else that energy, with confidence, integrity and trust, rather than doing that 'policeman job' you were talking about earlier, or checking up. I don't want to do that. As a start, you are talking about 'who am I really?'... I don't want to do that [Carlos agreeing], it's like an ordeal. Something has told me I have to do that from a very early age, so when I see I don't have to do it, it's lovely, it's really, really a great opportunity just to let things be.

Carlos: It's like you have taken a great weight off your shoulders, isn't it? You feel very ethereal and light…

James: …and you can live there right now. You talked about the worry of the past, or imagining the future. You don't beat yourself up about what happened, or the word I said that was wrong. So I said the word and look what happened – so it happened. But it's funny because another part of me – even as I say that to you now – is beating me up and saying 'Well that's just laziness that's slovenliness'. It's that continual battle with the superego and [learning] to leave it alone. But that is really nice actually, being able to play. You used the word 'playfulness' a bit earlier, there is a real playfulness. And you can pull all these things together, and in my experience Ones can pull lots of bits together and play with it, and tease and pull different parts and see what happens. I think that's what we can bring for people. I have really noticed that. I can be in a meeting with twenty or thirty different people and we have this ability to synthesise things and to pull things together. The detriment is, you then analyse things to death and put all those things that a patient could be presenting with and as a result don't do anything. But the real free thing, and the bit where you stand up and you are feeling really good about it – you know you are acting and helping – is that you can pull it together for other people. They can see you doing it and then they appreciate it and you go 'Wow! I didn't do any work then'. But people have really appreciated what you have done because you have pulled everything together and come out the other side with a solution.

Carlos: I think Ones can inspire people and we can also intimidate people. I have seen that, after the event. But inspiration… I think people can learn and feed a lot off of us when we are good.

Anne: You mean like in your role [James] with a meeting? It may be that you can lead the team on, you can analyse the problem, you can get a very good view of it and then actually lead them on with your idea…

James: And what's interesting, as you say that, I am thinking about something you said, Iain, about who you really are. I had the sense that when that is happening as a flow, there is a real quality to it – speaking from this experience I have had, the embodied experience. It was just a flow and the anxiety wasn't there at all in it because something else was acting, as opposed to just having to think up here [*touching head*]. I wasn't thinking it, I was feeling it. I was being it, and there was a sense of tiredness afterwards in these cases, but the quality of the tiredness is different to the quality of that real tenseness. It's a really delightful exhaustedness.

Carlos: It's coming from a different place, isn't it?

Iain: There is something I wrote down. I hope I can read my writing now [*group laughter*]. It was from the book *Facets of Unity* by A. H. Almaas who has written quite an in-depth book about the Enneagram, and this quote was about Type Ones: 'The potential is to see the world as it really is, without our perspective and judgments, our likes and dislikes. We have to let go of our mind. It doesn't matter whether we think things are good or bad. The moment you see that everything is perfect, you see your effort to make things better is pointless. Everything is co-emergent with Being. That is Holy Perfection.'

I thought that was very beautiful, I don't know how that resonates with you guys. This was written for Type Ones. The last thing written here, and I know it's a big jump in a way, it's basically saying everything is perfect the way it is and resistance to that is pointless and everything is co-emergent with Being.

James: I think in the best moments of my life, I can feel that and I can sense those, but a lot of the time... no. I don't believe him, he's not quite right on that, I know better. You know part of me is saying 'I know better. It can't possibly be meant to be like this'. So for me, I still have a lot to work on with acceptance, but I know from the glimpses I have had, when that acceptance comes, it's a much more beautiful place to be. It just does feel right and you are walking along under the sunshine and the leaves are falling in the autumn sunlight and you are delighted and you are not sure why and you really don't care that you don't know why. Or if you are miserable, you really don't care that you are miserable. You just are.

Iain: So when it's pissing with rain and you are late for the bus and you just fall in a puddle, how do you feel then?

James: It comes again to where you are at. So some days that's brilliant, there could be nothing better because, well, it's funny being wet but, on the other days...

Carlos: Do you find that it can trigger itself off very quickly, instantaneously? Like you could be fine and then suddenly something would happen and bang, it's like a trigger has gone off.

James: And there's a massive spiral downwards.

Carlos: That's right, and then you are in freefall at that moment and you can't come back until you have hit the bottom and then you realise what has happened. Many times, I have felt disappointed with myself after the event. I have said to myself 'I thought I was more advanced, I thought I had evolved more, but I haven't progressed at all. I am back right where I started!' [*group laughter and agreement*] That's the sort of thing going on in my mind.

Iain: That's a great thing to point out because yes, we all get this feeling, doesn't matter which Enneagram type we are. Sometimes we are back where we started, but at least we know that there is somewhere else to go because where we started, at one time, was where we thought the whole universe existed. You have a [new] perspective, which is a huge jump actually.

We have a couple of minutes left. I don't know if anyone has anything they would like to say in the last few minutes. Maybe to people who are watching, who have suddenly had the shock of finding they are a Type One, any words of encouragement, or warnings? Or they may be watching and are really pleased they have found out they are a Type One.

James: What has really helped me is the realisation that being kind to myself and being compassionate to myself about this self-criticism and not getting in that spiral, in that complete negative loop, that is a really good start. And by being kind, each time I notice something, however small… so by noticing the trigger, I may still go down that really bad path, but I have noticed the trigger and that's better than I was a month ago. Or a year ago. Being really kind to myself. And I have noticed that if I am being kind and compassionate with myself — but I may not act it out perfectly yet as my wife would probably say – I feel more compassionate to those people around me. Instead of just being angry or resentful, or judgemental, there is compassion, maybe [still] with judgement or anger, but with compassion too. The edge has kind of gone. These little steps, and just taking the time to notice that happening, have been really helpful for me.

Anne: I suppose you are showing that your self-knowledge is developing isn't it? In that you have actually identified something which before would just have been automatic. You are accepting that it has happened and you know you don't want to go along that track, you want to stop. Whereas before, you weren't even aware of it and it was an automatic reaction.

Carlos: With me, I remember being with my yoga teacher and ranting on about something that had happened, and he's looking at me from across the other side of the room and he has got a smile on his face and I am thinking to myself 'He is not taking me seriously'. And I finish ranting on and he says to me, "Carlos, you have got to learn how to forgive," and I said, "Okay." He said, "Not the other person, Carlos, yourself. You have got to start forgiving yourself for feeling this way," and it was such a slap in the face. I needed to receive that slap in the face and it was like the veil was lifted. I realised that the only way we can be free of ourselves is by forgiving ourselves.

Iain: Well, that's about a great place to finish. I really appreciate the three of you coming in today, Anne, Carlos, and James. I think you have given a feel of what it is to be Type Ones and for that I am very grateful.

To watch this interview please go to:
http://www.conscious.tv/consciousness/enneagram

Enneagram Type Two – The Helper

Discussion with Paul, Gill and Renate

Moderated by Iain McNay

Iain: Today I have in the studio with me Renate, Paul, and Gill, who are all Type Twos. Just to give you an idea of how the Enneagram works, Paul is going to give us a short introduction.

Paul: The Enneagram is an ancient symbol, many thousands of years old possibly, and it has nine points on it; and what we are doing here is talking about it in relation to human psychology and the transformation of the person. The theory is that there are nine personality types, and each personality type develops as a response to losing connection with deeper truths about ourselves when we are very young. By enquiring into our personality type, we can find the ways in which we have lost connection with deeper truths about ourselves and find a way back to wholeness through this ancient symbol. It's a map, or a system of psychology and spiritual understanding, which allows us to learn more about ourselves for transformation and liberation.

Iain: It's giving us clues to find out who we are and who we're not, so to speak.

Paul: Yes, it's helping us to get clear about how we are in relationship to deeper levels of our Being and how the personality relates to deeper levels of our Being.

Iain: How did you feel when you first found out you were a Type Two?

Paul: Well, I remember that I did a long questionnaire as well as reading books to try and understand what type I was, and there were maybe three types that came up strongly. But then I began to realise that the Two's pattern in me is of another order of magnitude, stronger than the other ones that I could see, and I was really curious. I didn't feel like I particularly wanted to be one type over another type. I just thought 'Well, this is going to be interesting. What does this mean about me and the way that I am in the world?' Curiosity was the main response.

Iain: Gill, tell us a little bit about yourself. What are your prevalent characteristics that suggest you are a Type Two?

Gill: I think I am a Type Two because I'm probably obsessive about supporting people, helping people, doing good things, and generally putting other people first before myself. That's what I would say are my views about why I am a Type Two, and I do it in all walks of life and have done it as long as I can remember, pretty much.

Iain: What are some examples of how you put people first before yourself?

Gill: With all my friends, at any point that any of them have a problem, I step in and try and fix it, even if they don't want me to fix it [laughing]. But it's this ability to really try and make a difference for somebody who might be stuck. In my profession, I have had to deal with lots of people in a bad-news situation, and I always take the view that there must be something that I can do to make even what might be an awful situation, better. For example, a friend of mine's son died and I travelled to Singapore to open a garden in remembrance of the child in a weekend. And that would be what I call my typical behaviour.

Iain: But you are also saying that you would help out even when the person didn't want you to help out?

Gill: Sometimes I think what happens as a Two is that you think everybody needs help, or needs some help. For example, if somebody is looking for work, I might try calling all the people I know of, but they might not actually want me to do that, but I'll do that. So I think sometimes one can overstep 'the brief' but it's a compulsion. It's not something that you actually think about. As soon as somebody is in trouble, certainly from my point of view, I think 'Okay, what can I do?' Then I go into who do I know, do they need money or whatever it is, that's what I do.

Iain: So you feel like you have no alternative, really?

Gill: No, because I couldn't possibly see these people who were struggling and not come up with something. Actually, I have a belief that if you think you can come up with something, you can come up with something. So you nearly always improve [the situation], however dire it is, I think.

Renate: Can I step in now? This pattern sounds very familiar [agreeing], to try to help people, or to try to make people happy. I think what drives us to do this is that we want to feel loved.

Gill: Yes, I am sure that is right, I am sure we do want to feel loved.

Renate: And to feel loved, we just would do anything and completely step beyond ourselves.

Gill: You are right. Beneath it, one does want to be loved, but I think a Two puts the other person's needs first and then maybe it brings this – people love you. But sometimes people don't love you when you are supporting them, especially if they are in a beat-up mode themselves. It's quite difficult to be a Two because you can help and people don't value it. People don't give you enough acknowledgements for being a Two, for trying to do what you think is a really good thing, and some people will take it completely for granted. So it's quite difficult being a Two because you expect some acknowledgement if you do something. I'm talking about something perhaps a bit outside of the norm here.

Iain: So you are a bit disappointed sometimes. You are doing something you feel is very helpful to somebody and they are not necessarily saying thank you, or acknowledging the fact that you have given them help?

Gill: Yes, because if somebody did that for me, if somebody puts themselves out for me, then generally, it's my belief a Two will over-thank and perhaps buy them something because they did something for you.

Renate: [*laughing*] We even try to pay them!

Gill: You expect something back, because you would give, so you expect. That's the way I see it as a Type Two.

Iain: Paul, what's the male interpretation of this?

Paul: Well, that's interesting. I can see myself, if I am being quite Two-ish. Say in a community context or in a group, I go into a helping mode to be a sweet, empathic, and helping type person just so that I can be included. It's my way of coming into the group so I can feel connected, so I can feel like I belong. Because I am really looking for other people for a sense of connection and wanting to feel I belong, like I'm part of it. In terms of a group thing, then I can see very clearly that I'm trying to get my needs for connection met. I am being a sweet and nice helpful person so that I have got a role, I have got a place. Then, in a one-to-one way, I would tend to take on a very empathetic character, so that I can have a connection, so that people would want to connect with me. Somehow I can merge and be in a bubble with another person and get something juicy from being in a bubble with another person. Something that feels supportive, somehow.

Iain: Do you feel it's easier for you to give than to receive?

Paul: It can be very hard to receive. For example, some of the work I do is donation-based work and people give me money. And they choose to give me money, however much they want to give, and it can be really touching and somehow really painful when you see someone actually choose to give you some money when they didn't have to give me any money but they chose to. It can feel kind of challenging. Also the giving: when I am giving, there are expectations there as well. So it's easy to give, but maybe it's not necessarily a straightforward giving; I am kind of asking for something as I am giving as well. I notice that sometimes.

Iain: Do you guys feel lonely inside? What's happening inside as you do these various things?

Renate: I remember if I didn't feel merged with somebody, I felt incredibly lonely and empty. It was such a longing to merge with somebody who was around… and what that also brought with it was that I completely understood and knew the person I was with much better than myself. I sometimes was surprised if their attention shifted to me and somebody said, "Well, how are you?" It was like a shock, I almost felt paralysed. I hadn't a clue how I was, I was so melted with my environment…

Iain: Your empathy went out to the other and in that you forgot yourself somehow? Or forgot to check in with how you were feeling?

Renate: Yes, it is a typically Type Two pattern to completely forget yourself. You don't exist for yourself, and that has a reason. I understand today why I became a Type Two. I had a mother who needed a lot of attention because she was a Type Two who gave a lot of attention in the same way. If my mother went shopping she would come home sometimes with five refugees and she would cook for them. We didn't have much money, but she couldn't help herself. So I had to work really hard to get her attention and her love. That is when I started to leave myself. I am much, much better now and I learnt to come back to myself. One thing that helped me a lot is, I remember a few years ago Sandra Maitri, my teacher, said, "Renate, Type Twos can only heal when they are alone."

Paul: That's interesting.

Renate: That's when I learnt to be alone. Which actually almost never happens [*laughing*], but sometimes, I shut myself away on a meditation retreat at Gaia House, or wherever… And she also said, "Then you need to learn to be alone with others, which means you are with others, but you are completely with yourself at the same time."

Paul: Yes, I can relate really strongly to that. I notice I can be a very different person with different groups like family, friends, and spiritual groups, and sometimes I wonder, underneath it, who I actually am. It's foggy and fuzzy and it's so much how I see myself: 'How should I see myself now to connect? What would be the best person to be, in order to connect, so that this person will approve and be loving, be open and want to connect?' I don't know if you [Gill] feel that. Do you feel that?

Gill: I don't have either of those experiences [Renate and Paul]. I am not good being alone at all. I don't feel comfortable in that situation, and I think that is very much why I go seeking others. Others who are in a weaker state, in certain aspects. I never choose to be alone. Ever!

Renate: You just said something important. You like to be with others who are in need of you.

Gill: Yes.

Renate: It is also very typical: we like to be needed [*Gill and Paul agreeing*], and the more we feel needed, the more we feel loved. I actually remember saying to Iain… this is a typical hand movement [*Renate touching Iain's arm*]: we touch people sitting next to us. It was very much at the beginning of our relationship, and I remember I so much wanted to feel loved by Iain, and I said one time to him, "If you could just tell me sometimes that you need me." He looked at me and said, "I don't need you. I like to be with you, but I don't need you," and that was incredibly devastating. It meant for me that he didn't really love me. It took me years to really transform that.

Iain: This wanting to find that somebody loves you seems to be one of the underlying themes here, and you interpret how that would happen, in a practical way, from the actions and words of the other person. You are nodding, Paul...

Paul: I have often found myself in a situation where I have been romantically obsessed and infatuated with a woman, and it seems like it's the be all and end all. It's the source of everything I need in terms of support and guidance and holding and connection; it can be a really big thing and yes, very painful, very painful. My experience of myself is in the image of another person. I often have an image of a woman right in the centre of me that I want to merge with somehow. A special other person becomes the most important thing and other things like friends and work become neglected.

Gill: Yes, I can relate to that, because if your instinct as a Type Two is to try and get attention or love, when you actually get it – and it's what you want coming back – it is an unusual situation. So then other people almost get dropped because it becomes nearly an obsession that you for once are getting something back, that you want back. But I think that happens in a romantic situation and all sense goes out of the window, actually [*group laughter*].

Iain: [*laughing*] It does with most people.

Gill: Yes, and even more so with a Two, because it's what you want the most, and all of a sudden the person that you want is giving it to you. But that doesn't happen very often.

Iain: I have a list of things that normally help people decide whether they are a Type Two, or not, and one quote here is 'I don't want my dependence to show'.

Gill: Yes, I... absolutely one hundred percent for me, because I genuinely do not feel like I want to depend on anybody.

Paul: I don't want to feel like a needy child. It's really hard to feel like that.

Iain: [*reading*] 'I often figure out what others would like in a person, then act in that way'.

Gill: Yes, yes, I do that too.

Paul: Like changing accents, depending on the accent of the person I am speaking to.

Iain: Really, you actually change the way you speak?

Paul: Yes, sometimes I can notice myself trying to sound less posh, or something.

Iain: [*reading*] 'I'm attracted to being with powerful or important people'.

Does that align with what you feel you do?

Gill: It can. I don't know that it's necessarily a trait that goes particularly with a Two, but again I think important people usually are charismatic, and there is something about their personality that maybe you might hope that you mirror slightly, and therefore I think the attraction to that type goes for me. I don't know about all Twos, but that does go for me.

Iain: And then I drew up a list, out of three different books, of people they would say are examples of Type Twos. So let's see how this gets past this important test: Mother Teresa.

Gill: Yes, yes.

Paul: I did meet Mother Teresa with my friend Goatie who was raised by her. I was eighteen so we went back after school to Calcutta and I met her very briefly…

Renate: What do you mean he was raised by her?

Paul: He was born in Calcutta to Indian parents and had polio, and his parents left him at the orphanage. They couldn't raise him, and she raised him, her and her sisters raised him. Yes, that was an interesting trip.

Iain: Do you feel she is probably a Type Two in terms of what you know?

Paul: I have no idea, but in terms of being a loving servant, possibly.

Iain: Okay, then we have – they are mainly Americans as they are out of American books – Barbara Bush.

Gill: I don't know enough about her. She does have a foundation, doesn't she? A very big foundation.

Iain: And that would be a clue for possibly a Type Two: helpful and philanthropic?

Gill: Yes it would, philanthropic. A very, very charitable nature, because if you are in a powerful position and you are wealthy, it's fairly easy to be charitable, but I think when some of the money goes, or some of the fame goes or the power goes, if you continue it's because it is who you are. I believe the foundation is still going.

Iain: Okay, Florence Nightingale.

Paul: Iconic.

Iain: I'll just read them out… you don't have to comment: Meg Ryan, Shirley MacLaine, Elizabeth Taylor, and Jesus.

Paul: [*smiling*] Jesus.

Iain: [*laughing*] He is in great company here.

Renate: I would agree he is a Type Two, but a completely transformed one.

Iain: What do you mean, Renate, by transformed?

Renate: Here comes [the Almaas teaching of] the 'holy ideas' of the Enneagram, which is kind of the Enneagram on a non-dual level, not on a personal level any more. We have here 'holy will' belonging to Type Two and 'holy freedom'. Holy freedom is grounded in holy will, which means – and I am trying to exercise that a lot – to surrender to the will of the universe, of God, or of Being. Aligning your will with the universal will – that is the ultimate transformation of Type Two: 'Thy will, will be done'. We know these words from Jesus. Not 'my will', 'thy will'.

Paul: When I was on an Enneagram course, I remember [one of] the questions we were studying for Type Twos was 'How do you manipulate?' And along with that enquiry into how we manipulate was the quality of surrender and coming out of manipulating into surrendering. That's what came to my mind when you [Renate] were saying that. Surrendering to how it is, rather than make it more healthy, more enlightened, more developed... into how it is.

Renate: Yes, Type Two tries to live up to a very angelic self-image. I even remember my mother used to dress me in angel dresses. It is a very high self-image that you try to live up to. That is why you try to help and try to please and make other people happy but – Sandra Maitri actually talks about the 'soul child' – Type Two's soul child actually doesn't want to have anything to do with helping people. We have to decide for ourselves. And that means all this helping is a very egotistic, self-gratifying thing.

Iain: It's a way of trying to get what you need, but somehow it doesn't satisfy the depth, does it?

Renate: No, because our Type Two depth is not the merging with the environment and the helping, it's a longing for our soul to merge with our Being. That's where the merging needs to happen, not on the outside.

Paul: Not through personality strategy [of merging with] another person, or group.

Renate: The merging with ourselves – at least in my experience – I mostly experience when I am alone. Then somehow everything collapses inside and I enter this stillness and Beingness, which I still find I am working on integrating in my daily life. That is what is meant by 'You need to be, or feel, alone with other people': you don't leave this [still, inner] space.

Paul: Can you feel like that a bit now? Feeling alone, even though you are with us here?

Renate: Yes, I am actually quiet here. Inside.

Iain: It's an inclusive place, rather than an exclusive place, isn't it?

Renate: Of course, yes.

Paul: I find that a really interesting point: being able to be alone, but be with other people, and quite difficult. If I am feeling irritable, angry, or moody, and I don't want to lose connection with you guys, or people I am with, what do I do with this? I have some need there for that to be attended to and acknowledged, and it's telling me that I need something... whatever that might be. But for it to be there in an inclusive way, where I could be myself, still feel connected, and still have my own self being here, which might be grumpy or pissed off or something...

Renate: It sounds like a major achievement, Paul, if you can be with other people and still feel what is going on inside you.

Paul: Yes, what it takes to get to that place is actually talking about it. So doing an enquiry with somebody, or a one-to-one session with a therapist, where I can literally describe that I am feeling in a bad mood to the other person and they are helping me stay connected, and yet I am describing that I feel yucky inside. Something that is not normally allowed is there in the space. Then there is a simultaneous sense of the connection and a more full inclusivity of my emotional life – they kind of co-exist.

Gill: I think I have an experience where I can relate to what you are saying. Part of my job has been to make people redundant – I am a human resources consultant – and you have to have that empathetic, supportive [approach], whatever you can do to help this person, but inside yourself of course you are feeling absolutely horrendous. You are giving bad news and you know that this person may not be able to pay their mortgage. So you have to protect yourself. You might go into this meeting with this I-am-here-to-help [attitude], but inside you are… actually, alone is the right word because there is nobody who can help you, while you are trying to help this person. When the meeting is over, it is not finished. They leave and it is still with you [*pointing to heart*], and you have to learn to try and not get overwhelmed by it. I think a Type Two takes that process very personally. Whereas in many, many companies you will find human resources [people] who don't. They will give the information – "This is your book, this is this, call this company…" – and then they leave the room and that's it. Whereas I myself will stay in touch with everybody, say, until they get work – it could take years. My best friend is somebody I worked with who I had to let go. Most of my friends are people I have let go. So I think a Type Two has that in them: to hold on to what is an uncomfortable position because more importantly you are helping them, than how you feel about yourself.

Paul: Do you get what you need out of that? At the end of the day when you have had all these feelings inside and having to reject people and lose and sack people.

Gill: Well, it's an uncomfortable thing you have to do anyway, and nine times out of ten it is not your choice, or your decision. But to actually have somebody say, "Well that was a horrible experience, but you did make it about as good as it could get," yes, that works for me [*pointing to heart*].

Paul: And how about you at the end of the day?

Gill: Everyone says that – "Who looks after you?" But going back to that statement about being independent, I will say, "I don't need any help," and with most of these [self-developmental] trainings I don't need any help, but there is a certain level of denial, I think. You are just human at the end of the day. You can't cope with all traumas, all dramatic things. I have had employees who have attempted suicide. It's not just that they haven't got a job, it goes way, way further than that.

Iain: I just thought there was a bit of a bridge here in terms of what Renate was saying and what you came back to, Gill. I just made a few notes from some of the Enneagram books and you may or may not agree with this, but it is something worth putting out there for feedback. [reading] 'The key is about developing humility, settling into yourself, turning attention inwards and giving yourself the attention that you crave from others, and that slows down the frenzied activity and you get in touch more with your actual experience'. That tends to be the thing with Type Twos: they are – as we found out earlier from all of you – not always in touch with their own feelings. It also involves distancing yourself from the superego, the part of the mind that is judgemental of yourself, telling you that you are not doing the right thing, or have done it wrong.

Paul: Being selfish…

Iain: Being selfish, yes. [reading] 'The more you open to the inner reality, the more you see your own humanness and the value of yourself as who you really are, not what you are trying to be'. I don't know if that is helpful at all in bridging this gap that is opening up a little bit.

Paul: Yes, definitely for me [Gill shaking head, group laughter], but not for Gill.

Gill: No, to be honest, I don't completely understand what you are saying, so that's why.

Iain: Okay, do you have any feedback, Renate?

Renate: [pausing] That's a big one. To be true to our own feelings and our own needs. That's a huge step. And be able to actually admit to that. I do sometimes need help too, and [ask] can I please have help.

Iain: To ask for that is big?

Renate: To ask for that… it's very big.

Iain: Because you are so used to being available for everyone else?

Renate: Yes, and when I learnt that… it actually touches me. What happened to me was, I started to feel so much love for myself [smiling], and in that moment the picture turned and I stopped seeking love from the outside because there was something in me which felt, in that moment, whole and round and all of a sudden I could say, "I really love myself, I love the way I am." Yes, that was a big step [laughing]. The love I felt for myself I would translate that into: Being recognised itself. My Being recognised itself in that moment, and in that moment… completeness there.

Paul: It was interesting that you used the word humility there, Iain, and I was wondering what humility has got to do with it. But I know one of the things I can find going on is feeling that I'm trying to be special for other people. I am trying to be – in a certain way – especially empathetic, loving, wise, deep, mature, all these things that I'm trying to be in a special way. The humility somehow is coming out of that pride about being 'more special' than other people and connecting with just the true specialness that, like you were saying, Renate. When I spend time with myself and then come back to the fact of this living Being, which is kind of miraculously happening by itself… it's a special thing even if it's confused and feels lost a lot of the time. There is still a specialness there that doesn't depend on you needing to think I'm special, or me needing to show off in a certain way, or needing to have a certain special role. It's just like 'Yes, I'm special just as I am', and tasting that. 'Yes, I'm loveable as I am', with all the messiness and the complications of the human heart and being as I am. But like you were saying, I find it really important to be on my own, to connect with that, and it's quite hard to take time for myself sometimes. Maybe I wouldn't look after that piece: I am not aware of how much I need to take care of myself and be on my own and connect, feel that self-love, rather than needing to posture in a certain way to get that kind of love from other people.

Gill: I haven't reached that point of yours [Renate] or yours [Paul], and I think there must be a maturity to a Two… and to get to the point where, as you say, either you really love yourself – which I wouldn't profess to myself – or you take a step back and separate the Two that you want everybody to see and the real person inside. I can't separate for whatever reason, so I see everything I do, as exactly how I am, and I know it can't be that way. I think this maturity comes probably from exploring yourself and doing the sort of things that you guys do, but for me I am more trapped [*leaning back stiffly*]. I like being a Two and I think the best thing is to help people. I have been successful in business, but to me that doesn't count for a single thing.

Iain: But does it sometimes catch up with you in terms of, it gets too much?

Gill: Actually for me, I don't know that it does.

Iain: Well, that's very interesting. In a way maybe you are an example of a Type Two who actually quite thrives on being that type and doesn't necessarily have the incentive to move forward and away from the essential fixation.

Gill: Yes, maybe. I think one goes back to the psychology of it all and why – the why I may be stuck as a Two, if I put it that way. I think it's much healthier to be where Renate is, where you don't have this dependence on everyone else's acceptance and think you are all these things. It's much better if you can be both: be that and also be happy in your own skin and love yourself for it. But I don't know how to be like that unfortunately.

Renate: You are right, Gill, it is a process of maturation, but my teacher in this process was life experiences of suffering, where I felt completely alone on my own. I also experienced that if I surrendered to whatever I was feeling – grief, suffering, whatever was there – and went deep inside myself and stayed with this feeling… it took me to the light. It took me to this place of love that was not 'I love'. The feeling was 'I am love'. Everything is love. Yes, it was life experiences.

Gill: I think your training and your exploration probably moved you that way, and the world that you are in is very different. I am more in the business world and practicalities and don't spend a lot of time, if any, on self-development, for the want of a better word. I am interested in all sorts of psychological things and counselling and all that, but I don't actually work on it. Like you said, you went through various emotions, through difficult experiences and let them go, by the sound of it.

Renate: Yes, that brings up the question in me: are you happy, in your life?

Gill: I am. I mean, we are human beings [*Gill and Renate laughing*]. I am not ecstatic about everything, but yes, I am. I am most happy helping people and I am not happy if I am not. And if I am not wanted, I am not happy. So they do go together, being wanted…

Iain: How would you feel with that, Paul? Interesting statement: you are not happy if you are not wanted. Would you say that is true for you?

Paul: It's not totally true, but there is some truth in it, definitely. Particularly if there is somebody I really want to like me; if they are being really approving and I am making them laugh and they want to be close and connect and merge and be playful, then I can be just in heaven. I can be really in this kind of heavenly state. So in that way, getting some loving and mirroring back from particular others can make me really happy. But then sometimes I do touch on what Renate is touching on, where I am happy as I am and less dependent on another person being a certain way, or me being a certain way for another person, so there's both.

Iain: We have about five or six minutes left. Let's really look at what you all feel the potential for growth is for Type Twos. You [Renate] mentioned that it is 'holy will'.

Renate: And 'holy freedom'. Holy freedom comes in the moment you accept that this is the way it is and you surrender your own will – you don't try to change – in this moment or that moment. It is incredibly liberating and that is the freedom. If I am in an Absolute state, or if I feel angry, and it doesn't matter, and you are aware, and you can accept it, that is freedom. To surrender to the movement of the universe, [to] the way it is without trying to change it and [including] also whatever is happening inside us… to allow all that without manipulating, without interfering… that is the transformation into freedom.

Paul: There is one thing for me that I feel is really important for the integration and healing for a Two. If I feel completely lost and feel like the world has left me behind at the side of the road, and I am not where I am meant to be, usually I can get very busy and try [to] force things and manipulate the world so that I get to a successful set of conditions. But I am also really interested in spending time with that feeling and opening to that sensation of feeling lost and feeling like the world has left me behind and I am not where I need to be, and other things come through that. That feels like a really healing place to go to, rather than getting busy and wilful about trying to sort it out: 'Okay [*eyes closed*] I feel lost, I feel left behind', and spending time with that.

Iain: It's that slowing down that is the key, and it takes the courage to stay with the effects, the repercussions of the slowing down.

Paul: Slowing down, coming back, turning inwards a little bit and being with the effect of it, the mood and direct experience of the state of 'feeling lost' *and* connecting with that.

Gill: [*laughing*] I don't want to put myself into that place. If I am abandoned, I'll use the word 'abandoned' as 'abandoned' for me is a very clear graphic word and I understand what it means. If I feel abandoned I am not comfortable to try and stay with it. Again, I am sure it would help in the long run, but at the moment I still run to where I am not abandoned, to the 'somebody' who will pull me back in. The way I do it – which I guess is slightly manipulative – is [ask], "What can I do to help you?" So I am not going to put myself through things. It's a pattern that I think the older you get, the more difficult it is to break it. If you have been playing that game for forty years, it's quite difficult really to sit there and put yourself through a certain level of suffering, because I think that is what you [Paul] were saying – holding on to that feeling. And probably that depends on the level of real suffering one has had along the road, and I don't choose to go back to some of those particularly difficult periods of my life.

Iain: Okay, we have two minutes left...

Renate: Well, [Iain], how is it to live with a Type Two? [*group laughter*]

Iain: It's more about you guys than me, but to live with a Type Two can be beautiful and also can be challenging at times...

Renate: Yes, because what a Type Two always does is – and I think it is most difficult for you [Iain] – we don't have boundaries; we invade other people's space.

Paul: Yes, it's true it can be invasive helping, can't it?

Iain: It's true, organising all of your clothes, your life, your possessions: 'Oh he doesn't need that any more, get rid of that'. So there are challenges to live with a Two, but there is a challenge to live with a Type Six as well, which I am. It's true of all the Enneagram types.

We are pretty much there on time and I would like to thank Renate, Paul, and Gill for coming along to conscious.tv.

To watch this interview please go to:
http://www.conscious.tv/consciousness/enneagram

Enneagram Type Three – The Achiever

Discussion with Maureen, Eleonora and Pat

Moderated by Iain McNay

Iain: I've personally found the Enneagram very useful in my life, and it's something I discovered many years ago. I'm joined by three guests who all know quite a lot about the Enneagram and their type: Maureen, Eleonora, and Pat. Maureen, let's start with you, tell us briefly what is the Enneagram.

Maureen: It is a big question, but in short in my experience, what I have found it to be is a map. It's a map of nine perspectives or worldviews that we have, and what that does is lead to a whole set of motivations, values, and then behaviours. For example, if I took a very simple one: two people walk into a room full of strangers. If you have a worldview that contains the aspect of 'Hey this is exciting and don't know who I'm going to meet, but I may find out something out here or meet somebody', then the person is likely to go in feeling excited. They are likely to be quite animated and talk to people, and that will bring on a whole set of behaviours. On the other hand, someone else might go in with more trepidation because part of their worldview is that connection with people is something very intimate and more personal, and so a room full of strangers wouldn't give them that. They might go in feeling apprehensive, or maybe bored, or not going to enjoy it, so that would set up a whole set of behaviours. Even in that simple example I can see that the whole thing is a mix. And while the worldview drives behaviours, then the behaviours also reinforce the worldview.

Iain: Let's just be clear, each person is basically one different Enneagram type and that influences how they are in terms of how they see life in certain situations.

Maureen: Exactly, yes.

Iain: I know there are nine different types, and one of the challenges of course is to find our own type.

Pat: Yes it is, because having a worldview like that is limited.

Maureen: What we are trying to do is – and the reason it's a map – if we can find where we start from, we can see what the confines are. Some call it a prison in a way, that we're confined within that worldview and believe it to be *the* perspective, whereas if we can broaden our perspective, then we have more choices. So the Enneagram helps us to know where we start from so we can move outwards.

Iain: And we can find our potential.

Maureen: Absolutely.

Iain: I know everyone has their own ideas and understanding of the Enneagram, but Pat, how does it help you in your life?

Pat: I came across it... must have been twenty-odd years ago. I found a book on the Enneagram and I thought 'It can't be that simple' – that I have a type and therefore I enact throughout my type. But the more I read about the Enneagram, the more I realised many sets of habits that I had developed as a child, that give me my personality, i.e., persona, [that] really can drive my behaviour. The Enneagram showed me that actually I could run my ego rather than my ego running me, which was very important – how my type helps me and how it hinders me. It's like nailing the jelly to the wall. So I started to study it, and as Maureen said, it is like a map: once you know the point that you're at, then you can take that and move yourself further into being more of who you really are, rather than how the personality make you appear to be. Personality is useful to have, but sometimes it kind of gets it wrong and starts to drive you and it's really important [to notice].

Iain: So you find out more of who you really are.

Pat: I believe so, yes. Because the ego or the personality can have a tendency to drive one, and I have been in many boardrooms to see two-year-old behaviour to know that to be true. It's getting the ego in perspective and that's what the Enneagram helps you to do.

Iain: Eleonora, how did you find out you were a Type Three?

Eleonora: It was quite a journey to find out I was a Type Three. First of all, I started off doing a workshop at Emmaus House with the Helen Palmer camp of the Enneagram.

Iain: So explain when you say 'Helen Palmer camp'. What do mean by that?

Eleonora: Basically there are various numbers of teachers worldwide that are teaching the Enneagram. And one teacher is Helen Palmer, and another two good teachers are Don Riso and Russ Hudson, and then we also have David Daniels; those are the ones I actually know. Claudio Naranjo is teaching the Enneagram too. How I got to find out about the Enneagram was through my spiritual path, and how I found out about being a Type Three was a really long journey because having done a lot of therapy and lots of workshops beforehand, it was really difficult for me to pinpoint exactly which type am I, as I could identify myself with many of the other types. It was through one of the workshops with Sandra Maitri – whom I forgot to mention and who is also a teacher of the Enneagram – and she absolutely pinpointed the fact that everything the Three does is [to] get value. Threes do not really value themselves for what they are, but they value themselves for the things that they do.

Iain: Let's have a practical example of that in your life.

Eleonora: [*thinking*] A practical example of that in my life… I can bend over backwards to do all kinds of different things. Do them fast, do them well, do lots of them at the same time, so that *you* can see how valuable I am to you.

Iain: It's like impressing people in one way.

Eleonora: It's more than impressing, it's really getting the validation that I, as an individual, cannot do for myself; so I have to get you guys to validate who I am, based upon what it is I can do for you. For me that was very key: the sense of lack of self-value. Not lack of self-worth, but value. So I do not know if you [Pat] want to add anything to that.

Pat: It's being driven really… I think Threes are externally high-acuity: they can read people very quickly, and there is a need to see the value reflected in somebody else's persona or eyes. And it would be quite nice if you told me I was pretty good as well; that would help. So there is a seeking to be externally validated, which for me was one of the things that made me realise I was a Three. It took me a while to actually accept that was an important aspect to motivate me to get and do things.

Iain: We know there are nine different types altogether and we all have an element of each type in us, but it's the predominant type that we are looking at. Pat and Maureen, was it quite easy for you to spot you were a Type Three, or did you go through a process like Eleonora did?

Maureen: When I read the Riso-Hudson book it hit me in the pit of my stomach. It was like 'Oh, how did they know? They must have been following me round for the last twenty years!'

Iain: So they know the intimate details of you.

Maureen: It really hit me, physically, and I was like 'Wow…' Partly a relief: here explains the things that have been conflicting in my life and the things I have been struggling with. Partly I was like 'Oh my god how did they know?' And in typical Three fashion – picking up on what Eleonora was saying about the validation – someone said to me, "Oh you don't look like a Three, you can't possibly be a Three!" I thought 'Oh that's all right then, I must be a Nine', and I spent a little while as a Nine because they had said so. Then eventually I came back to know I am a Three. What really did it for me was reading the book and hitting on the right type. I think when you read it, there are a lot of behaviours in all the types and you can tick them and say 'Ah yes, I get that one', but it's when it really hits you to the core, that's when you know that's your type.

Pat: It can often be the type that you least like to be.

Eleonora and Maureen: [*laughing*]

Pat: 'Hello, I'm not really like that!' There is almost a rejection of it.

Maureen: Often there is.

Pat: I'm not a Type Three for godsake… but actually I am. Knowing you are a Three can be very helpful because it helps you recognise how you drive yourself and at the same time drive others. I have a daughter who is a Type Four. We are always in a clash because I am continually trying to get her to do stuff, and she doesn't want to do it. So I have to recognise how what I'm doing is not a useful thing, or when it is useful. For me it was recognising how helpful it is to be a Type Three and how hindering it can be too.

Iain: For someone watching this programme who doesn't know anything about the Enneagram, [people] who are hopefully intrigued and want to know what type they are, what are the simple things and triggers they would look out for? What are the basic characteristics of a Type Three?

Maureen: If we go back to worldview, the way I would sum up a Three perspective – for me anyway, it may be different for my colleagues here – is the phrase 'It's up to me'. That has two things: there is one side that Pat talked about, the positive and the negative. The one side that is the American dream, you know, 'It's up to me; the pauper can be the President'. If I do it, if I put my mind on something and decide to do it and work hard enough and conscientiously enough, I can do it! So there is a lot of achievement, success, working hard, efficiency, those kind of words are within that. But then the other side of the model is, if it's up to me… the image that springs to my mind is Atlas, holding the world on the shoulders… *it's up to me*.

Iain: So, responsibility.

Maureen: Yes, responsibility, burden. If I let go who's going to catch it? Nobody. Therefore you get on a treadmill of 'I have to keep going'. I think that's more of the downside of Type Three, a drivenness, and you almost have to hide your heart from yourself. I think that's key for Threes, because if I really got in touch with my feelings, sometimes I might not want to do these things, it might be a burden, but I can't allow myself really to feel that, so I have to keep driving myself and driving myself. If anybody recognises those kinds of characteristics in themselves, then it might be useful for them to look into Type Three, because I think as Pat said, it is both positive and negative. There are great qualities, but there is also a great cost to being a Three.

Pat: It's fair to say that often Threes feel like the little hero, they take the responsibility of the family and may often give away their heart's desire. It's a fortunate child, the one who doesn't give up their heart's desire and actually does what they want to do; but a Three will quite happily give up their heart's desire to achieve whatever they believe is the goal. I was in corporate life for many years and did very well until I got to the top of the ladder and realised there was nothing there, there was no heart there, and that's often what will happen.

Iain: That's pretty scary to get to the top of the ladder and realise there's nothing there.

Pat: Well, yes. I perceived it at the top of the ladder, but it could have been the bottom.

Maureen: It is. That's the sadness of the Three and we don't like to go there because it is very sad.

Iain: So you discover this emptiness inside you.

Maureen: Yes I realised that a Three, if you can get in touch with that emptiness inside you, can feel like a polo mint, you know. It's all on the outside. On the inside there is nothing. There is no one home because you are doing everything for others...

Eleonora: ...[for] an adult or from the outside world, from your parents: everything about the child tries to be someone your parents want you to be, rather than finding your own heart's desire.

Pat: I found, after doing a lot of this work, that people... in fact it was my stepbrother who said it to me, "You're not the same person as you were before." And I said, "I have always been here, I just haven't been able to show you that I'm here." The work has helped me to be able to show who I am without the persona. I am not saying the persona goes away, but there is this kind of an awakening to some extent, that I'm more than just my type. I've actually got something else to offer rather than just this efficiency that's driving this competitiveness, this success... and that actually there is more to it. Often you don't get to see that side of the Three. Threes will often be sales directors, people who are at the top of their game.

Maureen: It might be interesting to say lots of famous people are Threes.

Pat: Yes, Tony Blair would be a good example. Threes are great at being able to think on their feet, to be able to spin a yarn. Sometimes that gets them into trouble because they haven't done the detail, but there you go. So, good at sales.

Iain: Well, I have a list here that I thought might be interesting. Tony Blair is not here actually, but Bill Clinton, Paul McCartney, Tony Robbins, Tom Cruise, Madonna, Sting, Diana Ross, George Clooney. This is a list that I took out from two different books, but they are all – as you mentioned with Tony Blair – very driven people and at the top of their professions.

Maureen: And also image-wise, there is a real image aspect to a Three. We like to look good.

Iain: Let's look at this image thing. You like to look good. What else about the image?

Eleonora: The image seems to be everything, and that's what I was talking about in terms of the lack of value. What you are appreciating about me is what it is I can do for you *and* the way I can look.

Pat: Chameleon.

Eleonora: The fact that I can be absolutely adaptable to any kind of situation and circumstances *and* I know what it is that you want as well! But inside, what do I want? Why am I doing this, what are my motivations? So that is what is missing in a sense.

Pat: The self-value that you [Eleonora] talked about...

Eleonora: Yes, the self-value, and really follow your heart's desire rather than trying to fulfil somebody else's dreams, or somebody else's expectations, or your parents' expectations and dreams.

Maureen: My example would be, I did work for Pricewaterhouse, which is typical of a lot of the consultancies, and the phrase always used was 'You are as good as today's project'. So you could have been brilliant on yesterday's project, last year's project, the last twenty years, but that doesn't count, it's only today's project that counts. So it's that constant 'Who are you today in the eyes of the people?' There is no history in a way for the Three, it's only today, so it's very hard to keep satisfying everyone's expectations because they are so wide and so dispersed, and even if they were happy with you yesterday we don't assume as Threes that they will be happy with us today unless we prove ourselves again. It's a kind of *Ground Hog Day*.

Iain: That's a lot of pressure on you guys.

Eleonora: It is a lot of pressure, even if it comes from the inside and not necessarily on top of perhaps the expectations of others. But it's also a way of being excellent in your own eyes and god forbid you make a mistake!

Pat: It's funny that actually you pick up on the person that you think doesn't like you, and put all your energy into trying to make them like you, and then when they like you, you can move onto the next one.

Iain: Really, is that how you feel, you can really tick them off?

Pat: It can be. I've got that one, that's good, I can move on, particularly if you are in a competitive situation. I think the competitiveness of the Three... there is focus too, like the train coming down the track. This is where I am going, I am going there and nothing takes you off it, so that's a bit of a difficult one, because you can run over people when you are so focused.

Eleonora: Before I actually started working from the spiritual perspective of the Enneagram, as well as other things, I used to say to myself 'I'm going to do that, even if it kills me. I will get that, even if it kills me or even if I have to run over somebody'. I don't do that any more, but I used *to* [*group laughter*].

Iain: You [Threes] are also never bored. Is that right?

Eleonora: We try *never* to be bored because – at least speaking for myself – boredom used to be a big issue. Now I'm not bored in the slightest, but I have different views on what boredom is. Certainly before I embarked on understanding more of myself, boredom was a big issue. I would do anything not to be bored.

Pat: To be bored means to be slowed down. That's not an option, and we've got to keep going.

Maureen: I was going to say, I think we are the 'human doings' of the Enneagram types, I think I have read that somewhere, rather than the 'human beings'. As long as we are *doing*, we are achieving what we want to, because then there is a chance of success. Failure isn't an option for a Three really, so we keep on the treadmill of whatever we have created for ourselves, whatever that is.

Pat: It's a little train that *could*, isn't it?

Maureen: Even if we are enjoying ourselves, we do it to the best.

Eleonora: I also find that energy-wise it's just so high. Sometimes, when I compare myself to my friends for instance, I think 'Oh I can keep going and I have left them behind a few hours ago'. Also, it's a way for me of feeling very much alive, and that energy keeps feeding on itself, and to some extent it gives life meaning. So yes, we are the *doing* of the Enneagram and the thing that we try to avoid is actually *being*.

Pat: But that's the 'workaholism' and then comes the big burnout. You work yourself into an early grave at that rate.

Iain: So that's one of the dangers: you burn yourselves out and have a bit of a breakdown.

Pat: I used to go on holiday and would be ill the minute I would stop work. The minute I would stop a project, or a project was over, I'd fall ill, because I would not allow myself to be ill or anything while there was a project going on.

Eleonora: I have heard that before. In fact, it is really typical.

Pat: And then I'm only ill for the time I am on holiday. Then I am back at work. So there is this kind of drivenness, this workaholism that Threes then discover. Actually you know you're going to burn out.

Iain: You are always doing lists of things to do. Is that right?

Maureen: I do them in my head. I don't write them down.

Eleonora: I do, I have to, and I have more than one list, as a matter of fact.

Iain: So you have lists of lists?

Eleonora: No, not lists of lists, I've got several lists in order of importance [*Maureen laughing*]…

Pat: Wow [*group laughter*].

Eleonora: It's true. Otherwise I don't get things done.

Iain: So you are impressed by this, are you, Pat?

Pat: Well, they are all in my head, my lists, but anyway yes…

Iain: I think we have quite a few clues if somebody watching this program wants to try and spot if they are a Three or not. You are driven, you are constantly on the go, ambitious, and you do lists.

Pat: We are good at what we do and we get things done.

Iain: And you mention shape-shift. Talk more about this, the chameleon you mention. That's a kind of shape-shift.

Pat: This was what Eleonora was talking about, an ability to be whatever somebody else wants you to be. I read somewhere once that even someone in a Buddhist monastery who was a Three would still be the best Buddhist they could ever be. There would always be this kind of jump to always be at the top of the game, top of the list. A lot of sports people, I can't remember them off the top of my head, that are driven, are that Three energy. You don't necessarily have to be a Three, but Type Three energy is about succeeding, moving forward, getting things done, task oriented. That kind of sums us up. Do you think that is fair to say?

Maureen: Yes, and I think it goes back to – it's what we were saying earlier about living on the outside of ourselves – looking for validation, and so we're looking to see who wants what from us. And then we are always trying to satisfy it. That's why sometimes people say that we are the marketeers, but it's because we are very good at having acuity as you [Pat] said, and then looking to see what they want and trying to give it to them. It comes back to there is nothing inside you, because if we give what we think the other needs, then we will be successful. That's success to us.

Eleonora: We will be successful, and we will be loved, and we will be acknowledged, because the thing that is missing intrinsically is that sense of not valuing yourself. So until you get that, you will always look outside of yourself for that kind of validation. And if you don't get it, you are going to go on over and over again, until you do get it. Even then, it's never going to be quite the way you want it. The key to this is valuing oneself first.

Iain: Okay, once you realise all of this, then what happens? You realise what this pattern is for you all. How does this start to change the way you see life?

Pat: That's a good question because I think for me when I had the realisation, it was 'Oh really, is that it?' I came to that recognition when I left corporate life because I realised that I could not burn myself out more than I already had done. For me it was burnout.

Iain: So, practical things: you left the job you were doing, and you decided that was taking you nowhere. So what did you do then?

Pat: Well, then I guess it was not a loss of hope, but of trying to find something more than just the image I thought that I was projecting. So really I had to slow down and spend some time looking at myself and knowing myself more, which is what I do now.

Iain: And how is that for you?

Pat: It's much more satisfying because I actually feel that I have more worth than I thought I had before. I can see myself as a softer gentler person than the person I was before. I wouldn't show that side of me. I don't feel so rejected. It's a strange thing to try and explain. I do know that when I slow down and smell the coffee, there is a sense of being here, and being present

Iain: That's a huge change.

Pat: Huge change, yes.

Iain: And you're happier?

Pat: Very much so, yes.

Iain: What about you [Maureen]? How have you integrated these realisations?

Maureen: I think I haven't had quite such a big road to Damascus as Pat. I think how it helps me practically every day is to know the characteristics and then catch myself doing it. For example, yesterday I was doing the garden at the front and it was getting dark and I wanted to do everything before it got dark, because success is doing everything. And if I had done three quarters of it and not the other quarter, that would not have been success because I couldn't tick it off my list. So I would have driven myself before, like 'It's got to be finished!' Then I said to myself 'Hey, I have a choice here, I can finish it if I want, but I don't have to'. Then I weighed up the pros and cons, and actually it made more sense to finish it off before it got dark. Before, I never would have had even that conversation with myself, I would have just driven myself. So it's about catching myself in very small ways, of things that I am doing to drive myself, and giving myself the choice. Of course there are bigger things, but it's in the minutiae of life as well.

Iain: It seems you relax a lot and you see what wants to happen, rather than 'I've got do this!'

Maureen: That's right, and then fun comes in. I know my triggers, I know when I'm too driven because I lose my sense of fun, everything becomes very serious: 'I must do!' I am very harsh, so when I'm not smiling and laughing I know 'Hey, relax, slow down, have a drink'. It's knowing myself more, knowing the little things in life, and allowing myself to have a choice, which is that worldview of not being constrained by 'This is the only way I can live'… and saying 'Hey, there are choices here'.

Pat: I think that is true to all the types because you actually end up being kinder to yourself; you're not beating yourself up so much. And what we all end up realising is that – like Maureen said – you don't have to do anything. It's a choice, and that's a huge, huge release…

Maureen: [*laughing*]

Pat: And we talked earlier about the burdens that we Type Threes have. I don't think there's that much of a burden [if] we don't feel we have to do everything for everybody else, and we start to do stuff for ourselves and don't feel bad about it, because within that there is shame – shame that I am actually expected to be validated externally. I think there is a huge shame that suddenly goes as well. That's my experience…

Eleonora: For me it's a question of beginning to appreciate all the gifts that this particular type has to offer – [it's] the same with every type. So rather than rejecting them, as I used to in the past – 'Oh this is wrong if I do it this way', or 'I shouldn't be driving myself', you know, a lot of internal criticism going on – now I recognise 'Hey, my goodness I'm rushing through things again… what's that about?' So it's through observation and also through light-heartedness. We can't change effectively, but what we can do is observe how we are, how we behave, and that we have choices. You can still go in that particular direction, rush through things and tick them off the list, or you can actually relax and laugh about it. The other thing is, looking at my motivations: 'Why am I doing this? Who am I trying to please? Who am I doing it for?' And to be clear about what it is that motivates me, in this particular moment, to do this particular thing. And 'Do I have to?' What's the internal conversation? So those are the aspects I found to be interesting. Also validating myself for the capacities that I have. And yes, they could be better, but so what? This is what there is, and this is what I can do, this is who I am… to some extent. When I say, "This is who I am," it's in terms of the personality: this is the kind of personality I have – it's not who *I am*, but it's the personality that I have.

Iain: I brought two books with me. I know Eleonora has brought a huge pile – we might get through some of them later – but I brought two that I really like. One is *The Enneagram Made Easy* [by Baron and Wagele] which is fairly basic, but for anyone who wants to take this further and maybe investigate what kind of type they are, this is a great book. It gives you a series of questions, some cartoons in here, and it's very simple. It's not necessarily always easy to find your type, and it makes it a lot simpler than some of the other books. This one here is by Sandra Maitri, who we have interviewed twice on conscious.tv, titled *The Spiritual Dimension of the Enneagram*, and she says one interesting thing, which I wanted to discuss with you ladies, she is saying that modern life is taking on more and more of the Three-ish quality. I thought that was interesting, because that seems to me to be very true. People are rushing around even more: mobile phones, Blackberries and everything… you can't get away from being a Three, can you?

Pat: Also it's a celebrity thing, this whole 'Celebrity Get Me out of Here'. That's very Three-ish, you'll get a lot of actors.

Iain: And the TV series 'The Apprentice' is very Three-ish, I would guess.

Pat: Very much so. I look at The Apprentice and try and guess what the type might be, not that I would know totally, but…

Maureen: And the whole Susan Boyle phenomenon, the fact that she was pulled from obscurity and became this huge superstar, that's a very Type Three phenomenon. That's also what we are valued for, being Threes in our society. In a way it's a very addictive type to be because we are applauded for it and we get a lot of success for it.

Pat: It's also shallow.

Iain: It's interesting for me that this is the way society is moving. Society is moving like you said, with the celebrity thing. We hide more and more, all of us, and as a society [we hide] what we really are and what's really going on, and we do what we think is going to bring us success. Then we think that's going to bring us happiness, but it doesn't work out that way [group agreement].

Pat: And I think that's what drives the doing-ness of the Three because we think if we do everything for everyone, and be the best we can be, conquer the Everest Mountain, everyone will love us and we will be happy. Well… hmm.

Iain: Might be, for a little time.

Pat: Might be for a nanosecond – if you allow yourself to appreciate it.

Iain: Also I have found in Sandra's book a couple of things which I thought were worth looking at, to see if you all agree. She was saying that Threes can have a very painful inner journey because the whole image thing is a lie and when they realise that, it's actually quite devastating. I think that's probably what you felt, Pat, when you left.

Pat: Painful, because you spend all of these years building this image and then when it fails it's like a piece of tissue paper, you realise it actually stands for nothing. The only thing that stands for anything is what you think of yourself and how you are in yourself, which is a hard lesson for a Three to come to terms with.

Eleonora: Yes indeed, it's almost as if everything you have done is worthless, actually.

Iain: Well, that's quite a deep statement to make, isn't it – everything is worthless [group laughter].

Pat: Shall we get the tissues out?

Iain: So the potential for the Three I gather is the nearest to the 'pearl beyond price'. Does anyone want to explain what the pearl beyond price is?

Maureen: Well I think the pearl beyond price is the transformation of our ego. Our ego is absolutely essential as we know it got us here, and it is a great development, but we have seen the trap we get into. The potential in living the spiritual life is to transform that into our spiritual life away from the ego. I think you said at the beginning, Pat, about being driven by the ego, it's about using that to move us into our spiritual journey. So I guess in that sense we do have a potential.

Pat: Yes, and I think the gift of the Three – all types have gifts – is hope. If we can get through our huge ego, then anybody can do it. There is a hope that through the Enneagram, and through our Three-ness, is this authentic hope. The shadow, if you like, of the Three is self-deception. It has to be, because in order to have a personality you have to self-deceive. Our shadow is self-deception, we lie to ourselves that this is okay, and sometimes stretch the

CONVERSATIONS ON THE ENNEAGRAM

truth a bit, like... the fish was this big [*demonstrating large size*], not this big [*smaller*]. When we become authentic, become truly connected to who we are, to our True Nature, then that is real hope. That is authenticity, which is I think what we all, at the end of the day, would call happiness. To be true and authentic to myself, to have *me* running my ego instead of my ego running me. I call my ego Rover. When it gets in the way I say 'Sit!'

Iain: Does it always obey?

Pat: Sometimes [*laughing*]. Like all dogs, they don't always do it.

Eleanora: Where I've got to, [as far as] living with [my] personality is concerned, is again through appreciating the fact that what's manifesting here – in terms of 'true nature' – is through this personality. I happen to have been born – there is something about nature versus nurture – with a particular type of personality, or with the blueprint of a particular type of personality, and then the nurturing that I have received builds up on the nature. So here I am. I am on this planet being given this personality-type and being as authentic and truthful as I can be, but it's not about destroying the personality or making it better, even. It's about being able to live with whatever I have and I happen to be a Type Three personality, and it is through appreciation that I see my true nature manifesting itself through this [type].

Iain: So when you [Eleonora] say 'true nature', what do you mean by that?

Eleonora: True nature is what's real about ourselves, rather than what we think is real, or the kind of persona that I want to portray.

Iain: So what's real about you now?

Eleonora: That I am here, that I am breathing, that I have emotions going through and sensation going through my body, thinking about... or even being confused about who I am right now. It's a combination of various things. Yes, there is the personality and yes, there is also what I am experiencing right now at a physical level and at an emotional level.

Pat: Yes, I think when I am teaching the Enneagram I visualise it almost like a jacket, so the more I know about my type the more I can unbutton this jacket and at some point even take it off and wear it lightly. It's always going to be with me, but the less I use my personality to live my life as it unfolds, the more likely I am to be able to live it in the moment and be present and be conscious of who I really am. But the personality will always be there; it's just how we deal with that.

Iain: It seems where we are getting to here is, you are all aware of something that is aware of the personality...

Pat: The inner witness, yes.

Iain: Using Sandra Maitri's words here, 'a constant which is nothing to do with the personality'. Would you say that is your experience?

Maureen: Absolutely. And if we take it back to the Enneagram, that would be the whole point wouldn't it? If we know that our starting point is the Three and we open up our potentiality to the other energies, the other worldviews, the other perspectives, then they are all available to us, and they are always available to us. But if we are in a limited worldview, we only think we have one perspective available to us. So if we can relax and open up to that, we have all those energies. I think that's what you [Eleonora] were saying, and we have access to them all.

Pat: Yes, it's like being in a box and you can only see out of this bit. And once you know your type, the box opens and you have the whole spectrum to play with, and then you actually start to understand how to relate, because the higher purpose of the Three is relating, connecting, being with people, and often people can't be with you because you are spending too much time telling how great you are when actually, when you stop doing that, people start to tell you or they see that you are great. It's getting the persona or personality in perspective and not letting it drive you.

Iain: Maureen, how are you feeling in terms of how you are finding your potential as you understand more and more about the Three-ish nature of your personality and you realise you are not just the personality?

Maureen: I think first of all, the 'polo mint' perspective has gone and I'm more in touch with reality and more in touch with who I am and what qualities I have. Before, I wasn't really aware of those, so I'm more grounded in myself.

Iain: When you say 'qualities', would being grounded be one of the qualities?

Maureen: It would be one of the qualities, yes. And seeing the strengths I have and believing that I have them, that would be the first aspect, but then the second aspect would be… sometimes other strengths are required. Like strength and straight talking for example that Threes are not so good at, but then realising they are available to me as well. It's being able to access those if it's appropriate, if an occasion arises when that is required, and so I have more freedom, more choice.

Iain: You are not so caught in having to please everybody, or receive approval. You can just tell someone what you really think.

Maureen: If that's required, yes, I don't mean in a crass…

Iain: No, no I didn't mean that…

Maureen: But yes, if that's required, that would be more available and easier to do, whereas maybe when I am caught in Three-ness – 'What would they think?' and 'Is it the right thing?' and 'What would their reaction be?' and 'Should I do it?' – there's this whole inner talk of whether I could even do it and whether it's the right thing, rather than just being present to 'This is what's required right now, let me do it'. There is no angst, no inner talk, it just flows. There is just much more flow, much more freedom; there's much more choice, there's much more relying on, rather than 'It's up to me'. If I go back to my worldview of 'It's up to me', maybe it isn't up to me, maybe there are other things around and I just can tap into them, if I am open to the possibility. If I am open to life rather than being contained, then things can flow much more easily.

Iain: Do you find that people who are close to you see you in a different way now?

Maureen: Yes. For example, my dad was ill and he has now subsequently died, but I gave up work and took a sabbatical to look after him in his last days. I know my friends were very surprised because I was the corporate woman on the treadmill running round the world every week, running workshops, coaching managers, and they were very surprised that I would do that. I was quite surprised as well, but I did it, and thoroughly. It was a blessing to be able to do that. So yes, things are changing for me.

Iain: What about you two guys [Pat and Eleonora]? How do you think people see you differently, if they do see you differently?

Pat: I think I broached it a while ago when somebody said to me, "You are not the same person as you were before." My stepbrother said that and I said, "Actually, I've always been here, I just haven't been able to show you." I think that's the difference for me. Failure was not an option. Now I see failure as really quite a good thing, it slows me down. I live my life in a much more relaxed state of being. If I have got to get a job done… and I do a lot of work at the moment with young offenders, then you know I have to keep very grounded when I am doing that sort of work. And that's been very good for me to know that I am not depending on them liking me, because actually most of the time they don't. You've got to stand up there and talk to them with absolutely no response whatsoever, and for a Three that's really hard, but at least that was really great. So yes, I think I am much more like Maureen was saying, more grounded and hopefully more authentic and living my life more meaningfully, with real meaning rather than just superficial meaning which is how I lived it before.

Iain: And Eleonora?

Eleonora: I have stopped trying to please anybody really. People around me have noticed that tremendously, because I am not as helpful as I used to be – always there and always in charge, that sort of thing. I've transformed my life completely since I first started finding out about the Enneagram, and subsequently I got involved in a spiritual path and a lot of stuff really changed. My life has turned around completely and I no longer try to please everybody.

Iain: Okay, I know you have a big pile of books and we've about two minutes left. If you give them to me I can hold them to the camera. We talked about the one by Sandra Maitri, *The Spiritual Dimension of the Enneagram*. Here is another one, *The Enneagram of Passions and Virtues*, which I have read. We have all read this so we can probably recommend this.

Eleonora: Then we have Helen Palmer – *The Enneagram in Love and Work*.

Iain: This is Don Riso and Russ Hudson who also do seminars: *Personality*

Types and *The Wisdom of the Enneagram*. This is a very [good book]. If somebody wanted to get their first [book], as well as the one you mentioned earlier, *The Wisdom of the Enneagram* would be [the] one.

Iain: Here is another concise one: *The Essential Enneagram*, by David Daniels.

Eleonora: Then we have Claudio Naranjo, *Character Neurosis*, one of the many books he has written.

Iain: He was actually one of the people to bring it to the forefront. The Enneagram system is five thousand years old, isn't it?

Maureen: The symbol is, but the putting the types [around the symbol] isn't. It was done by Ichazo in the seventies.

Eleonora: And we have *Facets of Unity*, by A.H. Almaas. This is just a small selection of the vast amounts of literature.

Iain: That's quite advanced, but a very interesting one. Of course Eleonora and all of you have read all these because you are such good Type Threes, is that right [*laughing*]?

Maureen: Iain, it even might be worth saying that if people wanted to find out about their type, there are a couple of good online questionnaires that they might want to take.

Iain: Do you want to mention those?

Maureen: The one I am particularly familiar with is the Riso-Hudson, which is Enneagraminstitute.com. And you can take it for about ten dollars I think online. It's very good, and that might be a good start point, and I think David Daniels has one as well, doesn't he?

Pat: I think so.

Iain: Ladies – Eleonora, Pat, and Maureen – I want to thank you very much for coming in and spending your time talking very honestly about your Type Three and how you're moving beyond your type. Thank you.

To watch this interview please go to:
http://www.conscious.tv/consciousness/enneagram

Enneagram Type Four – The Romantic

Discussion with Janette, Rosemarie and Phil

Moderated by Iain McNay

Iain: I have three Type Fours in the studio with me. We have Janette, Phil, and Rosemarie. Welcome, guys. Let's start with you, Janette, if I can ask you how you first heard about the Enneagram.

Janette: I first came across the Enneagram in the early part of nineteen-ninety-eight when I was working in the training and development area. I actually went on a week-long course in Bristol and I absolutely loved it. Straight away, I knew it was one of the models for me.

Iain: What did you love about it?

Janette: For a long time I'd felt that our personal and spiritual journeys were one and the same thing. They were part of the same continuum. But I hadn't found a tool that brought those two together in a very conscious way. So, when I came across the Enneagram, here at last was something that helped us, both on our personal and spiritual journeys. I was so excited that here was a model that really reflected something that I had been thinking about for quite a while and was needed. It really spoke to me deeply.

Iain: What is the Enneagram?

Janette: The Enneagram is a geometric figure. If you think about the word itself, 'ennea' is from the Greek word for nine, and 'gram' is for 'diagram'. So it literally means nine points on the figure. The Enneagram can be used in many different ways. The way we are focusing on today, for this program, is looking at personality types. But the Enneagram can be used as a model to understand many different things. So for example Gurdjieff, who brought the model to the West in the early nineteen-hundreds, looked at using the Enneagram to understand complex systems such as the universe and how all of that works. But today, we are working with the personality types. What that means is that the Enneagram can really help us understand ourselves and others in quite a deep way. It helps us understand our deep motivations, and also both our limitations and our potential, and I know we will be talking about that a bit later. Unlike a lot of tools in this personality area, the Enneagram doesn't put us into a box. In fact it shows us the box we put ourselves in unconsciously most of the time, and most importantly, it shows us the way out of that. It's very powerful in that sense.

Iain: Let's just briefly have the story of how you guys first heard of the Enneagram.

Rosemarie: For me it was through my husband. He was on training and those trainers were interested in the Enneagram. They held a weekend course and my husband said, "Let's go." We went along and thoroughly enjoyed that, but in fact my husband was also doing training and got very deeply involved in it. I was not so enamoured at the beginning, as Janette has been describing. There was a curiosity, but it was only about 'Hmm that's interesting'. But then it grew because I recognised how powerful it actually is, and I like the dynamic quality of the Enneagram.

Iain: How quickly did you recognise your type?

Rosemarie: Fairly quickly. I made a few other detours before I got to Type Four, probably one other particularly, but when I did the questionnaire, Four came out quite strongly.

Iain: It is quite remarkable how it not exactly nails you down, but it does give you a pretty good indication, when you really look.

Rosemarie: Yes, but it wasn't the one I went to immediately [*laughing*].

Iain: Phil, what's your story, with the Enneagram?

Phil: I came across it at a very similar time to Janette, in the late nineties. Having done a lot of work with other personality types, I had been teaching Myers Briggs for quite a long time – which is very valuable for what it is – and I think the Enneagram brings something different. I think to understand our complexity, the more maps we have to understand that complexity, the better. I don't believe any one [tool] is absolutely 'Oh that's the one'. The Enneagram brings something that Jungian type doesn't: more around the growth areas. For me, it was a route into more of a spiritual journey. Whether it has turned out that way or not, I don't know [*laughing*], but at the time, that is what I was looking for.

Iain: How did you feel when you found out you were a Type Four?

Phil: Reassured, because what was very powerful is the small examples of behaviour. Sometimes when I read the Type Four description I think 'Well, I'm not sure', but actually when you look at the underlying motivations and you see where your own habits of behaviour are coming from, that's actually very powerful. It's always easy to do something about, but to realise when you are sitting there, every single moment, not quite being satisfied with how that moment is, then that's the Type Four motivation.

In every moment, no matter how ideal you think that is, you are always thinking 'And it could be better'. It's the inability to sit with exactly what is, and just enjoy it. For example, I was on the Isle of Wight yesterday, it was chucking it down with rain, and I was visiting an artist, a potter I know. I was fascinated with her work, and what was constantly going through my mind is 'And I wish I was doing that and I have missed that opportunity'. Instead of actually just delighting in the engagement with that person and staying with it, it's 'Gosh, isn't this fantastic and why [*clenching fists*] am I not doing it?' That's the habit.

Iain: To some extent we all feel that, at different times. I am not a Type Four and I still feel that at times.

Phil: Yes, I am not sure what everyone else feels [*laughing*], but for me it's particularly the *longing* bit you read.

Iain: For you particularly, it is the longing that you are connecting with…

Phil: Yes, that can be at a huge level, or it can be just in that moment. Just not being satisfied with exactly what's happening.

Rosemarie: Now I recognise much more how in the past I would look and envy other people for 'Oh they have got this' or 'They have got that' and 'They seem to have got it together, why haven't I got it together?' I recognise that part of it. It's quite difficult when you look into your past and that's perhaps another thing as a Four, I tend to look back a lot at what has been and [have] dug into what has been but not enjoying things in the moment. I would say I do enjoy things in the moment, but not all the time. It's difficult to put all these things… it's like Janette saying about boxes. Often for me, it's a moving goal post. Talking about it now, I know when I was younger I would have been much more fixed in always looking for certain things and feeling a bit hard done by: 'Oh, why haven't I got that?' But that has changed. I am able to take a different perspective nowadays.

Iain: It's like the grass is always greener on the other side of the hill. Is that how you feel sometimes?

Janette: Grass is always greener [*thinking*]… to some extent…

Phil: I think when you say 'sometimes', that's important. [Rosemarie,] we are not locked into that habit of behaviour all the time. I think one of the advantages of the Enneagram is being able to recognise 'Oh hang on a minute, that's the type [Four pattern], so stay with what is'. So yes, there are times when we can just be with the moment and other times we take ourselves away from it unnecessarily.

Iain: Janette, what input do you have?

Janette: I think the sensitivity and introspection of Type Four are really key, and how that plays out for me is, I remember as a child – and still now, but certainly as a child – one of the things that used to puzzle me was how affected I was by things. I used to be very emotional at sad stories or hymns in school. I would be crying when everyone else wasn't and I didn't understand why I was so affected. And of course immediately – this is another characteristic of the Four – I turned it in on myself and I was the one who was wrong. There was something missing in me, or different about me that didn't quite fit. I think this is another aspect of the Four, that we look at the world and there is an instant comparison, usually on the whole a more negative comparison. As Rosemarie was saying, 'They have got it and I haven't' …there is something missing in my own way of being. Not 'They have got it' in the sense of they have got a nice car, or a lovely suit, it's something about their way of being in the world that as Fours we can often envy and often compare, and that then turns in on ourselves in quite a negative way. That's just one of the patterns, and there are other things around feeling unique and special and different and again, that being a double-edged sword. Of course we all are, every sentient being on the planet is unique and special and different, but from a Four perspective it's often that there is something set apart about me. There is something that is not quite fitting in with other people, and if I am an average Four then that becomes my identity, that becomes 'I move away from other people, I don't move towards other people'. This is a key element of a Four. I create a whole internal world around my feelings. Other types might say 'I think, therefore I am', with Fours it's 'I feel, therefore I am'. My feelings are my whole arbiter of how I am in the world so my feelings start to – if I am not careful, if I am not present and awake – take over and take me further and further away from reality, from the reality of engaging with you, with being here. I am off in some usually quite negative fantasy about what is actually going on in relation to me, in relation to my inadequacy.

Iain: Yes, it's interesting. We made a program earlier today with Type Seven and they are very feeling-oriented, but their feelings seem to come out. It seems the difference with Type Four is that you bring them more into yourselves.

Janette: There is a deep introspection with Fours. They are called, along with two other types, the 'withdrawn' types. What that means is that we withdraw in order to make sense of the world. So, someone says something, I am affected by it, I take it inside and start to make sense and meaning from that, often way off the mark [*laughing*], as I have learnt over time, but nevertheless as you say, it is an internal process. I don't feel I necessarily have to go out and act on it, but I am certainly doing activity inside with it and often a negative activity… there is some judgement about myself that is going on.

Iain: Are there any other clues for people watching this, trying to guess whether they are a type Four or not, that might be useful for them?

Rosemarie: I think Janette hit most of the key features there: the sensitivity, taking things to heart. An odd comment that someone makes [*hand on chest*] feels like a wounding. This [*pointing to heart*] gets engaged first before anything else, then this [*pointing to head*] takes over and builds lots of stories and creates that fantasy.

Janette: Taking things personally. Everything is a personal reflection on me.

Iain: That must be difficult actually. Quite a challenge, I would think, to come to terms with that. So when you realised that – and that was obviously valuable information – how did that affect your lives?

Janette: It was huge because again, I think one of the beauties of the Enneagram in general is that we often think we are the only one with that particular pattern, or that particular suffering. First of all, we can see that there are many other people who have a similar pattern, and that's both a relief and an amazing kind of growth potential *and* an embarrassment. There is a whole area of shame with Fours. It's a very interesting area of being ashamed of how we are and a fear of being shown to be inadequate in some way... I have lost your question. What was your original question? I am so interested in the inadequacies [*laughing*] that I have forgotten your question.

Iain: Overall, what I am trying to do – for people who are watching this and don't know their type – is to get a feel for it. I have made a few notes, from some of the books, of traits of Fours. Let me just read through this, and it is not necessarily for you guys to comment on, but you can if you like. You have touched on most of them: 'sensitive to critical remarks', 'ideals are important', 'always searching for your true self'. You are all nodding there [*laughing*]. 'Often long for what others have', which you have already mentioned. 'Experience dark moods of emptiness and despair'.

Rosemarie: Afraid so.

Iain: Okay, we will come onto that one later [*laughing*]. ' Feeling abandoned'. 'Don't like being told what to do'.

Janette: I think that is true of many types, but from the Fours' perspective – on not liking to be told what to do – I would say it is wanting to do things our own special way, and that being very important. For some people that is a very creative way and when I say creative, I don't just mean in a traditional artistic sense, although some Fours are artists, but not all artists are Fours. It would be some kind of personal creativity that would be important for the Four to engage in, to express themselves in that way. So 'I want to do it my way, with my own unique expression' is how that would come out. I think many people, no matter what type they are, want to do things their own way. But the particular flavour I think for a Four is 'with my own creative slant on it, whatever that is and whatever medium I am working with'.

Phil: It's interesting reading those words. I tend to think that if you look at those and try to use them as a diagnosis, that can be quite difficult. Personally I have found, and in discussion with other people, the best way is to start noticing what is it that I *do* – and where is that motivation coming from? Again, in the smallest little bits of behaviour, through to the big patterns. And

CONVERSATIONS ON THE ENNEAGRAM

the more you are aware of your habit of mind, where you automatically go, then you can start analysing: 'Well, is that a Four motivation, is that a Five or...' For some people, you read the descriptions and bang it's obvious and other times you need to get underneath it. The periods of dark depression... [you may say/think] 'No way, I don't do that!' But in its own little way, I will have periods where the dissatisfaction is greater than it is in other months. So I think everyone is unique in their behavioural expression of some of those patterns. For me, becoming aware of what it is that I do is a more important step than nailing down your type.

Janette: I would really agree with that. One of the teachers I was reading earlier on the train, coming here, talked about how our attention gets magnetised in certain directions and I really liked that. There is that draw [*body moving back and forth*] that we kind of have. So the whole way of working with the Enneagram as Phil said – and I think this is really important – isn't just about 'What's my label?', 'What's my new badge?', but actually it's a tool for self-awareness and for observing ourselves more and more honestly.

We haven't really touched on the spiritual journey, but I think the Enneagram is a spiritual tool, as well as a psychological tool. From a spiritual perspective, it's really knowing deeply the real truth of who we are, and the way through is to know deeply the way in which we deceive ourselves, or the way in which we think our usual patterns are our reality. We really need to be able to look at those, and our attention does get magnetised in certain areas and does get drawn off. And in the process – from a spiritual perspective – we get drawn away from ourselves. We lose ourselves in our usual habitual response, which is where the Enneagram is so beautiful in very specifically offering us a map to look at: 'Which cul-de-sac have I gone into now?'

So that ability and willingness to self-observe is really critical. Fortunately for us as Fours, I think one of our gifts is, with that introspection, to be very honest with what is going on within ourselves. I think we are able to land in that in a way that is perhaps more difficult for some types. We have the ability to be honest: 'This is actually what is going on here now.' And if we feel safe, we will share that in quite an articulate way, usually. I think that is one of the gifts of our introspective type. Self-awareness, as well, is another area for Fours that can be a gift.

Iain: Yes, I want to also try to keep the program as basic as possible. When you say 'self-aware', talk very briefly about what that is for you. How you practise self-awareness.

Janette: For me, at a practical level, I might notice that I have got some envious feelings about someone. I might be thinking 'I wish I had worn something that Rosemarie might be wearing today'. I can notice that happening, and over time, I notice that quicker and quicker. In the past, I might be withdrawing from her in some way. I might be pretending I don't want to talk to her, or just be too busy doing other things, when actually what I am doing is being envious of something about her. I can start to notice that happening and sometimes I might notice physical tensions around my shoulder, around my neck, a headache. So I can start to ask myself 'What's really going on here?'

Iain: It's the mental patterns that we all have, and we don't necessarily realise they are driving us a lot of the time. So it's a question of really trying to pull back and almost disassociate: 'Well, this is a pattern that I'm carrying'. Is that right?

Janette: I start to be able to look at it more objectively and not believe it so much. You know, I don't necessarily believe my own story, or I see 'Oh there I go again, here it comes up again'. Because these will be repeated patterns; it won't be the first time. So I start to catch myself in the act again – as they talk about in the Enneagram world – and I think that's really key. To ideally be able to see it as it is happening and the gap becoming closer, between my doing it and my noticing it.

Rosemarie: The *intention* of doing that... To begin with, I found certainly that you observe it after the fact. You think 'Ah that's just what's happened', and then that kind of goes backward in a way in the process, in that the more you have the intention of being aware of what is really going on here, at some point you suddenly realise it's happening while it's happening.

Iain: It takes practise doesn't it?

Rosemarie: It does take practise, yes. It's not easy.

Phil: Just picking up on what you said... the mental habit. I think for me, one of the very powerful things is that it's a mental, emotional, and physical habit. That pattern is embodied in the whole system. So being aware of 'How am I physically when I am mentally wishing something was happening and melancholy comes in?' You [Rosemarie] were saying, "Notice it." Well, if I then decide 'Woop there I go again, actually I don't want to go down that route', then one of the ways of breaking that is physically and emotionally. I don't think you can just think yourself out of it, I think it's the whole system and that, for me, is one of the areas where there is a lot of development work to do and understanding to do with the Enneagram. A lot of very valuable work I think could be done, understanding this whole approach. Am I making sense there?

Iain: Yes, the Enneagram is the framework to show you things, and there is a lot of work that goes on behind the scenes in the observation, the understanding, and the feeling.

Phil: Yes, it's the reality or awareness that my habit of personality is removing, or hiding me from. In that personality, I have got into the habit of doing it here [*pointing to head*], here [*pointing to heart*], and here [*pointing around body*]. Just trying to *think* myself out of it, in my experience, won't do it. You need to work at it, at all the levels.

Iain: I think you [Janette] mentioned the potential. Once you understand you're Type Four and you have become familiar with your patterns and the way you are operating, there's a potential for each person in their lives, and Type Four has a particular potential. I wonder if any of you want to talk about that. I guess it's also a personal thing insofar as it's *your* particular potential.

Rosemarie: For me, the potential is there for everyone. It's just recognising the fullness and the holding back that that creates. If I can recognise all those different things within me, then that releases me from following the same path and allows me to be more creative, to enjoy things even more. Personally, music, art, all of those things are really important, but to actually get involved in that and not use it in the way that I use it now, but to embody it as well as feel it, as well as think it; it's embracing all the things. That for me is what the potential is about. It's about recognising the wholeness of it all, and then it's all there for me if I'm prepared to let go of what are the most familiar things to me.

Iain: When you say 'let go', what does that mean for you?

Rosemarie: Letting go of this wounding. Letting go of 'That was meant just for me'; it is not. It's for everybody. It's letting go of the 'when I have my melancholy moods...'; it's recognising that I'm doing that. That I'm feeding it, I'm creating it. I'm digging a hole for myself that I can get out of. I can go for a walk, I can do something different and I have choices, I have possibilities. I don't have to do what I have done in the past and I don't have to make the past part of my present and my future. The future is there to be had, it's to be created, it's to be developed and to be inspired by.

Iain: It sounds like when you were all saying that you tend to bring your feelings inward. And it seems like it's almost the opposite process of your feelings coming out.

Rosemarie: I think for me, it is to trust. I don't know about you two. I mean trusting people that it will be okay to go out there and to be whoever, whatever, and to trust that people are going to be there and accept it.

Iain: How has that process been for you?

Rosemarie: It's a work-in-progress... I suppose it's going out a little bit, testing out. There are certain scenarios where it is very comfortable where you go, certainly in the spiritual work. There is a sense of everybody's there to support, so this is okay, this is safe. But other environments hmmm... it is a testing the water and seeing whether that is okay, for me. But it's an ongoing process; I see it as a journey that is just part of what life is

Iain: What are some of the challenges for you, Phil, in your journey from discovery to moving towards the potential?

Phil: Following on the potential bit, there is the potential of what the strengths of my type are. Actually, the sort of longing for 'wouldn't-it-be-great-if…' can be a very powerful motivation and great because it can drive you places. As well as 'What is the potential if I stop inhibiting myself?' And I drop the negative patterns and instead of sitting there thinking about it, I actually get on, [asking myself] what the right action is, and do it. So there are those two sides. The biggest challenge is that in deciding, or in thinking my route is to become that, then you create something really, really *special* and of course it is the same old habit again. You know, it will be wonderful *if…* and our habits kick in again and again and again. I think Fours are very good at 'I will be a wonderfully calm, spiritual being when I have done such and such'. Well, that's the Four pattern. You are not getting more spiritual though, you are just falling in the same trap again.

Iain: Yes, you have to be super aware to catch yet another hidden pattern.

Phil: Yeah, well, okay! Am I moving forward? Well, yeah. So that's good!

Janette: I think for me the potential is the adventure of being in touch with reality, whatever that is… so, to really meet reality and be with that, and be with my emotional responses to that, my mental responses, my physical responses, and let whatever I experience be okay. The potential in that is therefore that whoever I am with and whatever I am doing, I hope that I may enable other people to feel safe to do that for themselves. I think we all want to feel safe in the world and be acknowledged and understood. If I am able to really allow myself to be as I am, with all of myself here connected with what is actually happening – not what is happening in my fantasy, or what my dream world would be, or my ideal partner, or my ideal life, but actually, I am landed here now, physically, mentally, and emotionally – then that's a huge adventure. I am realising that is much more attractive and interesting than anything that I have going on in my head, anything that I have created in my own emotional fantasy about things, including my ideal self. I am not there at all, in terms of what is my ongoing reality all the time… don't get me wrong. But, it's certainly something I am glimpsing more of as a possibility. I do think that is not only facilitative and more joyful for me, but potentially is for the people that I am working with, or living with, or any people that I come across in relationships and for life in general.

Iain: Of course, for all of us really, it is a journey to discover our true selves, whatever that means for us at the time. And for you guys, it has helped the progression towards that. So, what has been the biggest stumbling block? I know this has already been covered in a minor way, but I am interested for people watching this – who are wondering if they are a Type Four – and who might identify with a particular stumbling block that you have had on a personal level.

Phil: Carrying on from what was said before, the biggest stumbling block for me is doing things because I am trying to be more *special* and different. I am learning the cello at the moment because I had a thing about 'Oh I wish I played a musical instrument as a child'. I had an opportunity to do drama, which due to other circumstances, I didn't, and I am now taking acting classes. I have a pottery studio at home, but how much time do I actually spend doing it? If I am not careful, I can set up all these special things – and it is just a habit – without deeply engaging in it. But that is making it too special again. Actually, just go out there and enjoy it. How many times do I actually sit down and just enjoy the cello practise because I want to reward myself, or just sit and play with some clay because I love doing it? That's the rare bit. I don't often do that. It's all about an image, if I am not careful.

Rosemarie: Yes, that does resonate with me. For instance painting: I am not a brilliant painter, but I have enjoyed it, but sometimes it is like 'Oh, if it's not that good, or not that special by the time I have finished it, is it worth my time doing it?' So I may actually – and I have – given it up. But I do enjoy doing it and I enjoy doing lots of different things, but there is that pitfall that if it doesn't get some kind of fantastic attention or something, then there is a danger that I decide 'Well I won't do that because I am not quite good enough at it'.

Iain: Is the need for external recognition part of it?

Rosemarie: Yes, I think it is. [Phil,] that is certainly something that resonates with me. I am afraid I do have times when I can spiral into being very melancholic. I hope I don't show it to people a lot. No doubt I do, in different ways that I haven't recognised yet.

Iain: Why do you say you hope you don't show it to people?

Rosemarie: There is a long story attached to that [*laughing*]... because other people don't really want to go there. That's me in my head and it's not a pleasant place to be, and it's of my making. Why would I want to suck people into that? But I do know certain things will trigger those moods, and if I allow them to really take me into them, then I'm not very productive. Luckily, I have always described myself as someone who bounces back, but I recognise I go down there. But in a way, I go down there to really battle it out so I can then let it go. It's a strategy for me.

Iain: I am not saying this is the case... isn't it maybe the challenge, or maybe the doorway to actually be in this melancholic state and simply allow yourself to be there not knowing what is going to happen? Whether there is a way out, or there isn't, and not wallowing...

Rosemarie: It is a challenge yes, and that is a choice, but on the whole I have found... and I would assess it now as quite unproductive. There are times... I can remember episodes when I really enjoyed it, but I can't get away from the fact that I have allowed it to be there.

Iain: You have indulged...

Rosemarie: Yes, 'indulged' is a good word, I think. But it's really not very productive. It doesn't really take me anywhere.

Phil: Productive for me therefore is 'What is the right action?' I can't remember whereabouts in the model that phrase 'right action' comes from, but it's this: 'What am I going to do about it? What is the thing in the next five minutes that I will actually take physical action about?'

Rosemarie: I think it can be quite informative… coming back to you [Iain]. I am not putting a label on it: 'That's bad!' I can be with it and that's one of the things about Fours. They can be with those very deep and dark areas, but at some stage I have to recognise that there is a world out there, and it comes back to Janette talking about fantasy and reality. If I want to engage in the world and discover more about myself and more about others and how to be in the world, I have got to get out there. I am hiding away in this little place [*pointing to body*].

Iain: How is that for you [Janette], this melancholic side of things?

Janette: I am just going back to this ongoing challenge that I notice for me. One of the biggest challenges is assuming that I don't have anything to offer, and so what I tend to do is often look at other people, idealise them, put them on a pedestal, look at all of their gifts and compare myself negatively. If I can't be like that person and do it their way… and of course in the process I am denying and not even turning towards my own gifts that I have to offer them. So, I notice that happening a lot and it still can be a tendency, which can be a culmination of withdrawal and melancholy. More and more I try to spot it and catch myself in the act. What I have also found is reality-testing things, actually going out and sometimes if I can, speaking to that person, finding out that they are a human being too, they have limitations, they have gaps. It's not all rosy for them. That really helps me have a reality check and take my own sense of myself back and say 'This is what I have to offer here'. Often I want it to be so unique and special and different that I am not really with the reality of what I am actually offering. So I have an idealised sense of what that means, and that takes me away from what I am offering now. That goes on quite a lot, I still notice.

Iain: What's it like for someone to be in a relationship with a Type Four person? What are the pros and cons? [*group laughter*] I am asking for a purpose, for those watching who may not know much about the Enneagram and may be wondering if their partner is a Type Four. We have heard it from your point of view, but what feedback do you get from your partners on how it is to be with you?

Phil: Because you are searching for an ideal in lots of different parts of your life then yes, I have had friends and partners say there is a sense of never being good enough, and that's quite shocking – that at some level, and it's been more than once – that is being put out… of not quite accepting the person, just for who they are.

Iain: Are you quite critical of other people?

Phil: I would say no, I am a very uncritical person. I don't criticise at all, but it gets felt.

Iain: It gets felt, so it's not so much put out there, but you are feeling it...

Phil: I think it's put out at a very subtle level. Yes, we can all be critical and I can be quite a perfectionist in some areas; there is a bit of Type One in me somewhere. The ability to pull people in and then when you get them very close, you have the ability to push them away. My experience is that it's a view of somebody and you can virtually morph them in front of you, and when I am fully into the Four pattern I can spot all the blemishes; equally when I am in the 'wow', then all I see is the good bits.

Iain: These are real polarities here, aren't they? And does that swing happen quite quickly from one to the other?

Phil: It can do. I have noticed – we talked earlier about it – how the habit needs a physical embodiment. Actually, if I am sitting in a much more grounded position [*sitting upright, feet planted*], I see the person for who they are. Whereas, if I am doing my false stuff [*slumping, head in hand*], I have experienced someone nearly physically change.

Iain: Say that again, that's really good. You were sitting in a certain way in that you were caught in your Four type and that's where...

Phil: ...I could start spotting that you've got more hair than I have and stuff like that.

Iain: [*laughing*] Only marginally.

Phil: Marginal, but I could pick it up and actually I fractionally noticed that just then. That's a habit of mine.

Iain: Really, that's really helpful to know these kinds of details.

Phil: ...much more here [*into the grounded position*], and there is a very different connection. It's me connecting to you for who you are.

Iain: Do you ladies feel the same, that you can switch like that?

Janette: Yes, definitely hypocritical of people. People not feeling understood. Ironically, I want to be understood and I don't give that time and energy to another. I know I can do that and yes, that sense of dismissing people that don't come up to some sort of arbitrary standard of how they should be, what they should be doing, how they should be responding to me a lot of the time, I have to say. On the plus side, I do think that Fours at their best are really able to hold a space for the other to really sense deeply into what's going on for them, because we are able to *be*. As Phil was saying, if we are more grounded in ourselves and are just able to be, just as I am, then I know that the other is more able to access how they are.

Iain: So, what is your different body position? We saw Phil's. Can you switch from one to the other?

Janette: Oh yes... it would be quite a disdain actually [*folding legs and arms, turning away, laughing*].

Iain: [*laughing*] You would even look away from us!

Janette: Yes, it's a kind of Miss Piggy; you know [*jerking head up and turning away*]. It's that kind of thing versus just being here really. Just being here sensing my body, being as fully open to you as I can be and of course being open to myself, allowing space for me to be, which in turn allows space for you to be. So I am not turning away, I am not twisting myself, I am not having a sort of paddy about how superficial you are, or lack of understanding, or lack of sophistication, all of that kind of stuff that I can get into.

Iain: How you are is also affecting how someone you are in contact with is too.

Janette: Definitely, both positively and negatively.

Iain: Yes, I think we forget that, but it is very true.

Rosemarie: I think it's amazing, how quickly we send those messages across, without saying anything, with the body positioning. They can be very subtle, you know a facial change. I do things with my jaw or my lips, which I have had comments on before like, "That's your jaw going, Rosemarie." Because there is a setness, which is like 'I am not listening' [*indicating invisible wall*].

Phil: You showed it earlier when you said you had created something really special.

Rosemarie: Yes [*laughing*]. You know they are not conscious, they just [*clicking her fingers*] happen.

Iain: I think they can become conscious.

Rosemarie: Yes, they can, it's just catching yourself in the act. But also, it's a pattern of behaviour, isn't it? Not always just sitting in one, but it's the softness that you move with, rather than the angular. There can be movements going on, but some movements are encompassing and there is a warmth there, an openness there, there is an inclusion rather than a barrier. Or I am over here and you are over there [*leaning back in chair*] and we are not going to meet.

Phil: I think, in terms of the bigger picture on this, that each person's physical emotional habit will be subtly different. All types have... each individual has a different mental, physical, emotional way of expressing their type. You can sometimes notice it in other people and help them see it by holding up a mirror, but I'd be very much against diagnosing and saying 'Oh that person is a Seven, look at what they are doing'... but useful when you just notice a shift in somebody. Often we are not aware of that shift happening in ourselves.

Iain: It does seem you are all on an ongoing journey with the Enneagram as one of your guides, so to speak...

Phil: [*laughing*] ...and just one other thing. It's noticing when that habit is not helping me because a lot of the time, that's me, it's who I am and it's the positivity I bring to the world. So, we can be a bit down on our type sometimes, or on our mental, emotional, physical habits. They are great, they are what help us operate in this world, and occasionally we might want to

CONVERSATIONS ON THE ENNEAGRAM

change them.

Iain: Yes, but isn't there a distinction between a habit and something that is truly an expression of us? The habit being something that is more acquired, rather than something that is fundamentally more tangible…

Phil: Yes, and I would still say that habit is very useful to me at times. I wouldn't want to get rid of it completely. I would be very uncomfortable working with anybody, especially myself, and say 'Get rid of that!' Just recognise when it is putting me in a box, or when it's trapping me and not enabling me to experience things differently.

Iain: Okay, we have about three or four minutes left. I don't know whether any of you wanted to say anything that you feel would be helpful to somebody watching this, which we haven't yet talked about on Type Four. Phil, have you got any quick points?

Phil: I suppose the main one is that some of the literature does make it into amazingly dramatic and artistic depressives and I just think 'Gosh, it overdoes it!' I think you can have the Four habit of mind done in slightly different ways than some of the behavioural descriptions. But that's just a Four saying I'm a *unique* Four [*laughing*], which is a habit.

Iain: Is there anyone famous that typifies the Four in terms of the more dramatic side? I usually read the suggested famous people, but I didn't do that on this occasion.

Janette: They reckon Michael Jackson was a Four, a lot of drama. People like Alanis Morissette and Martha Graham, the dancer. They each have their own unique expression, but there is something quite dramatic. And building on what Phil said, I think there can really be a danger… there is a huge range with all of these types and as we deepen into our spiritual journey, we do see all these different traits and styles, but I think it's very important to still be with the mystery of what's underneath all of that, to not know, really, who we are. And that's a particular irony with the Four, because one of the things you could say is a trait of the Four is having a constant question of 'Who am I and what is my true identity?' In a sense, as we go deeper into our journey with the Enneagram and other spiritual tools or practises we might be doing, perhaps we are more open to not knowing who we are, ironically. We are less and less sure about that. After the work, and the continued work that I am doing, I know that I am being more with the mystery. Again that could be a sense of excitement rather than a sense of emptiness, or a sense of lack. In the case of the Four, there is a potential in the mystery: that when we are trying to label ourselves or trying to say 'Am I a Four or not? Where am I on this spectrum?', *that* we can move away from.

Iain: That's a great place to finish, about the potential of the mystery. Thank you, all of you, for coming along and talking very openly about yourselves and your lives. I just want to show some of the books. If you have watched this program and other ones on the Enneagram, and you want to know more about the Enneagram and about what type you are, we have *The Wisdom of the Enneagram*, by Don Riso and Russ Hudson.

Janette: My personal favourite. I love it!

Iain: Good. This is one I always mention, *The Enneagram Made Easy*, which is a beginners' book but I still find very interesting. There are two more, which Janette mentioned earlier are on the spiritual side: *The Spiritual Dimension of the Enneagram* and *The Enneagram of Passions and Virtues* by Sandra Maitri, both good reads. And then by A.H. Almaas: *Facets of Unity*. Quite advanced and again on the spiritual side, but he does take it into a fascinating realm.

To watch this interview please go to:
http://www.conscious.tv/consciousness/enneagram

Enneagram Type Five – The Observer

Discussion with Angelina, Heather and Kilian

Moderated by Iain McNay

Iain: This time in the studio, I have three Type Fives with me, and they are going to talk about how it is to be Fives and the potential of being this type. On my right is Heather and then we have Kilian and Angelina. Heather, let's start with you. Maybe you can just give us a broad outline of what the Enneagram is, for people who don't know much about it.

Heather: At the very basic level the Enneagram is a diagram. It's a nine-sided figure – ennea-gram –and that, as a symbol, has been around for thousands of years. It was around at the time of Pythagoras and the Desert Fathers and so forth, but in the twentieth century it has also been used to map personality types, a map of the different drivers that energise us.

The idea behind the Enneagram as a model of personality is that we are all unique and that each of us has within us nine 'drivers'. Some of them might be the perfectionist, the achiever, the person who wants to be safe, or the peacemaker, and we all do all of these things, but within that, each of us – if we really look at the way we operate – know that there is one of those 'houses' that we *live* in. That's our home, for good and bad. There are great blessings to recognise in my type, and the blessings it brings, and there are also some bits to myself that I don't like. The more I can become conscious of what this type is – how it sometimes drives me and how I can perhaps take more control of it – the more choices I have. The better I know my type, the less I'm driven by it and the more choices I have about when to be in my type and when not to.

Iain: It's like 'Know your type, know yourself'.

Heather: Absolutely. I certainly have found that the Enneagram has helped me to understand bits of myself that were different maps. I had used a lot of personality maps before, and the Enneagram looks at slightly different areas that I don't think other maps look at.

Iain: And when you first found out that you were Type Five, what was your response to that?

Heather: [*laughing*] A kind of 'clunk' of recognition, which was both reassuring and 'Yep, all right, you got me'. Because, inasmuch as our type is something that we really value, [it] also contains parts of me that I didn't like particularly, and I went 'Yep, all right you got me there' [*hand on chest*]. So there was this kind of 'clunk' which gave me something to work with.

Iain: So there were certain things that you found out about yourself that shocked you a bit. Is that too strong a word to say: 'shocked'?

Heather: No I don't think 'shocked', but I work in management development and I'd used quite a lot of personality maps over the years, really useful stuff. I came across the Enneagram and thought 'Ah, here's another model to use with people'. I went on a workshop and… it [hit me] 'Thwack! You need to look at this one for yourself first, because there is more to this than meets the eye'. In my understanding of myself, I'd worked out a few things over the years, but there were some behaviours that were left almost like clinker in the bottom of the boiler that I didn't understand and would still get hijacked by.

Iain: Clinking in the bottom of the boiler…?

Heather: You know… in the old solid-fuel boilers where you had the [petroleum] coke going through and in the bottom you would end up with this load of clinker. There were some things about my own behaviour where I could still get hijacked by stuff and say 'I don't understand this', and when I saw the explanation of how the Type Five driver works, I went 'That's it, that's what drives it'. That's what explains all those bits in the bottom of the boiler that were still hijacking me and which I couldn't get a handle on. So it was a real *revelation*, more than a 'shock'.

Iain: You were finding, on a much deeper level, what was driving your unconscious patterns.

Heather: Absolutely, yes. Where some of the other personality things I'd looked at were looking at behaviour – and that is really useful – this really helped me to understand my motivation at a deep level and what was driving the behaviour.

Iain: Good. We will move across to the other bench there. I don't know who would like to start, maybe you, Angelina. When you first found out you were a Type Five, what impact did that have on you?

Angelina: I was really surprised at first at how accurate the description was of me and, in some ways, there was a sense of relief: 'Aha, it's a valid personality type to be like me!' Particularly, as you [Heather] said, the more unpleasant things that I always thought were strange about me. They were just there and they were part of this type. So there was a sense of relief about it and I actually found it quite comforting.

Iain: What were the main factors that helped you identify the fact that you were a Type Five?

Angelina: Some of the characteristics. For instance, Fives feel like they are observers of the world, rather than being in the world, and that really resonated with me.

Iain: An observer of the world means watching things go by, rather than participating. Is that what you are saying?

Angelina: Yes, or just analysing what's going on. Feeling like you're somehow detached, rather than someone taking part, and you're watching and trying to understand, *theorising* almost, about things that go on rather than just being there and in it. Feeling quite separate from things sometimes, like you are just watching, even watching yourself [*laughing*]... Does that make any sense at all?

Heather: [*laughing*] Makes sense to me.

Iain: Kilian, how do you experience watching yourself?

Kilian: I'm very much in my headspace. It can almost be like this rush of energy, right up into my head. I can visualise myself talking right now. When I'm being the observer, it's almost like I'm watching a film, there's a detachment from what's really going on. I'm actually aware of it right now – it's going straight into my head. I'm relying on what I know, instead of... getting contact with the self.

Iain: So this 'self' would mean more... your feelings?

Kilian: Yes, feelings and my body. Being the observer, you completely detach from your body, almost to the point of being completely caught up in your head. I don't know if you [Heather] want to say something more about that.

Heather: I can so relate to that on a personal level! I've said to people, on a number of occasions, for years my body was just this inconvenient thing, a pedestal, to stop my head from hitting the floor. And people said, "What?" But really, it was just a sense that what mattered was going on here [*pointing to head*] and this [*pointing to body*] was just the thing I carried [my head] around on. So I absolutely relate to what you're saying.

Angelina: It's quite interesting you say that because I never used to look after myself very well, and I took up yoga a few years ago because I started to see I needed to look after my car. I see that [my body] is the car that drives me around. I'm not my body, I'm the wheels. So yes it's an effort to look after my 'vehicle', as it were, but not to look after myself...

Iain: So you guys feel okay the way you are, it's just that you feel detached and not quite in the real world. Am I summarising this correctly? There's not a huge problem with feeling the way you are?

Kilian: Yes, one picture I have is a picture of a fortress and here I am surrounded by the walls of my fortress. Inside is what I know and then everything outside is the world – people, experiences, knowledge, feelings. I feel very secure and safe in my fortress and it takes an immense amount of effort to get out of that and to let experiences in.

Iain: So, why would you go out of your fortress?

CONVERSATIONS ON THE ENNEAGRAM

Kilian: Good question. First thing is to look for knowledge, to know and to understand.

Iain: Because there is a side of you that has this desire and is drawn towards understanding and knowledge?

Kilian: Yes, the seeking [of] knowledge is in a sense more about trying to find your place in the world. Trying to find your niche.

Angelina: I can relate to that in a way. Given half a chance, if I hadn't come across the Enneagram, I could actually live in my fortress quite happily. And now there is the Internet, there is no need to leave, but social life dictates that you have to go out and you have to meet... Going out, meeting people and things is fine, but there are certain things that take a huge amount of effort like turning up at a big event, talking to strangers. Even sometimes letting some of the things happening in the world touch you, like watching the news is something... on the one hand I want to know everything and on the other hand, really I hate it because it's like 'Oooh that horrible world has come and invaded my space and told me lots of bad things I don't want to know'. So there is a sense of 'You are safe actually in your own space'. It takes some effort to let the other things in, or to go out there.

Iain: And you are not great socialisers, are you? You tend to keep yourselves to yourselves. When I was doing my research for Type Five it said [reading]: 'they would rather sit at home and read a book on their own than go to a party'. I don't know if that's true for all of you...

Angelina: If it's with people I know well, I can be a pretty good socialiser, but the idea of going to a networking event, or something like that, really does fill me with dread. There are times when I am much more comfortable sitting with a book. So yes, that's where I would default to, the sitting with a book, which I used to get into a lot of trouble for when I was young.

Iain: It's funny you mention that. My sort of favourite Enneagram book is – I'll show these later [pointing to books] – *The Enneagram Made Easy*, and part of it is cartoons, which makes it very easy to identify the various types. And I remember this particular one for the Fives: there was a couple going out on their first date and they were sitting back to back with their backs touching, both reading a book, and the bubble coming out of their head to show their thoughts was 'This is my best ever first date'. [group laughter] Can you identify with that?

Heather: Absolutely. What I relate to absolutely is the basic premise for the Five – which is sometimes talked about in some of these books – that 'the world is invasive and intrusive and, if I let the world in, it will overwhelm me'. Fives have a reputation of being very calm and not showing their feelings and all the rest of it. But, there are some suggestions that in fact Fives *feel*. Well, we do feel things intensely, but that is quite frightening and I think that's what you [Angelina] were referring to, and therefore to save myself being overwhelmed by my feelings, I lock myself into my fortress from where I can look out onto the world, and my fortress is a lighthouse. I am up here [*pointing to head*] and I can see everything that is going on in the world, but you can't get to me unless you can get the door open downstairs, and then you have a lot of stairs to come up.

So here we are in our fortress and it's actually very scary to let people in, because we are not quite sure what will happen if other people's energy invades us. One of the concerns of Fives is always to manage my energy, and this is the thing that I recognise about going to parties. It took me until I was into my twenties to understand why, after an hour at a party, I would always end up in the loo. There is nothing wrong with my bladder, but it was the only place I could go just to be alone, and it wasn't consciously touching base with my own energy, it was just not touching base with all this energy that was going on outside. I just needed to be alone for a bit and then I could go and socialise again. Because my energy, my space had been invaded... You [Angelina and Kilian] are nodding there… is that true for you?

Kilian: Yes, both in relationships and social environments I find my energy gets depleted quite quickly unless I carefully manage it. That could be just the simple route of going to get a drink and then having space there on my own to recollect my thoughts, to recollect where I am and then go back into the fray so to speak, and re-engage with everybody and all my friends. Socialising is a constant balancing act.

Iain: Well, actually, it sounds quite intelligent insofar as, when you socialise you want to maximise it, you want to use that space for socialising, and if you are feeling tired, or not feeling like it, you don't do it. There is some sense, some intelligence in that.

Kilian: Yes, I think with Fives there definitely comes the realisation that the more withdrawn you get, [the more] you do need to go out and reconnect with people. We are not so caught up in our thoughts that we won't go out and socialise as such. There is a drive and that is something I have noticed. When I am caught up in books, or in doing something, when I have been incredibly focused and blot out everything else apart from what I am doing, then I realise... actually I do need to reconnect with everything else.

Iain: I've made notes from some of these books, so anybody that is watching who thinks they may be a Type Five, here are more clues. The first one is 'observing or reading, rather than doing', which you have kind of covered… 'Hard to express feelings in the moment': you have hinted at it and confirmed that.

Heather: Yes, I think that is certainly true for me. I am much more likely to know what I felt about something *after* the event. I need to go back and be on my own and then I can let the feelings come to me and also I will analyse, and this is not something I do consciously; I can't stop myself doing it. I will

CONVERSATIONS ON THE ENNEAGRAM

find myself analysing what has just gone on and then I will have a sense of what I feel about it. I am very often not in touch with my feelings at the moment at which it happens, unless something really socks me in the face and I think this is what, I as a Five, am scared of. Sometimes things do sock me in the face and they knock me totally off balance and so there is this feeling of either I am in control, or I am totally vulnerable. That's one of the reasons why I think Fives tend to protect themselves so much when they are in a social space, because it's this feeling of either all or nothing. I am either protected and in control, or I am utterly at your mercy, and that is not a comfortable place to be except with somebody that you are really happy with. I don't know if that is true for you [Angelina and Kilian], or not so much. That feeling of not knowing what you are feeling in the moment.

Angelina: Quite a lot of time I have to go off and reflect on something and then I will go [*frowning*] 'Hold on a minute, that really made me angry', but I wouldn't have been aware of it at the time. But there are other times when you have to go into situations, like funerals. I will cry more than anyone else at anyone's funeral even if I don't know them. I will just be absolutely overwhelmed by crying, I am quite famous for it [*laughing*]. But it's really uncomfortable and I just have to let it go because I can't do anything else about it. Most of the time I would keep away from things that have that intensity.

Iain: Just going down this list I made: 'gets lost in interests [*group agreement*], 'tries to conceal sensitivity to criticism' [*group concentration, Iain surveying*] …not sure about that one.

Heather: I don't know that we are any more, or less, sensitive to criticism than anybody else. I think 'Doesn't everyone take criticism personally?' Although probably I wouldn't react in the moment.

Angelina: Again, it would have the same [reaction]: 'Go away and think about it' and then I would also weigh up from whom it came, and if they knew what they were talking about, like a true Five [*laughing*]. Do they have the right knowledge to base their criticism on?

Iain: It's concealed sensitivity and a lot of people would react. It's trying to conceal the sensitivity to criticism.

Heather: Yes, I think the basic premise for a Five is that the likely reaction to any situation that is uncomfortable is withdrawal; physically if possible and if not, mentally. In a conversation, I will suddenly realise that I have actually, literally, gone walkabout [*pointing to head*] in the middle of the conversation. My brain has gone off to something else. I don't know whether you do that [*group agreement*]. There is a sense of being able to protect myself by withdrawing my energy even if I can't withdraw my body from a situation. So if there is criticism going on, the wall comes up, and I will be upset about it later.

Angelina: I agree, it would be 'Take it in, but not be present with it and then think about it later'.

Iain: Do you feel different from most people?

Angelina: Sort of. I know there are others out there, but I don't know many of them [group laughter], so I often do feel isolated and I get quite excited when I meet someone who has a similar interest to me, because yes, I do feel sometimes isolated in what I am like.

Iain: [reading] 'You are calm in a crisis'. Is that right?

Angelina: I am not sure. I think so.

Kilian: I would say, if a crisis is developing and I know and I am in my space and I have an understanding, a knowledge around the crisis, then I can use my knowledge to a great degree and rely on that information to really pinpoint exactly 'Okay this is what is going wrong. Cut it off right here. Spin the crisis on its head and really conceptualise what the crisis is. Take it out from its environment and really work at it up in here [touching head] and then… actually, you might want to do this, or do this'. That, I love doing. I get a real buzz out of doing that. Yes, it's almost like I look for crises.

Iain: You look for crisis?

Heather: I am hearing in what you [Kilain] are saying that when you have an intellectual problem to solve, you have the ability to take yourself out of it and observe it. I certainly recognise that in myself. I can be very calm in those situations where I feel I have the expertise to deal with it and I can be the expert. That's not about status for me, but it is about 'Oh, I know what to do here because I have got knowledge that will serve me'. But I can equally get totally thrown if I am in a situation where I don't have the expertise and then I get into a real panic. So when I have the expertise, then I can be calm in a crisis.

Iain: It's interesting, it just reminds me of the story of good friends of Renate and myself. We had lunch with them on Sunday and the story I heard... he is a Five, and a number of years ago they were travelling – I forget where they were – they landed somewhere, the plane had been delayed, and when they got there no taxis were available or anything. They were stuck at the airport at like two a.m. in the morning with no idea what to do, and he, being a Type Five, sat on his suitcase, took out a book, and read while all this chaos is going on round him [laughing]. Would you say this is the sort of thing you guys might do, or would you be more proactive?

Angelina: Would probably bring out a guidebook and start reading about where we can go, or look for information or something

Iain: Yes, there is a practical side to it, but doesn't get involved in the drama as such.

Kilian: It may be a lower-level Five that has a tendency to want to disconnect from the drama and just gets lost in one's own world again, the world of your book. But when it becomes the observer and the participant at the same time, then there comes that drive and that security to go out and actually search for that information which you need to then find out what the next move is.

Angelina: It's like problem solving. Crisis is problem solving but like you, I am fine when I have got options. Say my computer will do something weird and I'll think 'Right, let's try this. Let's try this. Let's try this'. Then as soon as I find I am out of my depth and I don't know what to do, then that's when I might have a bit of a reaction [*group laughter*].

Iain: [*laughing*] A bit of a reaction…?

Heather: I think some types enjoy the unknown much more than we do. So that story for me and how I would interpret it as a Five is that he needed that space of withdrawal, to sit and read the book, which just gave him a bit of space, and that he may well have then come up with some problem solving to take action and say what to do in that particular situation.

Iain: So, he was creating his temporary fortress and then was willing to possibly go out and…

Heather: Yes, and that may look very strange to outsiders because it is not an immediate [*clicking fingers*] 'Okay let's do this then'. I certainly know that if you can give me even twenty seconds sometimes to do that withdrawal, then I can usually do the be-calm-in-a-crisis bit. I don't know, is that something you are relating to?

Angelina: Definitely. It's like 'Can you just give me two minutes to think? And please stop talking and then I will come up with something'.

Kilian: That moment of space is so important…

Iain: Basically, as you were saying in the introduction, Heather, there are certain characteristics we incorporate into our personality that we learn when we are very young, which form the basis of our ego personality type, and there is also a potential for each personality type. Type Five has the potential to grow away from the control that the personality imprints have on us. Can you give me an example of how Fives are able to grow and not be so caught up?

Heather: I think the first thing is to notice that we are doing it, and that in itself is such an enormous [accomplishment] if I catch myself withdrawing and think 'You just did it again didn't you!' If I can do that with compassion for myself…

Iain: You don't judge yourself, you just take it as a fact that it has happened again.

Heather: Yes, then it already has less hold on me and therefore the boundaries soften. I think you probably get this impression from us about this fortress that is going on and that has thick walls… that it's hard. So the journey for a Type Five, as I have experienced it, is to soften these walls. I am not trying to demolish them with a pick axe in order to be somebody different, but if I can let them be a little more flexible, then I can still have my fortress, but I can get the benefits of going out into the world because I start to recognise that actually other people's energy can help me, not just invade me. So the potential – one of the things I can remember vividly from the end of my first workshop – was realising that for me the challenge was to *engage*. That was the word I took away with me on the first workshop – *and* with compassion. You don't have to do it all the time, but just open your doors for a bit, experience what it is like when you let other people's energy in, and do it with people who seem to be understanding and who are not going to trample all over you.

What I am looking for – if I am going to open my doors and engage with you – is that I want your energy to be quite gentle and respectful of my space. And my fear is if I open my doors, that you will come rampaging over my threshold on a big charger and that, I don't want. So I look for people that I can engage with, show and let myself be seen, show my emotions and tell them what I care about. But I am testing out first of all: 'Is this person going to be respectful of what I put out there?' So that is one of the opportunities for a Five, to experiment with opening my doors a bit. Is that what you [Angelina and Kilian] have experienced, as you have journeyed, with your type?

Kilian: Yes, and realising a lot of the times where I catch myself in the moment. The more times I do it, the easier it becomes and through that, I get a real sense of security.

Iain: What's the process, Kilian, of catching yourself in the moment? How does it work?

Kilian: It's really subtle. When we were talking before about observation, it's getting out of my space at that moment, and it's looking at 'Okay this is what is going on'. It's just for a split second, but that detachment is enough to recognise what's going on and then being able to not act on it, not act on the drive, and let it dissipate, let that energy, that kind of anxiety…

Iain: You have recognition that there is a pattern about to start through a thought or an action, and then you make the conscious decision not to follow that automatic reaction. Am I reading this correctly?

Kilian: Yes, it's a conscious decision but it's not a forceful decision. It's again using compassion to [say to myself] 'So what, I'm getting anxious', for example, 'What's the worst that can happen?' Asking that question really helps disengage from the negative energy and look for the positive in life.

Iain: Okay, [Angelina], do you have any observation on that?

Angelina: For me it was an awareness of what my traps might be, like the trap of trying to accumulate knowledge before taking action. I have learnt now that you don't need to know everything, you can't know everything, and it's okay to take action with what you have got. So that trap of over intellectualising things, and also catching myself in the act, is often when I start theorising rather than actually being there, or listening. I work as a psychologist and sometimes someone is telling me something and I think 'Oh right, that connects with that theory, or that sounds like that Enneagram thing', and I am off on my own little theory trip, and then I suddenly become aware that I am not really doing what I'm supposed to be doing, which is engaging with the person. It's catching myself doing that.

Iain: Yes, you bring yourself back and start again. It does seem that is the catalyst. It was the same when we were doing the Type Nine interview; it was very much about the element of awareness and understanding there are these patterns that we are not always aware of. They do control our lives, and just seeing when they come up, we do have a choice. You have to move quite fast and if you don't move fast enough, another pattern has come in there. But you have a choice of not moving with the automatic response and reaction, and something fresh, something new can be sitting there.

Heather: Sometimes the automatic reaction is absolutely the right thing, and to be within our type and to do what our type does naturally might be just the thing that is needed, and sometimes it might be working against us. So it's that awareness to actually have that choice in the moment to say 'Is it useful to bring a bit of *Fiveness* here or, actually am I not doing myself a favour by going down that route?'

Iain: [*laughing*] A bit of 'Fiveness'… that's a nice expression!

Heather: [*laughing*] Yes, one of the other things people often say about Fives is that we are stingy, and this isn't usually about money although Fives traditionally can survive on very little – I mean the minimalist is a Type Five. My personal sense is that I would be very happy with a tent to go wandering the world, as long as I've good food. I don't need to acquire lots of stuff, in fact I find myself clearing out a lot of the time. The stinginess is often with my energy, rather than with money, not putting myself into the world because of the fear that my energy will be depleted. The potential for a Five, therefore, is to take the risk that by putting myself out there, other people might actually feed my energy instead of depleting it. The potential for a Five then is to say 'If I can take that risk to engage, there is this flow that comes from this interaction and I don't have to do it all myself any more. There is joy to be had in letting other people come towards me and not feeling I have to protect my own energy levels all the time'.

Iain: I am just looking again at my notes… 'There is an inherent fear that nothing will come from the outside'.

Heather: Yes, that's the fear, so that's where the real risk is – to actually risk opening the doors – that something precious will escape if I open my doors and there will be nothing to take its place. I will be empty and depleted.

Iain: There will be more scarcity. As in when you open the cupboard that's not well stocked and will be even worse once you have opened it because everything falls out.

Heather: Yes, absolutely. That's right, and the cupboard is empty and I have no way of refilling it, and the idea that I might be able to get something to refill it from other people... when I am being in my Type Five, independence and self-sufficiency is very important to me because I can't rely on other people to refill my cupboard. So the potential is to just open my doors a little bit. If I am generous to others with my presence – and my money as well if you like – actually other people will be generous to me back and there will be this richness of interaction between us.

Angelina: [*laughing*] I was just theorising, can't help myself, I will have to think about that one. I relate very well to the withdrawing. That's one of my biggest problems: as a Five I withdraw from things very quickly. So as soon as I feel I am being overwhelmed by people or misunderstood, rather than open the doors a bit more and engage, I just back off instead. I don't know if that's exactly the same thing as you are talking about.

Iain: I understand Fives are often drawn to the path of contemplation and meditation. Is that something that you have found in your own lives?

Kilian: I love contemplating things, theorising and conceptualising. I can do that for hours, and meditation is the key to really disengage from that sort of mechanism. It's a respite from all the frantic energy that is going on in the head, and I find meditation really very useful and a re-engaging tool. A tool that helps me to re-engage with life effectively, with society, the environment, and with everything else. Meditation helps me to re-engage with the belly centre – if we talk about the head, the heart and the belly – it's very useful. I'd recommend it to any Five.

Angelina: It's really hard though, to switch off. I get a bit of presence when I do yoga, and you are doing a really hard balance so you can't think of anything except that one muscle in your toe that is making it all happen, and I find that releases me from the usual thing that is going on up here [*pointing to head*]. I find actual meditation really difficult. It's something I want to do more of, but [find it] really difficult.

Iain: So you are drawn towards contemplation and meditation, but the practise of it is not so easy for you guys?

Angelina: No, because I am sitting there thinking 'I wonder what this is doing for me? Is it calming down energy here? Is it changing alpha waves for me?' All this theoretical nonsense is going on. Sometimes you really get into it and you jump out of it and think 'Wow that worked, I felt really calm at that point. I wonder what was going on there?' And then think [*slapping head and laughing*] 'Oh shut up, give it a rest!'

Heather: [*laughing*] Yes, I relate to that. Everybody always thinks that Fives

CONVERSATIONS ON THE ENNEAGRAM

must be very good at meditation because we have this energy that's very still and so they say, "Oh you find it easy." And I say, "No, not at all." I certainly don't. Sounds like you [Kilian] have managed to get to grips with it.

Kilian: With anything it's practise, like a muscle really. The more you do it, the easier it becomes. There are days when I can't sit down and quieten the mind. There may be something that has grabbed my attention and it just fires off [*pointing to head*]. The other thing I find which really helps is getting in touch with the body. What you mentioned about wiggling your toe… any sort of kinesthetic work, martial arts, yoga, Pilates, and all that. Getting in touch with your body really, really, helps.

Iain: Brings you out of the fortress of the mind into the wider horizons that are connected to you.

Heather: Yes, it is grounding. Actually I'm just connecting my head to the earth, just getting the pathways going between my head and the rest of me. Even something like walking, just feeling literally the circulation in your body – that grounds me. It is really helpful for all the types, but I think particularly for Fives, to get in contact with the present moment, and doing something physical which is so totally engaging that I cannot analyse while I am doing it. It is a place of rest for me. I got involved, for example, in doing shiatsu which is massage, it's one-to-one, scary stuff. It's physical, very scary stuff and I have to be totally present in the moment and not be doing much of an analysis.

Angelina: [*laughing*] You have to touch other people?

Heather: Yes, touching other people. I did it because I had benefited so much from being touched in that respectful way I was talking about, and the challenge to do it with other people, really, was a challenge and a growth path. But needing to get into the bodywork and through that, then, hopefully connect with the heart, in terms of the three centres. If I think about 'I know I have got to get in touch with the other two centres [heart and belly]' – where am I going to start? For me, getting in touch with my heart: really scary. Getting in touch with my body: possible. Okay let's try that one first. I don't know, is that true for you [Kilian and Angelina]?

Kilian: Yes, feelings are definitely the hardest to get in touch with. They are there, it is just a case of firstly recognising them and wanting to dip into those feelings. I always seek a lot of safety in conceptualising and really relying on the mind to do one over on the feelings. It's definitely a lot easier to get into the body, and getting in touch with the body really allows the feelings to express. So I love dancing for example, and that's a great way of how I disengage with the head; or the head is busy listening to music, which is another of the things I really love. So body is busy dancing away and the heart…. you know, I can really get in touch with the emotions of the music.

Iain: How are the emotions, feelings, and touching for you?

Angelina: I am not always very engaged with them and they tend to creep up and surprise me sometimes, although they work away at an unconscious level and my behaviour will get a bit erratic. When it all becomes clear, it turns out that there has been something emotionally bothering me that I just haven't been aware of. So they do work at an unconscious level. It's quite hard to get in touch with.

Iain: And how is that? Are you okay with it, do you accept it, or is it something that you feel there is movement forward there?

Angelina: On the surface level I am okay with it, but I know it does cause me problems because sometimes you can make wrong decisions because you haven't been in touch with what you are feeling, or it can work at an unconscious level and you start behaving strangely without getting in contact with them. So it's something that I think needs work.

Iain: How is it to be a partner with a Five, those of you with partners, or past partners?

Angelina: [*laughing*] I'd like to ask him actually.

Iain: You don't know? Again that's a little bit Type Five isn't it? You don't actually know how your partner is feeling towards you and your relationship?

Angelina: [*group silence*] Go on, someone else jump in [*laughing*]. I haven't a clue how to answer that.

Kilian: It's a real learning curve...

Iain: Yes, you are in a fairly new relationship aren't you, Kilian?

Kilian: Yes, and she's a Type Seven, I think. Space is really important for me, but I am fortunate enough to be with a partner who actually recognises that. As a Type Seven, I think it's quite difficult for her, but it's a wonderful relationship, especially with that understanding there. Recognising that I need to go away and just be in my space and be disconnected, essentially to recharge my batteries and then re-engage. When I am there with her then, I am very much in the present moment and my mind is not elsewhere, just very much in the present. She has a really calming effect too.

Heather: My partner's an Eight, which is interesting. When I first got together with him I was struck by this life force from within him. I thought 'I want some of that!' I had an instinctive recognition that this ability to be there and engaged with life all the time was something I needed to do, and he could hold my hand and take me there. But, then of course, I withdrew, so his persistence...

Iain: So you withdrew because it was all too much for you?

Heather: Yes, and it took me a long time to work with it. Eights – 'the boss' – is a big energy, full of lust for life. It's 'what you see is what you get' and it comes on quite strong. Of course as a good Five, what did I do? Take three paces backwards. And his persistence in gently hanging around, not invading on a big charger, but not going away either... So what I would say to somebody who thinks they might be in a relationship with a Five is, take gentle steps in, but don't go away either. It's persistence because very often when people do the Enneagram and they learn about Fives, they say 'Oh we have got to be terribly respectful with you and not invade your space', and what happens is they pussyfoot about [*laughing*] and we don't want you to do that either.

Iain: [*laughing*] Type Eights don't pussyfoot about…

Heather: [*laughing*] Eights don't pussyfoot about. 'What you see is what you get', and by doing that they show us – if you are in a relationship with a Five – get your foot in the door and hold the door open very gently, but persistently. Don't keep saying 'Oh well, I will go away again then'. That doesn't work either because in our heart of hearts, we want to let you in; it's just that we are scared. So if you can put your foot in the door and gently say 'Is that all right, if I just stay here for a minute, is that all right with the door open? Okay, so what if I took another step further towards you, would that be okay?' And help us to build relationships in that way.

Iain: We talked earlier a couple of times about potential for Fives. How do you feel in your own movement towards this potential?

Kilian: I think there is an immense reliance on knowledge, but the pathway for growth for me is through learning to trust in myself and not having to rely on the mind to get me through a sticky situation; trusting on my gut instinct a lot more than what I am used to. With meditation and body work, my thought patterns are a lot quieter. Communication as well… it is a lot easier to communicate. I don't get caught up in my thoughts nearly as quickly. The more work I do, the easier it is to open that door and to really let the world in. With that, there comes a real sense of *groundedness* and a sense of *belonging* and from that space, to really make an impact on the world.

Iain: The sense of belonging is interesting because that's completely the opposite to the castle you were talking about, the fortress – and genuinely feel inside that there is a sense of belonging and you are moving towards that.

Kilian: Yes, it's very powerful. It's difficult, but I know it's possible and there is a lot of power in that, which is really appealing and it feels true. I don't know if you [Heather] want to say something on that?

Heather: Yes, 'belonging' is a word that is very important to me, and I desperately want to be in the group and not outside it, and taking that step out to be in the group… Why is that so hard? That's what the challenge is. I absolutely relate to what you are saying because if we can do that, I find now – in terms of how I used to be – that I can be more in a group and actually experience the joy of being in the group, rather than outside it. It's almost as if the castle fortress, for me, has become one of those garden gazebos that has four corners, but there is space in between and people can come in, and here I am! I am reclining on my cushions in the garden, but people can come in and out and we are enjoying interactions. So the whole fortress is relaxing as the years go on, and the awareness of what the pattern is has been central to letting it become more gentle and more open.

Iain: We have a couple of minutes left. Angelina, did you want to say something about how you are filling your potential?

Angelina: I think I am still on the learning curve with it, to be honest. I do get trapped by my *Fiveness* quite a lot still, but I do take time to look outside – literally outside the window – and just try and get a sense of what's out there and appreciating small things and being a bit more grounded, spending less time in my head and caught up with stuff. So that's what I am working on at the moment.

Iain: I am just going to run through these books here for people who are interested in knowing more about the Enneagram. *The Enneagram Made Easy*, by Renee Baron and Elizabeth Wagele, I referred to earlier, which is a very basic book but it's very good and even if you know a bit about it, I still find it very helpful. One that Heather gave me earlier, *The ABC of the Enneagram*, by Eric Salmon, which I hadn't actually looked at yet.

I hope you have enjoyed this and that you will seek out the other programmes on the Enneagram if you are not a Type Five and you are interested in finding out what your type is. Angelina, Heather, and Kilian, thank you for joining me in making this programme.

To watch this interview please go to:
http://www.conscious.tv/consciousness/enneagram

Enneagram Type Six – Fear and Courage

Discussion with Grahame, Judith and Lynne

Moderated by Iain McNay

Iain: We are going to talk about a specific type in the Enneagram, Type Six, and I have with me Grahame, Judith, and Lynne. Before we start, Grahame is going to tell us just briefly what the Enneagram is.

Grahame: The Enneagram, as a symbol, is about showing us the nine points. The word is ennea – nine; gram – points. The Enneagram of personality types, which is what we are discussing today, is a way of utilising that symbol, that map, and identifying certain behavioural structures, motivational structures about human nature. I guess most of us will have seen how different people act in different ways, and in some ways we see people act similarly to someone else and we think 'Gosh, that's just like so-and-so'. 'That's just like my friend'. 'That's like my mother'. The Enneagram of personality types has been constructed as a way of mapping these clusters of behaviour, clusters of traits. There are many kinds of psychometric tests out there that test things like traits, values, proactive or reactive, or if you are an introvert-extrovert. No personality structure is that one thing, but a cluster of that and many, many others. It is still only a map. It is still only a way of helping us to see the habitual patterns that we get ourselves into, the psychological movement and emotional patterns.

The purpose of that of course is to help us see some of the things that get us into stuck places, things that get in the way of us really showing up and being our 'true nature', our 'real essence', our 'soul' if you like. So it can also be seen as the way in which the ego structure – an aspect of our personality that has formed through our formative years – has taken on a certain way of seeing life, a way of taking certain aspects, interpreting what we are seeing and thinking: 'Oh, that must be that, because it links in with how I have seen my world and taken myself to be'. The whole point of doing that is to uncover, get rid of all that – not totally, it would never go completely – but to see through that and see our true nature, what is really, really us here, as the soul.

Iain: Without all the conditioning on top.

Grahame: Without all the conditioning, without the fears and the things that get in the way, the activity, the things we think we have to do, must do, should do, all of that structure. The Enneagram provides us with these nine basic kinds of domains – nine types — which actually are within us all. We really will see all the nine aspects of the Enneagram of personality types within us. We will see the Type Three within us, Type Four…

Iain: So there are nine different types, yet we are primarily one type, but we all have parts of the other types in us.

Grahame: Yes. The more we become identified with the ego structure, [the more] it takes on a certain dominance, because it means that we only stay in that. As we get loose from that, all those other aspects of the other types – the higher qualities – become more accessible to us, and we will experience the slightly less unpleasant [traits] of the other types as well, which is why you have that symbol with the nine [points]. I am not going to talk about that necessarily, but there are ways in which we connect through to some of the other types, specifically under stress, or in certain other conditions. But yes, we have the nine types, but there is one of them, which if we look closely enough, will have a bit more of a charge to it.

Iain: I must be honest with you, when I first discovered I was a Type Six it was more than a bit of a charge. I was reading something and I thought 'The person who wrote this *really* knows me'. It really hit home. But before we get on to that, Judith, why don't you tell us what are the clues to find out if we are a Type Six.

Judith: In the development of the young Six, very young usually, [there] has been some experience of a lack of holding, of a lack of support, and that has impacted the child at a very deep level. With this feeling of 'The world is not supporting me in some way', they begin to feel very fearful.

Iain: When you say 'lack of support', what would be a practical example of that?

Judith: A practical example of that may be that physically, their life was actually a challenge to them; they may have been physically very ill. It may be that the parents were rather inconsistent in their parenting. It might be that, in some way, they began to interpret repeated behaviours, or experiences in their life, as 'Okay, the world is now becoming, feeling to me, like a dangerous and uncertain place'. As that child begins to experience the world as an uncertain and dangerous place, they begin to see and perceive that their whole worldview becomes 'The world is a dangerous and risky place in which I need to be anxious and frightened and I begin to be wary and cautious and plan ahead and look for how I can *ensure* myself *before* whatever it is I am frightened of is going to get me'. A very nice little story that Tom Condon, who is a teacher of the Enneagram, gives is that Sixes are very much like zebras, and zebras out in the plains of the Serengeti are in actual danger of being eaten by a lion… and they intentionally get quite close to the lions, so the lions are within their sight. The zebras do that because if they run away too far from the lions, then they don't know where they are: 'The lions might creep up behind me and take a chunk out of my buttock!' And if they are too close to them: 'Well, now we are really in danger of being eaten', so the zebras keep the lions within their sight. And that is very descriptive of this whole Sixes way of being: 'Let me just be close enough to what it is out there that is frightening me, so that I am prepared, I can always be prepared for what I might need to do. I am ahead of the game'.

Iain: That's a good clue: 'someone who is always prepared and ahead of the game'. They are a bit nervous, from what you're saying.

Judith: Certainly there are a variety of styles within Sixes. Type Six is one of the problematic types in some ways to get a grip on, because they have a wide range of manifestation of their behaviour. Some Sixes are more phobic, they are more frightened, they withdraw, they feel frightened, they know they are frightened, they are very doubtful and uncertain, and they move away from things. Other Sixes are going against that fear: they want to in some way deny it in themselves and meet it head on. So they can become quite risk-taking, quite rebellious to try and prove to themselves – a kind of a muscling up against this deep inner fear and anxiety that's inside.

Iain: One of the books I really like, which is a very basic book, is *The Enneagram Made Easy*. I listed a few points last night just so viewers can get as wide a feel as possible on Type Six. 'Plagued by doubt'. This is something that I know for myself, sometimes. 'Always alert to danger', which you recognised there. 'Take things too seriously'. 'Very hard workers'. 'Loyal and supportive'. 'Good sense of humour'. They take things too seriously, but they also have a good sense of humour. 'Support people through thick and thin'. 'They either procrastinate, or plunge in headlong', which is what you've alluded to there. 'Exhaust themselves by worrying'. 'They overreact when stressed'. And as a Type Six, I can identify with all of these. I am not necessarily always overwhelmed by these things; maybe I was in the past by some of them, but they are all things I can recognise in me at times. Lynne, you are also a Type Six. I just wonder, when you first found you were a Six, how was that for you? Was it a relief? How did you feel?

Lynne: Well, I am like you, Iain. I doubted it, because doubt is what I do [*laughing*]. I wouldn't believe that I was Type Six. It doesn't look like any fun to me.

Iain: So did you go to a seminar to start with?

Lynne: I went to a seminar, and I sat as they went round and explained what all the different points were. By the end of the day everybody knew what they were, except for me.

Iain: So you were sitting there on your own, procrastinating and doubting…

Lynne: Yes, procrastinating, fearful, 'I don't fit into any of them'. And then the group leader, who was Eli Jaxon-Bear, said to me, "You are a Six." I didn't believe it.

Iain: Right, but you were actually displaying Six traits.

Lynne: Absolutely, absolutely.

Iain: Discovering you are a Six… has it helped you to know more about yourself and understand yourself better?

Lynne: Yes, yes. When you invited me to come here, I thought 'Great!' As you just described, no fear, just meet it on: 'Yes, I have never done anything like that, I am coming'. Then last night it's 'Who will be there, what will they be like, what will I wear, where will I sit, will I sit next to Iain, will I sit on the other sofa, which side of the camera?' On and on, just whizzing, whizzing. Then I caught it, and then I laughed, and then I relaxed. Otherwise, I might still be spinning.

Iain: So you realised that the Six in you was something that at one level you had some control over and you could watch it.

Lynne: Yes. I don't have to do that any more. It has been really helpful.

Iain: Let's go back to you, Grahame. I'll ask you similar questions. When you first found out you were essentially a Type Six, how did that alter the way you saw life?

Grahame: I came to the decision of Six through a process that was initially around looking at the centres [head, heart, belly]. We had had some teaching about the aspects of the different types and I am just thinking about this… and I am thinking 'Where do I spend my time, where do I spend my time, oh my gosh where…?' And ding! Light goes on: 'I'm up here, spending my time in my head'. I knew I was somewhere in the head and I wasn't sure between Type Five and Six. Some of the aspects that came out when I saw 'Yeah, this I can recognise in myself' I don't think necessarily changed my life in a great way at that point, because there was other training I was undergoing, but it became a constant thread. It was really on the teacher training that I began to see, more and more, how this structure gets in the way. So, what it did is, it started the process of awakening – which is for all people, for all human condition – that awakening moment. And one of the things that I've realised is that most of the Sixes, like two other types in the triangle, tend to be more revolutionary. Doesn't mean to say that we've got it, and we've got it all sorted out, but to get the structure and understand it and start to see it… but of course it is still very much a head thing. So the analytical side – what became more important was to catch myself in the act of seeing that. Seeing how I am thinking about the thinking about the thinking about the thinking, and the *overthinking* structure. It is catching myself in the act of that. Over the years it's made a huge difference to me.

Iain: And you, Judith, how has it helped you?

Judith: Those who've accompanied me on my journey with the Enneagram would be laughing heartily now because my journey to finding out I was a Six was a very long and tortuous one. In the end they named me a 'Ten', as a joke. It wasn't that funny, because I am a Six and because Sixes have great imagination: when I came to the Enneagram I really could imagine myself in very many places, and I could find all of those in me. There were certain types I just knew I wasn't, but I was left with quite a few that I thought I was and there is similarity of behaviour. In the end I got back down to Nine and Six and I worked for a very long time on myself as a Nine and it was really, really valuable work. I spent a long time trying to work out where I was on the line between Nine and Six – in that dynamic, which was my home ground. I began to see of course that my whole process in terms of that journey, and that questioning and that self-doubt… and every time I thought I'd landed with one, I'd then pick it to pieces – Six at work! I never felt secure and a sense of rightness of where I'd landed. All that work with the Enneagram really began to help me stand outside myself, to observe my process, to observe my type functioning, and then begin to [see] – first of all at gross level and then in subtle ways – how that was at work within me, and be able to then get a flavour of 'Okay look, this is happening again, this is something you need to relax. This is where you are at it again, this is where you keep banging your nose against the same wall, and so how about not doing that because it hurts'.

Iain: When I first found out I was a Six, it was actually an incredible relief. I thought 'Well, there are nine different types. A ninth of the population might essentially think a similar way to me a lot of the time. That's really good to know!' When I was a child I would be puzzled that I would feel so strongly about something, whether it was positive or negative, and other people seemed to be so indifferent to a situation or a feeling or an event. So, when I had that information, that I was purely classifiable, it was such a relief, and I started to understand myself a lot better. I started to have, ironically, more compassion for myself because I thought 'Yes, that's why I feel that, or react in that situation because that is my essential personality type and there are reasons for that'.

The other side of it, equally important for me, was I became very interested in the Enneagram, I got lots of other books – some of them are here – and I started to look at other types. Especially in my place of work, my world of business, if I found I didn't get on with someone, if I found them difficult, I'd look through one of the books and see if I could spot their type. I may not have got their type right, but it was really helpful because I'd find the main characteristics that I saw in the person and then I could work out how a Six would not react but relate to that. That was a big doorway that opened, so practically it's been a big impact on my life. My wife Renate and I often play the game when we've met someone: 'I wonder what type they are?' We may not get it right and it doesn't matter because we're exploring that person more, how we feel, how we understand them, and not just as a separate person, but our relationship with that person.

Lynne: I think for a Type Six particularly, it helps us make sense of the world and other people and gives us a little control back. If we feel we can understand ourselves better and can understand other people better, we are less intimidated, less fearful, we can manage better. Well, that's my experience.

Grahame: For me the biggest impact in learning the Enneagram has been understanding others — understanding certain situations others have been through, seeing through certain movements [actions], and understanding my own children. My own experience of this Six quality is a desire to understand, to know; that looking out for guidance, that looking for the answer, getting the books, the self-help books… maybe this book has got the answer. That's the movement of *Sixness*, which of course is part of what gets us into trouble: always looking outside of ourselves. The biggest other part of the whole journey for me – in using and working with the Enneagram – has been putting myself back in touch with my own instinctual sense of my own Being, the physical part. My wife and I completed a four-year training in Feldenkrais movement. I did it not to necessarily go out there teaching or using Feldenkrais, but because I realised the disconnection from myself with the physical being, which is one of the qualities of Type Six. We kind of walk around just up here [*pointing at head*]. One of the sayings that you hear people say is 'Wears his heart on his sleeve'. Now I probably in my own mind thought that I was pretty well controlled, that I was holding my emotion. Well, absolute rubbish! Everyone could see the coloration, the physiological changes, and that I was either worried or nervous. That comes out in certain ways, hand movements, whatever, so getting in touch with that is one of the biggest shifts for me. Certainly one of the recommendations I would say for anyone in the Type Six who sees this is 'How do we come back into this physical being?' Just to be here, to be present, instead of thinking about what's going to happen next.

Iain: Yes, [Lynne,] how is this feeling to come back into your body?

Lynne: When I read about Type Six being very mental I go 'Yes, that's where I live!' 'Not being very emotional' – that's not true. I am very emotional, but I don't live in my body. It's a tremendous effort for me to get into my body, to do yoga, and to breathe… just breathing. It's really hard work for me. It's only in the last few years that I've started to exercise, because we have to, as we get older.

Grahame: What I find is that I enjoy doing the Feldenkrais awareness through movement lessons, but I notice there is a real reluctance to do it. Part of me is saying 'I don't want to bother with that, I'll just go read a book or something'. Or even go for a walk, which is good physically, but to actually bring the attention into the physical being, into the movement, the functioning... but that is the work. One of the qualities of the work is to really be there. So it is interesting to hear you [Lynne] say that, because it's something I often notice, even now after five years.

Iain: How do you find this fear and courage? Because there is fear on one side, but the potential of the Six is to have courage. How has that impacted your life practically?

Judith: I remember doing the first enquiry around courage and my whole body having a reaction to that, because there was an inner knowing that all my life I had been fundamentally courageous and frightened at the same time, and that those had been in tension inside me. One of the things that a Six has tension around is authority. They place it outside themselves and they give away their own authority, they give away their own power, they give away their own strength, and they place it out there. And I began to see – well, in fact I didn't begin to see, I just knew – that's what I'd done, that's what I was doing, and that to be really walking a path of courage was to begin to take all of that back and own who I was, all the time, the part that I was disowning. There is an aspect of being a Type Six where you disown your own power. It feels a bit like 'Okay, I might be too powerful, I might be too forceful, I might be too much in here. So, I'll push it out there, where I can give it to somebody else'. And then I am in tension with that, so the whole journey of courage is the courage to be. It's that courage to really fully be who I already *am* and to find that.

Iain: And did you find that difficult?

Judith: Oh yes, tremendously. I'd had enormously challenging experiences in my life, which had seriously, profoundly challenged my courage. And those were transforming experiences. I went to the bottom, really at the bottom of what lies at Six, and that's because life brought that to me. It was only right at the bottom that I found the courage was there. I had to get to the bottom to find that what was at the bottom was *me*. It wasn't somebody outside, it wasn't my husband, it wasn't my family, it wasn't even God. In that depth, I found that there was *me* and that *me* had enough.

Iain: It was there, but it was hidden.

Judith: It had been hidden, or I had hidden it.

Iain: What about you, Grahame, how are you with fear and courage?

Grahame: One of the ways that I recognised when I first heard it talked about was an underlying sense that I might be told off. That somehow or other, I have to be careful because I may have done something that someone could reprimand me for. It is slightly different from just being good or evil, it's like

'Am I responsible for something?' That would be the fear part. The courage that I experience more and more now is this trusting in myself, trusting in my own being, which comes from the presence of being in this moment. In other words, instead of thinking of that future part, instead of thinking 'Have I checked everything? I've got the SatNav coming up here today... have I thought about what I'm going to say?', which would be a very typical Six [behaviour]...

Iain: Do you trust your SatNav? [*laughing*] This is the question. I don't trust mine either! I have to double check it [*group laughter*]...

Grahame: ...It is becoming more aligned to this moment. I am here, sensing into my physical reality of now, and realising that I don't know what's going to happen, I don't know what's going to happen from one moment to the next, and seeing that that is the thing to trust and that I can never know what's going to happen. If I get out of my way, things turn out pretty well, and that's the courage part, because [not knowing] can be very frightening. If I don't have a plan, if I don't have a strategy, if I really don't know what I'm going to walk into – that's the stepping off into the unknown, which is the courage that for the dominant Six feels very much at the core of the basic fear.

Iain: And you, Lynne, do you have a story, or a feeling for us on fear and courage?

Lynne: All I can think is, it's becoming more confusing to me. Because as I get older there are new fears that come with getting older, and there is more courage that comes with getting older.

Iain: The body doesn't do what it used to do, does it?

Lynne: And it doesn't want to be uncomfortable. The nervous system doesn't want to be pushed too much; I've done that, I don't need to go there. It's becoming a more wavy line. It moves differently.

Iain: We were discussing earlier some examples of famous Sixes, to maybe give people a context, and I had written a few down beforehand from books. There are two recommendations from you guys. We've got Robert Kennedy, Bruce Springsteen, Mel Gibson, which is maybe fairly obvious, and Richard Nixon. That was a surprise to me. Diane Keaton, and then one of you said Woody Allen. That almost typifies the neurosis, let's say, of a Type Six, and Tom Hanks. They are some of the famous individuals that probably people have heard of.

Grahame: I think Woody Allen films in particular bring out the humour side of the Six. A lot of comedians make fun of it and often people in relationships say, "I'm married to a Six," or "I have a Six brother. How do you deal with them?" Humour is a great way of defusing a situation.

Lynne: I read recently that Woody Allen likes to work within a small budget on his films and they're always low budget. That's because people will always give him a little bit of money to make films and he can keep on making films then. Also he feels safer as he's got a limit to work within. Very Type Six.

Grahame: I am thinking about Tom Hanks, in terms of other examples behaviourally, and the character in *Saving Private Ryan* that he plays... there is something for Sixes around home which has a sensitivity, a charge. There's almost a yearning to be home, whatever that is. It can take the form of our actual home, so it can be a very precious, very sacred place. In the film there's that moment: "Actually what I want to do is go home." That was really what he was going to do, go home. But of course then there's that other part that comes, which is the duty. So the Six quality also has a sense of duty: 'Well okay, I am responsible, but really, I'd rather just have gone home, but you know, I will do this'. Of course ultimately, what's our real home?

Iain: Maybe we can now step up a gear in terms of the overview, which is also very much part of the Enneagram, in seeing our potential to move beyond the neurotic side and the conditioning ego side, to our potential and [be] more in alignment with who we truly are. Do you want to talk a little bit about how you are seeing your own process in moving towards that alignment?

Judith: Yes, I certainly began to truly acknowledge for myself the gifts that I had. Sixes have real difficulty in acknowledging their gifts. They have difficulty with success. If you are successful, you're going to be out there and visible. So, it makes sense within the Six style to have difficulty with success, and part of that is a difficulty with recognising what your true gifts are. I began to recognise – and it was brought home to me in life – that my intuition was a real gift to me and that I hadn't followed it. I had followed other people's advice instead. I'd had very strong intuitions and then other people had said something and I took myself off my own path. So, I got in touch with the gifts of the mind and I fell in love with my mind. I fell in love with the aspect of my higher mind, which was informing me, but which – because I kept doubting it – I wasn't listening to. When I began to fall in love with my mind truly, instead of just playing about in it, then I began to access a greater self-wisdom.

Iain: What form did that self-wisdom take?

Judith: It might be in very small ways; I'd have precognitions about things. I did psychic development for quite a while and I began to take notice of them. I began to listen to my intuitions about other people without hanging on to them too much, without dissecting them and analysing them. I began to listen to the clues and the intuitions that came to me, say in relation to somebody else, and I came to realise that in fact there was a *me* that was talking to me all the time, that – if I settle down inside myself and listen to – had some really good, wise words to tell me. But I needed to practise and continue to need to practise [*laughing*] the settling of anxiety, or overthinking, or overanalysing, to allow that to come through.

Iain: Yes, as we were saying near the beginning, it comes down to

CONVERSATIONS ON THE ENNEAGRAM

understanding yourself more. When you understood yourself more, things could settle down.

Judith: It's a bit like we've made a cake of ourselves and we've over-egged it, or we've put in a bit too much of this or a bit too much of that. And to begin to get a feel for which ingredients have I just added a bit too much of… 'Am I a bit too salty now? Am I a bit too acidy now? Oh boy, that was sweet!' To get the flavor of yourself and really get a lived experience of 'How is that working *now*? Right in this minute, how is that at work?' And to catch oneself. Self-awareness is everything.

Iain: And you, Grahame, how is it for you to go on this journey of your potential?

Grahame: Picking up from what Judith was referring to about success, one of the characteristics of Sixes is to have this amnesia of success. Forgetting the things that went right in my life and only concentrating on and fixating on those things that have maybe gone wrong. Like the criticisms in feedback forms that come from some of the workshops I do. Out of eight people, seven people give a lovely glowing report, they loved it, and then one person makes one little comment, which may not even be a criticism but something they didn't particularly find sat with them, and that's the bit that will niggle and stay with me. I overthink and think about and chew it over and obsess about it. That certainly happens a bit and I catch myself in the act, but the potential part is the *awakeness* of that clarity, of just being able to let go of that and stay in this present moment. I mentioned earlier about the physical connection and this trust in myself. One of the things I've started to do – which I have always enjoyed of others, like art, writing – is believing in myself that these have a place. They mightn't have been magnificent, but they are worthy of putting out, worthy of showing without feeling any criticism or judgement from them. That's the potential, to not have that sense of always having to justify what I've done, what I'm doing. Just be who is here, be myself, be whatever this spirit, this soul that is manifesting in the world is, and allow that to blossom.

Iain: Lynne, I want to ask you the same question.

Lynne: A little different perspective for me, because when I first understood the point Six, I saw it as a template, a blueprint. I looked around the room and I saw other people who are also Sixes and how it fitted on them. And as I was driving home that night, I saw how it fitted for me, and it was who I used to think I was. I used to think that template was Lynne. When I saw that other people had exactly the same template, I was then able to ask 'If everybody who is a Six has that, then that's not Lynne. And who is Lynne? Who am I really?' It was a moment of profound awakening for me because I saw that I was not the Six. Then who was I really? And it took me to the essence.

Iain: And what did it feel like to go to the essence?

Lynne: Tremendous freedom. Freedom, liberation, peace, joy, excitement, bliss, happiness, relief.

Iain: Sounds wonderful.

Lynne: Yeah, it was great [*laughing*].

Iain: And are you able to still have that reference point in your day-to-day life?

Lynne: Absolutely, it is always with me. I am very grateful. It's been a tremendous tool for me.

Grahame: That quality of realisation, of *awakeness*, is something that Sixes when they get it, they really get it, and it's discriminating between the qualities of alertness. The alertness can be more fear-based, which would be… if you walked along an alleyway and you hear steps, there's that kind of 'I've got to keep an eye out, I've got to keep an eye out'. That's an alertness that's more fear-based. But in awakeness… 'I am here. I notice without having any judgements around it, without having any fear around it'. That quality is available to all people, to all human beings, as a high quality of Type Six. Just like every other type has a high quality and they're all available to us.

Iain: It seems that there are almost two levels of value here. There is the value of recognition of the patterns, the neurotic patterns, the programming, and seeing how that doesn't always serve us for the best, and seeing that we can approach things in a different way because our understanding is deepened. And there's also what you [Lynne] touched on quite beautifully, quite dramatically, that something really quantum can happen when you see that it is just a template, and that something else is the real you. You get beyond the mind, from 'Well, I can be a bit less fearful because I understand the dynamics' to 'There is something else there'.

Judith: The personality then becomes the vehicle of who you are and instead of being 'I am a personality and the real me exists somewhere else', there is the core self, there is who I am, and I have a personality, and my personality can then become much more open and porous. The soul can shine through my personality. And so my experience was that those aspects of Sixes which were constraining, limiting, tight – the space inside it got a bit too tight – became a gift. For example, questioning: there is a real gift in doubt. Doubt and questioning allow you to explore. There is a great curiosity, a childlike curiosity. If you think of a tree and you're investigating this tree, a Six is quite happy to go right to the end of a twig. They'll follow that thought right to the tip of that twig, wherever it's going, whether it's going in a positive or negative direction, because they want to know. There's this intense curiosity. And then when they get to the end of that twig, they think 'Okay, found that one out, I'll do another one'. There's a great freeing up of the joy of questioning. There's a joy in searching, there's a joy in being curious. So, it stops being a questioning because 'I need to feel secure and safe' and starts being 'Oooh, let's find out what's here'.

Iain: In a way there is value in what we could call the negative traits, but it is maximising that value.

Judith: It's transforming it.

Grahame: I think that it's always important for people watching this programme, and I would always offer to anybody that comes prepared to listen to me gabble on about the Enneagram: don't take my word for it. Don't take my word for anything. In fact, I wouldn't recommend anyone believe anything until we can prove it for ourselves and to experience it now! For a Six that comes as a natural 'Oh, right, I can doubt this stuff'. But there's a difference between doubting it and then looking in the books to support my doubt: 'What do you think about this? And what do you think about that?' That's one of the characteristics of Sixes, to go around and ask everyone what's the right thing to do, to store that and then to go back and use them as references. Of course, no one is going to agree with each other, which leads to that kind of confusion. There's a difference between that and saying 'Okay, that's an interesting point, let me see if I can prove it like a good scientist, a good sort of Sherlock Holmes would do. Let's test it out, observe it in myself'. Then when I find something which is a truth for me, that's where the courage comes, and to trust that. Because the next step would be for the Six personality to come back in and say 'Well hang on, I've had that experience, I've had that, I'll just check that out with my guru, or with someone else, to see if that is actually verifiable'. That shift is the single little shift to catch, away from myself, from trusting my own experience. And it is only my experience, it doesn't have to be everyone else's experience. That's the other part, not to become 'Oh, this is the way and this is the only way'. When Sixes get that, they can be an incredible inspiration to people and say, "What's your truth?"

Iain: Yes, it's interesting because I know one of the ways that Type Six is classified is 'the questioner'. In *The Enneagram Made Simple* book, the title that they give is 'the questioner'. I've always been a questioner. I know in business, one thing I always do – and I've done well in business – is that when we have a new project my Type Six always goes to 'What's the worst thing that can happen?' not because that is the only scenario, but because that is quite a good starting point when you look at a new project. If the worst thing happens, is it going to bring the company down? No. If it's not, we can go up a stage. So you are looking at something from a very grounded point of view; i.e., you have looked to the downside. Many people in the business world go racing ahead, they haven't really checked out the possible potential downside, and they get in a mess. For me, there is something very sensible and intelligent sometimes about Type Six, and it's the excess which can bring us down if we haven't got that understanding and awareness.

Judith: All our type structures seem intelligent to us. They are centred around a worldview, and we compensated for that which we had lost touch with. And so they were sensible, they were intelligent ways. If you feel that you're unsupported and you can't trust the world, then why not be frightened? It's very logical, and yet the problem was that that became an overcompensation and it becomes our reality. We begin to get so constricted into that particular view and it becomes an overdoing. Of course, then we're out of touch with the other possibility: that the world and the universe and people and our environment and us will always be there to support us. They are of themselves supporting. And so it becomes very binary: I'll choose this reality, and that means I am not choosing that one.

Lynne: People listening to this hear us talking a lot about fear and doubt and anxiety and courage. One of the things I learnt through identifying all that in myself was the antidote for it, which for me is faith. Some people call it trust, I like to call it faith. And that brings me tremendous peace and has helped me calm myself.

Iain: What does faith mean for you, Lynne?

Lynne: Very interesting question, which is what a Six would say. What does faith mean for me? That there is something much bigger than myself, much greater, and that my little pinprick of fear and anxiety is only that.

Iain: It shows you a bigger perspective?

Lynne: There is a bigger picture and the bigger picture is good.

Grahame: I think that's a very nice description of another aspect most Sixes will recognise and actually feel that there is a great grace and joy in being part of something bigger than ourselves. I think that the ego version is the kind of allegiance, or rebellion against the authoritative aspect, the kind of structure that's thinking 'I have to be, who can I trust?' Whereas that whole idea of we are all one, we are part of that and that's the honour, certainly speaks to me. The other thing that I just wanted to pick up from what you [Iain] were saying is that even the worst thing that can happen – and I know that it's not just Sixes that do that – for me that's a Six mental strategy that becomes one of the personality strategies that is always used. Now, I think for anybody watching this, maybe doing life coaching, this is the value of understanding the Enneagram and the different types, because when we have a sense of what's the normal default strategy of the personality structure, we know the one not to use [laughing]. As you'll see throughout the series, different types are going to have different strategies. We have seen it with Type Three earlier – having an outcome, always having a goal. That can be very useful for a Six and it can be part of the antidote, because the Six is always in that 'away from' [stance]: I don't want this, I don't want that. It's like being sent to the supermarket with a list of all the foods you don't want to eat. What do you come back with? You don't know; that's part of the problem. So, to move to having a goal is useful. Now, equally, [on] that strategy you mentioned –

'Think of the worst thing that can happen, and where are we?' — there's a whole series that Dale Carnegie did in how to stop worrying and start living, many years ago, and it's very valuable. But if you gave that to a Six, what is happening is you are giving that structure the very thing which takes us more and more deeply into the personality. So, it's the one strategy that I wouldn't recommend someone use as a coaching strategy for a Six, because that's already happening, that's the default mechanism. If we can get clear on that, any sort of assistance we are giving to friends, advice... if we have a sense of that, one to say would be, "Okay, we know you are doing that already. You probably do that really well, all the time [*laughing*], so let's look at something else."

Iain: Yeah, the example I was trying to give – for me anyway – was the way of actually ending up doing something that was new and creative, and maybe had a risk element, by looking at the possible downside. But the thing I'd like to ask about, in the last five minutes, is to look at lack of holding. You [Judith] introduced Type Six and you were talking about this lack of holding when we were very young. Of course that brings up what you mentioned: trust, basic trust. This is very much part of the progression of the Six towards its potential – this basic trust. I just wonder how that has manifested in your life.

Judith: Lynne put faith beautifully, and what I would say about faith, first of all, is to distinguish it from belief. Belief is somebody teaching you something, or somebody saying, "This is how it is," and you say, "Yes okay, I believe it." Faith is a gnosis; faith is an experience inside, which you described. Faith is that: the experience of self, of something which is known. It is really grounded in something very solid, very real. Faith is an aspect of reality. I was pondering faith yesterday, and I was reminded of when I was a little girl. I was a little girl who had a great deal of faith. I remember going to church and the vicar saying, "Believe in God," and being completely baffled. It was like saying to me, "Believe in your mother." Of course, she is standing next to me, why do I need to believe in her? I already had that; they were telling me something which I *knew*, because as a child I was close to it. On my journey I left it behind in some sense. That is what faith brings back. It brings back to you that experience inside yourself of the greater reality of who you are. We are not just our personality. I am not my body, I am not my thoughts, and I am not my emotions. I am more than all of those.

Iain: And you *know* that.

Judith: And you *know* it. It's not that you believe it, you know it. You have a real experience of knowing that there is a constant. There is a constant, eternal self, essence, soul, whatever one's frame of terminology might be, that means whatever it means to the people watching this. But there is something which remains, always. And that is both in me and greater than me, and it is that connection that you described so beautifully, that connection with that. And that experience for me, really, was like I remembered. I remembered who I was, and day-to-day life is about continuing to remember that. Remember who you are. That's right, you remember that. Be that.

Iain: You did already know, but you'd forgotten, so it was like rediscovering, remembering.

Judith: Yes, in Enneagram terms, I fell asleep. I fell asleep to it.

Iain: Good. We've almost got to the end of our little journey here with the Enneagram. Are there any books, quickly, that you guys would recommend?

Judith: I would recommend two websites from my training, which is Helen Palmer and David Daniels' Enneagram Worldwide. And the other one is Enneagram.com, which is Helen's website. Enneagram Worldwide is of the whole school that I was taught in, and it has a wealth of information.

Iain: Wonderful. Judith, Grahame, and Lynne, thank you very much for coming along and joining conscious.tv this afternoon, and I really hope you found it useful. I certainly very much enjoyed it. I was able to really participate in this as Six is my type.

To watch this interview please go to:
http://www.conscious.tv/consciousness/enneagram

Enneagram Type Seven – The Adventurer

Discussion with Daniel, Nina and Chris

Moderated by Iain McNay

Iain: Today we are going to look more closely at Type Seven. I have with me in the studio three Sevens: Chris, Daniel, and Nina. Let's start with you, Chris. How did you first get to hear about the Enneagram?

Chris: I first got to hear about it through a friend who's very much into developmental work. He brought a book round to my house one day and said, "You've got to read this, this is you," and he was showing me Type Eight at the time. So I read a lot of the Eight and I thought 'Yes, that's definitely me, but some of that's not quite on the mark'. Then when I nudged over and read the Seven in depth and understood the Seven, I thought 'Oh bloody hell, that's definitely me!' – those traits and that way to be.

Iain: We should explain the Enneagram of course. Why don't you tell us briefly what the Enneagram is?

Chris: The way I think of it and the way I describe it is that the Enneagram is a system for psychological and if you like spiritual growth. I think of it as a road map, a map to allow you to see aspects of yourself, your traits, the unconscious things that you do, your habits and your patterns that play throughout all of your life that for the most part we are unconscious of. We don't really become aware of them unless we have some sort of system to highlight them. And I describe it as that, as a system of growth that enables us to become more conscious of the things that we do, more aware of the self and what the self is, so that we can move along in a more harmonious balanced way, dealing with life and things that come up. That's the way I think of it.

Iain: When you first realised you were a Type Seven, how did that impact you, how did you feel about that?

Chris: Enlightened and psychotic at the same time. When I really got to understand it, firstly it made total sense with the traits of the Seven, the way that I live my life, the way I think, the way I feel, the way I interact; also, the more dysfunctional side, the things that I do when I'm stressed, where I lose energy. It really highlighted that.

Iain: Let's start with an example. When you say 'dysfunctional and lose energy', just give us a practical example of that.

Chris: I'll tell you what, why don't we start with the good side first [*laughing*] because that's more fun.

Iain: And that is also very typical of Type Sevens.

Chris: Exactly, yes, we don't want to start with the negative side too soon. So the traits that I can really relate to being a dominant Seven is that very optimistic, very high energy, always looking for new experiences, variety, and joy, enjoyment and happiness and pleasures and opportunities.

Iain: Exactly how you come across now – you're really living this.

Chris: Definitely the best place to be on the Enneagram obviously [*laughing*]... and then the slight downside to it is that if you're continually looking for more experiences, more pleasures, more stimulus, then you tend to not be able to be present in the moment. And because you're constantly looking for more experiences, more information, more knowledge, more things to give you some sort of energy, or where to put your energy, you can struggle with being in the moment because of the anxieties that you might have to face by being in the moment. The subtle little emotional pains that we all have to deal with day in and day out. As a dominant Seven you're trying to avoid those a little bit and not be here in the moment with those, and experience them and then potentially get the benefit from them. You'll be off, on to something else looking for more and more pleasures. In a way, the here and now spot, the 'live here now and be here now' and all that caper, is a mild challenge sometimes.

Iain: That's a great start, thanks. Nina, let's look at your story. How did you first hear about the Enneagram?

Nina: It was very similar to Chris. Someone came along and said, "I think you should go on an Enneagram course, I think you'd enjoy it," and so I went along. No one was saying I was an Eight, it was more... was I a Nine or was I a Four? It took me a long, long time because even though I love laughing, got a great sense of humour, that side of it, I'm not an instantly jolly person. I'm quite a serious person and so the Seven kind of fun, upbeat stuff, didn't instantly resonate; it took a while. I think it's exactly what Chris was saying, it's the ability to link, to make connections everywhere, to see, to meet people, to be able to join them. It's that kind of networking skills; it's the excitement of realising one bit of learning that you have, could link up with another bit of learning that you have. All of that is going on all the time. You've this very busy, active mind, and so it took me a long time to realise that I was a Seven.

Iain: A long time is like weeks?

Nina: Yes, a long time in 'Seven terms' [*laughing*]. Yes, it's probably just a weekend.

Daniel: Excruciating... a life sentence!

Nina: Yes, it was one of those times when I got really bored [*laughing*] and then it just helped me enormously. I suddenly understood why I've been sabotaging my life and my careers all the way down the line.

Iain: Explain that in more detail. You felt you've been sabotaging your life and your career, and so how did discovering being a Type Seven help you out of that?

Nina: When I got into the Enneagram I was in my forties and I'd already had my first career as a graphic designer. Then I'd written 'How To' books, but even though that sounds like a career, they were how-to books on looking after your home. They were how-to books on the Royal Family, they were how-to books on stain removal...

Iain: Hang on... you wrote a how-to book on the Royal Family?

Nina: Yes, it was all about the Royal Warrant Holders, how to live your life like the Royal Family. So I'd had experiences in lots and lots of different fields, and anyone else would have stayed an expert in one field, but I'd written a book, got bored, moved on to the next topic. I'd covered fifteen topics of books and was never sticking. Every time something was about to happen that I could write more books about on the same subject, I went 'No, don't want to do that, done it!' You know, 'been there, done that'. I think when I realised that that was a really deep part of my personality and I was going to carry on doing that forever, I started thinking about what I love doing and how I could put all the things I love doing into one business – something that would actually be exciting enough to sustain me throughout everything.

Iain: You went deeper into yourself to see what you really wanted and then you came from a different space, is that right?

Nina: Absolutely. It was saying let's not just do things for instant gratification, let's actually think about what's going to reward me long term. Something that's big enough that all the things that I get interested in can come into it and be part of it. That was an enormous help.

Iain: To slow down a bit, less frantic, is that right?

Nina: Yes definitely, less frantic, less after a kind of instant hit... it became a much bigger, more conscious, process.

Iain: Daniel, with you, how did discovering you were a Type Seven affect and change your life?

Daniel: I think it gave me a framework around things that I thought weren't normal, that I was supposed to deal with and eradicate actually. I understood they were part of my character... and a great example is choosing a table in a restaurant; it can be quite excruciating. I sit down and I think 'I'm on the wrong table, that table over there is so much better'. And to be given the space with my partner, to say, "Okay we can move there and you're allowed one more move." It freed me up to be me; that was part of my nature. I really resonate with what Nina's saying career-wise, of thinking I was supposed to become a specialist in something, but finding I would do something once. I'd like to learn it, I'd like to maybe do it a second time and be good at it, but after that I didn't need to do it again; I was ready for the next thing.

Iain: This process of change, was it difficult for you?

Daniel: No, I don't think so... it was freeing up what was already there rather than trying to change into something. I think I'd been trying to change; this allowed me to be me, so there's an excitement in that.

Iain: It seems both of you – in fact all three of you – pretty quickly got real value out of finding you were a Type Seven. It improved your life.

Nina: I really enjoyed hearing about the table. My husband now says, "You choose the table," because he's just so used to me not liking several tables and having to try them all out, so yes...

Daniel: And it's best being able to share dessert, because I hate limiting myself to one dessert. If I could share dessert with everyone on the table, I'm done.

Iain: You're dreaming of these restaurants you can find sometimes that give you almost compilation desserts. There are eight desserts on the menu and you can have a little bit of eight all in one deal!

Daniel: I love those.

Chris: Do you think it is nature, or is it more like learnt traits?

Daniel: I think it is nature, and my teaching of the Enneagram is also that it's nature. Unlike the Myers Briggs for example, where we can change types, in my understanding we don't [change] our Ennea-type. It's part of how we've dealt with our development, and it's the viewpoint we'll always have.

Chris: But is that nature, or the environmental nurture?

Daniel: Again, I think it's nature, it's how we deal with the separation from the breast. I was reading Sandra Maitri on the way here and she describes it in that sense, and because the painful quality of the Seven is always pursuing an experience we think we've had... I had that great dessert at one point in my life and where will I find it again?

Chris: Right, right.

Iain: And you want to better it somehow. It's almost like it's out of control isn't it? It's like greed and gluttony.

Daniel: Yes, and part of the life journey of the Seven is finding the nourishment that we had on the breast, because I remember feeling really loved and warm there, but where do we find that in life?

Iain: Interesting. I want to go back to a few basics for people that may be watching this, have never heard of the Enneagram before, and are just wondering whether they're Sevens, or not. I would just explain that even if you're a Type Seven you still have parts of all the other types in you. It's not as if you're just that type, but you are mainly that type. I wrote down a few quotes taken from books I was looking at for my research. Type Sevens 'enjoy life', are 'uninhibited', they're 'optimistic', they're 'busy and energetic'. And you all three display those qualities. They 'take risks'. I guess coming on this programme is a risk to some degree. You 'like to keep moving', you're 'easily bored' – you've all pretty much covered that – you 'like yourselves'... Do you like yourselves?

Chris: I love myself! [*laughing*]

Iain: Daniel, you're not looking quite so sure about that one?

Daniel: Yes, I think it's because of that green-grass syndrome for me: 'Oh but it would be better to have that quality'. So it's that sense of 'Ah, dark hair. No I think I'd like lighter hair, lighter hair seems like more fun'.

Iain: You like yourself, but yourself could always be better.

Nina: I don't know about liking myself, I love talking about myself.

Daniel: Oh yes, centre of attention thank you [*laughing*] – coming back to me.

Nina: Exactly, don't think that necessarily means I like myself... I like hearing myself think and talk. My husband's a Type Nine: the radio's always on in his world because he doesn't want to think, he doesn't want to hear himself think. I never have the radio on; it's always so I can enjoy my thoughts. I enjoy bits about me, but I don't know that I necessarily like them.

Iain: Just going down my list to try to cover as much as we can what Sevens are like: 'They're idealist and want to contribute to the world'. Is that something you connect with? You 'love excitement and travel'. There's 'not enough time to do what I want' – you very much covered that. You 'like being outspoken and outrageous'.

Daniel: Oh no [*laughing*]...

Nina: Yes, definitely.

Iain: How would you be outspoken and outrageous as a Type Seven?

Nina: Okay, this morning, in my business we had a breakfast for corporate clients. Once, when I was in a corporate [meeting] I was talking about what success meant to everyone in the room, and there was a lady there who, to my amazement said, "Well, success to me is having a Brazilian."

Chris: I think that's a type of coffee [*laughing*]...

Nina: Now, I was absolutely amazed. I was amazed to hear her talk about that in a mixed public arena, so by repeating that story [in this morning's meeting] to some quite high-powered corporate clients, that's what I'd call being slightly outrageous. With my grey hair it's probably not what they'd expect...

Chris: Good ice-breaker...

Nina: Good ice-breaker yes. I think with the risk-taking and the outrageousness, I'll want to go slightly further than everyone else. We're having a walk or a picnic, I'll want to push down the beach. We're in a boat, I'll want to row a little bit further than everyone else. It's that kind of thing: "Let's just do a little bit more." Maybe that's a bit outrageous, I don't know.

Wearing outrageous clothes, but probably not as outrageous as Type Four...

Iain: I've a feeling Chris would have a good example here.

Chris:: Of outrageous?

Iain: Yes, how would you be outrageous as a Seven?

Chris: [*laughing*] Is this an X-rated show? I mean outrageous, it depends what you call outrageous – I personally think that is outrageous.

Iain: That's what I'm getting at, something that you would naturally do that other people might be shocked in a minor way by, or even in a major way!

Chris: Outrageous? I don't know... I don't know if I'd really call things outrageous. I mean outrageous would be stripping off and running down the middle of Pall Mall whilst waving a banner saying 'I fancy the Queen'. That would be outrageous, but other than that, it's just normal behaviour.

Iain: Yes, so you're naturally outgoing, and other people might have slight inhibitions about doing something that for you would be quite ordinary.

Chris: Yes outrageous... depends what you mean by that, but getting up in front of people talking, for instance, I'm very extrovert in my energy structure, and so those sort of things that are considered generally more extrovert and out there a bit, are very easy for me. It's very comfortable for me to be that way. If there were a thousand people and you had a little group and somebody had to go up and tell this group good or bad news, it wouldn't bother me. I would volunteer to do that sort of thing, and then if they said, "You'll have to dress up in latex to do it, just for kicks and giggles," I'd say, "Even better, that'll be fun!"

Iain: Okay, so far [the conversation] has been very 'up', but there must be a side of the Seven that's challenging for you. I know Sevens can get ungrounded, they can get lost in things. Daniel, you hinted at this earlier – what is the challenge of being a Type Seven? What are the things that you find difficult at times in terms of your development?

Daniel: I think for me it is being present and accepting what is, because under stress Sevens go to Type One, which is the 'perfectionist'. So there's that desire in me, if I feel stressed, to want everything to get perfect. It's very hard to accept where I am at times, to enjoy where I am and the job I've got rather than to dream of 'the perfect job'.

Iain: What helps you in that situation?

Daniel: I think now, knowing that this is a tendency for me, knowing that the fantasy of the perfect job isn't perfect – that it is a fantasy... and I guess increasingly, letting my energy come down to remembering to breathe almost, and to experience what is going on around me and detach from the story of what might be.

Iain: You mentioned being present. Describe in a practical way what being present means.

Daniel: I don't know. What is being present? Certainly around my spiritual teaching it's physically being aware of my body. It's being here in this room, enjoying being with the three of you, rather than moving off into 'What's my journey home going to be like? What am I going to do when I get home? How I'm going to tell people that I was on TV?' – and I can even feel my energy change when I talk about the different things. So for me that's being present, and remaining present I think is really tough as a Seven – at least that's my excuse. Meditating I find excruciating and actually, I meditate now on my push-bike as a way of having movement and practising being with myself.

Iain: You don't close your eyes...

Daniel: No, no...

Chris: That would be a skill!

Daniel: That's the advanced meditation. So, yes, that's some of the pain for me of being a Seven.

Iain: We could say with being present it's very much feeling the body as you mentioned, about being here, about being aware if your mind is taking you away somewhere else... You also mentioned earlier: acceptance – accepting this is what's happening and that's it. What's happening: the four of us are together in a studio in West London and we're talking about Type Sevens. Chris, you're really bubbly and full of energy – is there a side of you that you find difficult at times?

Chris: [laughing] More than one... I definitely resonate with what Danny said about being present; it's very easy not to be present, it takes a bit of work. Overwhelm is something I experience a lot of, whether it could be having fifteen or twenty windows open on my computer and doing one task, then I've clicked on an email and before you know it I'm half hour into a programme and totally forgotten what the hell I was doing, which when you think about it, it's quite mad. Yes, I can very easily get consumed with doing lots and lots of things, and that can make me quite inefficient in getting the task done.

Iain: And how do you focus yourself?

Chris: I have to give myself a talking to, I have to say 'Hang on a minute, what's going on here, slow down man...'

Iain: There's a side of you that's wise and that wise side is saying 'Slow down' – in fact what Daniel's saying: 'Be present'. Is that right, is that how it works, or is it different for you?

Chris: Yes, I mean more or less. For me one of the big components of being able to be functional and as present as possible is exercise. I do a lot of exercise so that I have a good physical outlet for energy expenditure, and when I've had a good exercise session then it's much easier for me to be present. I'm much more centred mentally, emotionally, and physically, so then the living in the now is a lot easier. But, generally it's what Danny said. Being present is not easy for anybody, never mind if you are a Seven Enneagram, but it's a challenge anyway for anybody. So that's the game. Being right here, right now, is easier said than done.

Iain: Nina, how's that for you?

Nina: Yes, I definitely agree with both of them. What does it for me is two things: reading and writing. I find those really calm me down, especially reading and Mozart. Listening to classical music, or any music, really brings me right to the present very, very quickly, so that works. I think the difficulty Chris touched on, the overwhelm when your mind is spinning with ideas – your computer's flashing with all sorts of different things that you've started and haven't finished. But the thing that probably is the most difficult is something that Danny mentioned, is the idea of going into perfectionism. So it's very tough for people around me because I suddenly [say], "Oh my goodness you're dirtying the kitchen and you're just boiling an egg!" and snap at my husband for doing something which is really irrelevant in the grand scheme of things; but I've just gone into Type One, seeing him making a mess, and get very upset about it. And that part of being a Seven is difficult for everyone around us, that we can lose our temper very quickly. I don't know about you guys, but for me, one second later I've forgotten about it, and they're still going – especially if they don't know me very well – they're going 'Phew what was that? That was just like a tornado', and for me it was just nothing. I was just cross, I vented my crossness, but it left everyone else around me reeling. I think that is very hard for people, and I find it very hard. I know now there are certain things... my husband cooking... I'm just not there. I know now what my trigger points are, but the only way for me not to do it is to set myself not to get annoyed with certain things, and it is when I'm stressed.

Iain: So it can be a challenge to be around a Type Seven especially in a close relationship?

Chris: [*laughing*] I wouldn't have thought so...

Iain: What would you say?

Chris: I wouldn't say that, Iain, myself. No more of a challenge than anybody else, I think it's a pleasure!

Nina: It's a pleasure ninety-nine-point-nine percent of the time, but when I lose my temper... luckily your loved ones get to know you well enough they know it doesn't mean anything, but it can be quite a formidable force as it were. But maybe that's just me, I'm not talking for them.

Iain: So the anger for you guys is an expression, and it's clearing something and then back to your normal life, so to speak.

Nina: Yes, about a second later.

Chris: Short and sweet...

Nina: I don't bear grudges; basically I really like people, I love meeting new people. I'm impossible to interview people: if we've got someone that we need to hire, I can't do it because I would have everyone. I can see the strengths in everyone and I can see exactly 'Oh they might not be so good at that, but they'd be *brilliant* at that' and so it makes them exciting. On the whole it's quite fun to be around a Seven because there is that real desire to find a positive in every experience, in every person, in *every everything* really. It's a fun place to be.

Chris: [*laughing*] Sold!

Iain: You're all doing a great PR job for being Type Seven, I have to say. One of the things about the Enneagram that has been very useful when I discovered my type was, not only did I learn that there are a lot of people on the planet that function very much the same way as myself, but also that there was a potential of my type insofar as I didn't have to be stuck in certain behavioural patterns. There was a higher way of being myself. Nina, I wondered how that's affected you, seeing that potential, moving towards it and living the potential of Type Seven.

Nina: Gosh, it's what we were touching on earlier, realising that it's a freedom to be who you want to be; and the potential of Sevens, it's about finding... [*pause*] I think you should go to Danny on this one. I'm just trying to think. No, no, I'm just trying to think! Well it feels like most of it is potential because there is so much energy and there is so much desire to do lots of good things. Ways of helping people, ways of creating fun, harmonious situations. So the potential is to keep as grounded as you can, so that you have the energy to do these things.

Iain: What I'm trying to get at – and maybe this doesn't apply to you guys – but when I was doing my research earlier, one of the things I wrote down about the potential for Sevens was 'To move forward, they have to confront their emptiness and barrenness, they have to see and confront how much they live in their minds'. I wonder, can you relate to that?

Nina: Yes definitely. Well, Chris and Daniel are obviously wonderful, working out and going on their bikes and everything... I find that I don't even notice I've got a body.

Iain: You see, I'm interested in this, and as I say I'm not trying to put something in that isn't there for you guys, but this emptiness and barrenness, is this something you can relate to?

Nina: Yes, definitely, I think boredom is a real key thing. There is a real desire not to feel bored.

Daniel: [*laughing*] Yes.

Iain: Boredom for you is barrenness? Is that right?

Nina: Yes.

Iain: Describe boredom for you.

Nina: I don't know that I have it so much now, because I think I've got more resolved. It's something that I would dread a lot as a child, that feeling there's nothing to do and what am I going to do, and sitting for ages. I think now, if something sad happens I can feel very, very desolate as if I'm in a very barren landscape, with nothing there, grey skies and just a feeling of emptiness and uncertainty as to how it's going to get filled, ever!

Iain: And are you okay with that feeling now?

Nina: I'm much better with that feeling, yes.

Iain: Is that something that before you would try to jump over and try to get away from?

Nina: And not want to lie there crying, but want to actually move into something positive, and I'm now much better at just saying 'This is it!' and it doesn't last terribly long. In a way, I often try to get it to last longer because I think I will learn more about myself if I can stay in that unhappy space, but the happiness tends to kind of bubble up quite quickly. I think it is a good learning place, when it happens, so I don't mind if it does happen.

Iain: Daniel, how is the emptiness and barrenness for you? Is that something you connect with?

Daniel: Yes, a lot. I've a rowing machine and I never use it. I said to someone, "The problem is, it's boring, it's excruciatingly boring… I tried music video." And they said, "So what's wrong with boring?" And it had never occurred to me that boredom is something I could allow to exist. I presumed I was always meant to fill it, that it represented a lack of stimulation rather than being a state in itself.

Iain: So you judged it as a bad thing?

Daniel: Yes, it was a really tortuous place to be. I do really relate to that barrenness and I think that's almost the moving tables in the restaurants. It's like I sit at this table and it hasn't completely filled me up, I still feel an emptiness, and so maybe that table is going to satisfy me more.

Iain: What I'm interested in is, can you stay with the barrenness, and does it change without you doing something?

Chris: Jesus, Iain, come on! Move on, this is just a nightmare! Sorry Danny… continue…

Daniel: Can I stay with the barrenness?

Iain: I'll come on to your list in a minute, Chris [*laughing*]…

Daniel: I still judge it as a bad place to be. It's not a place that I want to be and stay… like the nature of this discussion [*laughing*]: I'm thinking 'Let's move on to the fun bit!'

Iain: You see, according to these books, this is the gateway to freedom for you Sevens.

Chris: If you believe them…

Iain: [Chris,] tell me about your barrenness [*laughing*]. I think I'll blink and I'll miss it!

Chris: What's the question? What's the specific question?

CONVERSATIONS ON THE ENNEAGRAM

Iain: Okay let's change it.

Daniel: No, make him suffer as well!

Chris: Bring it on!

Iain: How do you see your gateway to your potential as a Type Seven?

Chris: I think inevitably the gateway to express more potential, more expanded awareness, more expanded consciousness, the way I see it as a dominant Seven, is to slow down and be more aware of that present moment. You could say that about any type, but I think specifically of Sevens due to that desire for constant stimulation, always looking for something else, and being somewhere else and having something else, and feeling something else, and seeing something else, and all those things. The more I'm able to be totally present in the moment, and anything that comes up, accept it and let it pass, whatever comes up, experience it with non-judgement and non-attachment, then inevitably that is the gateway – from the way I view it – to expanded awareness, expanded consciousness.

Iain: How does that work practically for you?

Chris: [*laughing*] Carnage, doesn't work at all! I'm just good at waxing lyrical. I've read lots of books. Absolute bullshit!

Iain: Are you being totally serious there?

Chris: How does it work practically? I often say on a day-to-day basis [that] I have a range, an emotional scale from totally enlightened bliss and really present to everything that goes on... to absolute dysfunction and madness where you've completely lost the plot and everything in between. I think practically, it's just work. It's not that easy, you have to have a set of practises that help you live as presently as possible.

Iain: You're theorising. I'm trying to feel another side of you, you see...

Chris: So the question is what?

Iain: How practically do you realise the potential of a Type Seven by going through your gateway? And maybe the question is not appropriate for you. I'm not trying to pin you down.

Chris: How practically do I experience it? Like I say, on a day-to-day basis I can be totally present, totally aware, totally really in the moment and be an interconnected part of a grander whole, and really live from that space, walk that space, breathe that space; then the next thing I know I'm half an hour down the road and I've totally lost that way of being and I'm all over the place doing lots of things at the same time. That's the reality of my day-to-day, week-by-week breathing and living on this spinning planet.

Nina: I think often, even though Sevens like talking about themselves, they don't like thinking deeply about themselves because there might not be anything there. I think that is what can keep us more superficial, because that might be the emptiness inside. When we experience things, we don't do them in the same kind of in-depth way that maybe a Four or a Six does. We are living more on the surface and enjoying fun and superficial things, and maybe we're not as in touch with our emotions as other types are.

Chris: I don't know about that 'superficialness' as compared to other types yes, but as for not in touch with emotions… I don't know about that.

Nina: The 'superficialness', if you start digging deep, if someone does really start asking us about the dark side, it's hard for us to talk about it because we're not quite sure we understand it. We don't really like going there.

Chris: Why would you?

Nina: Yes, why would you? I think that's maybe why you're having difficulty with the questions because it's something that we find difficult to express ourselves.

Chris: Yes, plus Iain's throwing his own type over the questions, you know what I mean? So it's not right or wrong, that's how it rolls.

Daniel: I'm wondering too about the path of integration which from Seven goes into Five. I tend to always generalise [that] the Seven is quite extroverted and the Five is quite introverted. I think the Five is quite self-sufficient and likes to bring knowledge and calm – and I find that state. I've often been confused whether I'm extroverted or introverted because I have this very bubbly outgoing bit and then I need to recuperate, and for me that's the feeling of going towards the Five, of recharging, finding my self-sufficiency. I don't quite connect with the bit about not knowing myself, or not wanting to know myself. I find there's a lot of enquiry for me and yet I also get to a block and say 'I don't want to go to that bit'. I think part of my potential feels it's around *joy*, it's how I take the fun of being a Seven, but to experience it as joy rather than just stimulation, because it feels like there's a lot of fun to be had as a Seven, and to truly allow that fun rather than looking for the next fun.

Nina: I know exactly what you mean about the introversion/extroversion. For example my Monday to Friday diary is always absolutely full, and if it isn't absolutely full I'll wonder why. But if I've anything booked in on Saturday and Sunday it really upsets me: that's my real personal time when no one is allowed in, and I just want to be. That's the Five, I'm going into my Five, and you know holidays, just want to be with a book on my own, reading quietly or listening to music or something on my own. Definitely there's the public bit, which everyone's allowed a part of, and then there's the very private bit, which is really just for me.

Iain: I feel it's coming out now, maybe the phrases I used weren't the most helpful phrases, but you all have – I know Chris will come back in a minute – a quiet side. Is that right, or would you say a reflective side? And it's helping to balance all this activity of going, going, going… doing, doing, doing.

Daniel: Sometimes, that transition can be quite rapid and it's taken me a little while to realise the world can't always read that. It's like 'Yes, yes, loving the attention, loving the attention! Hey leave me alone, leave me alone!' And people get jarred by it. For me that's quite a quick movement. I don't know how rapidly you [Nina] feel it.

Nina: Oh yes, instantly, I don't like talking on the phone at weekends; just really don't want to pick up the phone.

Daniel: Oh my God yes, and everyone says, "Why don't you answer the phone?" I'm having 'me time'.

Nina: Yes, exactly, so there's this very, very selfish side that you just absolutely have to regroup. Chris is looking... any of this resonate, [Chris]?

Chris: Yes, I know what you mean...

Iain: You say you know what they mean, but does it resonate?

Chris: Yes, I definitely like those quiet times when it actually feels nice to be on your own and recharge. I know what you mean about the phone: quite often I don't bother with it, picking it up, whatever. But yes, those reflective times and meditative times are very, very useful. I find an energy balance in them, so I know what you mean.

Nina: And I think it's not even reflective or meditative for me, I think it's just going to have to be on my own, and yet there is a real dread about it, before going into the weekend; the thought that I've got a blank diary is very, very, scary: what if I get bored? So there's 'I am dreading this' and yet the moment that it happens I just think how wonderful that I have this time to myself, but it's definitely not easy...

Iain: It takes courage to allow this [alone] time, because I think you're right, in our modern life you have to really put in your diary a line through the day; otherwise it does get filled up.

Nina: And there is a fear that I'm going to be on my own, lonely and unhappy, and I don't want that to happen.

Iain: You still have a programme in there that says – and Daniel's nodding as well – that if you're on your own it could be that you're lonely and not happy.

Daniel: I think that's the barrenness that you're referring to in your question.

Iain: You guys seem pretty well-balanced, I have to say.

Daniel: Oh, thanks...

Chris: [*laughing*] Just the power of the Seven!

Iain: I think we should explain a little bit about the other influences... you mentioned Type Five. Now, as I understand it, the major influences on Sevens would be the adjoining types: Six, which is a more fear-based personality, and Eight, which is a more domineering, bossy personality. Are you aware of those influences? You've [Nina and Daniel] mentioned the reflective side. And you're [Chris] more on the Eight side, would you say?

Chris: Yes, I'm a strong Eight. The number of times I've taken Enneagram tests, or read the themes and dominant traits of Sevens and Eights, [Type Eight] is very, very close for me. It almost feels like fifty-one percent Seven, and forty-nine percent Eight. I resonate a lot with the dominance and the drive and the pushing forward and not hanging about, not messing about, of the Eight. I feel that very much in my way of being and energy structure, so I have to be aware of that. I don't feel the Six so much; in fact the Six sometimes drives me mental – the whole energy around that... Sometimes I think 'Jesus, come on, let's get going!' but hopefully I'm aware of that.

Iain: One of the things I've found so valuable, when I first found out about the Enneagram, and I am a Type Six, which is why I drive you [Chris] crazy, is not so much learning about myself that's been very valuable, but also learning about other people because it's so helpful in relationships. I've said this before on these programmes: if I have a problem with a person, I try and work out what type I think they are. I might get it wrong, but that doesn't matter, because it can still help in my relationship with them. I'm now putting my head in their head, or my heart in their heart, and I'm finding out why they are the way they are. I think that's a fantastic thing for me [about] the Enneagram. I don't know whether you've found value as well in understanding other people's types?

Daniel: I do, a lot. I'm in business with three others. We've a Four, an Eight, and a Six, and I think it's really helpful seeing the energy as we work together. The Six is quite risk-averse and quite conservative, and it's easy to dismiss that, until you really allow the understanding of the fear-based, whereas the Eight is quite action-based: 'Can we keep moving, can we keep moving...' Then the Four is more emotion-based. So I think it's a really powerful framework for observing people, and certainly my superego is quite caught up in right and wrong.

Iain: What's the superego?

Daniel: It's that inner critic, and I think Sevens have quite a strong inner critic.

Iain: Let's get this clear, when you say 'inner critic' what you mean is, that it's an internal voice criticising yourself...

Daniel: It's a constant judging that this is wrong and this is right, that that answer is wrong, that Nina's answer is better than my answer... that constant dialogue.

Chris: That's going more towards Type One, isn't it? The dysfunctional [side of this type].

Nina: Yes. I was just going to say, I would feel that when I'm stressed, but not otherwise.

Iain: Let's just stay with that, for people who don't know what the superego is, maybe that's very helpful. I actually do know, I'm just asking the question to bring it out.

Daniel: My superego's saying 'Oh now I've said the wrong thing because Nina doesn't think it's the superego!'

Iain: So we all have this internal critic we picked up from our parents when we were very young, and...

Daniel: Yes, and from society; society's rules, our parents' rules.

Iain: And we've learnt to criticise ourselves, which isn't actually very helpful.

Daniel: No, it was really helpful when we were very little, we needed that: "It's wrong to jump in the road, it's wrong to play with matches." But in adulthood we have a more innate sense of what's appropriate. But yes, certainly I've still got this constant voice evaluating.

Iain: I wonder if Chris has. Have you still got the superego, or have you passed all that?

Chris: Oh, well beyond it [*laughing*]. No, I can resonate with that a lot, that inner critic... that there's a better way to do it, should I do it this way, blah, blah, blah. I can resonate with that a lot. I have to aim, as much as possible, to let that be and move beyond that, but it's definitely there...

Iain: You've put it to one side, you let it keep chattering away, but don't give it any kind of attention or notice, is that right?

Chris: I wouldn't say I let it keep chatting away. I aim to acknowledge it, and then just let it go. I don't particularly want to hold on to any of those good or bad traits for that matter, but I can. That definitely resonates, and sometimes it's very annoying, it really is; under stress situations it can amplify the stress. Sometimes it's just easier to let that go and observe it and perhaps acknowledge it, easier than others.

Iain: I'm looking at the clock and we have about three or four minutes left.

Chris: [*laughing*] Champagne then!

Iain: That's a good trait isn't it for a Type Seven? They like their Champagne, they like their high living.

Nina: A bit of a generalisation here maybe, I don't really drink very much and I personally don't like Champagne...

Iain: You like other fine things though, do you?

Nina: I love eating...

Daniel: The sin of the Seven is gluttony, and yesterday's chocolate really attested to that, and I think that's part of this constant feeding of desires, new experiences, food...

Iain: It's one of the dangers of being a Type Seven – you get...

Chris: [*laughing*] ...indigestion!

Iain: You can get too much food, too much alcohol, too much sex, too much of everything. But it seems that you guys are all pretty much on your journey to at least recognise that and move beyond too much excess... and enjoy what excess you have.

Thank you all for coming in, being very forthright, and being very much your type, which is brilliant. That's what I was trying to get out of you – be yourselves – and you've all done that in your own unique way, thank you.

To watch this interview please go to:
http://www.conscious.tv/consciousness/enneagram

Enneagram Type Eight – The Challenger

Discussion with Phil, Lynne and Christine

Moderated by Iain McNay

Iain: We have three Eights in the studio who're going to share what it's like to be a Type Eight. We're going to have a general discussion to help you spot whether you're a Type Eight or not, and also look at its potential. On a personal note, this is quite a good programme for me because I've often had difficulty with Eights in the past. Especially in business, I haven't always found them easy, so let's hope they behave themselves and I learn from this as well. First of all I'm going to show you four books that we can all recommend: *The Enneagram Made Easy*, which is a very basic one, *The Wisdom of the Enneagram, The Spiritual Dimension of the Enneagram,* and *Facets of Unity: the Enneagram of Holy Ideas.*

I'm now going to introduce our guests. We have Phil, Christine, and Lynne. Christine, you're going to start by giving us a brief summary of the Enneagram, how you see it, and how you were introduced to it.

Christine: Sure. The Enneagram is a model of the human condition. It's a psychospiritual model which at the same time is both old and new. The 'old' is that it synthesises and incorporates a lot of teachings from philosophers, some of the major religions and mystics, and the 'new' is that it was also developed in the last century to incorporate a lot of modern psychological theories and ideas. It's represented by a nine-pointed geometric star and these nine points represent nine basic personality types, or programmes, that we as human beings have within us. We have all nine of them, but we tend to hang out in one particular type or domain – a 'default programme' if you will. That is our response to how we react to and engage with the world. This default programme covers things like the values that we've developed as individuals, our beliefs, the meanings that we've attached to our experiences through life, and our view of the world. Most of this initially is very unconscious programming, and what the study of the Enneagram does, it enables you to become aware of that programming, aware of your own beliefs and values and how you view the world. It gives you an opportunity to explore the meanings that you've attached to your life and your life experiences. It helps to create a space for you to interrupt that programming so that you have a choice about whether or not to continue behaving in the way you've always behaved, and thinking in the way you've always thought – or to have choice and freedom to change how you see the world and therefore how you make your way in the world.

I first came across the Enneagram about ten years ago, when I was training to be a coach, but my real direct experience of it came when I trained as a 'journey therapist'. It's a fundamental part of Journey Therapy training and continues to be one of the main building blocks for that training. My experience of knowing that I was an Eight came during that training.

Iain: Good. How has being an Eight impacted your life? What have you learnt on a practical basis?

Christine: The first feeling I remember having was a sense of relief. A lot of things started to make sense about looking back on my behaviour and the things that I'd focused my attention on through my adult life. Also with that came a sense of shame because some of the darker aspects of the Eight personality programming are quite difficult to face up to and deal with.

Iain: That's a great place to start. What are some of the darker aspects of Type Eight programming?

Christine: In the past I've been very driven, very driven with my career, very ambitious, very goal-orientated. And I know, and can recognise, that that drive means I can climb over people, walk through people in getting to my goal, that my focus is on my goal and on what I want.

Iain: Do you find you're quite ruthless in a way?

Christine: It's not a conscious ruthlessness, it's a conscious focus that means you don't see anything else, you just see where you want to go and what you want. Another aspect of that is I need to be in control, I need to be in control of my own destiny. In the past I've not taken kindly to taking orders from other people, particularly if I don't have a sense of respect or trust for them. When I worked in business, those are two of the aspects that I became aware of. When I looked back, I realised my programming and the game that I'd been playing.

Iain: A subtitle for Eights is often 'the boss', isn't it?

Christine: Yes, and throughout my career I have ended up in those positions and deliberately aimed for the next promotion, the next whatever, in order to be in control.

Iain: Okay. Phil, let's move on to you. How did you first discover the Enneagram?

Phil: When I met my wife about twenty years ago, it was love at first sight for me. I was very much in love, but we had lots of fights. We would get into big fights. For my commercial career, I'd done Myers Briggs training on other personality-type issues, so we went on a Myers Briggs course where the Enneagram was advertised. My wife and I didn't get much out of Myers Briggs, but we went to the Enneagram course and it was such a sense of relief for me to see that my fighting as an Eight was just a personality structure that I was lost in, rather than being me. The shame that Christine was talking about was awful. When I got into a fight I'd be fighting to win and if I did win I'd feel awful… terrible. At work, or in relationships, it was a dynamic I found myself in, and I got a sense of relief when I heard the Enneagram's way of looking at my personality structure.

Iain: Did you change after you understood more about how your personality worked? How did that affect you on a practical level?

Phil: On a practical level I guess it's affected me in lots of ways. Ultimately I guess I've changed my career because I've always been 'the boss'. Ever since my early twenties, I've been the boss of whatever operation I was involved in, and I would act out because I would have a very clear focus on what needed to be done and what was the right way to get something done – and to get success and achieve goals often at the expense of the people in the team. Although I could lead and inspire the team, I would often hurt them. Getting the job done could be really quite brutal at times and… I kept on colliding with this sense of shame. We'd done the job. I'd be getting applause for having led a team to a fantastic place and I'd be feeling awful because of what I'd done to make it happen, or what I felt I'd done. A sense of shame… so in the end I've changed careers. I can't trust myself to be a boss and now I'm getting a different kind of pain altogether. I've actively chosen not to be the boss of where I am at the moment. I'm working as a therapist in a team.

Iain: Isn't that a cop-out in a way? You changed your career, that's fair enough, but can't you be a boss and a good boss as a Type Eight?

[**Phil**: [*sighing*] Yes.

Iain: Maybe Lynne can come in.

Lynne: I really resonate with what's being said, and I've taken a different path. I'm a chief executive in the public sector and I'm on my third chief executive role. And what I've had to do… because of anger… the thing that you haven't mentioned and that I've always been very much aware of, is 'very quick to get angry'. I think I'm just speaking it as it is. Everyone else thinks they've been completely erased out by me because I'm like 'I was just telling you how it is', but they've gone away feeling completely pole-axed by the energy and the aggression. It wasn't conscious aggression, but it was received as such. I found the Enneagram twenty-five years ago, and at our best Eights are servant leaders, we move to Type Two, so we're able to serve. We understand that people are important, and I've had to consciously work at that, yes, and at getting the task done because we can see how to do it, you see. We've got this laser beam and we can see the big picture and you just look at a situation and see 'Yeah, that's where we go', and you assume everyone else can do it too. That was the revelation of the Enneagram for me: understanding there are eight other ways of seeing the world that are not mine and they're equally valid. This was the really hard thing for me as an Eight because we're always right! In our shadow, or at our worst, we're right, and nine times out of ten we tend to get it right. So my work has been very much [about] how do I get into the servant-leadership style which is saying 'I am here to serve a higher purpose', which brings in the spiritual dimension of the Enneagram and putting all of that energy, that focus, that drive into higher order than just getting my own ego-needs met. But I think rage, impatience, anger, wanting people to have done it... we're so fast as well. We do things very quickly, very immediately. We come from the gut. We're very intuitive. It's not all bad... though we are the bad boys of the Enneagram, we're also fun.

Phil: I've taken a different approach to that change, and my approach is the fact that – you talked about the Two and the Eights' relationship with the Two – I've very much denied...

Iain: Just [to] explain for people who don't know, Two is obviously another Enneagram type known as 'the helper'...

Phil: ... the 'soul child' of the Eight, where the Eight comes from. I've very much come to realise that I've denied my Two [aspect]. I guess by denying my Two, I didn't want to take the risk of connecting emotionally and being vulnerable with another. I needed to be in charge of my relationship with whoever I was with, and I didn't want the risk of being a servant-helper. [That] was an awful thought to me, [being] in that role. I've come to learn in a different way and by working as a therapist now for ten years, I've learnt to be in that role, but with connection and with heart. I've come to terms with my fear of vulnerability when I'm emotionally connected to somebody.

Iain: That's a big step, isn't it?

Christine: Yes. And I don't think I could have done that if I hadn't become a therapist either. I think I needed to get out of the business environment and – very similar to Phil – move into a different way of being. The big thing that has come for me is I want to be of service, and the challenge now is: what does that *mean* in everyday life? Practically, *how* do you do that? I think that has come from reconnecting with my heart and what's important to me. I've found a great joy in being with children. I've never had children; I've always concentrated on my career. Independence and kids – would be a problem balancing that, and I've found great joy in spending time with children. I've got involved with a charity now that's about helping children, and that's been absolutely wonderful... absolutely wonderful. It really helped with the heart connection and that sense of being able to be open to the feelings of joy — and some sadness because some of these children we work with have difficulties – and having the courage to sit in that emotion and not push it away. One of the most difficult things I've found as an Eight was sitting with love, sitting with people that love me. A lot of the spiritual retreats and the work that I've done on myself over the years, I have found it quite hard to be in a room with people that are basically loving me. It's almost a physical burning…

Iain: You are saying it was hard for you to respond to that?

Christine: Just to be there, never mind *respond*. Actually be in the room with it. It's very intense. It has got easier as I've progressed, but I'm very aware of it, very aware of it.

Iain: For people who are watching and who don't know much about the Enneagram, and think they may be a Type Eight, what other clues would they look for in terms of beginning an investigation?

Lynne: I think it's that needing to be strong, which [feels] compulsive. You believe that you have to be strong and you hide that vulnerable inner child away. At some point in our lives we just felt we were on our own, we had to do it. We were the ones who were responsible and it was down to us and I think that's a huge feeling. Also, the thing that really made me understand my Eightness is I can't bear people telling lies around me. There's something about truth and justice… it's almost like you will put yourself right out there on a limb to make sure that the underdog is being protected. We're very protective of the underdog, and the other thing for me was the compulsive confronting. It's almost like you can't help yourself.

Iain: Talk more about that.

Lynne: I've an anecdote. On a train in south London, a gang of youths slashing the seats. Everyone else moves to the other end. Before I even think about it – and yes, I am a teacher, I started out life as a teacher – I'm [shouting], "Put that knife away! Stop doing that!" It's only when they turned round that I realised the danger that I'd put myself in, but I didn't get to that until a lot later. In the moment it's almost like you see something wrong, or some injustice, and you try to sort it out or you step in. It's almost a compulsion.

Iain: So what happened?

Lynne: Well, nobody came [towards me]. They stopped. They actually stopped, because I think there's an authority in an Eight that people often respond to. They did get off the train behind me. They stopped what they were doing and they sat down. They looked a bit sheepish and then they followed me off the train, but they didn't harm me in any way. But when I thought about it, when I got in, I was shaking from head to foot, but it didn't stop me at the time. There's nothing between the event and the doing. It's like [*karate motion*] kerchunk!

Iain: You are not consciously thinking 'I'm being courageous'. It's compulsive. You have to, because you feel that's right.

Christine: That's what I meant about the programming. It's so automatic, you don't even realise you're doing it. And I've certainly never backed away from a fight. Particularly if I think about my work context, if one of my team is having a hard time, or is being badly treated by somebody, particularly if they're outside the department, I would wade in. I would not hesitate to protect them. Loyalty is really important. I feel very loyal to the people that worked for me. I feel very loyal to my clients now, but I expect that loyalty in return so there's a double issue... Loyalty is very important along with the truth and the courage, but it's not a conscious thing, or it wasn't a conscious thing at the time; but that's another common value I think for Eights. And injustice: I cannot tell you the number of campaigns that I've got involved in, right from Greenham Common many years ago, right the way through. Now, the Internet's brilliant, because you can sit and sign a petition and write a letter to your MP almost automatically. Well, I'm there doing it! I'm venting my discomfort or anger at the injustice that I see, but I'm aware. Now, the difference is that I'm really conscious that I'm doing it and I'm choosing. There's a space that comes up that develops and you think 'Okay, do I really want to react to this? Or do I not? What do I choose?'

I think the other big part of recognising you're an Eight is the amount of effort you put into something. I used to go through doors at work apparently, and people would say, "We always know when you're coming through a door, because the door bangs open." It was all about putting too much effort into something, something simple like opening a door. It can also be something complicated like restructuring the department, so I would work eighteen-hour days to get this done and put all this effort in, and then come out the other side of the event and crash. I was exhausted and needed time to recover. I used to choose jobs and projects that actually reinforced that pattern, so if you feel you're putting a lot of effort into something, or trying to achieve something, pushing the rock uphill, that's another key aspect of an Eight: you don't stop, you just push harder.

Iain: I'm looking at some notes that I've made to cover all the possible clues. I've written down 'can't stand being used or manipulated'. Is that something...?

All three: Oh yeah!

Lynne: Oh yeah! We can smell it a mile off. You can feel it. You know when someone's got that energy even when others can't. And sometimes that's when we're seen to be vengeful, or having personality conflicts. But we know it's there, you can just sense it.

Iain: I also wrote down 'making decisions is not difficult'.

Christine: Oh no, and don't bother me with the facts. I'll do it on my gut, thank you very much. The number of times I've said that in my business career:

"Don't confuse me with information, my gut's telling me what to do…"

Lynne: If anything, we make them too quickly sometimes. That can be a weakness.

Iain: [*reading*] …'self-reliance is important'.

Lynne and Christine: Oh yes!

Iain: You mention the thing about working hard… 'like excitement and stimulation'.

Christine: Yes, that's the killer, that one… that need for intensity. I'll give you an anecdote. My cat went missing a couple of weeks ago and she was gone nearly forty-eight hours and I felt double guilt because we'd been away. We came back and I [said] "Oh, the cat's gone, that's it, she's been run over, we're never going to see her again!" Husband, who's a Nine with a very positive outlook: "Oh, she's just got trapped somewhere." But I was having this really emotional response to the fact that the cat was missing. I put so much into this emotional response… and she walked through the door at ten o'clock the following night. And he said, "See, she was just trapped somewhere." But I'd invested so much emotion and intensity imagining this cat gone and the feeling of loss around this cat… such intensity!

Lynne: We haven't mentioned the word 'lust'. We lust for almost everything. My childhood memories are of always being told, "Enough is enough now, Lynne. Is enough never enough for you? Enough's enough" …my mum's a Nine. So there's something about 'enough is never enough' for us and we have such a lust for experience. I'm an Eight with a Seven wing as well, so that constant keeping options open, trying things out. And my energy is boundless. I'm never ill, very, very rarely. And it just seems to keep coming and coming, and I've got the boredom threshold of about two minutes and just love being stimulated. The intensity can be exciting, but I'm married to a Nine, and I spent the first few years sort of prodding…

Iain: You're both married to Nines, that's interesting.

Lynne: …and prodding, to make sure there was somebody home: 'Come out there and meet me, meet me!' because if you're not doing that, you don't care. And there is a sort of pathetic side of that. It isn't just about strength, there's something in there that's saying 'Come and meet me'. As an Eight woman, I also scare people. People used to be very scared of me and I never got why. And there was something for me about needing people who can meet me. I love it when somebody stands up to me and I can actually let my guard down and not have to fight back, but most people are terrified of Eights because we tend to keep upping the ante, but as we get more healthy we want to be met, or I want to be met by somebody who can hold their ground and…

Christine: …and speak the truth. I think that's another…

Phil: When I [was] in the commercial world, I would consciously employ department heads who could push against me and say, "Phil, you're saying it wrong, you're completely wrong." And they'd fight me, they'd be happy telling me to my face, "A load of rubbish!" Because what would happen, if I was working with the technicians, I would scare them. I would freeze them and I couldn't communicate like that. So I would consciously recruit people to run departments who could fight me and could work with [others] in a more heartfelt way, in a more subtle way.

Iain: But isn't there a difference between fighting you and standing up to you?

Phil: No, not for me. I accept there is, but for me… no, if you're pushing against me we're having a fight, I enjoy that. A fight is not a negative statement for me.

Iain: You see, that's very interesting. I said at the beginning of the programme that for me Eights have always been very challenging, especially in the business arena. One of the things that I've done in my life – since I've discovered the Enneagram – [with] people that I find hard to get on with, I do a bit of research and I work out what I think their Enneagram type is. In a way it doesn't matter if I get it right or not. I get enough clues somehow and I feel I understand them more. I've found with Type Eight that the best way for me to deal with them is I have to prepare myself, because to go straight in and have a fight is not natural for me. It's like 'I'm not going in to have a fight, but I'm going in prepared to be strong and hold my ground'. That's how I do it. And I think that's probably something that a lot of people have to do with Eights because it doesn't come naturally. You're in their face for them to come back and be in your face. It's something you build up to, or learn.

Phil: My preparation as an Eight is in the service of a completely different dynamic. My preparation as an Eight is because I know people look to me as a leader. People will follow what I say and I've got to be really careful what I say. I don't want a quick decision if it's not properly informed so, in Enneagram-speak, I would go to my Five. I would do an awful lot of research to avoid the shame I felt of making a mistake. I didn't want to lead people in the wrong direction. So I would do an awful lot of work to protect myself – that's what my preparation would be – from the shame of taking people in the wrong direction, because they'd follow me. People I worked with would tend to follow me wherever I went, and that's a big responsibility.

Iain: As I listen to the three of you, the feeling that I'm getting is that you haven't necessarily fundamentally changed yourselves, but you've refined yourselves and you've used your basic energy-personality in a more intelligent way. Would you agree with that?

Lynne: I think that's so because when I first discovered I was an Eight, I didn't want to be an Eight. I rejected it, but now I'm glad I'm an Eight. It's as if I can celebrate the good things about me, and I've completely toned down the other aspects. So yes, I think that trying to be more intelligent, having choice, having space, and being conscious about the impact... I've used the Enneagram in three organisations in which I've been the chief executive and it's very similar to what Phil was saying. It was like 'Well, if you want to share in this, you'll find out about me because I really don't want to be these negative things, and I can find out about you'. What I discovered is that people did make stands and they did say to me, "We can prepare for you now, Lynne. We get that it's not malicious, we get that it's not intentional." It's exactly what you [Phil] said: "We can prepare because we understand the fabric of the Eight and how we can come and make a stand with you." I saw teams change; my relationships with the senior team improved drastically because we were all consciously using the Eight and coming to very high performance as a result of that.

Iain: Was this toning down hard for you?

Lynne: There's a part of it that was very difficult because you can get high on some of this – the intensity, the relief of a good fight, you know...

Iain: So a good fight is something that brings you relief?

Lynne: Aliveness. It's about aliveness and it gets the tension out of your system.

Phil: It's a physical feeling. I'm sixty-four, I'm an Eight, I'm not playing golf, I'm playing squash. Golf as a game is far too low-intensity for me. I don't get anything back from golf. That intensity is there, and after a game of squash... aaah [*sighing*] I'm empty.

Iain: To understand you better, when you appear to be having a fight with somebody – and I'm not saying the three of you do this now – but when you did, was it a similar feeling like after you've had a game of squash, or whatever sports you guys do... that relief and relaxation you can have after having a good run?

Christine: It's a discharge of energy, and what I found is I had no problem finding the words to wound. Even my father when he was alive used to say to me – and he was an Eight, "Your command of language when the red mist is down, and the way you can speak and put sentences together to wound..." I wasn't even aware that I was doing it. It would just come – bang! I never do it again, but I know that capacity, that potential is there, and what for me has worked is self-reflection. I go into Five – the point of disintegration for Eights if you get really stressed; you can withdraw to see what's going on and work out a strategy for how you're going to come back into the game. For me a lot of self-reflection, reading, and meditation have helped me tremendously to create that space, and I don't consider it to be fights any more. I'm looking for a win-win-win. A win for me, a win for the other person, and a win for the universe – that was the big shift for me, to change that perspective. That's how I recognised I could let go of the need to discharge that energy and always win and always be on top. For me, the service piece is about leading people from behind. That's why I'm a therapist and a coach. It's about helping others to become self-leaders. That's how I serve, and if they can take something from me and my experiences of training and being a leader in previous jobs, then that's how I discharge that. That's how I discharge that energy now, and it's a much healthier, balanced, and integrated place to be. But I do know that if at any point I'm not having a particularly good day, and somebody crosses me, I have the potential to lash out.

Iain: One of the books I showed earlier by Sandra Maitri talks about the 'animal soul' being very basic in a Type Eight and you have this animal side. As in when you were telling us about the train – the guy with the knife – you go out there and you pounce without thinking. You're saying that never really goes, you just understand it more and it's more in balance.

Christine: And you have choice. If you really work with the Enneagram and other [methods], you create freedom for yourself to choose, to respond in a different way, and for me that was the blessing... that was the blessing.

Phil: One of the gifts of Type Eight is this huge availability of energy, strength, and durability. I used to direct that outwards into my defences, into the world of structure. What I've learnt is, if I can direct that inwards and nourish my heart – which I used to deny – I'm more whole, I'm safer, I don't act out in the same way at all. I can still feel a rush sometimes when I see something going wrong. I still feel it's my responsibility whatever's going wrong, and I have a responsibility to do something about that. I still feel the pull of that, and it's learning that it's not all my business – I can't do everything I'm pulled to do – and it's something I have to accept. That's why I liked and I was really drawn to *Facets of Unity* which talks about that struggle for an Eight. I do get a real sense of what Almaas talks about, and I do feel when I'm connected [that] I'm connected to everything.

Christine: To the universe.

Phil: To the universe yes. I understand that.

Iain: How does that feel, Phil? You've got two dynamics going on. You haven't lost contact with your animal soul, and yet you have this feeling that you're widely connected. How does that balance feel in you?

Phil: It just brings me joy now. It doesn't bring the red mist any more. It nourishes me. That slight rewiring of the programme to feed the energy into my heart before I engage my head and do something... brings joy.

Lynne: It's a kind of equanimity. The word 'equanimity' is coming up for me... One of the things that really worked was training as a spiritual healer and being able to learn how to manage energy so that all this energy that was coming through me – realising I could channel it – I didn't have to do something with it. Also 'presencing', literally feeling my legs, my feet, and sensing into the body. There's a calmness and an equanimity and a sense of expansiveness that absorbs the energy in a way that the intensity isn't coming out through the personality into *doing*. It's taken me years and years to know how to be. I really was a 'human doing'.

Iain: And what were some of the key steps that helped you on that journey?

Lynne: Meditation was hard for me, head meditation. I was a Theravadan Buddhist for eleven years and I never really got it. I had a 'living daylight' experience where that energy was everywhere.

Iain: What's a 'living daylight' experience?

Lynne: When I got filled with light, oneness and unity, I could feel I was part of the whole universe. I trained as a spiritual healer with the Federation of Spiritual Healers, and that helped me to ground myself in whole new ways. So energetic work, bodywork, which I would avoid really, and kundalini work. Bodywork has the most powerful impacts on me, but I will avoid it like anything. I have to work really hard to be in my body.

Phil: To give control over to someone, to give your body physically over to someone to control – as I would characterise it as an Eight – getting somebody to do bodywork on me physically is a big stretch. I have to go into myself there and really consciously reconnect, to allow myself not to tense.

Christine: It's interesting because we are body types, but the one thing that I think the three of us have in common is 'I don't want to do this'. I've just re-started yoga after many years because I just couldn't cope with it [at the time] and I recognised and understood why, and I think it's a sign of giving myself a little pat on the back that I've actually managed to sustain going to yoga. I think the other thing I've learnt is, at the core, our biggest fear is fear of being controlled, and I recognised that that's a double-bind. My fear of being controlled has controlled me all my life. And the minute I realised that, it started to fall away and dissipate, and that sense of connection and oneness started to become much stronger and I laughed, I actually laughed when I was on a retreat and this came out. I started giggling because it really is very silly if you think about it, to get caught up in that kind of delusion, or illusion. I found that very helpful.

Phil: The whole issue of vulnerability was a big issue. It really was a smack in the face when I realised that for me to be defending all the time, making things right, sorting out the things that were from the outside causing wrongness, meant that I had to perceive myself as a victim. That was a big part of the unravelling of my connections with that because I'm not a victim. But to be acting like I'm defending against the damage you can do me means I have to believe that *I am* a victim. And that for me was a huge letting go, of 'I know I'm not a victim'. Absolutely.

Christine: It's letting go of the story… the story of who you are.

Iain: When you say 'letting go of the story', talk more about that.

Christine: It's the victim thing, isn't it? In my case I could talk about a very happy childhood in lots of ways, but then aspects of feeling as the eldest that

CONVERSATIONS ON THE ENNEAGRAM

was responsible and had to get out there and prove myself... somehow there's this story you attach to why you are who you are and it's a pile of crap, to use a very Eight phrase. If you can learn to let go of that and accept letting go of that, and step into that space where it's unknown – 'If you're not this, then who are you?' – stepping into that space and being courageous enough and being vulnerable enough to explore 'Who are you?' And the answer is presence. Once you can do that, whatever type in the Enneagram you are, it just brings such freedom, joy, and love and deep stillness. It's characterised for me by a completely deep stillness. It's the complete opposite of what you were doing if you were operating from the Eight personality type. The last thing you are is still!

Lynne: I think that's right. And we tend to be big body types and clearly the three of us are, because we're carrying the weight of the world. I think part of the story I really identify with – and I'm the eldest – is being so responsible, being so strong; it's down to us. And I know I pad myself out in order to be able to carry that because I feel stronger. Also, letting go of that and being vulnerable, beginning to realise that actually you're not right all the time, you can't control it all, and you can't carry the weight of the world on your shoulders. It's just silly, but we really believe that.

Iain: Some people would say that being vulnerable, when you're [Lynne] a CEO of a big company, is a pretty difficult thing to do.

Lynne: And it is.

Iain: How do you find that balance?

Lynne: I had to go into therapy. I had the experience of 'my usual way's not working' and feeling very vulnerable and I hid it, so I went into therapy. Then what I realised is, as long as I'm authentic... for me the big issue was about vulnerability and authenticity and realising that if I'd made a mistake, instead of blustering my way through it, I actually went out to the staff and said, "You know, I think I got that wrong. How can we do that?" – expecting that they would react against me. I got the opposite effect. The leadership theory now is right up into authentic leadership and self-awareness, but in those days – I'm talking twenty years ago – it wasn't. But I gradually got an experience that as I showed those parts of myself that were less sure, I really got that I didn't have to know everything all the time and that people responded very well. Now, if I'd been incompetent, or I was saying I got it wrong all the time, I think it would have been a different reaction. But this was showing I was authentically saying, "I don't know how to do this," or "How can we do that?" I might have gone into my office afterwards and cried my eyes out, or shaken thinking 'I can't believe I just did that. I can't believe I just did that!' Instead, I was just staying with it.

Iain: People respond in a positive way to your honesty?

Lynne: To the sense that this is honest, this is real. Because with an Eight, what you see is what you get. But I don't underestimate the challenges because there are pressures on you from your board, from targets around performance, but my sense is if you're on this journey of self-awareness and wanting to get out of the traps of the Eightness, or any type, then staying with this honesty and truth and seeing 'We're in this together' instead of 'I'm here on my own'.

Iain: The other two guys both changed their careers, and you [Lynne] talked about going to a spiritual healer and you trained in therapy. Was there a point where you thought 'Well, maybe this isn't my vocation to be a big boss'?

Lynne: It's really interesting. I have spent my life saying, "I'm going to leave!" I'm an ordained interfaith minister. I constantly do my spiritual work by training, and then when I get to the end of that training I realise I want to stay where I am. I even wanted to be a nun at one time [*laughing*]. Well, they wouldn't have me anyway and the novice mistress said, "Not your vocation." I'm in further education and I've been a principal of a college, so my true vocation professionally is serving students for second chance and further education. There's a bit of duality with me: I'm always going to leave, but actually business and leadership is as much my spiritual path as going out into a different arena. Having said that, I've just moved to Glastonbury! [*group laughter*]

Iain: We have about ten minutes left and I'd like to use this as effectively as we can. I'm particularly interested in the clues that people watching this can pick up on how to move forward if they identify themselves as this type – the practical things that they can do if they're stuck in their patterns. Everyone has their own path and their own way of moving forward, the potential of this type.

Christine: There's a lot of stuff out there about the Enneagram, the books you've talked about and all your programmes, in terms of trying to bring [the Enneagram] to life. The other thing for an Eight that's a real growth point is asking for help. Eights don't ask for help and that's been one of the biggest reliefs for me. If you are watching and you are an Eight, that's going to be a real challenge – asking for help, seeking someone out that you can talk to, going into therapy, which I did as well some years ago. That was a huge thing to do because it meant asking for help, paying for it, and admitting that there was something not quite right. Something wasn't working well. So I would suggest: find people that you do trust, whose wisdom you trust, and talk to them. Take time out to think about what it is you want, take some quiet time. There's plenty of retreats and things that people could do as a starting point, and just be still for a bit and see what comes up. It's very scary as an Eight, but I think that's a key part of it.

Iain: One of the things for me, when I discovered my Enneagram type, was understanding other people. I was intrigued and once I discovered what I was, I wanted to read about everybody else and work out how they worked as human beings, what their difficulties were, and as I said earlier, how I could relate better. I think that's probably quite an important step for you guys as well, to truly understand how other people function.

Christine: I think there's a note of caution with that, that you don't nominalise somebody and say, "Oh, you're a Four, you're a Six, and you're a Three," [as if] they become the number. We are not the numbers, but certainly in terms of my training as a therapist it's helped me understand other people's maps of the world when they walk through the door: 'What might their key drivers be? What might their focus be?' It's given me a huge amount of compassion, which I think is another thing, getting in touch with that heart side. That was quite painful when that arose, when that started to bloom, the sense of pain that you felt for other people's pain. Again that was something I had to get used to sitting with and not pushing away, particularly as I was training to be a therapist. So I think that's one of the key aspects that comes with it. Understanding and awareness of other people has also brought out compassion for me.

Lynne: I think listening to music that makes you cry and finding things that you can feel in your heart... because one of our shadow sides is we can perhaps cut off too quickly and easily, so I think heartfelt practises. They don't have to be complicated, just things that make you cry, things that make you feel connected to others, things that make you realise – because people are not objects – that they have their own way of being. There is something in us that needs to respond to where they are and how they are. I think that's a really important element.

Phil: The Sufis say 'this ocean of tears', and often I found that in the early years when I started to meditate, to reconnect with my body I would go through a layer of tears before I would connect at every meditation. It was a lot of sadness for the heart to process, and what was most useful for me in the early days, when I would act out, when I would respond and start an argument, or a fight, was learning what I call my 'skiing technique'. I'm afraid of heights so I learnt to ski and, going down a black slope, the best way to ski is to put your weight down the steepest part of the slope and then your skis work and you're safe. But every instinct of my body was saying 'Cling back onto the snow!' Then of course your skis get light and you're all over the place. This 'skiing technique' is when every part of me says 'Okay, I'm going to fight now!' That's a call for a fight, and every time I felt that, I came to recognise it and I would do the opposite. I would just contact my heart and that's how I bought myself *time*. Not that I dishonoured that red energy in me, but I honoured a different part of myself and gave it time to join up so I wouldn't get lost again in a fight. And that was really scary, scary, scary, scary!

Iain: I did a bit of research and I wrote down some well-known people who are Eights. Funnily enough, quite a few of them are dead now. Golda Meir, John Wayne, Martin Luther King – very different from John Wayne, Nelson Mandela, Charles de Gaulle, Bette Midler, and the one that made me really laugh was Sarah Ferguson. I'm not saying it's definitely true, but this is to give people a feel for some personalities who are Type Eight.

Lynne: The very first Enneagram workshop I went on, they went round and they were saying, "Oh, Mother Teresa," "Kennedy," then they came to the Eight and they went, "Saddam Hussein!" [*group laughter*] In the early days, it was often said that the Eight was a sort of negative figure, and I think bringing out that there are very positive Eights, whose leadership can be quite amazing, is great!

Christine: In my discussions on the Enneagram in various groups – I think it might be an English trait – the English have a tendency to focus on what's wrong and what needs fixing, and I think in the interest of balance there are gifts that the Eights bring, as there are gifts that every Ennea-type brings. I think anyone watching this, thinking about or looking to diagnose themselves from the negatives, give yourself a break and look at some of the positive things you bring to the world because you can end up in a very dark and gloomy place if you don't, if you're just beginning to understand this work and want to explore it more. There are gifts.

Lynne: I think that's right, and the most liberating thing for me in the very early days of discovering the Enneagram is that the Eight was no better or no worse than any other type, which was such a relief to me because I think we do harbour that we are the worst type and we really are bad on some level. The notion that we're no better, but we're certainly no worse, was a complete liberation for me.

Iain: One thing I wrote down that I've just remembered, that I picked up from one of the books was that Eights 'have the power to inspire others to be heroic', which kind of ties in with what you're saying. They have this leadership quality and others will follow and be inspired. If you're in your courage, your innocence, and in your vulnerability, others will follow.

Christine: That's my deepest prayer for my clients, when working with them, that they feel inspired to face the difficulties that they're dealing with and the courage to change.

Iain: We're going to have to finish there, but I want to first thank you all very much for coming along and sharing yourselves. I think it's been a very helpful and interesting programme.

To watch this interview please go to:
http://www.conscious.tv/consciousness/enneagram

Enneagram Type Nine – The Mediator

Discussion with Dottie, Cate and Sam

Moderated by Iain McNay

Iain: Today we'll be talking about Type Nine, and in the studio we have Dottie, Sam, and Cate. Dottie, tell us a little bit about the Enneagram for people who're watching this programme and don't know much about it. What is the Enneagram?

Dottie: I think the Enneagram is open for anyone to interpret in whatever way they choose, but as I understand it, when we're born – and maybe when we're still in the womb – we interact with our environment and in that interaction we start building up patterns of behaviour, programmes. Over time these programmes will develop into what we think we are and who we think we are. Our personality is mainly developed through our interaction with the environment, and what the Enneagram offers is a model, which has nine basic personality types.

Iain: So everybody has to be one of these nine types pretty much?

Dottie: Everyone is basically one of these nine, but the other thing about the Enneagram is that the symbol of the Enneagram is a circle, and so there can be movement within that circle. Although you are basically one type, there is movement within the circle. You are not just defined by a list of 'This is who you are'. There is movement within that circle.

Iain: So we would also find part of ourselves in the other types.

Dottie: Yes. I think when we talk a bit more about the Nine, we'll be looking at what the driver is behind the Nine behaviour and why it is as it is. To me that is fundamental: finding what the driver is, what it is that makes you be a Type Nine, and what's driving that personality. Through studying the Enneagram, hopefully you find your type. For some people it's really easy. Certainly for me, as soon as I read the Nine, I knew that was me. Some people have no idea and it takes them time to actually… they really need to visit all the different types to find out which one fits most comfortably for them. One of the common things that you feel when you first find out your type is 'I thought everybody

CONVERSATIONS ON THE ENNEAGRAM

felt like me'. Then you discover that they don't. Or you realise 'Some people feel like me, but some people feel completely different to me'. That understanding of not just yourself, but of other people as well, is really helpful in life. But I find the Enneagram does not define you. I think some people see it as something that can give you a classification: 'You are a Nine'. I don't think the Enneagram defines you. You find how much you have defined yourself and at the same time, how much you have defined other people. That gives you more compassion and understanding both for yourself and others.

Iain: It can help in your relationships with other people, can't it?

Dottie: Yes, very much so. Initially it's 'This is all about me and it's fascinating', but then you learn about how other people are different and you understand what's driving them, and that leads to much-improved relationships.

Iain: Because if you understand someone else better, to some extent, you can put yourself in their shoes and realise why they are the way they are.

Dottie: Yes, but you can take the Enneagram at whatever level you want. It can be a self-development, self-awareness tool, but as I've gone through it, for me is more about the spiritual aspect and its potential for transformation.

Iain: We'll come on to the potential later. How did you first hear about the Enneagram, Sam?

Sam: I was living in Thailand in a Buddhist monastery as a monk, and we were introduced to it there as a tool for learning more about ourselves. We used it as a community – well, some of us were more into it than others – to look at our interactions with each other and how we could improve our interactions. It's very, very helpful and complementary with the meditation and study of the Buddhist teachings. I've used it and studied it quite a bit – and then eventually came to England and did a course with Judith Priest and Tim Luckcock. It's been very useful in my marriage and in my relationship with my wife who's a Type Four, in being able to unpick why things might be going wrong and see how I'm contributing to the dysfunction, to the odd dynamic. That's a very, very useful tool.

Iain: When you were in the Buddhist monastery, were you interacting with the other monks and discussing your types?

Sam: Yes, sometimes formally in workshops, but as we were interested in it, we would also use it to look at the dynamics.

Iain: The image I have of Buddhist monks is that they keep themselves very much to themselves. They meditate a lot and don't speak much, but obviously this was quite a modern monastery, was it?

Sam: Yes, the monk who introduced it to us, Santikaro, is now in America and not a monk any more either. He saw it as a tool for spiritual development. I remember him saying once that the Enneagram may be as useful as meditation and as useful as the Buddhist teachings, but definitely very helpful as a complementary thing.

Iain: Because when you're meditating for long periods a day, you can get very lost, can't you – in your inner world? And this must give more of a perspective.

Sam: Yes, and as solitary and relatively quiet as we were, we still came together to do a bit of work, and around mealtimes and projects outside. Very useful.

Iain: Cate, I know you've been working with the Enneagram for a long time now as part of the school you're in – I think for almost twenty years? How do you find you've changed during that time using the information you've learnt about the Enneagram?

Cate: You'll notice I'm not going to answer your question directly first, because listening to what you asked Sam, I realised the relief of reading about the Enneagram and feeling that somebody really understood what it felt like inside. It was *Facets of Unity*, written by A. H. Almaas. How he understood the sense of deficiency and lack was just such a huge relief. And recognising a lot of the traits I have, like going towards the other more than thinking of myself because that's a way of not feeling the emptiness and being fascinated by other people… that's how I felt I was relating to others.

Iain: What do you mean by 'not feeling the emptiness'?

Cate: I think what I'm learning – and it's still in process – is that going towards others is my nature, but not negating myself at the same time. What is difficult for me is to stay with myself when I'm with another, and to really feel into myself. That's what I find difficult.

Iain: So you lose, not your agenda but your own desire, or what you would like to do when you are with somebody else?

Cate: I don't know what desire is. I mean, I just lose… I always remember the first time I really noticed how much I did this. This was years ago, I was driving with somebody who I was a bit frightened of actually, she was an Eight. It was when we were running a centre and I was driving her along and as usual asking her a mass of questions, which was very interesting, and she suddenly said, "And what about you?" I couldn't get out of the car and escape this question and it was *terrifying*. So the focus on myself is… frightening, but I'm getting much better at staying…

Iain: Is it frightening because it's unfamiliar and you don't know how to deal with it?

Cate: I suppose for a long time it was so difficult to feel myself. The only way I could feel *filled* was by going out towards the other. Even before I'd done any spiritual work, I remember my biggest fear was to be in solitary confinement and thought 'What am I going to do if I've just got me?' What's helping more and more is the work I've done with the Diamond Approach and also more recently doing meditation with Dan Brown – Pointing the Way. Before in meditation, I would just sit and come to the most wonderful spacious place, very smooth, very calming, and [now] having to be more alert is really helping me.

Iain: So taking that same issue to you, Sam… you were in a monastery where you were very much encouraged to stay with your process. Were you able to develop what was right for Sam, when you were given that space?

Sam: Possibly a bit. I started to wake up to the fact that it was more comfortable for me to stay in that spaciousness, as you called it. I remember once, over a period, realising that there was this great feeling of inner peacefulness, a sort of an inner smile. For a long time I mistook that as 'This is what it's all about', but for me – I think actually for most Nines – it's not about that. It's about knowing what I want, knowing my agenda as you put it, when I'm with other people, and being able to act on that and not feeling like I have to put it all aside and go with what the other person wants – really knowing in the first place and then acting on it, acting on what I feel.

Iain: Dottie, what are the other factors people might want to look for, if they think they might be a Type Nine? What are the clues?

Dottie: If I can describe where I think the driver of Nines is – and it's looking at the essence of the Being of Type Nine, again going back to birth or maybe before birth – [it's] the belief that we are all loved unconditionally. There's this sense of everyone being loved and being in a state of unity, almost like a non-duality. That's the perfect Essence that we move further and further away from, as we develop our personality.

Iain: We move further away, because that's the way the rest of the world is. Is that right?

Dottie: Yes, because that's what we learn and that's how our life is. You start off being educated, being domesticated by your parents. You pick up all the societal beliefs and that's who you think you are. But underneath it, this desire for being loved and for that sense of unity is still there. What the Nine then does is try and recreate what that sense of love, unity, and kindness feels like. They try and recreate that in the way they live their lives, and they will do anything to avoid conflict. They make themselves invisible because that gives everybody else space, and this is how they are trying to create that love. But it all goes a bit wonky because the Nine goes into the state of being asleep to themselves, as it's described. This not knowing what I think, not knowing what I want, not knowing what I feel… but finding it so easy to tune into someone else. Nines merge with other people. You know what other people are thinking and you know what they need before they do.

Iain: They're [Cate and Sam] both nodding.

Dottie: So you do it. You find you're then living almost vicariously because you're living through somebody else. It's recognising that you're not returning to that wonderful initial state and that you're making a false copy of it. Recognising that and then going 'Okay, this is who I really am' and starting to wake up to who you are. When I first discovered the Enneagram, I realised that if I'd got something challenging to do, I would actually start feeling really,

really tired. I could almost fall asleep and 'I'm so tired, I have to go and lie down', and realise I'm not really tired, I'm just avoiding something here because it's going to upset the equilibrium that I've created for myself.

Iain: It must be quite a shock when you recognise that you've created this kind of false image.

Dottie: Absolutely. It's a shock, but I think as Cate and Sam were saying, it's a revelation that somebody else feels like this, it's not just me. I'm not lazy, I'm not all these negative labels we put on ourselves. It's not about being lazy, it's about this lack of self-awareness, and I can do something about it. I don't have to fall asleep. When I first started meditating I would literally go to sleep.

Sam: Yes, big problem.

Dottie: Yes, whether that's particularly for Nines… I think it can be for anyone. But for Nines yes, it's a wonderful space. It's the duvet thing, isn't it? That's a real Nine under the duvet.

Sam: What you were saying about not knowing what you feel, I remember when I was little, people and my family asking me, "What are you thinking, Sam? What are you feeling?" And being really frustrated because I couldn't answer that because I didn't know. And my wife, who's a Four, she's extremely in touch with her feelings and just can't get that. "How come you can't say what you're feeling?" Yes, that's very typical. Another thing that's fairly typical – I speak for myself, you're probably all enlightened, or highly evolved – is that Nines can spend a lot of energy dissipating anger, or not appearing angry. It's a very powerful force.

Iain: You feel anger, but you don't put it out there so people can recognise it. Is that what you're saying?

Sam: Well, especially people who know you well do sense it coming off you, but…

Iain: You hold it back?

Sam: Hold it back, yes. There's a dream I had once where a very dark character, who I knew in the dream, came out at night only. He wasn't evil, but he was really strong and powerful. I went to meet him, he was scary. I woke up from that dream – I was writing my dreams down at this point – and wrote 'I must meet this character' and it was this…

Dottie: …almost like the shadow Carl Jung talked about, isn't it? This aspect of yourself you don't want to acknowledge.

Sam: Yes, and later I did meet him in a way, in something that happened about a week later in my life. I was able to express, for the first time, feeling very pinched between two people who I was very close to. I'd felt pinched for years. One person would run the other person down with me, and then the other person would do the same, and I felt very squeezed in the middle and tired of understanding them and not expressing how I actually felt. I was able to express that for the first time in fifteen years and it was fantastic! It really shifted something in me and it also shifted something in the whole dynamic.

Iain: So when you say 'it was fantastic', what was the feeling then?

Sam: I don't have to hide any more. I don't have to keep my feeling or my understanding of the situation to myself. What I say matters, what I feel matters. I can express that, it's valid and essential in the functioning of my relationship with those other people.

Cate: I agree now that's happening, but I remember the first few times… anger… my partner in particular used to say, "You're angry." I would reply, "I'm not angry." Then five minutes later, "I jolly well am angry!" But what happened for me the first few times I got angry, it was terrifying. I didn't feel that sense of… it was more like I totally destroyed them. The guilt afterwards… and what I realised was I only got angry when I was pushed. I could accommodate, accommodate, accommodate, and then suddenly it was all too much. And so it came out in a very… I couldn't believe it was me. Now I'm beginning to be able to do what you've [Sam] done. But I don't think anger for me is still easy.

Sam: It's not easy for me either and I hate it, really.

Dottie: There's anger and there's losing your temper, isn't there? Being able to say, "You're making me really angry."

Cate: Exactly. It's very different to the aggression that it's coming out.

Dottie: Because we're so accommodating, I find that people think that's the way we are and they can go on doing it. So if they push you and push you and push you and certainly take advantage of your good nature, that's when you can go into this passive-aggressive and the aggressive starts to come out. Also, I don't know if you guys are the same, but Nines can be really, really stubborn. People think we're so easygoing, then all of a sudden we'll just dig our heels in and they won't be able to move us.

Sam: Going slow and pretending not to understand.

Cate: Yes.

Iain: I wrote down from a couple of books a few clues for people that might still not be clear whether they might be a Type Nine or not. I'll read them all through and you might want to comment: 'often feel in union with nature and people'.

Dottie: Yes.

Iain: 'Making choices can be very difficult'. 'Hard to know what they want when they're with other people'. We've covered that. Here is a quote: 'Others see me as peaceful but inside I often feel anxious'. Is that something you go along with?

Dottie: Yes.

Iain: Okay. 'When there's unpleasantness around me I just try to think about something else'. Is that something you guys connect with?

Dottie: Yes, I think we're quite into diversionary tactics. Doing something else or thinking something else if we're in a challenging situation – just zone out.

Sam: Or losing yourself in detail of the work or small, easy tasks instead of addressing the bigger stuff that might, in your mind, lead to conflict or lead to difference of opinions.

Iain: And then you get stubborn when you feel controlled?

Cate and Dottie: Yes!

Iain: 'Tend to put things off to the last minute, but usually get them done in the end'.

Dottie: Yes, yes, procrastination.

Iain: You're all ticking the boxes there.

Sam: I don't know if there's anything on that list about this paradox of wanting to avoid conflict, but in the attempt to avoid it, actually creating it. For example, if in a situation I have a difference of opinion, rather than expressing that, I'll agree with the other person, go along with them and decide to do something. Then down the road a few days or weeks later, I can't sustain their position, which I've taken up, and so in the attempt to avoid conflict I've actually created it, and it's a pain.

Dottie: You've taken that into yourself in order to keep the peace, but the conflict has remained within you. That's where you say you've actually generated conflict, it's actually in you. They're quite happy because you're agreeing with them.

Sam: Then it blows up: "Why didn't you say that?"

Iain: But Nines are also known as the peacemakers, so you obviously have this quality of being able to get together parties that are not getting on, and to help be the catalysts for peace.

Cate: Seeing both sides.

Dottie: It's very easy to tune in to other people. We can pick up the vibe about what's going on and therefore – but not in a manipulative way – we steer things to a more peaceful space.

Iain: You're really feeling how they feel, you can understand their mindsets, and then I presume somewhere appears a clue of how you can bring them together in common interest.

Dottie: Yes, you're looking for a common ground. If you've got two people standing opposite, you look for the common ground that everyone can stand in. It's that sort of thing.

Iain: Well, that's a great quality!

Dottie: We've said a lot of negative things about Nines, haven't we? But there are lots of positive things about being a Type Nine.

Iain: I don't know how much you want to talk about it now, Sam… You work for an organisation called the Prison Phoenix Trust. In fact you run the organisation in the UK, which helps to teach meditation and yoga to prisoners. So you must find quite a lot of conflict situations coming up. I presume your Type Nine peacemaker ability helps in those situations?

Sam: Yes, I think in any situation where you're leading or managing people it's a great skill to have. The challenge is to not only try to go with that easy skill of tuning in to what other people think, but knowing what you think and putting that into the equation. If you don't have that, then it's difficult.

Iain: Swimming around without an anchor, aren't you? You've got to find your own anchor.

Sam: Exactly, and know how you feel and what your take is.

Dottie: Sam, does that take an effort on your part to actually think 'Okay, what is my stand here? Where am I?' – so that it's a conscious thing and not an automatic thing?

Sam: It does take effort, and one thing that helps me is to think at the beginning of each day, or at the beginning of each week, what is important to me because I know I'll be hit with all kinds of pulls from other people and situations arising, and I can very easily get drawn off what is important to me. So yes, it takes effort. What's important is not something that I can easily remember.

Iain: Something else I wrote down in my notes is that 'Nines are often non-judgemental and accepting'. Is that something you all feel you are?

Dottie: Yes, it's all part of the same thing really. It's trying to have this environment where everything is nice and there's no conflict.

Cate: Then you feel much better, as long as everyone else is happy.

Iain: But if it's genuinely non-judgemental, that's really quite a quality.

Dottie: Oh I think it's genuinely non-judgemental – I think partly because you understand where the other person's coming from. You're not judging them because you know there's something that's driving them.

Cate: As long as what Sam has just said is also in place, it's truly so. It's not a by-passing so that you don't have to get into…

Dottie: …avoiding.

Cate: Yes.

Iain: You're also good listeners. Is that right?

Sam: So they say [*group laughter*]. Yes, people tend to tell us that we're good listeners.

Iain: But do you enjoy listening to people?

Sam: It's easy. It's a way of making the situation feel harmonious. I'm not sure about the judgemental bit. I think that maybe it's because I have Type One wing that I come across as judgemental sometimes… I don't know. Do you [Cate and Dottie] have that? Or do you genuinely feel not judgemental?

Cate: I distrust my non-judgementalness sometimes. I feel that I've sacrificed truth for harmony if I really, really look at it. And I'm really trying to be absolutely more… and that means feeling myself more, to really know.

Iain: Can you give a practical example of how the situation may appear less harmonious if you were more truthful to yourself?

Cate: The example that comes up [happened] a long time ago. I lived running a small growth centre with two other people who were together, and sometimes it got pretty difficult. Now, for me the whole thing was to keep things harmonious even if I could feel and I could see what was going wrong; it was more important not to rock the boat. My Type Eight partner would come in, and for him the whole thing was to see the truth and what was really happening. I used to get terrified of that – that my whole existence might disappear if things were rocked. Now I really see the moments when I have to stand and say, "This is what I feel." I can do that more now, but it's still frightening because [of] that tendency to want harmony and smoothing things over – particularly when I get very anxious – to feel smooth and silky.

Iain: Let's talk more, Dottie, about the potential for Type Nine. You talked in your introduction about the ways in which Nines can move forward from let's say the neurotic patterns we all learn when we're very young.

Dottie: From this whole set of programmes?

Iain: Yes.

Dottie: I think the key is awareness and using the Enneagram as a tool. If you're aware of what your behaviour is, then you can start to do something about it.

Iain: Let's keep it very basic. What does awareness mean to you?

Dottie: It's like the story I was telling you about, that when I have a challenge I will feel sleepy. This is just a behaviour pattern kicking in – this is an avoidance. But having the awareness that this is a pattern of mine, and that I feel sleepy when I'm challenged, means I can go 'Ah! I've clocked that, I'm aware of it'. That's a pattern of behaviour. It's recognising when the behaviour is driving you. Something like the falling asleep is a classic one. So I think the first thing is awareness.

Iain: And you've got to practise being aware, haven't you?

Dottie: You have.

Iain: It's like a muscle that needs to be used.

Dottie: Yes, it's what Sam was saying earlier. When you have to consciously think 'Okay, today this is what I am'… it doesn't come automatically. Also in terms of potential… I've lost my train of thought now, what was I going to say? [*laughing*] That's very Nine-ish!

Sam: I think we have a huge capacity to act and to act decisively and to carry other people along with us. The capacity to see where they are, to see what they're feeling as you move forward a project, or decision, is great and it's perfectly possible to act and to come to bring your position forward.

Dottie: Looking at the physicality – and I think other Enneagram programmes have explained how the Enneagram types fall into ruled by the head, the heart or the gut – the Nine is ruled by the gut, down here [*indicating belly*], and that refers to how disconnected or to how connected you are to your body. In Nines the tendency has been to be disconnected from the body. So what's important for Nines is to get into their bodies, to actually physically be present. That may be through grounding exercises, it may be through doing physical exercise, going running or doing yoga, t'ai chi, chi gung. All these activities are really good to give Nines the sense of being physically present, and that's being down in the gut, which in yoga you call the hara. And I can't remember what it is in chi gung, but there's a similar word for it. It's this sense of being grounded, of being very physically present, and that's really important in terms of developing the potential for the Nine.

I'm sure there are lots of other modalities that help, but fundamentally the Enneagram gives you an understanding of where you are. I remember I was driving through London, which is something very unfamiliar to me, and I got completely lost. So I rang up a friend because I was going into that 'Eww!' sort of state, and I said, "Can you help me? I'm lost." He asked, "Where are you?" and I said, "I'm lost! I don't know where I am!" And the Enneagram is a bit like having your SatNav, because what it says is 'This is where you are'. It gives you an understanding of where you are and it can guide you to where you want to be. There will be different ways of getting there, but the Enneagram can be part of that process. There may be other modalities that you use in order to achieve that, but at least the Enneagram is there to show you where you are and how you can move forward. You can move out of this space of being inertia, like the oyster at the bottom of the sea that sits there and the water washes round it. But it's a nice thing I feel about Nines… you're the oyster, but if there is stimulation – the grain of sand is that stimulation – then the oyster will create a pearl because Nines are capable of achieving amazing things. We're not all asleep, but you have to wake up in order to do it.

Sam: I don't think it's a steady linear progression upwards. Over the last couple of months, there've been lots of ups and downs, and the nice thing for me about connecting with a sense of self, or sense of identity, is that at the same time my relationships to other people are richer. They're more… I want to say 'profound', but they're richer, they're more alive. Life in general is more alive because of that tuning in to oneself.

Iain: Practically, how have you done that?

Sam: How do I do it? Communication with people who know me well; to think together. Meditation is very, very useful in rising, or bringing awareness to what the internal processes, or internal dialogue, is. Not shying away from conflict, not backing away and going to the usual modes of trying to avoid it or get out of it, and to face difficulty.

Iain: It takes a degree of courage, doesn't it? Would you say that was an issue for you, Cate?

Cate: Definitely. The other thing I was just thinking, particularly when I get overwhelmed, my tendency is not to do the most important thing. I'll procrastinate, I'll do everything else. To realise that and to sit down and think about what the most important thing is and not run away and do all the other things... to focus on what is really important and to face that... And for me it is so much about awareness and so much about facing conflict and daring to say things that I didn't use to dare to say... and the aliveness that comes with that.

Iain: That must be quite enjoyable.

Cate: It is, hugely. And 'focusing' to me is a word that I really, really need.

Dottie: The expression 'Where the attention goes the energy follows'... if your attention is out here, that's where your energies go.

Cate: Yes. It used to be and still can be, when I'm sort of panicky, that people could follow what I'd done. I did this, then suddenly I thought of something else, so left that not finished, and then did the next thing... and to really finish something is...

Iain: I was reading in some of my homework – and I can't claim to have read all the books — but I was dipping in and out the last couple of days on Type Nines, and the words 'real action' came up quite a bit. I don't know if you want to talk about what 'real action' is to you. Dottie, you seem to be fired up by this word [*group laughter*].

Dottie: When you first start learning the Enneagram, this is what you're meant to be doing: 'real action'. And you think 'Well, what is it?' To understand what real action is, there's a quote from Almaas explaining what it is. Real action is connected to being in your body, to be actually grounding yourself in the body. Real action is when you know what to do without having to go through a process of thinking. As you study through the Nine and as Sam was saying – 'I have to *think* at the beginning of the day: this is what I'm going to do' – it's still a thought process. We haven't got to the stage of *knowing* which is the '*right action*' that we're working towards. Although having been working with it for a number of years, I'm now getting glimpses of that 'Oooh, I knew what to do and I did it!'

Sam: Without thinking.

Dottie: Without thinking.

Cate: It happens.

Dottie: It just happens. And I'm finding that I'm doing that more and when it happens: 'Ah, that's what it feels like'. So in a sense it's easier to do it again because you know what it feels like.

Iain: It becomes familiar.

Dottie: It becomes familiar because that's what you're working with, isn't it? When you're doing any sort of development it's the negative if you like that has become familiar, so I stick with that. Then it's actually changing that, so that the positive becomes familiar, and then it becomes easy. It's going through the barrier that Cate was talking about: the fear of making waves by saying what I want. It's the fear of saying no to somebody, because [*low whisper*] they might be angry with me. So going through that and finding that the world doesn't fall apart, it's okay… and the more you do it, the easier it becomes. And then you get the positive reinforcement of 'That feels good!'

Cate: Particularly when you were talking about right action… the more present I can be [the more] it happens. So there's none of this [hesitation]. I mean, I can easily dip into that again, but somehow it is extraordinary how more present I am. It can just happen. I don't have to go through all this procrastinating…

Dottie: I think the wonderful thing is when you're looking at the other types in the Enneagram that may be listening to us and thinking 'I don't feel like that at all, I have no problems making decisions', it's recognising how different we are from other people, isn't it?

Iain: I think that's one of the great values of the Enneagram. I know when I discovered my Enneagram type it was really quite a relief that at least a ninth of the people around the world do function and feel maybe in a similar way to me, but I didn't always realise that. I felt that maybe it was just me that was odd and different from other people, but when you realise that about eight percent of the world's population is roughly your type… So how is it for people to be close to Nines?

Sam: Frustrating probably a lot of the time because you can go along with what they want to do. Type Nine will go along with what a partner or friend wants to do and then discover that actually the Nine doesn't want to do that. So that's frustrating. Not being able to know, really, what the Nine is feeling is very hard.

Iain: Knowing both of your partners, who seem to be quite opinionated and spirited people, I guess you tend to be drawn to people who are more in touch with their feelings. That's something that maybe attracts you to them, because they seem to be more assertive and in touch. Would you say that's true?

Sam: I don't know if there's a better type, or types that Nines tend to be drawn towards. I can't comment, I don't know.

Iain: I wasn't thinking about a particular type. It's that knowing both of your partners, yours [Cate] better than Sam's, they just feel that they're… yours [Sam] is very in touch with her feelings. Norman is, certainly…

Cate: [*laughing*] …assertive!

Iain: 'Assertive', shall we say? Yes.

Cate: I think yes, because I always remember my father saying, "Why are all your friends much stronger than you?" And I never really thought about it. He said, "What is it?" and I think for me, being with somebody who is really able to say what he thinks does help me. I also feel very safe because I know exactly where he is... there's a sort of honesty about it.

Sam: That's certainly true for me. I appreciate knowing exactly where...

Cate: ...where you are.

Iain: Yes. And that's very useful for a peacemaker to know exactly where one person is.

Sam: Yes, and that uncertainty I have is taken away by the certainty of the other person.

Cate: What you say is very interesting because I think people come towards Nines... because I always think I'm boringly unthreatening. But then probably with other people there's this incredible frustration.

Sam: 'Who are you?' 'Where's the person?' 'What are you actually?' 'Who's there?' That's what I fear.

Dottie: My first husband used to get really, really cross with me because he'd say, "What do you want to do?" I'd say, "I don't mind, what do *you* want to do?" And one of the things somebody said: "What's good for Nines is that you give them a choice." If you say, "What do you want to do? You can do anything," it's like 'I've no idea'. But if you say, "Would you like to go swimming, horse-riding, or mountain climbing?" they'll go, "Oh, I think we'll go swimming!" So when you're given a choice it's much easier. Somebody's actually giving you something to choose between, rather than 'Oooh that's just all too much to have to choose'. But yeah, he used to get really angry with me. I think he was an Eight and I became more and more invisible. You've come through your relationship and you've found your strengths, but that marriage ended because I'd almost disappeared. I really had, because he was very strong and I just gave in.

Sam: I think it's probably mind-boggling to some other types that Nines don't have a sense of identity, they don't have a strong sense of self.

Dottie: It's the unity, isn't it? If you think about duality and non-duality, the Nines want this sense of non-duality. That is complete unity and a loss of individuality to a degree, isn't it? If that's part of us, then you can see how you've lost that little bit that's 'me' somehow. Does that make sense?

Sam: It does, the whole non-duality thing is very interesting. How does a person who's a Nine fit into that non-duality? How does a strong sense of self exist at the same time as this non-dual reality? That's what I'm trying to crack.

Dottie: You know the Rumi poem where he says that you're the drop of rainwater and the drop of water falls into the ocean and it becomes part of the ocean, but is also still that drop. That's the bit that fries your brain, isn't it? That you are connected, but you are also connected and separate at the same time. That's what's tricky.

Iain: We have about three minutes left. Any last comments you want to make?

Dottie: Iain, can I ask you a question? What do you think about Nines having had this talk?

Iain: It was very interesting how I felt during the interview because usually I'm quite assertive in these programmes. I try not to be. I try and let them flow, but I felt my assertiveness going. I was becoming Nine-type [*group laughter*].
Dottie: You're entering the Nine energy!
Iain: I thought that was interesting how you guys had influenced a part of me – which of course, as we were saying at the beginning, we all have each type in us, it's just one type is predominant – and I was feeling very Nine-ish: 'Shall I ask them this?' 'Shall I go there?' And I wasn't quite sure [*group laughter*].
Dottie: Well that's a wonderful expression of what Nine-ishness can be like, isn't it?
Iain: Yes, it's good because one of the aims of this series we're doing on the nine different Enneagram types isn't to come up with all the right descriptions and the right answers, but it's to give viewers a feel for these types. I think that came across very well here.
Dottie: Good.
Iain: Any words of wisdom from the other side of the bench there?
Cate: It just makes me think when you say that, how easy it is to be with other Nines. I always remember ages ago there were four of us in a car leaving a retreat and the car obviously wasn't… smoke was coming out and goodness knows what, and two people immediately – I think there was an Eight and a Six – got out of the car and said, "We can't go with you!" The driver was a Nine and I was a Nine, and we decided to just go and we had such fun: 'Oh well, this is what's happening, so let's go along with it'. And I was suddenly thinking when you said you'd become more Nine-ish that…
Dottie: Do you sometimes find that – oh sorry, I might be wandering somewhere else – when you're with a group of Nines you're not trying to be anything else? Do you sometimes find it tiring if you're with a lot of people because you're holding the space for everybody and… Eww!
Cate: Well, I like being with people enormously, but it's very relaxing if you let them get on with it and you're still part of it all without…
Sam: …having to do anything.
Iain: I think we're going to finish on that note. Really appreciate the three of you coming in to be on conscious.tv and share your 'Nine-ishness' with the world.

To watch this interview please go to:
http://www.conscious.tv/consciousness/enneagram

CONVERSATIONS ON THE ENNEAGRAM

Tom Condon
Living the Dynamic Enneagram

Interview by Iain McNay

Iain: My guest today is Tom Condon. Tom has written a book which we found interesting, and we thought we would get Tom along whilst he is in the UK for an interview. The full title of the book is *The Dynamic Enneagram: How to Work with Your Personality Style to Truly Grow and Change*. At the moment it is an ebook, but it will be coming out shortly as well, as a paper book.

The Enneagram is something I heard about twenty years ago, and I found it extraordinarily helpful in my life, not only in understanding myself better, but in understanding my relation to other people. There are many different ways to look at the Enneagram, and we are going to cover Tom's book and focus very much on the personality style to truly grow and change. For people who haven't heard about the Enneagram, Tom, why don't you just give a brief three-minute summary of what the Enneagram actually is?

Tom: It is a system of nine personality styles on one level. There is also another way of conceiving the Enneagram that is different from strictly talking about personality. The one that I deal with, and the one that is best-known and that people respond to a lot, is a kind of compact system that describes nine different personality styles and their connections and interactions. In that description, what you recognise are nine ways of perceiving reality: nine ways of apprehending the world and kind of specialising in a certain style of perception, a certain skew towards how you perceive and interact with the world around you. I would say, in one sense, what the Enneagram is describing, when it describes someone's personality style, is a reality strategy, a strategy for making your way through the world, a picture of the world, a map of the world that you have internally – an internal representation that allows you to predict events and know where you are, know who you are, in a world where other people seem to know where they are, or who they are. It has got to do with a worldview basically, and how people see themselves and how people subjectively see the world around them and perceive, as well as feel, the world around them. Within that, there are talents, resources, abilities, and things that come naturally to you that maybe don't come as naturally to other Enneagram styles. Then the Enneagram also describes typical illusions you are prone to, pitfalls and things that motivate you, and ways in which you are blind to other potentials, other dimensions and other ideas.

Iain: When we had dinner together last night, you were telling me that you first heard of the Enneagram over thirty years ago and at that point there weren't actually any written books on the Enneagram. And you were educating yourself about it from notes from seminars that people had written. It must have been exciting to get involved in what has proved to be a very helpful tool at quite an early stage?

Tom: I got involved in NLP about nineteen-seventy-seven and liked aspects of it very much and still do. NLP is a bit of a mixed bag because it has a kind of shallow, opportunistic, sort of sociopathic dimension to it, but actually the original formulation of it was based on the study of effective psychotherapists and people who helped people change. The guys who created it came up with a number of techniques that were common to a lot of therapies, and also with a way of understanding the inner subjective experience in terms of the senses – how someone has a problem, how do things look, how do things sound, how do things feel when you are having the problem, and then also applying techniques towards creating solutions. NLP had a lot of good stuff in it, but it was also inherently shallow and it lacked. It was not a good system for working with the whole person, or comprehending the emotional ground, or the subtext and inner dynamics that generated problem behaviour. About the time I was realising this about NLP, I came across the Enneagram, and the Enneagram at that time – I lived in Berkeley California – was taught by Helen Palmer and Claudio Naranjo, and a few other people. Most of the people I knew were therapists and they were all sort of involved in the Enneagram. They had all heard about it. There were no books, there was nothing in literature, it was all... Helen would do ten-week courses – and I went to one of them – where she would interview people who all had the same Enneagram style and do panels. It was very illuminating and it was very obvious that they all shared the same strategy.

Iain: How did you find your own style?

Tom: Through notes mostly, and what happened was that most of the therapists who went to these courses that I was describing would keep the hand-outs. And then people would also go to the courses, they would make notes and have their own reactions, and they would mimeograph those – they had mimeograph in those days – so the stack of notes grew and got to be about four or five inches thick before any of the books ever came out. I would read within that about the various styles and it was instantly obvious to me what my style was, which was counter-phobic Six. There was already, at that young age, a mountain of evidence to indicate that I was a Type Six.

Iain: Were you okay to find out you were a Six? What was your reaction, your response?

Tom: When you find out your Enneagram style, truly find out… because people will vacillate and sometimes it is a process. I always tell students a good indicator is the one that kind of makes you sick to your stomach a little bit.

Iain: So you feel it here [*indicating gut*], but not necessarily a good feeling?

Tom: Some sort of physiological…

Iain: An 'Oh dear!'

Tom: Yes, 'Oh my God!' is how it is, rather than an 'Aha' experience. Yet, when I came across mine, it was uncomfortable, especially relating to the downside of it, but it was so obvious and right away really helpful because you started to realise this is a pattern. There is a name for this, there is a name for the type of suffering I have inflicted on myself. There is a rationale and a schema and a kind of unconscious drive to do it and to reproduce it and you know… there's that Chinese saying: 'The beginning of wisdom is to call things by their right names'. And so that was a good first step.

Unfortunately in those days all of the material, since it was generated by therapists and since it was generated by people who had spiritual practises that emphasised the *'via negativa'* – which is to say, you kind of blast the student with insight and shock them down to their toes – most of the descriptions were negative in those days. So the name for Sixes was Coward [*laughing*]. So [*shrugging*] that was a little hard to wrap your arms around and kind of enthusiastically affirm. Nevertheless it was pretty plain.

Iain: Interesting, because when I first found out my type, which was also Type Six, it was I think about twenty years ago, and I found it an incredible relief. The basic reasons for the relief was that first of all, I thought that there are other people like me [*laughing*]; that means one person in every nine – as there are nine types – is functioning in the same way as me. Yes, because often I couldn't understand why I responded so differently to other people, in different situations. So that was kind of positive, and of course at that time there were more books out about it. Then, it was all the information about how to be with that and, as your book talks about, how to grow with that, use that in a positive way to your advantage, to find out more about yourself. And that, as I said earlier, is the key for me: finding out more about myself and about the other. Now, one of the things that you say in your book – and you mentioned this also in your introduction – is that the Enneagram is an inner map, but of course everybody's is an incomplete map, isn't it?

Tom: Well, and also to the degree that you are caught in the pattern of your Enneagram style, it is an old map. It is one of those maps of the New World that they had in Europe before they had fully explored the New World. Or a better example is there was a map of California that represented it as an island – an early map based on the perceptions of early explorers. They soon realised it wasn't an island, but it took one hundred and fifty years for them to actually change the maps. So it is like you have an inner map – I think of it as almost an inner flat Earth – and you are sort of sailing on the ocean and trying to avoid sailing off the edge of your flat Earth because that is also the edge of your self-definition, of your capabilities, and of your inner subjective universe.

Iain: Is it, in effect, a map of how we see life based on how we were brought up and on our experiences?

Tom: And what we adapted to. How we handle those experiences when you are caught in them. I mean, it is more than that. You are born probably with a temperament and a predisposition to certain Enneagram styles. Some people insist it is genetic and that you are born with your Enneagram style. I would question that just simply because I have identical twins in my family and they don't have the same Enneagram styles and we won't know until there is a blood test in any case.

Iain: Yes, you are raising an interesting point here which is a little bit controversial in the Enneagram world. Some people say it is genetic – as you say, you are born with it – other people say it is to do with conditioning right from very early childhood.

Tom: My wife had the best comment on this at one point. She is a Nine, she said, "I may have been born a Nine, but I definitely learned to be unhealthy." I thought yes, that kind of captures it because at least in my work and the work of a lot of people, the emphasis is on how to grow and change and evolve out of stuck points and rigid patterns, ways in which you over-identify with one aspect of your personality and under-identify with another. Where you kind of have an ideal, but it is defensive. Ones will identify with being good and right and virtuous. Then, the capacity to sin and make chaos and break the rules, that's sort of pushed away and becomes a shadow. In doing that, you are then making an inner defensive arrangement that protects you in certain ways when you are growing up. Maybe the One grew up in an environment where there are high standards in the air, or there was a lot of criticism in the air, or it was just implied that you had to really do your best. So the person internalised those high standards and tried to push away other aspects of their personality – making them into a shadow, basically.

Iain: It is as if we construct in our minds these boundaries, don't we? We construct an understanding of how we see life to be, and it is that which inhibits us in later life. Those boundaries may be useful when we are very young as it protects us, but as we get older they become redundant, but we don't realise they are redundant.

Tom: Well, it is like getting addicted to pain pills or something. The thing that saved you in the first place, or relieved your pain, or allowed you to adapt to whatever your family circumstance was, whatever your early experience of life was, what role in your family you were expected to play, all these things can have a defensive cast where the self gets warped, or misshapen. And there is a shadow that goes with it and then the thing that saved you turns out to be the thing that gets in your way some decades later.

Iain: So it worked once and then it stopped being effective.

Tom: Right, but we get attached to how it worked, and parts of ourselves get time-locked as well, where you reach some barrier when you were a kid, where you found circumstances overwhelming, or extremely painful, or just confounding. And you start to do things to yourself that happened to you the most, and in doing that it has an element of control that comes into it. Then you find out later that you are still generating something that corresponds with the low side of your Enneagram style and you're baffled by it, and various Enneagram schools have names for that. They call it a compulsion, or a fixation or a habit, an emotional habit, but there is some logic to it as well. There is an underlying drive. There is an underlying will within it to reproduce it, because at some level you believe in it as a method.

Iain: Is there an example you can give from your own life? Something that served you when you were younger and then you had to really be aware that as you got older that didn't work the best for you any more?

Tom: Well, Sixes scare themselves. I grew up around Irish alcoholics who used to drink and fight, and I remember developing a sort of strategy where I would sit at the dinner table and if I saw people starting to drink I started to, in my own mind, predict what was going to happen in twenty minutes... because things could go crazy, you know. Somebody, when they were drunk, could have an argument about the peas at dinner. A lot of it was just nonsensical, but it was also kind of unpleasant. So as a Six, one of the things you do is, you start to imagine negative scenarios and kind of anticipate and fantasise, and the defensive logic behind it is that you are trying to prepare for what might go wrong, or what might happen that would be unpredictable in order to be prepared for it, so that you can handle it in a strong way. But the paradox of it is that actually, when you scare yourself, the more you scare yourself, the more you feel helpless and kind of young and resource-less. So it has this back-to-front quality.

Iain: Yes, it takes your own power away. When you are young you are powerless, when you are older you actually have some power.

Tom: Well, when you are young maybe it makes sense to give away your power in a circumstance where your power is going to be taken from you anyway. But when you are older it is like you are giving away your power to imaginary authorities, or other people, or conspiracy theories, or something like that. When you are doing that, you are missing a piece of yourself. You react to your own power out there in other people, and have a self-image of being maybe young and helpless lurking within it somewhere.

So Sixes are unusually contradictory among Enneagram styles this way, but all the styles have a sort of ruling paradox built into them. Style number Three are quite performance-oriented and image-oriented. When you scratch down to it and summarise it, it is like the person believes 'In order to be loved for who I am, I have to pretend to be who I am not'.

Iain: Yes. In the book – you use an interesting word for me – you talk about being in a '*trance*' a lot of the time.

Tom: I use that term in a specific way because I have a background in hypnosis, and it sounds like a loose metaphor, but actually when you look closely at the inner subjective experience of different Enneagram styles, especially when people are caught in their patterns, they actually have trance-like characteristics that correspond with studies of official hypnosis. For instance, certain Enneagram styles are prone to amnesia, and hypnotic subjects sometimes will be prone to amnesia. Other Enneagram styles are prone to the opposite of amnesia which is hypermnesia, where instead of forgetting things, you remember things in very unusually sensory-rich and vivid detail. Style number Four will do that. Sixes will do it too, where you remember some awful thing that happened in the past. Or a Four will be nostalgic for a time when they were twenty years old and in love for the first time and life had a certain kind of beauty, and they remember the smells and the song that united them with their beloved. And there is a lot of sensory-rich detail in it that they get preoccupied with as they sort of take themselves out of the present. So when I say a 'trance', it is really like an open-eyed hypnotic trance and there is a lot of correspondence with it.

Iain: It makes sense that we are going through life and we are partly hypnotised by our early beliefs, and it stops us seeing reality, doesn't it?

Tom: It does, and then what I do like, about disciplines like NLP and working with hypnosis, is that they pretty much approach working with the inner life and approach working with problems as things that we create ourselves. That we make this stuff up, that we are self-generating, even if we are generating from an unconscious level. You can read in Enneagram books – sometimes the wording in Enneagram books is kind of fatalistic and passive and it sounds like something that has just descended upon you, that you are stuck with, like a scarlet number on your forehead or something. I find it a lot more useful to approach it from the standpoint of how much of this is learned behaviour and how much of it, if it is learned, you can overwrite and unlearn. You can delve into the depths of it and find emotional stuck points, and maybe feelings you couldn't handle earlier in life that you can now manage because there is so much more of you, or free yourself in a variety of ways. I don't know that there is a limit to that, and that then tracks over into how people experience the Enneagram spiritually too – what they open up to as they grow and change. Old themes fall away and old conflicts get resolved, and then you have the sense of living less of a story, less of a script, and have more of a sense of being in the present and responding to life and aware of the vastness of life around you.

Iain: And the richness that comes with that.

Tom: Yes, living a more complete life.

Iain: Tell me more about yourself insofar as how that has affected you as a human being. You have been on this long journey with the Enneagram, and you gave an example earlier of something that was helpful when you realised it. But how do you generally feel? You talk about being a counterphobic Six. How do you generally feel about life now? Has your view fundamentally changed?

Tom: Ah yes. It has fundamentally softened and lessened compared to where I came from. When I first came across the Enneagram I was pretty much in a mode of perceiving danger wherever I looked, and the counterphobic style within Type Six is to go against the danger.

Iain: To jump over it?

Tom: Yes, and I would literally do things like jump off bridges onto moving trains.

Iain: Really?

Tom: Yes, and climb hotels.

Iain: What, you climbed hotels on the outside?

Tom: Yes, they have these ladders that go up the side.

Iain: Wow…

Tom: I would do things like that, and part of the reason for doing it, apart from being young, impulsive, and reckless, was that I always had the sense that I could do it. You understand, it was a calculated risk, but when I would do things like that, I then would be free from fear for a few days.

Iain: And is that what happened, in effect?

Tom: Yes, it was. It was like expunging the fear. And then the habit, the un-dealt-with habit of scaring myself, would creep back in. I would do something daring on Saturday and then by Tuesday I was starting to get a bad case of nerves.

Iain: This is a very interesting point. I guess this applies in its own way to the other types as well. You can do something that in a way takes you out of the habit of that type, but on the other hand, you have almost got to do your homework as such, in understanding and working in a less dramatic way just to loosen up and lessen the effect of the history of the type.

Tom: I would classify different approaches to working with something like an Enneagram style in maybe a broader way. If you think about it in terms of therapy, or change, or trying to evolve in whatever way appeals to you the most, or is necessary the most, there are approaches that involve going against the problem. What I am describing is certainly that. I was going against my own fear. Sometimes, it is recommended in Enneagram books that you create counter-examples to your normal experience, quote-unquote 'normal experience', and you maybe make more space and gather more life experience that contradicts the tendency you have when you are maintaining your pattern. So it is good for that. It is not so good for really getting over it, if that is all you do. Because if you just go against the premises of your style, or the tendencies, or the compulsion or what have you, then a lot of times you just strengthen the conflict within you – sort of like isometrics. And then there are other approaches that involve standing back from your style. Certainly a lot of dissociative meditation techniques are like this, where you are trying to witness the pattern and see it, rather than feel it for example – and where you are trying again to expand your awareness so that you are not taking your own behaviour personally. Not taking your own pattern personally, and maybe seeing the workings of it and the intricacies of it without reacting quite so strongly in your body, for instance, and in your feelings. Then there are other approaches...

Iain: Let's just take that, because that's an interesting thing I would like to follow through with you. We have had a lot of people on conscious.tv itself who have talked about how they sit and see they are not the body, they are not the thoughts, they are not the emotions. And there is a certain freedom in that, and it is a huge realisation because you realise at that level that you are not just the body, the thoughts, and the emotions.

On the other hand we've got the day-to-day reality that we have the vehicle of the body in which to live our life. It is something that I didn't get for a time, but now I see more and more the importance of yes, you want that realisation because that realisation is showing you the bigger picture, is showing you who you really are, but integrating that realisation in day-to-day life, that becomes really the key. Certainly from reading your book, there is a lot of advice, a lot of ideas of how you can do this process of integration, but understanding the humanness more, it doesn't just go away, does it?

Tom: No, it doesn't, and we are incarnated and we are living in the world and our bodies have a lifespan, and certain things bring health and certain things don't. It is a little like a self-image. To me a lot of this work involves realising you are more than your self-image, more than body, but you are also your body. If you can handle it, it is like having two contradictory ideas in your mind at the same time, and you know both are true at different times.

There was a Rabbi one time who said, "You should go through life with things in two pockets and when you come into a new situation you can reach into one pocket and pull out a little note to yourself that says 'The world is made for me', and then the note in the other pocket says 'I am but ashes and dust'." He says the trick to life is knowing which pocket to reach into at which time.

Iain: [*laughing*] And knowing that either one is not the total truth.

Tom: Right.

Iain: You also talk about the Void in your book, which is something I've certainly experienced from time to time in my life. Just talk us through how you see the Void.

Tom: People don't really evolve out of their Enneagram style and turn into another style, or have no style – I would say – any more than they evolve out of their nationalities, but as you grow and change, you wear it more and more lightly and in doing so, you are more and more open. There is less and less in the way of you and the world around you, both externally and when you look inside... Internally there is far more space. People start to have spontaneous experiences of the Void, of the *mysterium tremendum*. And we were talking a little bit about the difference between maybe looking at the night sky and seeing it almost as a ceiling, or a kind of umbrella that has little pinprick lights in it, versus occasionally, when the stars are out in a remote place for example, you look into the night sky and you feel the distances in your body. You feel yourself kind of sucked up into space in a way, and that is quite a different sort of apperception of what is around us. But you know, we are on this tiny planet, we are all very involved in our lives and rightly so, and there are a vast number of cultures, and the cultures all have a history, and yet we are in a suburb of the Milky Way galaxy. There are a hundred billion other galaxies, and the new telescopes are showing us more and more distance, strangeness. Something in us defends against that and yet at the same time, as you grow and change, you start to open up to wider and broader and deeper and further realities.

Iain: You talk about the Void being intense, formless, and beautiful. But it can also be frightening and unnerving.

Tom: Well, most people have a dual reaction to it, and I would say our unconscious minds protect us from the perception that we are surrounded by infinity. I mean, that is something that people seek because extinguishing the self means extinguishing its suffering. So we go towards experiences where we are getting in the flow, where we lose ourselves – experiences that are immersive, that take us out of our normal frame of mind. And then at the same time, if we go too far, we are sort of sailing on the edge of the flat Earth. And then there are those waterfalls that were talked about in medieval times: down below there are dragons and rocks and the ships break up on the rocks and the dragons eat the sailors. There is something in the unconscious that then guards that boundary and we contract and maintain our worldview.

Iain: Yes, because we believe somehow that if we go past the boundary, which we have constructed, we will perish.

Tom: Yes, and in a way that is true, you know. It is like an ego-death which is different from physical death, but on some unconscious level we are not making that distinction a lot of the time.

Iain: You also talk in your book about families and how we carry our families around with us. Just explain that a little more.

Tom: I think it is the family therapist Salvador Minuchin who said that families create specialists, and what he meant was that families are systems and that there are roles to play within families and functions to serve within families that are based on whatever is needed within the family for it to function well. So someone comes into a family and they are, to a certain extent, type-cast: it depends upon what the family needs. Does it need a hero, does it need a screw-up, does it need someone who makes conflict, someone who avoids conflict? Families create specialists in this sense, and so you can sometimes see pretty clearly that a family doesn't cause someone to have a certain Enneagram style, but you can see that the role that they played in their family of origin comes out through the expression, especially of the problematic, of the low side of their Enneagram style. Then the tendency is to recreate that – sort of invisibly and unconsciously without realising it – in your own family as you grow up and create one, but also maybe in your work place. For example, seeing the boss as a kind of parent, relating to co-workers as you might relate to a sibling, that kind of thing. It is all very subtle, and some of it doesn't matter because it works very well, but sometimes what you start to realise is that you are carrying with you a field of experience and you are filtering the world as you find it through that field and relating to people in ways that are familiar –and also setting up new situations that are presumably untarnished. You come in and you sully them up with unconscious assumptions and expectations and requirements, and you know things have to go this way and if they don't, it means that. And there is a way in which all of that stuff is grist for the mill, for stuff to work on, and to catch yourself in the act and maybe to unhitch from.

Iain: It really is work, to get to the bottom of this, isn't it? One of the things for me was that a lot of the time I found the work truly fascinating because I found as I looked at myself more and more, that I was interested in finding out why I was the way I was. Not only was it practically helpful, but the inner journey is an intriguing journey, just as going on an adventure and walking across mountains. That inner journey is interesting because certain people take to it naturally, other people just resist it. I don't know whether you have a feel for this, in all your years of experience, about what are the factors that really encourage someone to follow the inner journey, as opposed to ones who are just trying to ignore the whole thing and get by?

Tom: Motivation to change is really an important thing and there are no rules about it. There is no book anywhere that describes who should change and how much, or whether they should change. For most people, it has to do with how much they are suffering and maybe the inkling that they have somewhere a hand in their own suffering. Then that leads them in certain directions to seek out methods and to seek out contexts where it would be safe and where it is encouraged to grow and change. Some people grow and change, in my experience a smaller percentage based on a kind of aspiration and curiosity: 'I wonder what it would be like if I went beyond this?' This sort of thing, where there is more of a positive motivation, you might say, to change. Then within the Enneagram styles there are different considerations as well. There are certain Enneagram styles… when people are caught in their pattern, they suffer a lot more. Sixes for example, Ones for example, Fours for example, and then there are other Enneagram styles who have defences that make them feel better. Sevens will reframe things and find the positive in difficult and painful experiences and kind of jump to the positive benefit a little too fast, when they are caught in their pattern. And what does that do for motivation if your way of coping is to generally make yourself feel better? You might not get as distressed as you really ought to, about something that you have a tendency to do, or create, or hang on to. Style number Nine, for example… one of the things I will ask in workshops sometimes, is that I will ask the Nines to tell me the first number that comes into their mind when I ask the question, "How long do you expect to live?" And the number is almost always eighty-five to a hundred and ten. What does that do for motivation?

Iain: It is a bit optimistic, isn't it?

Tom: Well, they may be right. Some day there will be a medical – if there is ever a blood test or something like that – there may be a medical work-up of the different styles. I wouldn't be surprised if Nines on average live longer, it is a type B personality. You handle stress pretty well. There are a lot of things to suggest that might be true anecdotally, but if I am in my middle sixties and I am going to live to be eighty-five, a hundred and ten, and there is something I am doing that is affecting my life, or affecting my relationships, or I am in a conflict with somebody in some way, or I have a bad habit, or I have something I have to change, but I am going to live to be a hundred and ten…

Iain: [*laughing*] Then there is time to do it?

Tom: Yes, you know, what is that, forty-five years… why rush into this thing?

Iain: So which of the types, when you ask that question, gives the answer with the least number of years that they have to live?

Tom: Ah, I haven't asked the other styles that question so much. There are styles where the future seems shorter… like style number Four. A lot of times they will say, "Well, I don't know how long I will live, but the past is what is in front of me, not the future." When Fours are in their trance, Sixes too, when they are in their trance, they will be focused on the past rather than the future and have trouble thinking about the future.

Iain: You also talk in your book about there being two versions of the Enneagram, in a way. There is the Enneagram of Personality and the Enneagram of Everything. Can you explain how you see the distinction there between the two?

Tom: Well, I am speaking out of and operating with and working with the Enneagram of Personality, and then there is another sort of version of it, which is kind of inherited from Gurdjieffian sources. Fourth Way sources and other people have had a fair amount of input into this, that looks at contexts and various aspects of life in terms of the Enneagram and also has a lot of symbolism attached to it that I don't personally find very useful. I don't really even know how to describe it well, except that it is quite rarefied. There are people who use it, who get a lot out of that, so I don't have any problem with that part, but it has more to do with a spiritualised approach that is basically framed as 'Here is how to reach your highest potential and here is what your highest potential is'.

Iain: But that is also what you are working with in the Enneagram of Personality, isn't it?

Tom: I would say so, but I don't really try to formulate what those things are too closely. I am not very theoretical basically.

Iain: So you're going stage by stage practically, and seeing where the adventure leads people.

Tom: Also allowing for approaching change at various levels from neurotic stuck points, to evolving beyond your worldview in a broader way. So I always think that working with biography is a complement to working with a spiritual practise and vice versa, that they are not contradictory even though some people will kind of polarise that way, into one or the other. But they both have their advantages and if you only do one or the other, then they both have their limitations. You know that if you only work in a psychiatric way, a psychological way on your biography, then you can be like Woody Allen who has been in therapy for forty years...

Iain: It seems, from his films, that nothing has changed.

Tom: Yes, it doesn't seem so different. And then if you only work in a spiritual way and ignore biography, biography comes up and bites you in the ass sometimes. People will sometimes get into spiritualising their ego, so it is like I am trying to be spiritual and I have these high-level spiritual aspirations and you know these other little dark details in life are not me. But other people in your life have to deal with them if that becomes a shadow.

Iain: We have just over five minutes left. Let's use that in a practical way, insofar as somebody who is watching this and has never heard of the Enneagram, but is a little intrigued about what you are talking about and would like to find out more and maybe their type. What would be the starting point for them?

Tom: There are tests, and there are some relatively good ones. They are only about seventy percent accurate in my opinion, and partially that is because you have certain traits in you. You not only have a central Enneagram style, but you have secondary Enneagram styles, secondary connections that show up, that start to make sense once you learn the system. But you also have the Enneagram styles of your parents within you. Everybody knows that you introject your parents. Well, that also includes their parents' Enneagram styles, and tests can't really measure that because it is not consistent. A Six doesn't always have an Eight father and a Two mother, and so it can be a little confusing, but what is a good starting point is to begin to expose yourself to the material. Maybe take a test, but take it with a grain of salt and try to begin to think about and to observe in day-to-day life: 'What are my reactions?' 'What are my motivations?' 'How am I seeing the world?' 'How am I perceiving things when I have this particular reaction that seems like it relates to being a Nine, or seems like it relates to being a Two?' Something like that... and beginning to fish for what your own motivations are. It is almost like a thought that you think all day long. Something that you keep returning to, a kind of meta-pattern that your unconscious is generating, but also is attached to. In trying to do that, then the difficulty can be that not everyone is a psychologist for one. Secondly, it is almost like a fish trying to see water, or a human trying to see the air, because basically what you are trying to do is ask yourself 'What are my basic unconscious assumptions about reality?' And they are unconscious for some people, and yet sometimes you might begin to think about what you were like when you were twenty years old and what you were going through.

You know, there are sometimes periods in life where something like an Enneagram style is more apparent and more vividly expressed, and that can be helpful too. Also this system won't make you honest; that is something you have to bring to the party. So if you can be as honest with yourself as you can, that really helps quite a bit and then – as we were saying – motivation. Sometimes people will come into contact with the Enneagram and it is like 'Oh, that is interesting', and it sounds like a bunch of stereotypes to them, and maybe that is a consequence of who is teaching it. Or maybe they met somebody at a party who had gone on an Enneagram workshop and now they are type-happy and they are running around typing everyone in sight. But occasionally someone will come into contact with the Enneagram that way, think nothing of it, and then come into contact with it a couple of years later and it blows their mind and just shakes their tree.

Iain: I was saying at the beginning that one of the things for me was understanding other people better, especially people I don't get on with, or who I don't seem to get on with. I will have a go at working out their type and I might not get it completely right, but in a way it doesn't matter because I feel that just the act of trying to understand them more… opens up something in the relationship. Then, if I have got the style right and I read up about it, I am more understanding of how their mind is working and why they are the way they are. Isn't that the basis of nearly every conflict and every war? It is a lack of understanding of the other and having a different viewpoint… also not being willing to listen to someone else's viewpoint.

Tom: Wars are also situations where two groups of people are sort of identical and they accuse each other of being what they believe they are not. There is this kind of shadow play that is going on, and you know people on both sides of a war behave abominably. So there is a recognition of your own shadow within it sometimes. But also, the ability to step into other people's shoes and understand the world from their point of view is a great thing because you de-vilify them, for one thing. It is a lot like… I am an American, I come to Europe and operate in a bunch of different cultures in Europe, and there are guide books for what to do and what not to do in different cultures such as 'Always be on time in Switzerland', 'Never do this in France'. And it is appreciating differences in nationalities. You can decide you don't like certain Enneagram styles, but that is not really the point. The point is, this goes on whether you like it, or not. If you decide there are certain Enneagram styles you don't like, that can also be an indicator of something that is unintegrated within you.

Iain: Yes, and I think, again for myself, that if I understand the other better, I actually end up understanding myself better, and there is that point when the understanding starts to drift away and you actually feel you go beyond the understanding and there is a connection there.

Tom: You have compassion for yourself just as you develop compassion for others.

Iain: We have about two minutes left. I don't know if you want to squeeze in anything we haven't covered that is important to you?

Tom: One thing I would like to underline is that when people are doing their 'Enneagram style' – quote-unquote – when they are especially caught in their pattern, there are typical sensory qualities that go with the different styles and that make up the illusion of being within a subjective universe that is quite compelling, that goes with the low side of your style. Beginning to identify those can be really helpful because you begin to realise 'Oh my gosh! I am doing this to myself somehow'. But also – we talked earlier about living a story – it is not just a verbal story, it is a story that has visual components, and it is a story that has kinaesthetic components as well, both in the emotions and in the body kinaesthetic, which are a little different from each other. So when a person is in their Enneagram trance, they are seeing the world a certain way, they are talking to themselves a certain way, they are feeling a certain way, and all of those sensory qualities are recurrent. They are things the person is unconsciously inducing and re-inducing in themselves. As they start to realise that and start to work with it, it can really be very helpful to opening up and to dropping old defences and resolving past conflicts and battles and so on. But you also alter your inner experience of yourself. Another way to put this is: I will sometime ask people in a detailed way, in workshops, to identify what are the sensory components of the low side of their Enneagram style and then, for contrast's sake, what are the sensory components of the high side of your Enneagram style. What is it like when you are at your best? What is it like when you are functioning within your style, and what do you identify as the high side of your style, even based on descriptions you have read? What is it like when you are not an Enneagram style? What is it like when you've pretty much escaped the mortal coil of it?

Iain: In simple terms, it is going into the feeling of the style.

Tom: Not just the feeling… the subtleties in the feeling. Like when Fives scare themselves for instance – the fear is in the middle of their chest, it is not in their kneecaps – and beginning to really identify and specify. It is also like when people say they have a fear of flying. A lot of times that is an umbrella term and then when you go into it more deeply with them, some people will say, "Well, I have a fear of turbulence." Another will say, "I have a fear of take-off and landing." Another will say, "I have a kind of claustrophobic reaction to being locked in a metal tube with a bunch of strangers." And so those are really different problems although they all come under the umbrella of fear of flying. What I am talking about is specifying and beginning to discern and discriminate between what it is like when you are at your worst, what it is like when you are at your best, and what are the sensory components of that. It helps a lot.

Iain: Okay good. Tom, thank you, it has been interesting.

Tom: Thank you.

Iain: Thank you everyone for watching conscious.tv. Here is the cover of Tom's book which is *The Dynamic Enneagram*, available as an ebook and will shortly be available as a physical book as well.

To watch this interview please go to:
http://www.conscious.tv/consciousness/enneagram

Tom Condon
The Enneagram and relationships

Interview by Eleonora Gilbert

Eleonora: Today my guest is Tom Condon. Tom has worked with the Enneagram since the nineteen-eighties and with Ericksonian hypnosis and NLP – Neurolinguistic Programming – since nineteen-seventy-seven. He uses these three tools to bring about change. In a moment I will ask you how you do that. You are the author of a couple of books, as well as fifty CDs and DVDs. You have taught over eight hundred workshops worldwide and you're the director of The Changeworks. You're based in Oregon.

We're going to talk about one particular book, which is *The Dynamic Enneagram: How to Work with Your Personality Style to Truly Grow and Change.* It's only available at the moment as an ebook, as a serial, but it will be available in the summer [2014]. Also you have written *How to See Enneagram Styles in the Movies.* That was your very first book.

What we're going to be talking about today is relationships, including how the Enneagram and the other two tools that you're using could be supportive of how to be more authentic in relationships. Before we start, could you just give me a little synopsis of what the Enneagram is and what Ericksonian hypnosis is, and NLP, and how you work with these three?

Tom: The Enneagram is a system of nine personality styles, kind of arranged in a circle. It presents nine central personality styles that people have – that the unconscious mind seems to favour in human beings. Then, within that, there are interconnections and subtler, finer distinctions that matter quite a bit, especially in relationships, as we'll probably talk about. But it is basically a very deceptively deep system that shows you your central preoccupations and beliefs and unconscious assumptions about the nature of reality – who you are within that vision of reality, your sort of subjective worldview, its contours, and its urgencies. Also it talks about what motivates people, how people are motivated differently from within different Enneagram styles.

I've worked with the Enneagram for a long time, but I've also worked with NLP and Ericksonian hypnosis, some Gestalt therapy, and imagery. My principal interest when I first came across the Enneagram was in applying various methods to it to help people grow and change from within the purview of their Enneagram styles. The Enneagram especially will show you your talents and your resources and your capacities and potentials, and then it'll also show you the good news and bad news. It'll show you the low side of your style and how you go wrong with confidence. The ways you get stuck in repetitive patterns that seem to have some meaning to you – or once had some adaptive purpose in the past – and that now are just behaviours, or assumptions, or patterns that get in the way, and block things like having a more complete life – but also block intimacy, for instance, get in the way of relationships. So these other disciplines besides the Enneagram are all technique-oriented, all method-oriented. Then the Enneagram is a superb diagnostic system and it seemed to me they needed to be married, so to speak.

Eleonora: Right. And I think you're unique in actually using these particular three tools.

Tom: So far. At least in the little universe of the Enneagram.

Eleonora: In your book, you talk a lot about the parental points as being influential in how we relate to one another.

Tom: Well, you have a central Enneagram style, and then you have connections to generally four other Enneagram styles, in the way that the system is formulated. The Enneagram is easy to learn but difficult to master, and it takes a while. But you can apprehend it pretty quickly and get the basic idea, and even maybe get to your central Enneagram style pretty fast. And then, if it interests you and you have some motivation and some ongoing curiosity about it, then you can add in these other subtler distinctions. They make a world of difference as well, and one of the distinctions that I like to emphasise and encourage people to have identified, is the Enneagram styles of their parents. Because once you identify your central style and some of these other connections, you also have the Enneagram styles of your mother, your father, or whoever was your basic caregiver through time. Those are operating too. Those are in your behaviour and in your reactions sometimes, like sides to your character.

Eleonora: Yes. I had not come across this particular distinction before reading your book. And one of the things that I was definitely aware of is the fact that we can come from the perspective of having two superegos sitting on our shoulders, in addition to our own superegos (the two superegos of our parents). So to identify them even more clearly as the types of your parents, I found that particularly useful.

Tom: Well, it's something people know in real life – when they grow up and have their own children, and they start talking to their own children in the way one of their parents talked to them, and maybe they vowed they would never talk to their own children that way, but it pops out. We introject our parents. We have that inside of us. And that means as well that we introject their Enneagram style. Maybe those Enneagram styles overlap with our central style, or maybe some of these other connections I was talking about, which tends to then strengthen and intensify the experience of that style. Or maybe there's no connection – at least in terms of the way the Enneagram formulates things. The other thing about it is, within each Enneagram style there's a tendency to over-identify with certain aspects of your personality and under-identify with others. One is like an ego ideal. For instance, style number Eight emphasises being strong, and so they're in tension to their own weakness, in tension to their own vulnerability, or to a level of their experience where they're a little bit lost and don't know what to do. And so they overcompensate.

When you carry your parents with you, or when you figure out the Enneagram styles of one of your parents, how you relate to that in yourself may be shaded by how you relate to it in your parents, in the actual person. For example, my style would be counterphobic Six. My father was an Eight and we didn't get along when I was young. We fought a lot. Now, during that period of time, I denied that I was anything like him. And of course, looking back on it, the stronger I denied it, the more I was like him. And that's because it was a shadow for me, and I was trying to create a boundary. It's something young people go through anyway and teenagers go through, where you're trying to separate and establish your own self-definitions somehow. But at the same time, I had somewhere inside of myself an Eight streak and gradually I realised this. Gradually – it took me a while to manage it, and to learn to accept it and stop reacting out of the low side of it and start finding my way to the high side of it. But this also parallels how sometimes you can have a conflict with a parent, and then as you both get older and grow and change, you kind of get together. You forgive each other, or you become friends after all, or something like that – which is in fact what happened with my father.

Eleonora: I was going to ask you if you actually had improved your relationship with him, or whether you also needed something from him to change, in order to be able to meet.

Tom: I think, for myself, I just accepted that he wasn't going to change. And that was all right. There was a way to manoeuvre with that. But what was even more salient was dealing with my own Eightness. And that became an advantage. The high side of Eight has got a lot of resources and capacities, and it's especially helpful for a Six. It's got a kind of honesty, a kind of motive force, and a decisiveness that cut against the neurotic tendencies of the Six style.

Eleonora: In your book, you also mention how families have an ego, and an ego style, which you'll either meet, or go against. Can you say a bit more about that?

Tom: It's hard to talk about without sounding over-generalised. And people will talk, for example, about different countries having different Enneagram styles. You can say that certainly in a broad-strokes sort of way and also you can recognise it. You can recognise France as having Enneagram style Four running through it, but it's more precise to say that cultures have Enneagram styles influencing them and shading them. It's not always definitive which one it is, but they're there. Also, if you go over to, say, a business context, a lot of businesses will have Enneagram styles running through the assumption of the business, and the culture of the business. Usually it's the Enneagram style based on the founder or founders of the business.

Eleonora: Right.

Tom: And then if you apply that to a family, it's a similar idea. A family has a mini-culture within it. There can be assumptions within the family and group beliefs about what's a 'good way' to be, and what's a 'bad way' to function. And you can see an Enneagram style running through it. If you have, let's say, a family of high achievers, a sort of Three-ish family, and there's no room for failure within it, then everybody's living in tension to that, in some way or other, or living in reaction to it anyway. Maybe the family is unbalanced that way, and so it needs a failure. So one child comes along, one of the siblings is a screw-up, and everybody else is in polarity to that. It can be that kind of thing. Then it can be useful understanding your family through the Enneagram. You can start to look at where you meet, and this applies to one-to-one relationships too, and friendships. Like I said, everybody's got a central Enneagram style, and then there are these secondary connections that are like sides to your character. Sometimes you find in families that somewhere within the secondary connections, everybody's meeting within a particular Enneagram style. That sometimes is quite instructive and informative too. You start to catch yourself in the act. You start to take everyone's behaviour less personally. You start to recognise 'Oh, there's a name for this, this is a pattern', or 'Oh look, the family is sinking into depression again, everybody is meeting in Type Four, and it happens every year when the weather's bad', or something like that.

Eleonora: It can be quite helpful, actually, to be able to identify that.

Tom: Yes, it's quite helpful. It's quite helpful. Like I say, it's not something that you arrive at overnight. You have to be interested in this and have some sort of motivation for it, some sort of need or see some use for it. It's possible to encounter the Enneagram and underestimate it. Or it's possible to hear about

CONVERSATIONS ON THE ENNEAGRAM

it from somebody who's enthusiastic but doesn't know what they're talking about and think that it's a bland silly thing or another set of stereotypes, but actually it's way deep.

Eleonora: Yes. The more I read about it in your book, the more I thought 'Gosh, there are so many aspects to be taken into account'. On the one hand, I felt there is so much to know; it's not just about your type, you need to take into consideration all of the types… so [there's] the feeling of 'Oh my goodness, this is a lot'. But at the same time, I also really appreciated the various distinctions that you created, because I was then able to see, in my own life, in my own family… and both [overwhelm and clarity] were there.

Tom: It depends on the kind of use you have for it, and motivation. I often recommend that if people are studying the Enneagram, and really want to get into it, over time, treat it like a hobby. Treat it like something that you allow yourself to enjoy, and you come back to from time to time. Or something happens in real life and you look it up in an Enneagram book and see how the two correspond – and to add in some of the distinctions that we're talking about, over time, rather than trying to drink the entire ocean.

Eleonora: That's right. I think I came across the Enneagram about fifteen years ago, and as I said, it was very useful to see what kind of type [I am], even though it took me quite a while, several years, to actually get into my actual type.

Tom: And that's a process too.

Eleonora: It is definitely a process. And for some people it seems easier than for others. For me, it wasn't particularly easy. I went all over the place – not quite all over the place, but certainly I went through two other types in addition to my own. But the thing that I found really, really, an eye-opener were the subtypes. Can you tell us a bit about the subtypes?

Tom: People describe the subtypes differently. In fact, they also call it something else. In some Enneagram books, they'll call them instinctual subtypes, or the instincts. I can only give you my version of it, and mine is shaded by the use that I find with the material. Basically, what it's describing are preoccupations, sort of self-preoccupations that you can have within your central Enneagram style – how these are then expressed, and how these influence and shade your expression of your style, for example. And what they mean by subtypes is: they say there are three categories of subtypes, and people generally tend to favour one or two… over-favour maybe one in particular and under-favour a third one. They deal with three different realms of life. One of them has to do with 'self-preservation' and it means that on some level, a person will – no matter what their Enneagram style – be especially preoccupied with the material details of life: making money, food, survival, having a house, paying the bills, the details of life that preserve life and keep it going.

And there's a high side and a low side to each of these, in their broad aspects. The high side of being a self-preservation subtype would be that you really take care of business. You keep things running in your life and live a healthy life – maybe make money, or are prosperous in whatever way you define that, and continually attend to, and have a part of your consciousness preoccupied with maintaining the material side of life. What's true with all Enneagram styles is that there's a tendency, when you get caught in the pattern of them, to over-use your strength, to get into a defensive mode, and then the low side of an Enneagram style comes out. And it's the same with subtypes too. On the low side of self-preservation, somebody could be so focused on self-preservation that it's to their detriment in some way. In other words, making money and having a house and having food is all that you care about. In doing that, then it's like you're sacrificing your life in order to have your life. There's no art, there's no love, there's no spirituality, there's no broader context – there's just survival.

Eleonora: I have a little example. You just reminded me of a friend of mine who has three freezers – not just one… clearly she is a self-preservation subtype.

Tom: You can think of survivalism that way too, you know, on the low side of it. Also, there can be a paradoxical thing within this where somebody is so preoccupied with self-preservation that they maybe accumulate a lot of money and a lot of material security, and then they go bankrupt. Something like that, where they go in a kind of cycle. So it's just an over-emphasis.

And then the next subtype that the model describes is what they call 'intimate' subtype. They sometimes call it 'sexual' subtype. I'm not crazy about the word 'sexual' because it's misleading, at least in my experience. What the intimate subtype describes are people who specialise in one-to-one relationships. And in one-to-one relationships, they have a capacity for multilevel connections with their close friends, for instance, or with a partner, or a mate. Within that capacity, there's an ability to recognise the singularity of that other individual and be so closely connected to them sometimes that you could be out around the rings of Saturn, floating in space, and you wouldn't know it because you're just involved intensely and connected intensely.

Eleonora: [*laughing*] I 'm smiling because I recognise so much of this happening.

Tom: So yes, that's another sort of knack and also another style of attention and of motivation. Somebody who is motivated for material security in self-preservation terms might not be motivated by the same thing that an intimate subtype is motivated by. And on the low side of the intimate subtype then, it can mean that you put too much emphasis on relationships. You freight them up with expectations, or dependency, or what the other person does matters too much. Or the search for love, the quest for love, can be kind of…

Eleonora: …all-consuming.

Tom: Well, consuming and then it never quite 'happening'. You want it so badly you prevent it from happening.

And then the third distinction they make in subtypes is where there's someone who's predominantly a 'social' subtype. What that means is, when you close your eyes, when an intimate subtype closes their eyes they might see one person, or have a conversation with one person in their mind. When somebody with a social subtype orientation does that, there's a group and they are intentioned towards a group, conceiving of themselves in relation to a group, preoccupied with social causes in some ways – a feeling on the high side of life that your personal welfare is connected to group welfare. It's like the Buddhist saying about 'no one can be enlightened until everyone is enlightened'. And the identification with the group is quite strong and voluntary. I'm a social person, I'm a social entity and I exist within this broader context, and the welfare of the broader context is important to me. If somebody is more caught in the low side of that kind of orientation, then they're prone to have conflicts between personal freedom and community – individuation versus what the group wants: what my true standards [are], who I really am in my heart of hearts, versus how I am perceived in a group context according to some values and norms that are external to me. And so you can get lost then. I mean, on the low side, you could join a cult or something like that, where you're caught up in a group context that takes you away from yourself, but is comforting on some level, or matches your expectations of who you are and what the world expects of you. Also you could go back and forth about the group. You could be a partial joiner and partially pull back from it. You could exist on the fringes of the group, on the edge of the group, and kind of enjoy the group energy. The group could see you a certain way, and then you could over-identify with how they see you. Things like that.

Eleonora: That doesn't sound very freeing.

Tom: Each one of these has a high side and low side, basically.

Eleonora: Would you say that these particular subtypes are actually learnt, or is it something that somehow we come into the world with, just like our own type? Or is it a preference that we come into the world with and then nature and nurture do their work?

Tom: Personally, I don't think you're born with an Enneagram style. It's just my opinion, but I think that nature and nurture aren't really separate. They need each other. You're born, certainly, with a temperament and a predisposition and it probably predisposes you to several Enneagram styles, but not all of them.

Eleonora: I see.

Tom: And then, based on what happens to you, you may at some point unconsciously form an adoptive style. In terms of the subtypes, I find those a lot easier to track back into someone's experience of their personal biography. Quite a bit easier. And it's helpful for people to understand because part of what you're putting your finger on is 'What are the defensive stances that I took on early in life? What are preoccupations I developed based on the pressures around me, or based on what kept happening to me, that I unconsciously then thought, well, I better keep paying attention to this? It's especially important. This is where my salvation is, in some way this is where my defensive safety is'.

Eleonora: Or the strategies that I may have developed... to make life more comfortable.

Tom: To make life more comfortable, or just maybe live in that family where there's all that pressure to succeed, or some other family where there are other pressures. Or maybe you were singled out for a certain kind of treatment. Whatever keeps happening to you, when you're young, is what you then start to do to yourself. So, in this case, it would be getting preoccupied, sometimes unconsciously, preoccupied with one of these three subtypes. And then, like I say, there're really twenty-seven of them – that's nine Enneagram styles and three subtypes for each one. And they come out really differently, in different styles, and they shade the expression of the style – such as people in England from the south versus the north, that kind of thing.

Eleonora: So in relationships, is there a way that perhaps the [subtype] stacking order might work better with your partner, or with your family, or in a work situation?

Tom: Well, one of the questions that come up with the Enneagram is, "I'm a Four, what would be the best type for me to marry?" And the answer is: a healthy type, and one that loves you. Part of what that means is the Enneagram can really describe what the interactions will be if you're a Four and somebody else is a Seven or an Eight. It can describe beautifully, and with great insight and depth, what it'll be like when it goes well, and what it'll be like when it goes wrong. And it's pretty much the same with the subtypes. It's more about using it for insight into whatever's going on, but there's not really exactly a recommendation.

Eleonora: I wasn't thinking about recommendations. I was thinking more in terms of creating distinctions to recognise where my subtype is, perhaps, in opposition to my partner's, my husband's, my friend's subtype. So that instead of going against the other subtype, I might actually have an understanding: 'Oh, I see, it's very important to you to have such, and such, and such...' if you're a self-preservationist. My self-preservation is at the bottom of the stack.

Tom: Right.

Eleonora: It would mean absolutely nothing [to me], but that's where the conflict arises. For some person it's important, for the other person it's absolutely meaningless.

Tom: Well, what's interesting, in the context of the Enneagram, a lot of times subtypes are more salient in close relationships, and more meaningful and influential than differences in core Enneagram styles. It can really matter.

Eleonora: Can you say more about that?

Tom: If somebody is, for example, very preoccupied with self-preservation, and somebody else is very preoccupied with the intimate one-to-one connections, if they don't find a bridge, then those two things will be the things they argue about over and over again. If you've ever been in a long-term relationship, you notice there's a certain repetition to some of the things you wrangle about. And the subtypes explain it beautifully.

Eleonora: I certainly saw my sticky points when I was married – being a one-to-one, married to somebody who's mostly self-preservation... definitely there were areas where we just couldn't meet at all. It was painful, really, and then when you realise 'Oh my goodness, is that all it was?' — the simple recognition that 'You have this particular kind of preference, and if I come towards you [in your preference], then there's no problem any more'...

Tom: Yeah, you find you're operating out of different values, even though you don't think you are. And sometimes there're ways to bridge that, or sometimes there're ways to bring that out in yourself, or in the other person. It depends on what else is [going on] in the relationship and how much you want to stay together, and things like that. The other thing to note about subtypes is that they're sometimes contextual. Sometimes you'll go through phases in your life where you are occupying one subtype, or reacting out of one subtype much more strongly than you might in general, or in a long-term sort of way, or maybe that you already have been reacting from. Most people's experience of the subtypes is that they're characterological. But somebody could be very self-preservation oriented and then fall in love. And until the chemicals wear off, they'll be reacting much more out of their intimate subtype. Or somebody else could go into a social context of some kind – join the Army or something. Suddenly they're in a group of people where, if they'd been a shy computer hacker before, well, the social instinct part of it, the social reaction's going to come out and be expressed in a way that the Enneagram accounts for rather nicely.

Eleonora: Would you say that, once we become more aware, we somehow shift or change in our subtypes as well, or create perhaps more of a balanced [personality]?

Tom: Well, people will look for that sometimes, but a lot of it depends on the individual and what they're going through and what they need, and what they want, what they're motivated to have for themselves. One way to look at it sometimes is 'I'm really strong in intimate subtype and I'm kind of weak in self-preservation; maybe I ought to educate myself' — generally speaking, working with subtypes like the Enneagram, or, if you broaden it, to living a life where you grow and change and evolve – they're getting over illusions, going past limitations, and going past blocks and stuck points. And then, on the other hand, there's also taking responsibility for gaps in your education. Learning about whatever you're missing sometimes becomes a helpful thing, if it's quite conscious and deliberate.

Eleonora: Let's see. I've made a few notes here. Yes, cultural influences. I'm beginning to see more and more how much these play into our lives. I was just wondering if you wanted to say something about it.

Tom: Well, like I said before, there are Enneagrammatic strains and influences running through different cultures. It's not something I try to define too tightly, because you get into cliché and stereotype country pretty fast. I do actually make an analogy between Enneagram styles and nationalities.

Eleonora: Yes, I liked that, because I thought it was very graphic and very descriptive.

Tom: It's like saying an Enneagram style is your psychological nationality, and, when you encounter people, or know people, not within your Enneagram style, it's not unlike the difference in nationalities because an Enneagram style is deeply unconscious. It influences and shades a lot of your perceptions, and at the same time it's ultimately not the only thing you are. It's ultimately not who you are in your heart of hearts. Yet it could be very meaningful, and it's also not something that you grow out of, or evolve out of. What it is, is something that you can wear more and more lightly, if you're an expatriate, for instance. And I think that's a parallel with the Enneagram as well. As people grow and change, the low side of their style, the kind of rigidity and repetitiveness of the pattern... it's defensive. If you work on it, you drain the defences of their intensity. You still have an inclination to think a certain way and not another way, of course, but you wear it much more lightly. The more lightly you wear it, the more open you are to the world around you, and also the more available the talents and the high-side capacities and typical resources that go with your style, are. Those are available to you much more.

Eleonora: What comes to mind also is more openness of the heart. We've been describing the model and we haven't really spoken about the heart: the falling in love, the love and appreciation that we have for friends and co-workers. I imagine, in terms of my own experience, the more I wear my type lightly, the more open I become... as the defences of my particular type [lessen].

Tom: You know, we also have fewer shadows too. Which is to say, there are fewer instances where you react negatively to somebody else in an automatic button-pushing sort of way: 'Ah, that person pushes my buttons'. I go to

Enneagram conferences, and I've been to a number of them in America, and one of the things you sometimes hear as you're walking through a crowd is somebody talking about the styles that they like and dislike. "Everybody loves Sevens. But I don't like Twos, you know, I always want to keep them at arm's length, and they're coming up to my elbow." That kind of thing. And the person is talking about different Enneagram styles in a way I actually term 'educated bigotry' because you're taking a part and judging it and mistaking it for the whole. But also, when a person talks that way, what they're really saying is 'I have those styles in myself, latently perhaps. I like my own Sevenness and I don't like my own Twoness, and I haven't made peace with it and I haven't integrated it'. They're talking about their own shadows – both white shadows and dark shadows.

Eleonora: Yes. That's a danger that I've certainly found when I first learnt about the Enneagram. There was a tendency to pigeonhole people instead of actually creating more freedom and more liberation around one's own façade and perhaps develop more compassion and more acceptance. There was a narrowing down of people and labelling. So quickly... and dismissing so quickly, which I then felt...

Tom: Well, if you label it and then dismiss it... There's a cartoon I saw years ago which showed a man in hell. He was shovelling coal into a wheelbarrow, and the flames of hell were in the background. He was whistling, whistling a happy tune while he was shovelling coal to fuel the fires of hell. And a couple of devils are standing there with their pitchforks, and one says to the other 'You know, we're just not reaching this guy'. If you use the Enneagram to label, and then to dismiss, or to decide who you like and who you dislike, it's just not reaching...

Eleonora: It's not what the system was designed to do, really.

Tom: No. And furthermore, that can be tied to desire for control, desire for a way of pushing away the implications of what it might be telling you because this is not for sissies... the good news and bad news part of it. You know, when you identify your central style sometimes, it can be a shock and there's a gruesome aspect to it, as well as the good news.

Eleonora: Yes. When it comes to conflict – I'm thinking in terms of one-to-one relationships, or in families – how can knowing the Enneagram help in conflict resolution?

Tom: Well, it's saved a lot of marriages, I figure the Enneagram has. And where it really does that is in situations where people are basically bonded and have a strong affectionate feeling for one another, but then there're aspects of each other's behaviours that drive them crazy. A lot of times, learning about the other person's Enneagram style and realising that that person's crazy-making behaviour (a) is not personal to you, and (b) is somehow attached to their view of the world, and a kind of trance that they're in – what they then believe is necessary to do in order to manage, and cope with, and live in that view of the world… it helps a lot, it really helps a lot.

You know, there's a broad answer to that question, which is that it makes you more compassionate – or can, if you'll allow it to. You might have Enneagram styles that you don't relate to at all, that you don't have any connection to, and that just baffle you. Say, you're from France, but you're damned if you understand people from Malaysia.

Eleonora: [*laughing*]

Tom: That kind of thing. But gradually, as you work with it for a while, it helps quite a bit. It helps at least just to remind you that there are vastly different worldviews and that other people are not just doing what they're doing to get to you.

Eleonora: Right.

Tom: That's a good point. It gets harder to answer that question until you consider the individuals involved and what their individual styles are, and also subtypes will influence as well. But generally speaking, it works pretty well for building bridges. Also, there are some things to measure, like in a marriage for example: 'What is your rate of change, versus the other person's rate of change?' 'How well do you assimilate new information and get over old limitations?' 'How motivated are you to do it?' And within the context of a relationship, there is a way in which you rub up against each other a lot – perhaps literally but also figuratively – and, if you're both attempting to stay connected and go towards one another, you tend to eliminate little things that are in the way.

And the Enneagram really helps with that, sort of catching yourself in the act and seeing how you're maybe putting some barrier in the way in the present that used to be a necessary and effective thing. Now it's just something that gets in the way, to protect you from things that happened in the past. As you do that, there's also the fact that in the studies of long-term relationships, where the two partners pronounce themselves satisfied, a lot of times they'll say they focus more on what they can give, rather than what they can receive. And they're not doing so much bookkeeping: 'Okay, what did she give me vs what did I give her?' There's more generosity and an emphasis on giving, and you get a lot more back.

Also, they have noticed, in those studies, that people tend to say that they see the other person in a positive light – almost no matter what. But they're realistically aware of the other person's limitations. It's like the truth plus ten percent, or something.

Eleonora: Could I ask you, in your relationship – I don't know if you've been married just the once, or more than once – has your understanding of the Enneagram made you perhaps a better husband, or a better father, or maybe none of the above?

Tom: I've wanted to be a good husband. And I don't know. I would say that it's all of the things I just said, being able to change places with the other person. One of the things it helps you do is anticipate what a person's response will be and in doing that, in anticipating, it's far easier to not only deal with the response, but also not take it personally. You sort of know where they're coming from.

Eleonora: I think not taking it personally is quite a thing to bear in mind.

Tom: Yes, it's lovely. That part of it is really nice and then, the more you learn about your own style and your own patterns as well, you take those less personally too: 'Okay, we're caught up in a kind of shadow place this afternoon and we'll work it out'.

Eleonora: I've interviewed a couple of other people about relationships, but coming from the spiritual side of relationships. So in other words, there are not two personalities that are interacting here, there is something that is beyond the personality. And yes, we're not taking the personalities to be one thing and spirituality as being two separate things – we're all one Being expressed as each person. But we've been talking about the Enneagram, coming from the perspective of the personality. In your work, do you also include what is not-the-personality?

Tom: I don't define it very tightly. And I'm not really comfortable with a lot of the spiritual language, because it's...

Eleonora: Tell me why not.

Tom: Because of my training in hypnosis.

Eleonora: Say more about that. What does that mean?

Tom: Well, what it means is that you are trained in hypnosis to talk to people in a way that sounds specific, but is actually really general. And you're trained to use a certain kind of language that is abstract and noun-based. It's what writers call the passive voice, what editors call the passive voice that they're trying to cure writers of all the time. Hypnotists do this on purpose. So they speak in an abstract way that's nevertheless structured. I can speak to a large crowd of people, and speak in this sort of process-oriented way, using this language, and everyone in the room thinks I'm speaking to them [individually].

Eleonora: Right.

Tom: And that's the method. Unfortunately, then, what also happens... you actually don't know the meaning of certain words after a while, because they're open-ended and you're very aware of people making their own meanings. And there's a lot of spiritual literature that is written exactly this way. When I look at it, I see not only the language of trance, but also the sequences and some of the methods and so on. I think I'm like somebody who's been trained as a magician, to do magic tricks, who then sees somebody doing something and who claims it's paranormal, but I can see the trickery in it.

Eleonora: I see...

Tom: I think it's like that. But anyway, that's one reason I don't talk that way, because I don't know what the words mean exactly. Also, I don't tend to chunk in big abstract terms. Most of the work that I've done, and most of what I pay attention to and emphasise and value, I guess, is experiential. So I'm more after the experience of it without nailing it down too tightly and without describing it in a way that for me is only abstract.

Eleonora: So, if you were to advise people... you said earlier, "Find somebody that loves you and..." what else did you say?

Tom: Marry a healthy type and one that loves you.

Eleonora: Right. Well, that might be possible and it might not be possible. But anyway, given what society is today and given where marriages are today, where we have far more divorces than we did fifty years ago, what words of advice could you give us?

Tom: Don't listen to me.

Eleonora: [*laughing*]

Tom: That'd be first. And... I don't know. We're talking about types. But everybody's an individual and so it's really hard to generalise. It depends on what you want. It depends on what you're ready for. It depends on the phase you're at in your life and what would mean the most to you. But if you meet somebody that you have a strong connection with, and you want to stay together with them, a lot of these things that we've talked about can be useful considerations, really useful things to learn about and to apply and just absorb into your knowledge base, but also use to modify your reactions, for example.

And the other thing that is really salient in relationships is how much you work on yourself, because you can get locked into wanting the other person to change, or just reacting to them out of your own torment. And I've certainly done that. At the same time, what's really needed is somehow more self-to-self, rather than self-to-other. You've got to come to terms with your own shadows in some way, or put some fears that you have at rest, or be willing to go beyond certain limitations. Be willing to be ten percent braver some of the time, with whatever you define and experience as a risk for you.

And then, there'll oftentimes be a dynamic in relationships where a couple will take two different polarised positions and then when one of them changes, the roles reverse. Somebody who's critical, for instance, following the other person around criticising their behaviour, maybe they work on that and they mellow out. And then the other person starts to become critical because now they've got a chance, now there's room for that in the vacuum that the other's change had left. So there're dynamics like that, but generally speaking, I think in relationships you're working on relating to and reaching out to one another, but you're also dealing to some degree with your own shadows and your own barriers to being able to reach out to one another. That's good work. In an odd way, that's part of being together.

Eleonora: Yes. So we owe it to ourselves and to the other.

Tom: Well, I don't know about 'owing' it. It depends on what you want. If having a deepening and more interesting connection to somebody is part of your definition of a good life, then it's worth it. People change when it costs more to stay the same than it costs to change.

Eleonora: Absolutely.

Tom: Like a cost-benefit analysis, to use a gross materialistic metaphor.

Eleonora: Tom, it's been lovely speaking with you and exploring this. I'm just going to show your *Dynamic Enneagram*, which will be available in the summer of twenty-fourteen. Thank you, Tom, for joining me.

To watch this interview please go to:
http://www.conscious.tv/consciousness/enneagram

Helen Palmer
Relationships matter:
The Enneagram tells us how

Interview by Eleonora Gilbert

Eleonora: Helen is an international best-selling Enneagram author and teacher of psychology and intuition. She is the author of two best-sellers: *The Enneagram: Understanding Yourself and the Others in Your Life*, and *The Enneagram in Love and Work: Understanding your Intimate and Business Relationships*. We have *The Pocket Enneagram* – I used this a long time ago – and *The Enneagram Advantage*. Also a lovely book, *Inner Knowing*. You've edited this book and put together a number of essays by renowned psychologists and writers. It's a really neat book...

Helen: That one is my favourite...

Eleonora: Is it? Oh right! I can see it becoming my favourite too. Helen is the co-founder with Dr David Daniels of the Enneagram Professional Training Program offered by Enneagram Worldwide. You've been in this business, if we can call it a business, for over thirty years.

Helen: Yes.

Eleonora: You're currently teaching one programme a month, and you've also been involved in the writing project on *The Diagram as an Eternal Guide to Spiritual Evolution*. You co-chaired in nineteen-ninety-four the first International Enneagram Conference, held at Stanford University with Dr Daniels, and are the founding director of the International Enneagram Association. There is plenty more that I could say about you, but I think we'll leave it at that.

I've done, in the past, a number of interviews based on relationship and consciousness and being more present to what is real. We talked earlier about the importance of relationships and how 'there are no boundaries'. You travel all over the world and you seem to be encountering similar kinds of problems across various different cultures. Would you like to say a little bit about that?

Helen: Well, we have Worldwide, which is the house of our professional training. People come to our country and train with us and then go back to their own country. This has been going on for over thirty years so there's quite a proliferation of the material. What I notice about it is the marked tendency when the Enneagram first comes into a country, such as mainland China, or South Africa, or several countries in South America, the recapitulation of the problem that we had in the United States when the first books came out. My first one, *The Enneagram*, came out in nineteen-eight-eight, which is over twenty-five years ago, and the impact that it made was *tremendous* at the beginning. People were so anxious to know their own type and how they could better interact with other people of different types. And again the spiritual material got quite downtrodden, I thought. At the beginning when material that is suitable for a certain level of consciousness comes out, which is that you're ready to work on change, and this is not a universal theme: 'Someone else in the relationship should change, not *me*. If *you* would change, I'd feel a whole lot better'. So we go to work to change the *other guy* instead of being able to witness these pattern-like ways in which we inhabit a relationship. We're oblivious, until attention turns inward and you begin to reflect, or begin to recognise your own situation and what *you* bring to a relationship – because you can certainly change that, but not affect the other in the direct way of expecting them to be able to witness themselves. So when the books first came out there was this higher order of consciousness – nothing invented by us, but being renewed. The Enneagram is a renewal of a very old teaching and the timing is beautiful because the world is in such conflict.

Eleonora: Yes it is.

Helen: And we see that within ourselves, the conflicts, choices we have to make between work and love and relationship and being a success... things that the previous generation never had to face, really. And many interactions in the world [are] dreadful. Collisions of cultures, different levels of culture, and they don't understand each other. So when the first books came out in eighty-eight, they had an immediate impact because of the promise that they held: that we have a map that can guide you into self-reflection to understand your own idiosyncrasies, your own pattern-like way of sorting information, and that it is vastly different from somebody you might be relating to, or the culture that you're in. You may be vastly different than the surrounding environment. So the material started to degenerate almost immediately. And I hate to say that, but it really started to take a dive, almost immediately, into a kind of pop-psychology cocktail party: "Well it says here that you look like…. and your appearance is such that your outer behaviour is such that I think you're a type… certain type." And that was very hard for those of us that were involved in this. It was very hard for us to witness, and inevitable.

Eleonora: Why do you say inevitable?

Helen: Because… in order to make itself available to survive in the reality of these conflicting different environments where the material landed: different socio-economic groups, different races, different religions… America, for its many difficulties, is one of the true melting pots. I think that's a significant contribution, but the cultures themselves don't accept these materials. You know… "Why are you so self-involved, looking at your type?" "Why aren't you productive out here in the workplace?" "Why aren't you more of a success?" "Why are you so inhibited this way?" That could be something that you could actually work with as material, psychological material which can be observed, and so you have a choice about being on automatic, or taking the choice of a more liberated view. Eventually it took hold, much to my delight, in the business community.

Eleonora: What sort of period [in your life] are we talking about here? You've been in the business for over thirty years…

Helen: Right. I was a teacher of psychology and intuition for years before I ever met the Enneagram. But intuition, which is the objective knowing unfiltered by type, by type structures, by this illusion of our identity – we have a capacity for clarity which can be trained. That's what spiritual material is about. It's about training to be able to not see through and sort through the identity, but be able to participate in *relaxing* our own identity so that we come to a truer ground inside of ourselves. So all of those filters of perception begin to relax and you begin to see the reality of what you're actually facing instead of the *subjective* reality that you previously saw.

Eleonora: Right.

Helen: That's how intuition can be trained. So the ten years prior, teaching psychology at university level and also having private classes in intuition training, when I met the Enneagram it was a godsend, because it put together the psychology of type and what the filters are by name. It named the filters for the normal and the high-functioning person, whereas where I came from way back when, anything to do with psychology was something about deep pathology. You wouldn't want to say for example that you were going to a therapist, especially in a working-class family at the time that I was teaching psychology, because it was pejorative. The Enneagram isn't pejorative, it's organised for people who are in evolution, who are trying to be able to work with themselves in a definite and helpful way.

So it talked about the psychology of type, or at least that's what I read into it – the structure of type – because that's what psychology is. It's a structure of understanding the thought patterns, the emotional patterns, and the somatic patterns that we call our identity. They vary according to the type of person that you are. But it also had the liberating effect of advising that we practise a simple breath observation practise. It implied this, when the Enneagram first came: that there is a place of silence inside of yourself that is always unfolding in the present moment, which is rapidly taken over by the patterns that move you from past to future, bypassing the present moment. So the aim was to be able to develop presence and single-pointed attention in the present moment which has, as we now discover, huge health benefits. The recent science, based on brain research, has done nothing but to strongly support the personal perceptions that we had but couldn't legitimise in any coherent way. We had no way to explain it, or to justify it, and you needed justification at the beginning.

Eleonora: You started talking earlier about the fact that the introduction of the Enneagram was taking off, but then somehow it kind of nosedived. Where are we now with that?

Helen: Well, it definitely hit bottom – at a certain point where it became the parlour game, and the 'I know your type better than you know yourself', and the arguments about what *your type* is. It was childish and trivial, but the best that we had. That lasted, I would say about ten years.

Eleonora: Right. And now? [2014]

Helen: Now, since it bottomed out so to speak, all of a sudden the differences among us [are acknowledged], partly because of the world situation… but it's imperative to understand that you are not seeing the same reality as somebody with whom you relate.

Eleonora: Yes. Very much so.

Helen: It's an amazing insight for most people, who assume that what they see is consensus. So the differences among us have become so apparent that people now talk about how they see the situation, and they expect to hear an alternative point of view from somebody who holds a different position.

Eleonora: Would you say – from understanding now the various different patterns and how we see the world from these particular patterns – that people actually get on better? Or do you find that it has not made that much difference? Not just in terms of relating, but also in terms of their own personal growth and moving from a particular perception of themselves to being something far greater…

Helen: The key word you used is *pattern*, because most people think 'Well, if I have an opinion', which is really a concept, 'if I have a fixed opinion about something, well, I could change that. I could understand your other opinion based on the differences between us'. But *pattern* is something else and it needs another perceptual sense. It needs an ability to turn attention inward and to be able to perceive the pattern-like way in which your mind sorts information. Now we're getting somewhere. Now we're getting into spiritual material because you begin to turn inward and reflect upon not just an opinion, which is an idea, a concept that's buried in some part of your pre-frontal, mechanical brain, but you begin to notice, when you turn attention inward, the pattern-like way in which your mind actually is structured – for example, someone who is rooted in an instinct to 'move away' from people… or if you are the type of person that is rooted in an instinct to 'move against' people, or to 'seek security' in making contact with people; now, these are inborn instinctual responses. Now, I'll make a very long story short, but those instinctual responses are buried in the back of your brain and they come out of the animal kingdom and they come out of evolution, and they haven't gone away. You cannot at the same time be seeking security by contact with people and also opposing them and, also moving away from them out of insecurity and fear. You can't be taking that movement all at the same time, but you have a first-tendency response. That's at birth. That's innate. So you don't come into the world new, you come into the world with a certain bias, which is neurologically wired.

So the first-tendency response is part of how you read the [Enneagram] diagram. There are three types that are 'instinct moving away' and fear-types, 'instinct moving against' that would be the anger-types' first-tendency response, and 'instinct moving toward'. Most people would say 'Well I have all three', because you do, but there is a strong proclivity to move in one direction rather than the other two. So with that neurological wiring, you interface with the environment in which you find yourself. Now, somewhere between nature at birth and nurture in the environment, a relationship forms and you learn to adapt, which is the technical word to have an adaptive strategy, to be able to interface successfully with whatever environment you have. We know this because adults report the environment and how they made their way so that they could be secure.

So the hub of relationship is this automatic response that we have. It's very important to know the type of person you are because it explains a whole lot about yourself, and it isn't better to be a 'seeking contact', or 'being against', or 'being away from'. It isn't better to be one or the other. It's the way we are.

Eleonora: Does that change over time, over our lifetime?

Helen: It depends on your circumstance because, as an adult I would say I am a lot more angry that I ever was as a youngster – as a fear-type. But you have those adaptations and I don't see any reason why they should go away.

Eleonora: I presume that these adaptations are in order to survive.

Helen: These are survival strategies. In the animal kingdom you see it very clearly: the animals that run away, the ones that stand against and go toward in an aggressive way, and the ones that seek contact in the herd or the pack or the group. Anyway that's the beginning of things; it's not the end of the story. But all this interface means that you have, as an individual, a pattern-like way of behaving that's on its own, automatic. Very hard to accept. This was one of the reasons why the Enneagram had to prove itself over time, because it's just very hard to accept that we are on automatic and that we don't have choices about what we do. You know ninety percent of our behaviour is subcortical. We don't know about it until we go looking, and there is this ability that we have as humans – it dignifies us from the animal kingdom – this capacity to internally reflect upon the patterns that drive us. Then, choice begins to open, and it's a great relief if people even get that far: 'I have something to say about this... I can change'.

Eleonora: I'm trying to connect various different things based upon what you have just said. Earlier we talked about also the 'witnessing consciousness'. Can you say more about that?

Helen: Self-reflection is identical to witnessing consciousness. In the Christian sector it's called witnessing consciousness. In the Vedanta it's called self-reflection. It could be called the inner observer. The word 'observer' is confused with 'I look in a mirror and that's what I observe out here'. The adaptation that you have is to turn attention inward and actually begin to reflect upon your thinking. It's not just *what* you think, like the conclusion you come to, but there is a pattern-like way which a brain sorts billions of bits of data. It supports by focusing attention on a certain sector of reality that was your survival when you were young. Now, we were speaking earlier, and you said you would be a Type Three, you were inclined to that direction, and I'm a Six. So, the way that your mind focuses is toward success and accomplishment and connection with people that can be earned by that. Mine, on the other hand [*laughing*], is to move back, step back from contact and evaluate, to think. So we operate from very different centres of...

Eleonora: We come from different places completely; we see the world differently.

Helen: We come from different places. One is in the head and the other in the heart, and it isn't that we don't enjoy or understand each other, it's just that at the beginning you would assume that I was dealing with the same patterns that you were dealing with and was interested in the same thrust, you see. So it's that assumption, especially in interpersonal relationships, because of appearance, because of education, because of the language that you speak, because of so many factors, we somehow think that everybody is doing the same thing here.

Eleonora: However, that ability of witnessing consciousness somehow puts a stop to that automaticity of projecting onto the other my worldview.

Helen: Yes, the assumption that we have... [*laughing*] I mean, we insult people on a daily basis without realising it on the assumption that we have that they ought to enjoy this: 'Let's have a very deep talk about what we think about things'. The Six would say this is intimacy to us, and it can be really off-putting to many other types. But we don't know that. So, the interpersonal level depends on being able to observe oneself, and that is not selfish because with self-observation comes a huge amount of insight into the situation that we face. Self-reflection means to turn attention inward and to be able to notice the patterns of thought that arise in you and to notice what the focus of attention might be, that all of these thoughts, emotions, sensations are dedicated to. The focus of attention means that you… metaphysically, you attach a point of concentration on something. This naturally organises the field of all those billion bits of data into what is coherent to you. You will be reading a different kind of information out of the same room that I will be reading.

My thing would be 'Okay, now where is the difficulty here and what must I do to counteract this?' That would be the naïve Six view, and for the naïve Three it would be 'What is positive here and how can I exaggerate and bring that forward so everybody can participate in it?' You are moving toward contact and I am not. But each of these is an intact worldview, and each from its own position is correct. It's a truth.

Eleonora: Yes, it can't be otherwise, because this is my experience. And that is your experience…

Helen: [*agreeing*] … and it's true for me *subjectively*. It's true, but only partially. So all of these partial truths, if you begin to reflect internally, you begin to realise that 'Well, there are some things that I could change here. I might have a choice actually. I am not an automaton that is on automatic, I can witness these things. I can witness the structures of my own neurological pathways'. Now isn't that something? Because the emphasis that I have put, at least on the Enneagram, has been the witnessing of the patterns rather than separating from the patterns, and emphasising the other necessary factor, which is: *to be in the present moment without any patterns*. That is the practise of presence.

Eleonora: Yes, and that is the difficulty.

Helen: It is the absence of patterns that is emphasised particularly in the traditions of Zazen and Vipassana, which is taking the United States, at least, by storm. This is very helpful and necessary, and now we have evidence-based research which is fundamental to supporting this whole enterprise of having a choice. The enterprise of having a choice is what we are all about here, because then we can participate in raising our level of consciousness.

Eleonora: When you say 'choice', first of all there needs to be a certain degree of self-awareness of the particular pattern and acknowledging that there *is* a pattern, that there *is* a difference between us… so say more about the choice.

Helen: Yes. Well, it's the fundamental proposition of the whole thing, that we humans have a role in evolution. That our consciousness can evolve and we can participate in raising the level of consciousness within our self. That is the proposition. That is mysticism, which is at the core of every world religion, is the mystical component of the fact that we have a definitive role in an evolutionary spectrum, but it's not out here [*hands at arms-length*].

Eleonora: [*laughing*] That's right.

Helen: [*laughing*] It's not out here. I can't change anything. I can't change anyone in a relationship no matter how dear they are to me. I can't change them!

Eleonora: Absolutely!

Helen: But I can have a part, a choice about how I manage myself in a relationship, so that I can perhaps influence them, by changing myself. There is enormous power and importance in the one who goes first. The one who goes first is mighty, because it requires self-change in the absence of any feedback whatsoever that it's going to be beneficial, and you don't want to lose the relationship because you are so attached to it, so it sets up a huge amount of tension. The idea [is] of moving into oneself and *relaxing* the patterns that drive us, especially getting to the point of self-witnessing, or the self-reflection where you can notice the internal cues and signs of the body, the emotions, and the conditioned mental patterns. So, I've emphasised that because I have to put out that many people have described and discovered their type out of a book, no previous experience: 'Oh that's me' by process of elimination, 'I don't do this, I don't do that' process of elimination, 'all right this is it!'

Eleonora: And then buy it, and believe it.

Helen: Because it's true, but only partially. There are eight other versions of the truth, but the ninth is me. So, the fact that they could recognise out of a book descriptions what is going on internally to themselves means that they have an awake self-reflective capacity, or they would not have been able to accomplish that feat. That's very heartening to me. So I would say what got us off the bottom of the deterioration in the first phase was [that] enough people were saying, "No, don't tell me what I am. I'm certain. You are looking at my appearance, you are not seeing how I am organised inside because I have gone looking."

And then it becomes almost miraculous the amount of choice you can make. Whether or not you do it... is your own free will. Many people stop right there. In the business community the Enneagram is so strong with the executive coaching, with team building. Properly handled it's like 'Oh my gosh I've managed you so incorrectly, I'm sorry'. The Three might be bobbing and weaving, changing position to whatever works, always with an eye on the goal, but the process of how to get to the goal changes. Well, tell that to a Type One who already has a fixed goal that they are moving towards, step by step, in a very precise way. They simply don't understand each other: 'You are bobbing and weaving and I don't understand what you want – would you tell me?' And from the other side it's like 'Well, why do you stick in the old when we are on to the new?' Now, those are just team-building techniques and they are marvellously important.

Eleonora: So when people see that in a work situation, then what happens?

Helen: Well, it's not exactly my area, but I certainly have trained a lot of business people in the Enneagram, and what happens is, depending on how it's handled, it can be phrased as an asset: "You have a great skills set," for example, "but I don't know why you just dig in, Mrs One, when I start to change the agenda," the Three might say.

The One would say, "I dig in because you've changed your mind. Obviously you're not in charge of things." You see? So once explained, then when the 'dig in' comes for the One, they can recognise 'All right. I can stay inside. I can be present. I can watch what happens. Is this effective or not?' without jumping to a premature future conclusion. And on the other side, the Three might say, "Well, when you dig in like that, I feel I'm doing something wrong and I want to get you back again. I want to get back into connection with you, emotional connection with you." [*turning away from imagined One*] 'I will just come in and be present and restrain myself and go about and see if my idea works... [*noticing imagined One*] Oh, they came along'. It can be used in a very strategic way, but all of that is on the horizontal plane of daily living. It is not a spiritual moment.

Eleonora: Absolutely. That's what I wanted to ask you next, because when it comes to business I think the focus is certainly not about transformation. Not in a business sense.

Helen: And it should not properly be there.

Eleonora: So here we are in a business situation, let's say, and the individual actually recognises the difference between 'myself' and my other co-workers. Does it stop there? Or do you find that there is...?

Helen: I would be congratulatory. I would say, "Now that we've found out that when I look like I'm moving too quickly and changing my mind and you feel 'dug in', you can turn your attention inward and find a point inside of yourself where you're relaxed. That's huge. We both have to take the same medicine. Nobody's right here, because each view is correct from a certain subjective viewpoint. Nobody's wrong here, but if when we feel this rising concern... if we could both just take a pause, come inside ourselves..." I mean, it is so uncustomary for anyone to centre themselves in a business setting. And I'm all for the introduction now into the business community – still horizontal plane, nothing deep, spiritual at all, but for basic attention practises, to shift your state of consciousness so that you're not going into a premature judgement of the conclusion, which would have happened if you hadn't introduced the pause. So staging it in that way, we're almost there in the business community, but 'change your state of mind'? This is just bizarre until it's introduced in the proper business language, which I don't actually have.

Eleonora: Right.

Helen: But it's the same principle that would happen in a spiritual direction session: "My relationship is in such difficulty, and this is how I feel inside." Well, you don't have to have those feelings right now. Those feelings are quite appropriate that you have, it's the adaptation that you are. That is your identity. It's quite appropriate, but if you really want to work on this relationship and take it to another level of experience, then those patterns of reactivity – moving away from, moving against, moving toward – they have to quiet down. And method: same method as in the business setting, but methods for bringing your attention inward and relaxing into a *pause*. Now, what guides this moving from patterns (head, heart, and somatic), into even a temporary silence, is restorative. You come to your senses because those automatic patterns are strategic for survival. In relationship, you're trying to be open to whatever is presented. You don't want to be on survival, defending. You want to be receptive to reality as it actually is occurring between two people.

Eleonora: If I were to look at my experience… for instance, when we talk about being in relationship with another, what is actually in relationship is the pattern, and what I find really hopeful is the possibility of not doing that. The possibility of really recognising that the divinity within each one of us is actually the divinity that we share, rather than focusing on what obfuscates what's truly real about us.

Helen: I would be careful of the language.

Eleonora: Okay.

Helen: It's very accurate what you say. I would be careful of the language. As soon as you bring divinity into it, though it's true, it is not true for everyone specifically in that language. I'm not chiding you in any way because I run into this all the time. The vocabulary that you can use, speaking to spiritual directors, is different than the marketplace. It's different than you can use with your beloved because the implication through [saying] the *divine within us* is somehow 'Well, you listen to my grievance first, and then we'll worry about what's the divine here'.

Eleonora: [*laughing*]

Helen: It's just the strategy, and this is I think the marvel of the programmes that you're running here is that you're getting people coming out of an old language base and finding the proper language-vocabulary for, because an individual couple is going to have their own vocabulary for this, you see? They need to be instructed about this. It's like 'How could I get the message across to you?'… And sometimes the wife or the husband might say, "I just need to say stop, I'll come back to you in twenty minutes." Another partner might say, "I need to settle it right now." Another partner would say, "I need to find where I feel so nervous about this thing. I need to just get my nerves under management." You see it's very important to tailor the vocabulary to the couple that wants to really evolve. Now the other thing is, nobody is really aware that it's one big reality out here. They're on the horizontal plane, so the language of the Enneagram... I think one of the marvels is that with the right vocabulary you can reach almost anybody with this. It's for everyone.

Eleonora: Yes.

Helen: And on a global basis [*laughing*] it's incredible. You work with a translator and you have a group of let's say Type Sevens under interview. Chinese Sevens, and you have something in your ear which is translating the Mandarin, or the Cantonese, and you're coming to some sort of conclusion about what they're saying, and then you pass the question to the translator who gives it to the audience in general. It's like three languages going on: Chinese, American, Enneagram. It's like three languages and they say the same things that I am absolutely primed to answer because it's a universal template for change. I just adore the whole enterprise.

Eleonora: That's what I find so amazing... that the Enneagram goes across cultures as well.

Helen: Oh, no doubt! But the language now is to reflect upon yourself and your part in this. That's the first shift of attention, to internalise and begin to realise 'Yes, my attention is going to all the defects here. I notice that. I notice the absence of positives... but I'm very good on seeing the negatives', for example. Or 'I see all of the loss and the abandonment'. Meanwhile, the partner is just trying to have a conversation about their point of view. They're not abandoning anybody, but it seems that way from Type Four perspective. It seems that way and it's true from that *subjective* perspective. To be able, for each of the partners, to know their Enneagram type is a huge advantage.

The second thing is to share the willingness to go inside and get empty because the spiritual evolution and the evolution of the couple had a lot to do with being able to withdraw, to relax into silence where this is no past or future, there's just now, and to extend that present-time awareness. Then you realise you're looking at a different reality. The whole view changes and the first things that you see are the tension and the urgency and commitment in someone else. However wrongheaded it might seem to your ego structure, to your identity, they're trying very hard to have a relationship with you. You see their suffering and you realise you're holding up your end to keep it going – that suffering. So it's most important at the beginning for each of the couples to know their type, because that explains a lot: "Oh, I thought when you said that, this is what you meant and here I find out you had a totally different point of view."

Eleonora: It creates space.

Helen: Yes, well said, it creates space. And the space, when you come inside yourself and you turn inward, means that you have to have some pause practise going on to be able to receive the other and remember 'Oh, this is the man that I love. Oh! And I'm agitated inside. That's me'. And in agitation, whether you know it or not, those survival patterns will engage and everything goes into a misunderstanding. The change is: change your *state*, your internal state of mind into *silence*. And from the silence you can watch these patterns, and you keep coming back to the silence. You let the patterns go... and then you realise that you can watch for the outcome of things, and your timing improves, and your ability to notice something when the right time to say it comes up... you're useful!

Eleonora: Yes. This is a lifelong practise.

Helen: When the investment is big, like a relationship, it can go quite swiftly. But you're quite right, it goes in levels, and there is divinity at the end of it.

Eleonora: When we talk about the practise for instance of the witnessing consciousness, would you also recommend that taking time out – for meditation for instance – would strengthen that part of ourselves?

Helen: Yes, it's essential. It's essential, but not to make a big deal of it because once you know your type... this is why I value the system, because it's like a roadmap. You're not in there just looking: 'Well, I'm tense... no, I'm not tense'. You're looking and... The One is looking – and their focus of attention is criticality. The Two is looking – and their focus of attention is on other people's needs. The Nine is looking at everyone else's agenda and losing their own.

The focus of attention is what drives the sorting system of brain so that, if you know that focus of attention, you know the way you're wired. You have a very good little codebook so that you're not going in just in general 'Oh I need to get away, and relax', which is the way the general public assumes it would be like. No, you don't need an alternative life. You need to know the patterns, the focus of attention, and you need to recognise through witnessing consciousness, which is a stage of development, but it is the witnessing consciousness that can go all of the distance to freedom.

Eleonora: We talked earlier… that you do see the Enneagram as a path, as a spiritual path.

Helen: I do.

Eleonora: It was [for me] up to a point... again, speaking from my own experience, there was a lot of talk, about fifteen years ago when I first became involved, that the Enneagram was a spiritual path, but I didn't find it that way because I felt it was somewhat finite. Somehow it didn't offer beyond the recognition of the patterns. But how I hear you now...

Helen: Well, you got to start somewhere... and I'm pretty responsible for that.

We had to start with the types because without the type recognition you don't have the capacity to realise that you can also witness.

Eleonora: Yes, of course.

Helen: Now, I would say that this is an approach that I take where self-reflection, the reflection on the patterns, doesn't stop there. It means that you can recognise and relax the patterns that you have, more or less on the spot. Rather than awakening five days later, two hours later and realise 'Oh, I did it again'.

Now, what this does strategically, inside, is to relax lower-order prefrontal patterns, neurological patterns, and limbic patterns – emotional patterns that are wired together. It's like a loop tape. You have an emotion, you have the corresponding thought. If you have the thought, you have the corresponding emotion. They're quite tied together as a reaction. You can actually change those reactions by introducing a pure level of consciousness that never gets conditioned. And this can be called variously according to your culture: the 'inner witness', the 'reflection of the self', the 'inner observer'... You call it what you like, those are just simple words that describe the ability to recognise when you're going on automatic. There's a huge amount of energy and life-force called '*the vice*' actually, or the passion of the heart, in the Enneagram, which is now going to engage and recreate itself, pattern-like; though it might be totally inappropriate to the present, it is historically the way we are wired to relate to things.

All of that energy can be relaxed in the present moment, which brings your attention to a spiritual level of consciousness where you are more objective in being able to see reality as it's actually taking place. That is called intuition. It is a recognition, it's not thoughts, because you're in the present moment and extended in silence. It is a recognition of the reality that you actually face, as in a relationship when all of a sudden you relax your 'I want my say'. You relax that and you begin to get into silence, and you begin to see the suffering of the partner, which is real. They're trying to maintain this relationship and it's very touching. And that encourages you to go a little deeper into yourself and realise 'This is a state of mind' because your energy starts to flow. Your consciousness starts to elevate in the sense that you are focused on reality as it's actually unfolding in present time instead of through this fixed filter of illusion, which is your identity structure. Now, that is why it's a spiritual path. The first thing that has to happen is 'I have to get rid of *me*, my identity'.

Eleonora: Yes.

Helen: And I would put in the fact that the Enneagram was developed not as any kind of psychological system, because psychology has a history of just barely over two hundred years old. This is out of ancient times, this renewal of the Enneagram map. It's a map of the obstacles, as it was originally used, to prayer and meditation and to deeper presence in the present moment, because what comes up is, as soon as the identity is triggered, 'Oh [*sighing*] I'm going into silence, deeper' – a new level – 'Oh [*sighing*] what's going to happen?' And the survival strategy activates. But by relaxing that survival strategy you pull energy away from prefrontals and limbic activity and back into the ability to tolerate deeper silence. When thoughts come, let them go.

Eleonora: Is this the area of work that you're focusing on, now?

Helen: Oh, that's how I entered this whole thing. One would suppose that I am deeply steeped in the psychology of type. That was an area that I taught for a long time, psychology of personality, but it's not my interest.

Eleonora: What's your interest now, in the evolution of the Enneagram?

Helen: I think it's very important... now, this is a personal, you know... others would have other wishes to the Enneagram.

Eleonora: Sure.

Helen: I put a lot of value on the work of Desmond Tutu.

Eleonora: Really? Say more.

Helen: He's about the reconciliation of hostile opposites. I'm a long-term peace activist and Desmond Tutu is my local hero now. Before, it was Mahatma Gandhi, but Desmond is with us and he has instituted a method. I don't know if we have time, a couple of minutes?

Eleonora: Yes, we do.

Helen: There was a time in his country when [people] who had committed heinous crimes, atrocities against their own people, were imprisoned. Too many prisoners. And he had the idea in concert with others: 'We can repatriate these people, because there's nowhere else for them to go. We either execute them, or we rehab them and put them back where they came from because no one else will have them'.

What a brilliant idea, to repatriate people who were accused and guilty of crimes against their own people. And this has so much to do with human relationships, which is your question. He has a method where the previously convicted are brought in and they are faced with their accusers in the very town where these atrocities were committed. And the ground rules are: we bring in a bank of fair witnesses from another town that wasn't involved and we're going to sit here until everybody has had the chance to speak their piece. Their view. Their truth. Their subjective reality. And the first, of course, are the accusers and they want vengeance. "You did this to me!" I mean, these are machete [wounds].

Eleonora: I can imagine.

Helen: So horrendous... they re sitting there with their mutilations. But the accusers have their way. And that could go on for days. And the witnesses are witnessing and speaking among themselves and the accused are silent. This can go on a long time and here's Desmond in his Episcopal Archbishop's robes presiding in silence over this whole interaction. Now, you could see this as an affirmative force and a negating force [*clapping fists together*]. No hope. No reconciliation. No third-force reconciliation. And then the accused come forward. These are now grown men and women and they say, "They took me when I was seven, eight years old. They stole me from this place and we were told that you had sold us. That you knew. We were told this. We believed this. And we were told that if we didn't commit these crimes in other places as we grew up that they would turn upon us, because those that are outcasts have to band together." It's a bonding technique and it's very powerful. That was my understanding of the material that Desmond Tutu is bringing forward. And the reconciling view is the shock that you see in this small documentary that I saw. The shock that you see on the accusers face. They never knew. They never could take in, because they hadn't known the reality of the other. Which is what, when you're receptive to it... which is the ground rules, and the ground rules held: there will be no retaliation. So the accused were free to speak. No retaliation. And the... "I was eight years old... and all I had were my friends, so we made our way in our world..." as we do.

Eleonora: And the resolution being...?

Helen: The talking back and forth resolves the situation. You don't have to do anything. In a receptive field of reality you don't do anything except wait in a certain state of mind. Not in a thinking way, however justified those thoughts might be. Not in an emotional way, however justified it might feel to want retaliation. You are empty. And I'm sure there was some instruction going on about the state of mind of listening to this. And the ground rules held.

The last shot on the documentary was amazing to me. It was one of the chief accusers, a woman whose husband had been killed in front of her eyes. She was going to... there was only one well – quite symbolically – there was one well and everybody has to get water out of that same well. She's going towards it with a jug, and coming back was the one that she had accused. And they passed in complete silence. And then the cinematographer asks the woman, "What did you feel about that?" She said – and this is such good neural science, "I'll never trust him. I don't like him, but I'm too busy about my ordinary business and I don't think about that." The memory remains. It must, because it happened. You're not going to take away the memory from those prefrontals, but the limbic relaxes. The emotional charge just went out of it. And that is healing.

Eleonora: What touched you was seeing first-hand the possibility of listening, for both the accuser and the victim, their story and where they were coming from in committing what they had done, and also in being present to the possibility perhaps of... forgiveness. I don't know, I'm using my own words...

Helen: No, no, forgiveness is great. Forgiveness can be 'I don't care about you, but I'm not going to do anything to you'. That's a good form of forgiveness given the situation, and that will change over time into more of an acceptance.

Eleonora: Yes. What you're talking about is really the possibility of changing the brain pathways.

Helen: Yes.

Eleonora: And that's what you find of the work of Desmond Tutu – so powerful and so healing – In the same way that the Enneagram also gives the opportunity and the possibility of changing these brain pathways.

Helen: Which is why I'm so stuck on this psychological structural approach, because you can change the structure voluntarily... and get a different one. Choice... it's such an inspiring thing to me. We can choose to be different and, yes, the memory is still there, but it doesn't engage.

Eleonora: We can change.

Helen: Yes.

Eleonora: We can change. I think that's really wonderful to know that we can really make these changes. We're also coming to the end of our time. Was there anything else you'd like to add quickly?

Helen: If you love your honey and he's being a real pain [*both laughing*]... change your state of mind and he'll be your honey who's trying to get a message across and you can speak to the message instead of getting reactive.

Eleonora: Wonderful, thank you, Helen. I just want to go through your books again: *Inner Knowing. The Enneagram Advantage. The Enneagram in Love and Work: Understanding Your Intimate and Business Relationships. The Pocket Enneagram.* And the other book, your... the bestseller is *The Enneagram: Understanding Yourself and the Others in Your Life.* Helen, it's been a pleasure to have you. Thank you very much for coming to London.

Helen: Oh, I'm delighted to be here and to be able to speak these things. It is very healing to me.

To watch this interview please go to:
http://www.conscious.tv/consciousness/enneagram

Ginger Lapid-Bogda
The Enneagram in business

Interview by Iain McNay

Iain: Our guest today is Ginger Lapid-Bodga. You're very prolific because you've written three books on the Enneagram: *Bringing Out The Best in Everyone You Coach*, based on the Enneagram, *What Type of Leader Are You?*, and *Bringing Out The Best in Yourself at Work*. Let's just start, as we normally do on conscious.tv, with how this all began for you in terms of your spiritual journey. You were saying earlier that actually you were about seven years old when you started to get in touch with what we might call the bigger picture.

Ginger: Right. I remember when I was doing my PhD work, at the University of California in Santa Barbara, the major professor there said that he didn't think people became conscious, or spiritual, until they were adults. And I think 'Oh well, that wasn't my experience'. My experience was of being brought into a family – the youngest of five children – and the family was highly dysfunctional. It didn't appear so on the outside, but inside there were a number of things that were very troubling. Being the youngest, I was watching everything and looking at it, and sometimes the recipient of a lot of this, and other times it was my siblings. I became very reflective. I remember even at seven years old thinking about the meaning of life. Thinking about why people did what they did, thinking about the potential of people to do their best and what sometimes caused them not to do so. I found a lot of solace in the solitude and the self-reflection. I remember believing at that time that there was a bigger universe, a bigger consciousness, and a bigger purpose to it all. I remember thinking 'I'm too young to know it yet, but I know there is something there'.

Iain: This was kind of instinctive?

Ginger: Yes, it was very instinctive. And I do think children have it. My son, who's now nineteen, was very conscious, had the same sense when he was four years old. I really do believe that it's out there. And it's in here [*gesturing to chest*].

Iain: Did you have relationships with other kids who felt the same way, or thought the same way?

Ginger: Well, I was raised in the late nineteen-forties, early fifties, and we didn't talk about those things [*smiling*].

Iain: Yes, true [*laughing*].

Ginger: I think that children now do talk about it more. I remember when my son was in third grade, his teacher saw this special quality in him, and they put him in touch with another child in the classroom who had the same quality, so that they could be together and just not feel like they saw the world in such a different way from other people. But I think there's an increasing awareness of the bigger consciousness that's available now that wasn't talked about then.

Iain: Did you feel isolated as such?

Ginger: I felt protected. I didn't feel isolated. I felt very protected.

Iain: You mentioned when you were at university – you were I think nineteen years old – you started to get political.

Ginger: I went to the University in Berkeley... in the nineteen-sixties. In my very first year – two months' start into it – the free speech movement: this movement started all the political activism in the United States. It was really about, ironically, computer cards, and we weren't computer cards with little punched-out codes, we were people. It was the beginning of a sort of political consciousness. My parents were politically active, so I had been active as a child in political causes, but it was a big awakening for me, and so I then got very involved in social actions, civil rights, and the anti-Vietnam War movement – and a little bit later, in the women's movement that grew out of the civil rights movement and the anti-war movement in the United States. I definitely was politically involved.

Iain: It was the same for me, when I was young. I also was very politically involved. Involved with the left-wing political movement in England. The way I saw things was, the system had to change and then people would be happier and better off, but it took me a few years to realise that actually you couldn't do it for people. People had to want to change from the inside. That was when my spiritual journey started. I had to go through this process of seeing that something else didn't work first. Was that at all similar for you?

Ginger: No [*smiling*]!

Iain: Yours was a different process?

Ginger: It wasn't like that. It's similar, but different. The best I can say it is...

my son, I love my son very much, a very wise child, and when he was five years old he said, "Mommy, is there a God?" And I said, "That's something you have to discover." And when he was seven he said, "Mommy, I've figured out the answer…"

Iain: [*laughing*]

Ginger: … and I said, "To what?" There was a two-year gap, but for him it was an ongoing process. He said, "God is something inside you."

God is also in the bigger universe, and the challenge in this lifetime for each of us is to connect with the universal force inside us and the universal energy outside us, and to make that connection. [pause] I feel that's true in terms of how I see consciousness, evolution, and change. If it's just all on the outside, in organisations, or society, or nations, it's not enough. If organisations become more conscious and if people inside organisations become more conscious, eventually they will change the organisation. But it takes a long time. So my focus is both the system and the individual and bringing the two together.

Iain: To follow your story in sequence… You got married…

Ginger: [*laughing*]

Iain: … and you married someone you thought was a prince.

Ginger: And he turned out to be a big toad.

Iain: [*laughing*] A big toad. That must have been a big disappointment?

Ginger: Yes, because the dream was very large and the reality was very harsh. I didn't consciously know this about him at the time, but he was very abusive, psychologically and physically. It wasn't the first time I'd experienced some psychological abuse because that had occurred in my family, but it was the very first time that I had experienced any physical abuse from anyone. And if I can put it into the late nineteen-sixties, seventies, nobody was talking about this. And I moved to a new city so I knew no one. I was in graduate school, but at first, I didn't know really. I got very disoriented by it and very discouraged and depressed, and then I started to realise that this was not how I wanted to live my life, and so I ended the marriage. But after that I realised that at some level I had chosen him, not knowing consciously, but unconsciously, and there was some energy in me that attracted him to me. That was the big beginning of my psychological [growth]. The connection between my psychological and spiritual growth was a big awakening of 'I want to live a life that is satisfying and rich in experience, rich in spirit, and rich in every' – money was never the issue of richness but – 'a very vibrant life, and I need to take responsibility for my conscious and my unconscious choices'.

Iain: Somehow you were almost relying on, or expecting to find, happiness in the relationship with him? And you realised that actually happiness has different roots.

CONVERSATIONS ON THE ENNEAGRAM

Ginger: It has to come from within.

Iain: Yes. That's a big lesson, isn't it?

Ginger: It was a hard one, but a rich one. I look back on it and I think it was one of the best things that ever happened to me because it really woke me up.

Iain: That's a great attitude to have.

Ginger: I feel blessed with that. But I suppose I had no choice, in a way. I had two choices, this or that. So given the choice…

Iain: There are a lot of people that collapse into the victim role and it affects them for years and years, and they maybe try and do some therapy. It takes a lot of courage, a lot of insight, and a much bigger overview to see 'Well, I get something out of this, even though it's very difficult, I can learn through this. I can grow and I can move forward'.

And then you were working with kids, deprived kids in poor urban environments. What attracted you to that?

Ginger: That was my social action. I believed – and I still do – that education is the path to choice, [the ability to] do what you want with your life, and do what you want in the world. So I went into an urban environment and I actually never thought of them as deprived, I just thought of them as poor and urban. Most of them were African Americans because it was in the city of Philadelphia. I had a blessed experience there. I made contact with all the families. I got to know the children. I saw the beauty in them, and the belief in them, and they were amazing learners. But I also saw how, if I set up the classroom environment – you see here we go into the system structure – in a certain way, they could get really motivated and learn, enjoy themselves, and feel fulfilled. I also worked on them individually, to find the best in themselves. It was again the system and the individual coming together. I still have contact with some of them. They're adults now, they're probably almost middle-aged.

I remember, I just got a Facebook message from one of them. His sister actually contacted me. His name is Lamont and he said he's doing very well, and he added, "I just remember your smile. No matter what was going on you believed in me, maybe more than I believed in myself, and your smile made everything okay."

Iain: This is probably the key to how you work now. You have the ability to spot a potential in a situation – whether it be in a kid, or in an adult, or in an organisation – and feed that potential so it can grow. Not because of you… but you're helping to see that it can grow on its own.

And then, I think it was in nineteen-seventy-two, you started working with businesses. How was that to start with?

Ginger: Interesting. It was interesting. I've always been involved with organisations, partly because I'm fascinated intellectually. I find the way they work amazing, but also because it's where people congregate. I've always

CONVERSATIONS ON THE ENNEAGRAM

been about trying to help organisations be more effective, more productive, more conscious, and more humane and help people in them be the same. For me, to be able to work in an organisation and do that, it's like... I'm a social subtype, so I like to help individuals, but I also [think] the more individuals that can be helped the better. What better place than in organisations?

Iain: Give us practically an example of some of the things that you actually did. What did you actually do with organisations to start with?

Ginger: Well, it's a thirty-five-year profession, so it can go anywhere from working with an individual and leadership coaching, to working with organisation restructure, strategy, organisation design, and everything in-between. But I don't come in as the expert. I come in as maybe an expert in processes to help them figure it out themselves. I don't help them, or tell them what their strategy should be. I help them get the information that will help them design their own strategy.

Iain: Again, it's taking the potential that's there and giving them a suggested guideline so it can evolve.

And then, I know in nineteen-ninety-two you were at Esalen in Big Sur and you went to do a workshop. You'd done all the workshops that were listed apart from one on the Enneagram. Tell us what happened.

Ginger: Well, I was just looking for a vacation.

Iain: [*laughing*] Not everyone goes to Esalen for a vacation!

Ginger: Well, my idea of a vacation is to go someplace that's very beautiful and also do some spiritual and psychological work. Sometimes it could be all by myself, but that's my idea of a vacation. So I end up in this Enneagram workshop that on the brochure says it's for beginners – that's me. I get there and it's advanced and I'm like 'Oh my goodness... everybody's talking about numbers...'

Iain: Did you know what the Enneagram was?

Ginger: No, not really. Somebody said, "You might like this." I had had a few friends from college who had gone and worked with Oscar Ichazo in Arica, and they had told me a little about it, but they weren't supposed to talk about it, so they said, "It's really great, but I can't talk about it." I was interested and I figured if I wasn't, I would not go to the sessions and just sit outside in the hot tubs and eat the good food. Anyway, the first day, all these numbers people were throwing around... I don't really like systems of personality because I feel that they can restrict people into not being all of who they are and we stereotype...

Iain: There will be people watching this programme that don't know what the Enneagram is. Just explain very basically what you learnt the first couple of days.

Ginger: Well, the first couple of days I learned there are numbers [styles] and people identify with them. But by the third day I went 'This is amazingly profound!' So I have shifted from 'I'm not sure about this' to 'This is pretty profound'. Would it be helpful if I explained the nine styles?

Iain: I'm just putting into context what the theory of the Enneagram is. There are nine different personality types…

Ginger: Yes. The theory of the Enneagram is that we have these nine different personality types and each of us is fundamentally oriented to have a certain worldview and a certain drive that comes from one of these nine styles, but we are not limited by our Enneagram type. In fact, it's not actually all of who we are, and there is a deeper self that wants to emerge beyond some of the restrictions of our Enneagram style. If we know our Enneagram style, it helps us identify our patterns of thinking, feeling, and behaving, and to see the interrelationship between the two, so that we can appreciate ourselves for what we do bring – also not identify with our personality, so that we can actually work on development in terms of expanding our patterns of thinking, feeling, and behaving.

With one of my colleagues, we first do our Enneagram types as the clothing we wear. It's not that we want to take off all our clothes, but that we can in fact change and grow. Even though our Enneagram style is something that we have [for] our lifetime, it's a continuous process of evolution and we are not fundamentally stuck in our patterns.

Iain: At this workshop you learnt about these nine styles. Was it quite easy to find your style?

Ginger: At first, actually, I thought I might be an Enneagram style Four. But as I worked, after about ten years of working with the system, I realised that the Fours and the Twos are very similar in some ways, and very different in others. I started doing all the development work for the Four. After a while it lifted and it wasn't working any more, and I found there was a Two underneath the Four. Because my family had been challenging, style Four had made a little more sense in that family system. But there is a story I'd like to share, when I left the Esalen experience.

I went to this for my own personal development, not just for a vacation. So I walk out of the room and literally, my eyes are wide open, but in my mind's eye I saw a blimp or a dirigible… you know, they look like an airplane, but they have no wings.

Anyway, it was carrying a banner and the message on the banner said 'Your mission, or your job is to bring the Enneagram more into the world'. I was taken, and I said, "But that's not my plan." And [it] came back a second time and it said 'It doesn't matter what your plan is'. And I'm like 'Am I tired, or…?' You know… twelve in the afternoon… "Well, that's good, but what am I supposed to do?" and it came back a third time and it said 'Just be patient and it will be clear to you'. So I said, "Well that's good because now I don't!" Then – couple of years – stuff started to happen and I realised what I was supposed to do. So, I feel I'm on some sort of plan that's bigger than me.

Iain: You then started to incorporate what you learnt from that Esalen workshop about the Enneagram, in your work and in working with businesses and individuals.

Ginger: Yes, but the interesting thing is that, after that programme, I decided I wanted to learn it better and deeper and, because Helen Palmer had been the leader of that workshop, I went into her training programme in California. Part of the programme to be certified was you had to type twenty people, and ten of them during this time had to be on tape so that you had somebody supervise. Now twenty people is a lot of people really. I started running out of family and friends who were willing to be typed and interested to be so. So I asked several of my clients. And it was my clients – after I typed them I would give them a book as a thank-you for their time – who asked me to work with them on how to use it in organisations. See, it wasn't my plan to do so, but my clients said, "Well gee, let's see if we can figure out how to use it with my team. Let's see how we can do this, let's see how we can use it for conflicts." So that's how my path evolved. It was through my clients.

Iain: Let's just explain, relatively briefly, about the nine different types. Just some clues about how people might be able to find their type. I realise it's probably not going to be detailed enough for someone to spot from this programme. But just a few minutes explaining, in a little more detail, what the whole thing is…

Ginger: The idea is that on the Enneagram symbol we are all human, and so there's a circle that relates to both our universal humanness and the fact [that] in some ways we have all of the nine styles within us. Yet, at the same time, we're more fundamentally wired to one of the nine. The reason for understanding which one is more our wiring is because once we understand it, it helps us clarify and become more conscious of our patterns of thinking, feeling, and behaving. Also, for each Enneagram style, there are certain development activities that work really well for one style and are not necessarily useful for another in terms of evolving, growing, expanding, and becoming more conscious. Shall I go through the nine styles very briefly?

Iain: Yes.

Ginger: What I'll try to do is give a business example. I find them rather amusing. I'll start with Type One. Enneagram style Ones believe that the world could potentially be perfect, but of course in reality they are quite aware that it's not. So, they feel that it's their job to improve themselves, other people, and circumstances. And this is, of course, lifelong work to try to keep improving things and making it perfect, because as soon as you perfect one thing, another thing pops up. And so, they are very diligent and responsible. To give you an example of an Enneagram style One: a manager, who had at least seventy people reporting to him, was describing this in a group. He said,

"I'm very good at delegating." His peers who weren't so sure if that was accurate said, "Really?" And he said, "Yes, I can delegate it to anyone who can do it better than I can."

They replied, "Well how many people is that?" And he said, "Two." Then his peers said, "What about people who can do it as well as you?" [He replied,] "Well maybe I could do this… maybe, but…" [They asked,] "And how many is that?" "Five." So I said to him, "Part of a manager or leader's job is to develop people who work for you. Do you think you could consider the possibility of delegating to people who could do it seventy-eighty percent as well as you, and give them that growth or stretch?" And he said, "I'd really have to think about this seriously." Now, he was very serious, but it was amusing to others, but it was very hard for him to let go of getting it done right and have the assurance that only he, or a few select others, could do so.

Iain: So, a clue for Type One is perfection.

Ginger: Yes, seeking perfection, but also knowing at some level that nothing is ever really perfect enough, because Ones will be the first to tell you they're not perfect. What works, what's important, is that you're constantly trying to make things more so.

Iain: Okay, Type Two?

Ginger: Enneagram Twos have this bigger sense that there's a bigger purpose to everybody's life and meaning, and so they feel that their job is to help people find that and hope to reduce suffering in the world, and to find out what people need and to satisfy it. They like to orchestrate and make things better, preferring to do it behind the scenes to out front – invisible. And so what they do is they focus on other people so much, organisations and groups and others, that they spend less time figuring out 'What is it that I need?' 'What is it that I really am about?' 'What is *my* bigger purpose?'

To give you an example, a high-level manager was saying to his managers, "I need some help. I'm very, very busy, could you do this for me?" There were eight or nine people in the room and one person said, "Yes I could do some if you give me a couple of days' notice," and another person said, "Not now, but next week"… go around [the group]… and the leader who was a Type Two said, "Well, I can help you now because I always give, I'll allow a couple of extra hours in my schedule just so I can help you." He was as busy as anybody else. Everybody was laughing about this, but it's the way Twos think. For him helping his boss was critically important, but of course he was exhausted.

And then, actually the same person had a difficulty in his life where somebody very close to him had died, and yet he kept going. People were saying, "Let us take care of you a little bit," and he was overwhelmed by it and didn't quite know what to do with all the support he got.

Iain: So they're focused out there, rather than also being here [*gesturing to chest*]. Okay, Type Three?

Ginger: Enneagram style Threes believe that they're looking for a natural order and flow in the world, a systematic way that things work moving forward and they can't quite find it; so they feel that their job is to create goals and get results and to create a plan to get there. In the process, they can end up being very high achievers and very successful, but they can – almost like a horse in a race with blinders on – lose sight about what's going on, both around them with other people particularly, and also what's going on internally with them.

Let me give you an example of something that was very moving to me. I'd been doing work with management teams with the Enneagram and its use in development, and one of the men in this group I think was a Three. He was pretty driven and pretty successful, and one day he arrived in this group, which had been ongoing, of leadership community. People looked at him and said, "You seem really different, what happened?" And he replied, "I'd been working on this focus-on-goals-and-plan, focus-on-goals-and-plan… and one day I looked outside when I was driving to work and there was this flower that had been there all the time and I'd never seen it. It was actually quite lovely. I looked at this flower and I thought my goodness this is beautiful – what flowers, metaphorically, am I not seeing in my life that my focus has limited me?" He has a son who was very young, three years old, and he said, "My son. I love my son and I'm being a good father I think, but I'm missing the moment with him, he's the flower. I need to be in the moment instead of focused on the goal, even with him." And it opened him up entirely and he's just as effective as ever, but there's a way that he knows what it is to *be*, and not just *do*.

Iain: Yes, they're almost too driven in a way. They're very focused, but too driven and again, lose the [bigger] picture.

Ginger: Enneagram Fours have a sense that they're wired, that there is a deeper connection between everything and all of us, but they can't quite feel it all the time, so they're constantly seeking it. One of the ways I like to describe Fours – their existential experience – is that they think whoever made humans, if we came through on the conveyor belt, one human, you know like in a store... one human, the next human… that we all kind of look the same, but there's one that's different, even though it looks the same – that's the Four. So they spend their lives trying to figure out 'I'm different'. Is it 'I'm different because I'm deficient or not good enough'? 'Am I different because I'm better than?' 'Or am I just different?' It's a constant process of trying to figure out 'Why am I different?' 'Why do I feel not quite like everybody else?' 'Do I like it, do I not like it?' It's all that, and eventually when they do their personal and spiritual growth, they realise that what's different about them is they *think* they're different. We're all different, we're all the same, but they have a liking of being different but are not sure they like being different.

So in the organisational setting, one of the things that often happens is that there's conflict and difficulties and people are emotional because we bring our feelings to work. Fours – as leaders or as players – actually like to listen to people talk about difficult situations. People can feel deeply heard [by Fours] and they can spend hours on this, whereas many other leaders or even co-workers would go, "Okay, I think enough already, we got to get back to work," but they really have a capacity and a pleasure in listening and really going deeply into things with people. So that's Four. Let me go to Five.

Enneagram style Five believes that it's possible to know everything. That's what they're seeking. They want to know everything that's of interest to them, but then, you know, it's an endless possibility of knowing. Their worldview is that, although you can know everything, the world is full of scarce resources, so you have to be careful both managing your time, your energy, your privacy, your relationships. They tend to lead with their minds and disconnect, or cut off from their emotions and their bodies too, in this pursuit of knowledge. Their lifelong task, of course, is to reconnect, because true wisdom or knowledge comes from knowing from the mind and the heart, from the full experience.

There's a wonderful Five leader I've got in mind. People would say to him, "I don't know you. Who are you? I want to know more of you." And he'd be like, "What is it you want to know?" So finally he's with his leadership group and this comes up, and he goes, "What is it you want to know?" and they say, "We just want to know you." I think in many ways they want to feel that he knows them, but they put it as [they want to know] him. So he said, "Okay, ask me a question." And one woman said, "When I say good morning how are you in the hallway, and you just say fine, I want to know more." So he said, "Do you really want to know what I'm feeling and thinking?" and she replied, "Yes," and he said, "Well, actually I feel it's a superficial comment. You don't really want to know who I am, or how I am. Maybe I had a bad day, maybe I had a good morning, but I'm supposed to just say I'm fine and how are you and smile at you. I don't like what feels to be more superficial interactions." I think that's a real good insight into the Type Five. On one level they don't like what you call social interactions, but on another level they spend a lot of time in self-reflection. Often they do know quite deeply, but they just don't share. They do have feelings, but they often go off later and reflect on them and experience them in a deeper way.

Iain: They keep it to themselves. Okay, now Sixes.

Ginger: Sixes are very complex individuals [*smiling*].

Iain: I'm a Six, so I know that [*laughing*].

Ginger: [*laughing*] I know you are. Sixes can be very different from one another, and the same Six can be very different at different moments. The basic rule of the Six is they're seeking meaning, certainty, and support in the world. They're looking for it and they can't exactly find it all the time, so they try to find it for themselves. They have antennae that scan: 'Well what's really going on here, in my heart? What am I feeling here, what's going to happen?' They like to be able to predict things and of course you can't, because there are so many things going on, but Sixes think they can. Some Sixes are more fearful, because they are looking around to see what could happen and do anticipatory planning. Some Sixes are fearful too, but they go against the fear to prove to themselves that they're not fearful at all. Some Sixes are in between, more fearful but can be quite bold, or not fearful at all but have some moments of fear.

I'll share a funny story about an Enneagram author who's a Six who's more on the counterphobic, or against the fear. At one point I was President of the International Enneagram Association and we were having a conference in Washington DC. And the alerts, after nine-eleven, would go to different colours. There had been a threat in New York and one in Washington and so the alert had gotten heightened and everybody in the country was aware of this because it was all over the news. So I'm the President of the Association, and he writes me an email three days before the meeting is to start, and I'm already in Washington for a board meeting. He's about this much taller than I am [*gestures half a metre*], which is sort of relevant to the story. So he writes, "I think you should write. Email all the participants who are coming to the conference – we're talking about three-hundred-four-hundred people – that the alert is heightened and that you can protect them" [*smiling*].

And I'm sitting there going... 'Oooh well, everybody?' You know what I mean, the desire, the fantasy to let people know... The fear came up, which you rarely see in this particular person because he doesn't show the fear and goes against the fear... and [he is] very tall, and I'm thinking 'I can't protect anybody any more than he can! He's this much taller than me anyway, and there are all of these armed guards around, so they're going to be doing it!' But the idea of telling authority that you need to tell people and you'll protect them, I found very amusing even in the less fearful of the Sixes. I just laughed and didn't send an email out [*smiling*], but it made a wonderful story. Can you see me protecting all of Washington DC against terrorists? I mean, what am I going to do?

So Sevens live in a world where they think the world is full of possibilities and a much bigger plan for all of us, but they can't quite figure out what that plan is. So they think it's their job to try to create all this planning of possibilities. It's an Enneagram style that seeks pleasure and stimulation and wants to avoid discomfort or pain. The idea in Type Seven is 'If things get a little tough I'll just think about what I'm going to do, or a new thing that can happen, or possibilities'. One of the ways I like to describe Sevens in work settings – because it works pretty well – is you think about the Seven mind as a computer screen where there are very few file folders. Every document is there on the desktop. So when one thing happens it makes them think of another very quickly because they don't have to go deep into the file folders. There's this [thing] called the synthesising mind of the Seven: 'Oh, that makes me think of this, and that makes me think of that...' They can put together innovative creative ideas, which are very stimulating and can often be very helpful in organisations. But their real challenge is also to focus on which of these ideas we could actually take to conclusion, which of these ideas really can be most useful to the organisation – and what the downside of the idea is, because they don't so much like to think of the downside of anything too long.

One of my very favourite clients – who has actually been an inspiration for my leadership book – a Type Seven – one of the ways he's working on himself is that at his senior executive meetings, he focuses people on the agenda. Instead of being the one to come up with all the ideas, he encourages others to come up with them and he helps focus them. It's almost like a psychological and spiritual developmental avenue for him and he just laughs at himself. What he did one day... Sevens often like to talk a lot and sometimes they're very introverted, but they talk inside their minds. A Seven I know doesn't stop talking. I spent about fourteen hours with him and he just didn't stop talking the whole time. I know another Seven who doesn't talk at all, but the chatter is still there [*gesturing to head*]. So this client of mine goes on silent retreats. Started with one day, two days...

Iain: [*laughing*]

Ginger: ... now he's up to seven. And he loves it, because he's found that the inside is just as fascinating as the outside, and maybe even more so. So that's the Seven.

Eights. I've had a lot of Eight clients and I have many stories about them. Eights believe that it's possible to understand true reality, the real truth of the world. They're looking for the truth and they feel that it's their job to do so, but inside they believe that the world is made up of two kinds of people: the tough and the weak. So they've learned to be the strong or the tough and hide their vulnerability, which they would see as weakness, and to protect other people whom they see as structurally weak. Interestingly though – if somebody looks like a victim to them, who isn't a real victim according to that particular Eight – they have disdain for people who victimise themselves in their mind, but want to protect those who are true victims, so they rise up to the occasion. It's about being bold, it's about being strong, and it's about being assertive, but hiding one's own vulnerability, one's own tender-heartedness.

When Eights get the Enneagram, it can be the biggest breakthrough in the world for them, because they love the moment of recognising that true strength comes from accepting and owning one's vulnerability as well as one's power. It's that meeting in the moment because they do love the truth, and the Enneagram can feel like that to them, but they have to be willing to be vulnerable in order to get there, which is...

Iain: It's quite difficult for them.

Ginger: It can be a challenge, but it can be a huge breakthrough.

Nines believe that the world is full of unconditional regard and harmony and yet there's all this tension everywhere, and they see it as their job to bring people together. So they become good listeners; they become facilitators. They like to draw other people out and bring them together. They don't like to create conflict themselves and so they meditate or harmonise, often at the expense of expressing their own true self, their own true voice, their own true thoughts, their true feelings. The developmental path for Nines is to find out what they really believe and be able to take a position and be able to follow through on it.

There's a woman in one of my groups for whom I have the greatest respect. She's a Nine, she's lovely, smart, and talented. One day she came to one of these meetings where we had been working on development for several months. People looked at her and said, "Maria, what happened to you?" She said, "Well, I'm forty-five years old and I was looking in the mirror. I looked and I said 'Maria, you're forty-five years old. If you're not going to speak up for yourself now, when? Are you going to wait until you're fifty-five, sixty-five?'" She just decided. She had grandchildren who were young. She said, "I owe it to myself, I owe it to my grandchildren, I owe it to... if not now, when? Now is the time." So she just started speaking her voice, saying what she thought, not waiting until the end of meetings to find out what other people thought and then say what she wanted in a kind of unassertive way. She was always a good leader, but she became an exemplary leader. So those are the nine styles.

Iain: Good. When you go into an organisation, into a business, are you pretty much scanning people to work out their styles, or are you patient with that? How do you get the information, and how do you implement that information?

Ginger: The only place I usually try to figure out what somebody's type is, is when I'm at an airport and I have a long wait and I'm bored...

Iain: [*laughing*]

Ginger: Then I'll see people walking along and go 'I wonder if that person is this type, or that type'. But when I go into a company, I actually have materials that help people discover their own type for themselves that are interactive.

Iain: So it's giving the power back to them again in terms of...

Ginger: It's a lot about giving the power back to them, but you know what else it is? The saying 'You can't judge a book by its cover'. Many of the types do the same things, but for different reasons. I've gotten more experienced with this and I may be a little better about guessing if a person might be this type or that type after I've been with them for a while, but you cannot [type]. I don't think anybody [can] and if they think they can, they maybe want to rethink this. It's so hard to tell from the outside what somebody's type is. So I have these materials that help people do it for themselves. They can be used individually or, even better, in groups. With the process of 'type-ing' – there are some cards and some other things – people get pretty close. Once they get more clear – they do activities with people – they can see how the different nine types respond to the same stimulus.

'What makes you angry?' 'What triggers your anger, how do you respond and why?' And 'What's the development?' Usually when we get upset, it's our own type that's getting triggered. So people can work on their own development, they can see how much their own responses are related to type. That's what I do in organisations or leadership: [I ask] "Why do you see it this way? It's your paradigm of leadership, versus that. Not right or wrong." Paradigms, by their nature, are limited.

Iain: Do people find it relatively easy to identify their own type?

Ginger: Well... easy? They have to do some work. They have to go inward and look at their patterns.

Iain: There has to be a willingness there, yes.

Ginger: They have to be, to some degree, self-aware enough to be able to see what their patterns are. Is that easy? Well, it depends on the person, but if there's enough openness and enough self-awareness... Most of the time I'll go into an organisation and I'll train people to use these materials and usually within about two hours, or less, I can get most of the people, whether they are leaders or non-leaders, eighty-five percent of them, to identify their type pretty accurately. But I'm very focused on what I do. The rest of them maybe need a little bit longer, need to do some reflection, maybe are confusing one type with another. Really there are people who can study the Enneagram for a month and then discover that they aren't the type they thought they were. Some people are a little more complex, have parental overlays, have a strong parent. So you think 'Well gee, I may be this type', but underneath you're this, with a little bit of that other type overlaid.

Iain: Yes, it's a tool for people to know themselves better. When they know themselves better they can act in a more intelligent way, and presumably they also get to know other people better too?

Ginger: It develops compassion and appreciation, instead of irritation and annoyance. But first of all, I do think of the Enneagram more as a map than a tool. It's a map to the inner interior. I've seen some people – I do not teach it this way – use it to just say 'Oh well, that's why I do this, this, and this', but not use it for development. So I think it's a map to the interior and a great opening for development and an incredible opportunity for compassion, both for other people and for oneself.

Iain: One of the things I do in my work environment – if I'm having a difficulty with somebody, or we're not seeing eye to eye on something, or we have a different style in how we approach things – is work out in my mind what their Enneagram type might be. I don't know whether I get it right or not, but it's almost as if I'm putting myself in their shoes: 'How are they thinking? How are they feeling? Why are they taking the position they are taking? How are they seeing me?' By doing that I find that I understand them much better. I understand why they're, in my eyes, being difficult, or not wanting to understand what I'm trying to put across. And it can change, it almost creates a field between us, because there is me trying to sit where they are. It's not always something that comes straight away and I don't always get the answer I want – but something opens up.

Ginger: I like that story, because whether you're right or wrong, at least you're considering that the other person has a point of view and it gives you something to do, instead of just reacting out of your own personality.

Now, I'm going to tell a story about this because I think it's a great story. If you imagine that you actually knew the other person's point of view, what their type was, and that the other person knew his or her own type, then think about how that conversation might go. There's a story that I love. I don't tell untrue stories because they're never as good as the real ones and I'm not good at telling fake stories anyway. So I had asked one of my key clients – two people, very high level vice presidents, senior vice president and a vice president – to come to an Enneagram conference to talk about the use of the Enneagram in their company and how we were doing it. There were about seventy people in the audience, and one of the audience members said, "How do you deal with the fact that the Enneagram doesn't have a multitude of research to show that it is a valid system and all the benefits and praise?" And one of the clients – he's a Five – just rose to the occasion and stood up. Normally Fives wouldn't necessarily stand up, but he took the microphone. He's a research scientist, one of *the* most respected, three most respected people in this very large successful company and he said, "I'm a scientist so let me tell you about research. You can make the research go any direction you really want it to, and you can look at the research process and find all kinds of questions about it. I know how to do that very well. So if you try to convince me about the Enneagram through research, I would be picking out the pieces of it, trying to find how it wasn't structured in a logical way. So I know about research, but let me tell you this. I'm a Five and there's a senior vice president of the company who's an Eight, and for the last fifteen years we haven't been able to get along, and it has completely impaired our senior leadership group from functioning. Once he

218

CONVERSATIONS ON THE ENNEAGRAM

recognised that I was into the Enneagram and knew my type and I recognised his, and we both realised that we were using it in our respective organisations, we had a conversation about it and about our relationship. In twenty minutes we were able to undo what for the last fifteen years had been a problem for us. And now, not only do we work effectively together, we've actually become good friends."

Iain: So they found a way of meeting and...

Ginger: That's what he said. He said to this group, "Don't tell me about research. Let me tell you about reality. This is what the Enneagram can do."

Iain: That's very interesting. We have to finish in a few minutes, but one thing I did note down was – you mentioned in one of your books – that the CIA actually used the Enneagram, which I found again quite fascinating. How did they use it, do you know?

Ginger: I don't know because I wasn't the person... I didn't really even know the Enneagram so well [then], but as I understand... I have to be careful ... a colleague did, and was to do their best guess at what the Enneagram type was of some of the foreign leaders whom they needed to deal with, to be able to predict behaviour. You see, the Enneagram can be highly predictive of behaviour. The issue is you have to know the person's style accurately. So you use someone who's a very knowledgeable Enneagram person to try to do this. That's the story. I don't know if they're still using it, but they did at one point.

Iain: Yes, it makes a lot of sense. Also I read in here the Federal Reserve Bank uses it as well. Is that via you, or just something you found out?

Ginger: They don't like it so much when we talk about it [*smiling*].

Iain: It's in your book.

Ginger: I know. It's okay, but they don't like to have the work exec talk about it. One of the branches of the Federal Reserve Bank uses it. They were one of the early users and they bring a number of Enneagram people in to teach them. When I go back tomorrow, the following week I'm going to be going up there doing some work with them. One of the people there really uses it in many great ways.

It shows you there are a lot of industries that can use it. My example of the Type Five and Eight story is from a very big biotech pharmaceutical company. We've got banking industry, we've got governments...

Iain: And is it on the increase in terms of...

Ginger: Oh definitely. Oh definitely. I think, ten years ago, if you took ten people at random who were reasonably educated and who worked, and you asked, "Have you ever heard of the Enneagram?"... mostly "No." Now, you take ten reasonably – you know – and you ask, "Have you ever heard of the Enneagram?"... one person vaguely, and three people, yes. One vaguely, but isn't sure what it is, the second person a little bit, and a third person would actually use it himself-herself, or know somebody very close who did. So its usage is increasing.

Iain: It's been very interesting, Ginger. Thanks for coming in. I'm going to just show your books again: *Bringing Out the Best in Yourself at Work,* and *Bringing Out the Best in Everyone You Coach,* and *What Type of Leader Are You?* So these are all books that are available to learn more about the Enneagram. Hopefully if you've been triggered by this programme you'll get one of the books and find out more about it and practically incorporate it in your life. It certainly worked in my life.

To watch this interview please go to:
http://www.conscious.tv/consciousness/enneagram

Sandra Maitri
Passions and Virtues

Interview by Iain McNay

Iain: Sandra has written two books on the Enneagram, and *The Enneagram of Passions and Virtues* is going to be the particular subject of our chat today. Sandra, for people who don't know about the Enneagram, give us a brief overview of what that is.

Sandra: The Enneagram is a system of nine different personality types. The basic principle is that as our personality — or ego structure — develops in early childhood, it develops based on nine different 'takes' on reality that are impressions on our consciousness. Those particular takes, or understandings, or fundamental beliefs about reality, in turn mushroom into a whole character type. We can describe nine types of structures of character in which there's a basic premise about reality and about ourselves, what we're like, what reality's like. As a result of that, a particular feeling tone arises, which is the 'passions'. This is what we're going to focus on mostly today, as well as a whole set of behavioural patterns that correspond to those fundamental beliefs.

Iain: And we're all basically one type, although obviously we have influences from other types as well.

Sandra: Yes, we can experience all nine types within ourselves, but one of them is strongest for each of us.

Iain: So that's dominant and is kind of guiding our personality, influencing our personality?

Sandra: Well, it's not so much influencing our personality, as in a sense it is the infrastructure of our personality.

Iain: So, it *is* our personality?

Sandra: Well, it's the basic beliefs about reality that shape our personality into how it is organised.

Iain: Okay, and we all have one of these types and we're pretty much – I was going to say stuck with that for the rest of our life – but I know we'll come on to how it can evolve. We're basically one type, from the time we're born, till the time we die.

Sandra: Yes.

Iain: There's not a transfer out, is there?

Sandra: Not exactly, no, although Oscar Ichazo, who's the one who brought the Enneagram of personality into the West, in the sixties, I think works with secondary types. His theory – as far as I understand it, I haven't worked directly with him – is that as we evolve, there may be a secondary type that makes itself felt within our consciousness.

Iain: I'm sure there are a lot of people watching this programme who want to know what type they are. Are there clues you can give people... without going into too much detail?

Sandra: That's difficult, that's really difficult, Iain. People pick up a book and they fix on one thing in each of the types and then, because they can identify with that, they think that that's their type. But to really know what your type is, is first of all to understand the Enneagram and to get the whole flavour of each of the nine types. And if you get that, then you can begin to really feel what you might be. For some people it is instant: the moment they hear the nine types they get a sense that 'Yes, that's what I am'. For other people, they're very, very hard to type.

Iain: When you meet someone, and spend a little time with them, can you pretty much tell straight away what their type is?

Sandra: Again it depends. Some people are easy to type and some people aren't, but after working with somebody for a while and starting to understand how they perceive reality and the kind of suffering that they go through, what the nature of it is, then I can get a pretty good sense of what somebody's type is.

Iain: You're sitting having dinner with a group of people and you're kind of checking them out to see...

Sandra: I don't really do that, I don't. It's usually only in retrospect if somebody asks me, "What do you think so-and-so's type is?" I mostly just take in people as they are, without trying to categorise them, or figure out what they are. Sometimes if I'm with someone I definitely get a strong impression, and it's like '*Oh* yeah, that person's a Seven, or a Two', or whatever.

Iain: I must say, I don't know much about the Enneagram, I only know some basics, but I find it enormously helpful, especially if I have a difficulty with somebody. It may be a business relationship, or a personal relationship, but if I know their type, or I think I know their type and I understand their type, then somehow I can understand them better and that helps our relationship. They may not realise that I'm doing this, or that I have this extra facility, if you like, that I'm able to access, but it's good stuff. It's very effective and it's very practical, and that's what I like about the Enneagram: it's so practical.

Sandra: Yes, I think it's very useful, mostly as you say to understand other people, as well as ourselves of course. It really helps us have compassion for others, which is so important for them and for us. It is important to get that other people are different than we are and to understand how they work, why they're operating the way they are – and not to take it personally. It's not about us, it's about how they're wired up.

Iain: Absolutely. The emphasis on today's programme is the 'passions' and the 'virtues'. What are the passions and the virtues, especially in relationship to the Enneagram?

Sandra: What we call the Enneagram of personality is a collection of different Enneagrams [that together map personality or ego structure -SM]. At the root is the Enneagram of the fixations, which are nine different fundamental beliefs about reality, as I said, and that corresponds to our mental, cognitive orientation to reality. The Enneagram of the passions has to do with the heart; it has to do with our inner atmosphere, the feeling sense of each of the nine types. Then there's a whole other set of Enneagrams that have to do with the 'instinctual sub-types', and those have to do with behavioural patterns and styles of orientation to life.

Iain: You mentioned two things: you mentioned the passions and also fixations. What's the relationship there?

Sandra: What's the difference? The fixations are nine fixed beliefs about ourselves and about reality, and they arise as a result of loss of contact with our 'true nature' in early childhood. The theory behind the Enneagram is that, as we develop, as we begin to be able to self-reflect, as our nervous system develops, hand in hand with that is the loss of contact with the depth [or spiritual dimension -SM] within ourselves. As we lose contact with the depth dimension within ourselves, in place of that contact we develop nine different fixed beliefs about how reality is, and those are the fixations. Out of those fixed beliefs we have a whole set of feeling patterns, or we could call them patterns of suffering, and those are the passions. They're reactive styles – is one way of describing them – they're passionate in the sense that they're knee-jerk reactions, responses to reality. So if something in particular happens, nine times out of ten, we're likely to respond with our passion, rather than with an objective response to the situation – to the extent of course that we're identified with our personality structure.

Iain: It's interesting that you use the word passion, because for me passion is something that I feel *passion* about. That can be my wife, it can be my football team, my business, walking, the things that I love, and I see it as something positive. That's maybe not the terms you see it in, and yet we're looking at passion here as something that is maybe, as you say, a reaction, a knee-jerk reaction to something.

Sandra: Yes. The Enneagram is interesting and unusual in that a lot of the terms are like codes. They're not necessarily referring to the meaning that we typically have for those words. 'Passion' here is really used in a very old-fashioned sense, like when we talk about the passion of Christ, the suffering of Christ on the cross for example, and the enormous amount of energy and pathos that was going into that whole process for him, as well as exultation of course. It's in that sense that the word 'passion' is used. We tend to use that word also sexually, with passionate desire. It's being used here in the Enneagram in the sense of tremendous force, tremendous energy behind these particular emotional states.

Iain: Let's run through some of the passions, and see what we're talking about on a practical basis.

Sandra: Beginning with point Nine, which is the point at the top of the Enneagram [symbol] and is really the basis of all of the other nine types – I think I talked about this in the last programme in some depth – we can see that what point Nine represents, whether it's the fixation, or the passion, or the instincts, is primary. If we took white light and refracted it through a prism, point Nine would be the white light and the colours of the rainbow would be the other eight types. So they're differentiations really, of this fundamental principle represented at point Nine. That said, here the passion is laziness, and the virtue is action. The passion here is pointing toward one of the forms of suffering that we humans encounter and experience, which is not attending to what needs to be attended to, being lazy about listening to ourselves, doing what we need to do in our lives. Whether it's balancing our cheque book, or doing our taxes, or doing things that we know we really need to do, and end up dragging our feet on, in fact sometimes even forgetting that we need to do it in the first place. That kind of procrastination is something that for many people is tremendous, tremendous suffering in their lives. So, of course for people who are Nines, laziness has to do with a difficulty in attuning to themselves, knowing what they think, knowing what they feel, really feeling what's going on in their bodies. It's a laziness in terms of self-attention [as well as attending to what they need to attend to for themselves -SM].

Iain: And they're probably aware of that, if they really look at themselves?

Sandra: Yes I think so.

Iain: It's not something that is that unconscious is it?

Sandra: No, it's not something that is that unconscious, although I think the depth of it, for most Nines, tends to be unconscious, just like all the other passions. There are levels of perception of them, and as we work on

CONVERSATIONS ON THE ENNEAGRAM

ourselves, as one investigates what's going on inside one's psyche, there are increasing levels of depth at which we can perceive the passions and increasing levels of subtlety also.

Iain: How does someone get from this laziness to action, which is the virtue?

Sandra: That's a good question. From the perspective of the work that I teach, the Diamond Approach, the Enneagram is really a map of… well, let's talk about the map of the passions and virtues. It's a map of the difficulties that one typically finds within ourselves. The 'virtues' are the end result of our work on ourselves, with those particular problematic areas. The virtues are also attitudes that we need in order to resolve that difficulty represented by the passions. How we do that depends upon the path that we're using to approach these areas within ourselves. The map of the Enneagram doesn't tell us how to do it, but it tells us what we are dealing with, and what's possible for us [as we work through those difficulties -SM].

That said, for somebody who is a Nine, or who has a great deal of laziness as part of their psyche, the virtue tells us that action is needed – action is the virtue – and action here means doing what we need to do. Action means, if we're unaware of what we really believe about something, it's doing whatever we need to do to find out what we really think, or to find out what we really feel about something, or to get what our body actually needs. We may need a particular kind of diet, or a particular kind of exercise, and that only happens by tuning in to ourselves, listening to ourselves. So, the movement of point Nine from the laziness to action is really a movement towards self. It's an increasing sensitivity to oneself.

Iain: It's moving away from the influence of the personality, back to something more tangible and basic. Would you say that?

Sandra: I would say it slightly differently, which is that the orientation of the personality at point Nine is outward, it's about other people, it's tuning into what's going on outside of oneself. The movement to the virtue is a shifting of the attention going out, to the attention going in. It's like that. That's a very fundamental principle in all kinds of inner work, whether it's psychological work, or spiritual work, that in order to grow and to develop we need to tune in to ourselves.

Iain: It makes sense, absolutely. That's point Nine done.

Sandra: Point One, the passion here is anger, and the virtue is serenity.

Iain: That's a big shift I have to say.

Sandra: It's a huge shift. And the definition of anger that Oscar Ichazo gave, I think, is the best description that really encapsulates what this passion is: 'standing against reality'. The anger here at point One is being upset that reality – whether it's our inner reality or our outer reality – doesn't conform to the ideas that we have about how it ought to be. Here it's our preconceptions about what ought to happen, and what ought not to happen, that cause us tremendous suffering. Each of us experiences that in the form of our inner critic, or superego. That's the part of our minds that's telling us what's right and what's wrong and what should or should not be happening. If we look at the virtue here of serenity, serenity is the absence of those preconceptions. It's a sense of receptivity to whatever's going on within ourselves, outside of ourselves, and an openness to a non-judgemental attitude to whatever's arising, which especially for Ones is a tremendous relief from a lot of inner aggravation and upset. Really the passion here of anger, for Ones, is experienced as rage and as upset and frustration, and the understanding of the passion tells us that that's rooted in our ideas about what should and shouldn't be going on.

Iain: And they're the voices in our head that, as you hinted, have been put there by somebody else in a way. It's what we've learnt along the way and isn't necessarily our own voice.

Sandra: Right. They weren't exactly put there by somebody else... that's kind of a Sixish thing... I'm sorry, Iain!

Iain: That's my simplistic language from my Enneagram type [laughing]... we'll get to Type Six a bit later. Where do we go from Type One?

Sandra: We'll go to point Two. The passion here is pride and the virtue is humility. Pride here represents having an inner picture of how we're supposed to be and if we look, as we go around the circle of the Enneagram, we can see that each point builds on the next. So we have an ego ideal as it's called psychologically, an inner picture of how we ought to be, and the pride is telling us whether we're corresponding to it, or we're not corresponding to it. It's an inner voice that's telling us 'Oh that was really great, that was really good, you did that extremely well... I feel really good about myself now', or 'God you are the worst possible human being on the planet!'

Iain: [laughing] It's a great extreme, isn't it, one to the other.

Sandra: Yes, but as I see it, both of them are part of the pride system because there's a self-evaluation operating. The pride in terms of whether one is special, or more wonderful than other people, or way worse. In both cases it's an exaggerated sense of self-importance and an exaggeration of importance about how one is seen by other people and how one is responded to, and so on. Twos are very, very concerned about whether they're accepted and loved by others. So the virtue here is humility, which means – according to Ichazo's definition again – *knowing one's limits*. To me, as a Two, it's always been an extremely useful definition because Twos get into over-extending, and pridefully over-extending: 'Oh, I can do this for you, or I can do that, or you know time's no obstacle', that sort of thing – a kind of inner override of any sense of limitation. Humility here is a realistic self-assessment; it's not false humbleness, which is a way that that term is often used, but rather it's a sense of bowing to one's true reality.

Iain: It's not trying to be superman or superwoman. It's saying 'I am a human being with finite resources and time'.

Sandra: Right... And 'This is where I am, and this is what's happening to me, and I don't need to inflate myself, or feel deflated because of where I am'. It's an accurate and an open recognition of where one is without judgement.

Iain: Yes, and what's coming up for me now... it's interesting. When I was reading the preface of your book last night and this thing you mentioned about brutal honesty, it just seemed that if we're honest with ourselves, we actually discover not only our Enneagram type, but also it's much easier to discover what our passion is and the possible way forward to our virtue. Unless we are honest with ourselves, there isn't much of a starting point then?

Sandra: That's right. I think that's the real beauty of the Enneagram. It lays out some very difficult material for each of us to confront about ourselves and there it is, and if we know that we're a particular type, it's pretty clear.

Iain: Even though it's embarrassing and we want to deny it – 'I'm not like this' – there the facts are, and we can either take it on board and decide we can do something about them, or we can try and push it under the carpet again.

Sandra: Exactly.

Iain: Let's move around. Do we go to Three next?

Sandra: Yes, the passion here is deceit, or lying, and the virtue is veracity: telling the truth, truthfulness – also 'something real' is another definition of veracity. Here, what's being pointed to is a form of suffering in which we delude ourselves, or deceive ourselves about what's really so, what's really true for us, who we truly are. It's connected to point Nine and actually it leads to point Nine if we followed the lines of flow around the Enneagram, but that's a whole other story....

Maybe we'll get into that another time. But here at point Three is the tendency that human beings have to not face what's so. It's interesting that you brought up about being brutally honest. This is where – especially at point Three – that need for honesty, brutal honesty with ourselves, is seen as a virtue. Threes as a character type typically deceive themselves about who they are and about what's important to them because they've taken on from others, from their culture and their family, a sense of who they're supposed to be – what the image is that they're supposed to correspond to – and so they end up kind of shape-shifting, changing themselves, becoming different, altering what's so for them, in order to fulfil that image. Each of us of course does that to greater or lesser extents, and the virtue here of veracity tells us that in order to truly know ourselves and to become at peace with ourselves, we need to get real about what's really true about us, what really matters to us, what we care about, what we feel. It's not so much a matter of listening to oneself as it is at point Nine; it's a matter of really understanding that it's much more efficient for us to be truthful than it is to lie our way through life.

Iain: Yes, it's also a lot easier isn't it? Because if you start lying you've got to keep up the pretence, which requires tremendous energy.

Sandra: Right, and on a deeper level, Iain, from a spiritual perspective, the passion here of lying is lying to ourselves about who we really are. In other words, deluding ourselves into believing that we are our personality. That's a fundamental and basic lie that all human beings tell themselves as long as they're identified with their personality as being who and what they are. In the retreat I just led last week, one of the participants talked about the personality as the kind of froth on the surface of ourselves, and I thought that was a very beautiful description of the matter. Deceit here is believing we are that froth, instead of the real substance underlying that.

Iain: Shall we move down to point Four?

Sandra: Here the passion is envy, and the passion of envy is having the felt sense that what others have is better than what I have. What's over there is better than what's over here, the grass is greener over there instead of here. The passion of envy as an emotional state is a very, very painful one because really it's a self-rejection. It's a sense of pushing away who I am and what I have and wishing to be different. It's a terrible form of suffering. The virtue of equanimity, on the other hand, is the recognition that how I am, how somebody else is, are equal – equanimity means equal. So, there's a sense that what's here is fine and what's there is fine.

Iain: Yes, they're very big shifts these, aren't they?

Sandra: Yes, they're enormous.

Iain: They're almost quantum. It's a tremendous challenge to someone who's really engrossed in their passion to think that's what I am and this is how I live my life. It's almost a hundred and eighty degrees, isn't it?

Sandra: It is, it is. A hundred and eighty degrees, but within the same bandwidth, dealing with the same level of problem, one could say.

Iain: Yes, there's a consistency of issue there, or major issue that you follow.

Sandra: Right. Yes, exactly.

Iain: I'm just looking at the time here, I want to make sure we get through them for anyone looking at this programme. Then we go to Five.

Sandra: At point Five the passion here is avarice or hoarding, which is a holding on to what we have or what we are, and the delusion of course – well, 'of course' for those of us who are involved in spiritual work and the recognition of the underlying principle that we're part of a oneness – the delusion here is that we're separate and that we have to hold on to what we have for fear of losing it.

Iain: We all feel that to a large extent.

Sandra: We all feel that, absolutely. We believe we're separate. Non-attachment, the virtue here, is the recognition that we're all interconnected and that what sustains us is something that is constantly replenishing itself, constantly available. So non-attachment then naturally arises the more we know that, so it's an attitude of allowing things to come in, and allowing things to go out, which is very difficult for Fives.

Iain: Yes, it's difficult for most of us actually and it's what the planet needs more and more now, isn't it, this oneness, everything being interconnected?

Sandra: Yes, the recognition of it…

Iain: … and intelligent use of our self and everything else. So, why is that particularly hard for Type Fives?

Sandra: Because the fundamental fixation, or the fixed belief about reality, is rooted in one's sense of separateness. So that's the bit of egoic reality that's highlighted for Fives.

Iain: That's extra strong in them?

Sandra: I wouldn't say that it's extra strong, but it's what the whole personality is constellated around. Any of the fixations could be quite strong, but it's a principle that the fixation of our type is the one that we're constellated around and that is given primary highlight, I would say.

Iain: So, Type Six.

Sandra: The passion here is fear, and fear shows up as anxiety, as doubt, as an inner sense of agitation, unrest. It's a felt sense that is ubiquitous in our modern world, where people feel tremendous survival anxiety, especially now I'd say, with what's happening in the world. And the Enneagram tells us that the degree to which we're identified with our bodies, with our physicality as defining who and what we are, is the degree to which – something like the Great Recession happens let's say, or other kinds of difficult health issues – our fear gets increased. The virtue of courage naturally arises the more that we're not identified with our bodies as being the end-all and be-all of who and what we are. That of course is one way of looking at the spiritual journey. It's a matter of increased non-attachment, increased recognition that who and what we are is not this form. That what we are *inhabits* this form, but the body isn't our ultimate nature.

Iain: Which as a Type Six, I understand in one way, but it's very hard to really absorb the true meaning of 'not being this form'. I think it's very hard for a lot of people actually. They understand that everything is connected – certainly some people do – but especially when you feel a threat, or what you perceive as a threat, it's very hard to just say 'Well I'm not just this body'.

Sandra: Right, but if you take an orientation when you're experiencing something as a threat, and you begin to question 'Who's feeling threatened? What's really being threatened here? Who am I taking myself to be… that can be harmed?'… then we can begin to unpack and unwind our beliefs about who we take ourselves to be. But that's a very long journey, as you say. Really I think that the realisation of the virtues is something that increases as one increasingly approaches enlightenment, self-realisation. And the passions really are with us in every step of that way.

Iain: It's an on-going process.

Sandra: It's an on-going process and with increasing levels of subtlety.

Iain: After Type Six we have Type Seven.

Sandra: The passion here is gluttony, and gluttony is a hunger for stimulation, a hunger for taking in. It's the result of a whole orientation that we have as long as we're identified with our personalities, which is that the goodies are outside of us and they need to be taken in, in order to connect with them. From a spiritual point of view, we see that the virtue here is sobriety, and it tells us that the goodies, as it were, in life are available within ourselves and that they're the result of turning toward ourselves and being with ourselves instead of looking out there for what's going to stimulate us, bring us a sense of excitement, or happiness, or joy, or whatever. That the true source of happiness and joy and excitement resides within ourselves and hence there's a quieting down, a soberness, that increasingly results in our consciousness as we realise that, as we turn towards ourselves.

Iain: Type Sevens, the ones that I know, do find it very difficult to change – I suppose everybody does – in particular because they're drawn into alcohol dependence and drug use and just getting hyped up about things, getting very busy and active – and that, really again, is a huge shift. I guess it either happens as a quantum thing, where you wake up... There's a good friend of mine, who was — I can't say drug abuse or alcohol abuse – but he was certainly living on the edge of being a Type Seven and he had a stroke. Of course that completely changed his life. He had to start to rebuild the way his body worked, he doesn't drink, he doesn't smoke now, he takes life much easier. It took his body, if you like, to give him the message. I'm not sure he would have got it otherwise. So, I know it's a very difficult thing for a Type Seven.

Sandra: It is, yes. Sevens are also a very mental type, so the gluttony is not so much a kind of physical drive towards our physical gratification and stimulation, it's more a mental kind of greed. It's a wanting of interesting ideas and titillation and interesting thoughts and making connections and all of that.

Iain: It's very much about stimulation isn't it?

Sandra: It's very much about stimulation.

Iain: Yes, for someone that loves stimulation, to say that they need to be more sober in all aspects is tough.

Sandra: Yes, because you're basically saying that what's causing a lot of your problems is going *with* that drive for stimulation. That, in and of itself, is making you suffer, it's keeping you in a state of inner unrest, basically.

Point Eight: lust – and it sounds very close to gluttony, except that here 'lust' is being at the mercy of our physical passions, our physical drives, whether it's our sexual drives, or our lust for life, or desire to kind of devour things. It's again the attitude of taking in what's going to satisfy from outside, but it's a matter here of completely devouring it, grabbing life and as much of life as possible and just eating it up.

Iain: Which on the face of it sounds an intelligent thing to do when you're younger, to simply get the best you can out of life. It sounds very passionate, it sounds as though you want the best of what's available. And I want to say, "What's wrong with that?"

Sandra: Well there's nothing wrong with that. It's just that when our drive, our passion to take in, becomes a fixation and it's the only way we can operate such that we're constantly trying to gratify our physical needs, then we become slaves of our appetites.

Iain: It becomes an automatic programme?

Sandra: Yes, and for Eights it very much is. It's being a slave to your appetites and not having any freedom from them. And the virtue, innocence, tells us that the more we become slaves of our appetites, the coarser our consciousness becomes. We can see that in people who are alcoholics for instance, or who are slaves to particular types of addictive behaviour, which is not to say that Eights are necessarily addicts, or alcoholics, or anything like that, but that what's happening is this kind of addictive passionate quality in which one can't say no to one's drives. And that has the natural tendency to coarsen one's soul, one's consciousness. There's a sense of density and grossness that gradually starts to take over. From a spiritual perspective, the virtue here is telling us that we lose our innocence. The more we are driven by our physical biological drives, the more we lose the openness and the transparency of our consciousness.

Iain: We have a few minutes left, so we can still very much talk about this whole relationship between the passions and the virtues. In the introduction to your book, you said – and it's very obvious now you have talked about it – that you really need to understand the passions before you can access the virtues. So it is very much going within, understanding the way you are – and I guess it helps to understand the way other people are too, and then that opens up doorways doesn't it?

Sandra: Yes, sometimes people work with the virtues as trying to take on certain characteristics. That is not the approach that I take to them. I think that, as you say, they're something that evolve naturally the more that we start unwinding and understanding the way that our structure works.

Iain: You mentioned earlier the Diamond Heart Approach, which I think you have seminars, and retreats you run in Wales and in the UK?

Sandra: Right.

Iain: And you work partly with the Enneagram on those retreats?

Sandra: Yes, it's a subset of the work that I do. The overall work that I do is about personal transformation and contact with 'true nature'. We go into the personality structure itself instead of trying to transcend it, which is the more traditional approach to spiritual work. We go into it, we work with it, we enquire, and what we find is that the personality has a natural tendency to loosen up and relax [when we engage it experientially -SM], such that we can get glimpses, increasingly larger glimpses of who and what we truly are.

Iain: In a way, the personality is giving us the clue. It's like when you watch detective programmes on television, they're looking for the clues and some spiritual schools say 'Oh, personality, must get rid of the ego', but in a way, what you're saying is 'No, the personality is giving you the insight into what really is more true for you'.

Sandra: Yes, the way that we look at the personality is that it's a mirror image of what is most true and most real about us, and so if we stay with this mirror image it will lead us to what it is reflecting within ourselves.

Iain: I wonder how we got there in the first place. Why would we do that? Why would we have this *something* that's real and then we build a mirror image? It sounds strange, doesn't it?

Sandra: Well it does, but if you look at things from a slightly different angle, you could say that the purpose of human life is about learning to recognise our true nature, and that the capacity to develop a whole structure that reflects that nature develops along with it: the capacity for self-reflection. As we unwind that structure, which goes hand in hand with our capacity to know ourselves, we have the possibility of our deepest nature recognising itself.

Iain: That makes sense. You also talked about, in your book, that there are almost two levels of understanding the Enneagram. It's understandable at the level of personality, but of course there's a much wider picture if one takes the wider picture of consciousness into account.

Sandra: Yes, right, we can look at all of the passions as difficulties that each of us faces in life, and we can also look at them from the perspective of difficulties that one faces on the spiritual path itself. So these are really two levels of discussing the same thing.

Iain: And they're both true and they both interconnect?

Sandra: Yes, they're just different degrees of, or levels of, understanding of the map. That's the great thing about the map of the Enneagram. It's relevant for the more superficial parts of our lives and it's also relevant for the deepest depths of our lives.

Iain: It comes back to this quality of my Enneagram type: the virtue is courage. But I think that really applies to anyone who's going to be watching this programme and who's going to say 'Well, this looks really interesting, but of course it's got consequences. If I'm really going to start looking and make changes in my life, I'm going to see something about myself I probably don't like and don't want to recognise'. It takes a lot of courage to go on this path, doesn't it?

Sandra: Yes, it certainly does. I think the thing that happens is that in a way you start seeing yourself under a magnifying glass, and so you see wonderful things and those get bigger, and you also see parts of yourself that are quite painful and difficult to be with. For a while on the journey the suffering seems to increase, but that happens on the road to its resolving through being the truth of our experience.

Iain: How is it for you, someone who has been doing this for a long, long time? Does the suffering still come up, or do you feel a little bit on the home run now, so to speak?

Sandra: It's definitely different. I've been working on myself for the whole of my adult life, since I was twenty. That was when I first started working with the Enneagram, so that's been many decades, and I won't say how many... [smiling]

Iain: A couple...

Sandra: A couple [smiling]. Definitely a couple and I live in a very different world than the world I used to.

Iain: I'm sure the hard work has been worth it, hasn't it? The courage and the brutal honesty and all the other things that you talk about in the book...

Sandra: Absolutely, yes. Some of us have to go for the truth of our experience and aren't content to live on the surface so... it's definitely worth it.

Iain: I understand that for myself...

Sandra: Yes, I know you do.

Iain: Thank you for coming along, Sandra, and chatting to us on conscious.tv. Sandra is doing these retreats in Wales and her website address will be at the bottom of this programme, so you can find out more about that. I found this book, *The Enneagram of Passions and Virtues*, really fascinating and she has another one as well, *The Spiritual Dimension of the Enneagram: Nine Faces of the Soul*.

To watch this interview please go to:
http://www.conscious.tv/consciousness/enneagram

Helen Palmer
The Enneagram:
Gateway to spiritual liberation

Interview by Iain McNay

Iain: Helen has written several books about the Enneagram. I first heard about the Enneagram – it must have been about twenty-one, twenty-two years ago – and I found it so helpful. The first book I read was this one here, *The Enneagram in Love and Work: Understanding Your Intimate and Business Relationships,* which is what I needed at the time. I still do sometimes. Helen has written other books – we have here *The Pocket Enneagram*, *The Enneagram Advantage: Putting the Nine Personality Types to work in the Office*, and *Inner Knowing*. Helen's still working, doing lots of Enneagram work and courses, and I think she'll keep going for a much longer time yet. Helen, when did you first actually hear about the Enneagram?

Helen: I remember where I first heard about it. I was teaching intuition training at a centre called Esalen, which was one of the few growth centres...

Iain: I've been there, yes.

Helen: ... in America, on the California coast. I was at that time interested in consciousness, and various presenters would go there and present their materials. I was someone who went back a couple of times a year to teach an intuition training group, and the word came to Esalen that there was material that was presented as an upgrade, or a new view, of the Gurdjieff work because it uses the same symbol as the Gurdjieff tradition, which I was very interested in. I didn't hear much about it further until a teacher named Oscar Ichazo announced this material as his own and indeed made good contributions to the material, and his student Claudio Naranjo, whom I believe you also know...

Iain: He's been on conscious.tv, yes.

Helen: …was also a trainer at Esalen, came back and began to teach a version, his own addition to what he had learned with Ichazo in South America at a training called Arica. Now, I never went to South America, but I was very interested in going to a class of Naranjo's, and at the same time that I was teaching intuition work, I was getting a lot of influx from unexpected groups of people like many, many nuns and priests who were on sabbatical leave for a year, or came to California to have a different experience, and they would train at the Graduate Theological Union. Now, this was fascinating to me, this group of people, because they were the first avenue that the Enneagram went down. The first real home that it found was in the Catholic orders. Naranjo was teaching and a priest friend of mine who was in my intuition work said, "Look, this is great Christian mysticism." That's how he saw it, though I don't think Naranjo did, but that was his view of this material. He enroled me to come to Naranjo's class, which was a nine-week course in which each of the types was presented, and Claudio Naranjo was doing a very good job of bridging – like a Rosetta Stone – bridging these types of people that were described, into psychological language without which I don't think it would have progressed very quickly. But in his class – I only took the one class with him – there were many, many people from my university where I was teaching psychology. So I had a double job. I taught intuition training and I also taught psychology and I was trying to bridge the two – two different states of mind: one, received wisdom – intuition, objective received wisdom…

Iain: So one's coming from up here [*pointing above head*] and one's emerging from here [*pointing to heart*].

Helen: Indeed. And the other is conditioned and cognitive emotional in nature. So between conditioned reality and unconditioned knowing, I was very busy in my groups trying to put these two things together. At the university where I taught, which was John F. Kennedy University School of Consciousness – the first school of consciousness in the US – many of the teachers came to Naranjo's class to discover this bridge that he was putting together between mystical traditions' view of the human person and psychological nomenclature. He was trying to put the two together.

Iain: Was that unique at the time, relatively speaking?

Helen: Oh, it was revolutionary, it was revolutionary. The word 'mysticism' was a bad word, which is why I was flooded with nuns and priests because those with mystical inclination – why they had taken on a vocation in the first place – were massively disappointed to realise that they had essentially a desk job. And there was no training for this inward turn.

Iain: At the time, how did you work in teaching intuition?

Helen: It's a very different state of mind than ordinary cognition or emotional

CONVERSATIONS ON THE ENNEAGRAM

life. The first move would be to get sufficiently empty, so that thoughts and emotions are receded in your field of perception.

Iain: When you say 'receded', mind is saying they're not prominent, but they're still there to some degree?

Helen: They are on the horizon. They are available on need, but they are not foreground in your attention.

Iain: Well, that requires a lot of work and time.

Helen: Not necessarily, because what I was getting from the Enneagram right early in the beginning of time was that the structures – the psychological structure – of thoughts, emotions, sensation, which we knew about, could be observed and witnessed internally. Which is what emptying practise is about, and I just use that word generally because I'm not steeped in the tradition of 'emptying' so I call it 'emptying practise', rather than Vipassana, or Zen, or one of the definitive versions of how to achieve emptiness.

Iain: Let's look at practically what 'witnessing internally' actually means.

Helen: Just to get silent and empty.

Iain: Well, hang on. That's easy to say, it's not so easy to do in this body in this busy world – to get silent and empty.

Helen: It's not ultimate silence or emptiness, but it is a recession of the structure, the typology structure that you have.

Iain: You do that by stopping what you're doing?

Helen: You can do it in two ways. One is the recommended first way, which is to come in and to find your breath and take a pause and be able to follow the breath in the pause because the breath is empty of internal objects. That's one way.

Iain: So let me do that. I close my eyes…

Helen: Turn inward and find the breath in the body…

Iain: Yes, when I do that, briefly my focus is on the breath, that's true, and then things have gone more in the background – thoughts, yes.

Helen: Yes, because the brain actually can only foreground one significant object of attention at a time. So what you're trying to do is to get the breath to be the significant object of attention – the internal breath. And you can get quite skilled at it if you don't put a tremendous amount of pressure on yourself that it has to be ultimate silence. None of that. Take a pause and come into yourself and relax down and just be with the breath for some little period of time and immediately you recognise 'Oh, I have these tensions in my body' or 'Oh, I have this mind that won't let go' or 'I have this emotion that's breaking me'. Something like that.

Now, from the perspective of the 'witnessing consciousness', the heart, the head, and the somatic constrictions are a restriction of life force. Somewhere there's been a tension in the body, or a re-creation of a habitual pattern that is stealing all the life force for itself, in its own automatic way, and it's our job not to get ultimately silent, it's our job just to attend to ourselves so that we can get our life force back. Now, this is not insignificant in terms of the Enneagram. The passions of the heart are actually automatic emotional patterns that arise all on their own because we are conditioned to have that set of feelings and they're attached to a set of thoughts – they operate in tandem.

Iain: I'm just trying to look at this, stage by stage. You're saying our life force has got constricted because of tensions in the body, which is stress I guess, in how we live our life, or how we've reacted to experiences that have happened to us.

Helen: Yes. Conditioned patterns start in very early life based on the instinctual first tendency response that you have to fight, to flee, or to seek contact. That's your endowment and then you interface with that primary tendency with the environment that you have. Patterning starts very early, very early on and so we become a type of person, which is a way of adapting so that we can survive most effectively in the environment that we have, based on the instinct that is most prominent in our lives. That's conditioning and it operates by reinforcement. A child looks for strategies – tries to find strategies that make them agreeable to other people and that create safety, security.

Iain: Yes. So much of the time when we talk about ourselves, really we're talking about our basic patterns, our basic conditioning.

Helen: Our identity.

Iain: Our identity. Which isn't who we really are, it's just something we've learned…

Helen: Yes it is. It is my conditioned reality and it is very suitable to the horizontal plane of ordinary daily living and it has done very well for us to keep us organised in an on-going survival situation, which is life. Which is life.

Iain: It's done its job but… Okay, I think we'll just go back slightly, just very briefly. What is the Enneagram? For people who are watching this programme and don't know what the Enneagram is. What is it?

Helen: It's a description of nine different personality types, which concur very well with modern psychiatry. There's no argument. It's a description of nine different personality types but with the agenda that psychiatry doesn't have, which is that these types are capable of higher orders of consciousness if you find a way to get there, and many ways have been brought to the planet, different ways.

Iain: Like a key if you like, a doorway, clues.

Helen: A key, a doorway, a method. Silence, or emptiness, is one of the methods. The other method is concentration. So between silence and concentration you have a key, because both methods stop the recurring patterns of identity that we have and bring you into the present moment, which is not conditioned.

CONVERSATIONS ON THE ENNEAGRAM

Iain: When you say 'silence', we have a feel of that from what we talked about before, but with concentration. Are you talking about concentrating on the silence, or concentrating on what?

Helen: Concentration is about objects. So you concentrate by bringing your attention over and over again to a single object, usually a devotional object, something that you trust, something that is important to you, but *one* object. The technique is to bring your attention over and over again to one thing only, which backgrounds everything else, because brain can really only hold – foreground – one thing at a time. So emptiness is one, it's an empty object you could call it, and the action there is to relax resistance and to go deeper into the breath that is empty and so create a kind of... a breath that is extended, an emptiness that extends in time. And this is extremely beneficial to the health system. The best research in consciousness lately is coming out of the neurological studies of vastly improved MRI scans, which got a whole lot better in the last fifteen years. You can see, by putting a neural net on an advanced meditator, the actual recession of blood flow and nervous excitement, excitation, from prefrontals and limbic areas – emotion and thinking areas – into a more neutral place inside of yourself. This is extremely useful for lowering blood pressure, for example, and the material that's emanating out of the work of, originally, Jon Kabat-Zinn is marvellous. It has health benefits, so it's a kind of evidence that silence is healing if you can just learn to relax out of – not force anything – relax out of the habit of our identity.

Iain: Yes. I know from what you told me, when we talked on the phone yesterday, that you were actually practicing Zen when you first heard about the Enneagram. What drew you to Zen?

Helen: This was a long time ago, Iain. This was not in the culture. This was so far out of the culture, the idea of going away on a retreat wasn't even a concept for most people. What drew me to Zen was turning off my mind. I'd started with a concentration practise. Knowing nothing else, I learned how to return attention over and over again to a single object of contemplation. And it happens to be my strength, rather than emptying. There's a whole tradition of concentration practise – Vedanta for example, and others that use active contemplation; but the active contemplation is to return to a devotional object instead of moving with – like into the future... staying with now, and it's conjoined with breath, which is in the present moment. Now this set me on a path – this concentration practise – and I don't know how this will sit with you Iain, but I was in my graduate school; I joined up with a peace activism group against the Vietnam War and I was quite dedicated to it. In retrospect, I can see what the draw was because I was so revved and... I lived in Manhattan, it was a very competitive school. To hold my own and do well was very important and so my general energetics was nervous and very high strung.

Iain: I know this for myself.

Helen: So, I needed a way out. Now, what I got out of the relationship with my Zen teacher was a whole lot of peace inside and not much understanding or sympathy with the fact that my visualisation process is florid, which is very suitable to concentration. To imagine inside a devotional object and return attention over and over again to the one great thing was quite natural to me, whereas peace and silence brought up 'What am I getting into?' because it felt alien.

All of that said, my Zen priest kept saying, "Too much studying, too much thinking, Helen," you know, "More zazen." Which did not speak to my situation, but I loved him and I loved the little ashram that he had. The little zendo actually. And then there was my mentor in college who loved the way my mind worked and I had a great relationship with him, my supervisor… "Zen? Leaving your head and your thoughts and your intellectual capacities?" He was appalled. He thought it was sort of magical thinking.

That was the time, and we were left to put together something that seemed suitable to ourselves. So I started a concentration practise with sufficient emptiness, or so I thought, and then I would introduce a single-pointed concentration object and again, I don't know how this will sit with you Iain, but one of my self-appointed jobs in the peace movement was to shepherd young men over the border into Canada, who were resisting the draft.

Iain: The Vietnam War?

Helen: The Vietnam War. And I was in sympathy with them. The peace centre in which I was active was housed in a church and I saw it as a kind of pacifist commitment. Now, right or wrong, that was a decision that I made, but what it did to my tension level was to really skyrocket the situation because this was illegal activity. We had a receiver on the Canadian side, because Canada was sympathetic to the exodus of draft-aged men, but some of these guys could very well have been underage and I was in my early twenties, so I was of age and there were significant consequences. You could get a five-year jail sentence for this. So the pressure – self-induced, I signed on for this – in retrospect, I put so much tension on myself.

Iain: It's interesting because I know, like me, you're a Type Six, which is a fear-based personality, and yet you choose something which is obviously a passion for you that ramps it up even more.

Helen: In retrospect I found myself pinned – because it was my responsibility to get them across – I found myself pinned in an old brown chair in my living room and I would be awakened late at night and I would go into this state of intense concentration and focus and I couldn't think my way out. In fact I couldn't think very well because I couldn't track, I'd been over the same terrain over and over again and it seemed like a guessing game: which post – which border post – you can get the car through successfully… because they were doing random checks and many people were turned back.

So in the midst of four a.m. and in the old brown chair, I would so concentrate on which one of the choices that I had, and focus on one and then the other, that I internalised into a state of concentration that was hyper in its capacity. And I found one evening myself focused on the choice to the extent where I let go. I relaxed into silence from great concentration, let go, and I entered a scene internally – all of this is internal – I entered a scene of the checkpoint and... 'This one is not safe and that one is. Let's go here'.

Iain: But how did you know it was all internal?

Helen: I knew it was internal because every now and then it would become so extreme that I would open my eyes and there would be like an overlay. I could still see the furniture in the room, but there would be this overlay – I actually entered the scene.

Iain: The reason why I asked was it all internal – I can't think of the word for it, but there was at one point – it's now documented – a whole department in the United States Army where they had these people that could look at defences in Russia when it was the Cold War. I forget the name of what it was called. It was a technique, kind of leaving the body... but yours, you were saying was a different...

Helen: No, I don't leave anywhere. I dig deeper in where I am. I never left anywhere but the *perception* is of leaving.

Iain: The perception – okay.

Helen: You see, that's what I think is a mistake, maybe not leaving but the *perception* is that you have left yourself and entered a new scene.

Iain: So you leave your conditioned mind?

Helen: Indeed – it completely recessed the conditioned reality. That would be my understanding. And so my experience was all internal as I understood it, but it had very good information and I relied upon that information for some period of time. I think I took the chance, I put the pressure on myself, the risk – all of that – to increase my capacity, which was my strength to begin with, of concentration. To become inseparable, non-dual with a situation which was not present and with great accuracy inhabit that, I would say, internally, in the imaginal world of reality. *And* I also noticed in this that the information did not come from increased immersion, it came from a place where you could let go and allow the dream to unfold on its own.

Iain: Let's look at this. There's a degree of emptiness, then there's a focus and then, in a way, there's a letting go of the focus.

Helen: Indeed, and that's where the information is because the focus has backgrounded your own interfering streams and you are in reception, which is where intuition occurs.

Iain: I think we all find this in life sometimes and I certainly find it now and again. You know, I am very focused on something and there is a kind of a letting go and then something resolves itself, something becomes clear.

Helen: Indeed. You've concentrated so much energy in the field of your perception that when you let go it sorts itself out. I completely concur with that. So when you say – what did I do with intuition training… I think that was our original thrust here…

Iain: Yes, but the whole subject is fascinating. Somehow it all ties together.

Helen: It is a secondary form of perception, unlike conditioned reality that goes from past to future in a conditioned way. It is a direct experience at a level of consciousness that most people are not interested in until they have an experience of it spontaneously. Then they want to get back to where they've already been, which was the majority of my students, particularly the nuns and priests who – in their prayer life of concentration and the letting go and being in reception of a response to their focused concentration on a single object of devotion – were avid to improve this, and they had been deprived of methodology.

Iain: Okay, but did the improvement of it take them into a real understanding, or experience, of the wider picture?

Helen: That was my job to try to re-create, to try to find, the lost and buried methodology. That's been my cause for forty years.

Iain: You mentioned in a couple of books that the Enneagram is so good that it can actually be a curse in some ways. Because you can understand yourself so much better, you can understand others so much better, but in a way there's a danger [if] you keep this in the horizontal plane; whereas the potential of the Enneagram, as we said earlier, is the key, the doorway to much, much more.

Helen: And I've been on that trajectory for all of these years, but you have to start somewhere, and I have trained, on a worldwide basis – my school is Enneagram Worldwide – we've trained thousands of people in many countries, many thousands in many countries in our history of twenty-six, or -seven years now. I am all for the people that have adapted, that have applied the Enneagram typology, which is the horizontal, how people are different in their ordinary conditioned minds – nine different views of reality, each one accurate to the individual who thinks and feels in a particular way. Subjectively it's truth and there is no other truth. Though you strive to understand the other truths, it is a concept. It is not something that you live with internally in your patterns. The Enneagram has been applied to many settings. Parenting – what could be more valuable, understanding your children? Psychological counselling – what could be more valuable than empowering a client to know themselves through knowing their type? And then the conversation raises in level of information exchange, in a fabulous way. What's wrong with people in couples counselling knowing each other's type so that they can interplay more easily? These are marvellous applications. The business world has taken on many applications and I train people like this, and I have no objection to the horizontal, *unless* it sacrifices the reality that I hold, that the very type structure that is adapted is the raw material for higher orders of evolutionary consciousness.

Iain: How did it work for you, in terms of you moving up the vertical? You started off probably on the horizontal like we all do and got excited about that. What were the gateways that opened for you on the vertical?

Helen: On a personal level it was that I got better at being an intuitive and I began to train people, and this was very important because in training people to be intuitive... you know, there's a lot of talent around. You know people that have had experiences and they were hungry for some kind of mystical training, they would come in for a series of classes, they'd get interested, I would teach them the Enneagram so that they would understand the mechanisms that they had and what had to recede. Fear has to go, Iain...

Iain: [*laughing*]

Helen: ...It has to be relaxed, so that they want to understand it as a structure, that it wasn't so personal, really. It was a structural adaptation that a Six Type has, and there are eight other structural adaptations. So I wanted them to know their type, but I also wanted them to enter the state of mind where they could get received information. That was very important, and for me in all of this I noticed the endemic problem of what is now called spiritual bypass.

Iain: There are even books called that now, aren't there?

Helen: And should be because it's just coming into the public view. I witnessed spiritual bypass, and I probably had some of it myself because I was much better as an intuitive than I was as a slightly immature Six.

Iain: Just to explain briefly, what is spiritual bypass?

Helen: Spiritual bypass is when you take on a spiritual practise and you find yourself attuned to it and you progress spiritually. This is just a simple image – on the cushion you're free. The patterns of your identity are recessed and you're in a state where life force is moving smoothly, which feels blissful. It's the beginning of bliss. You're in a state where your thoughts are not present, so any troubles, any opinions there, they're not there any more and you're in a state of emptiness and silence, or you're in a state of object contemplation if you prefer that path, where you're in reverie and internalising the object of your devotion which has a quality attached to it. If you meditate on a concentration object that is filled with love, then love is a quality, but that's not the same as joy, or the same as other qualities of Being because you can only do one thing at a time and you can't switch in the middle. So the road to non-duality is approachable when you have someone who is adept, somebody who has done enough practise to get skilful means, somebody who is rewarded by simply going to the internal realms because you can't not go there, it's part of your self, it becomes part of your identity. And then you go back home and life is as problematic as ever.

Iain: So we're talking about integration and embodiment of what we taste and learn on our spiritual practise. Is that right?

Helen: I do, I do. I would call it reconciliation because you would have the best of your intellectual pursuits and your emotional, horizontal commitments, and you would also have access to the terrain of higher qualities of Being. I would call it reconciling because the best of the two aspects of the human being, the spiritual and the mundane, come together but you can see each stream as independent from each other. I like that. But spiritual bypass is quite a bother because if you have done no psychological work – which is true in many people committed to a lifelong practise – without psychological understanding of the type, you're in a different territory, you're back in the conditioned territory of your type. The discrepancy is vast between these two states of mind, so the tendency is either to get grandiose like 'I'm better than you because I have access to these personal domains', which may not be exhibited in your psychological behaviour at all because that was back on the cushion, in a different state of mind.

Iain: This is a bit of a cheeky question but I'm going to ask it. Do you feel you're basically free?

Helen: That is cheeky [*pause*]. Let's see.

Iain: You don't have to answer it, if you don't want to.

Helen: The way that I hold myself is, I'm in balance. And I've been written up a lot as an intuitive in the United States. My state is good, it's demonstrable. It was a lot better when I was younger than I am now because I haven't been doing sessions, day after day after day, but when I was cranked up, I was very good. And you know intuitives have different kinds of capacities, so the capacity I had was to read into other people and to do past and future and I asked always for feedback. Over that thirty-five-year span I got feedback from clients. If there was a prediction, I want to know. I want to know if I was projecting or not, so I would give audiotapes. I started out when it was reel-to-reel recordings, that's how far back, but that was the property of my clients and I would forget very quickly what had transpired. But I asked for feedback and I always knew that I had done really well if the family members, who were described as background characters in the tape for my client, all called up and wanted sessions. The feedback was important to me and I've always been very disciplined about that because without feedback you can't be certain, and without certainty you can't go deeper. And that was my commitment to that.

Iain: How does certainty feel?

Helen: Certainty in my inner planes? It's very rewarding. So in the inner planes, I would say I'm more free than the way that I want to hold myself in

243

CONVERSATIONS ON THE ENNEAGRAM

the outer planes because my commitment is balance and I've never said I'm the best psychic in the world, or the best intuitive in the world – ever.

Iain: That's the highest thing – balance. Yes.

Helen: Because each intuitive has a tour de force and they're much better at it than somebody else who's equally competent in another area of focus. But I know the way between my psychological type, which I treasure because it's the vehicle, and refining the vehicle brings you into a better level of balance. Refining the vehicle brings you into better balance, and I know the way back and forth between my prefrontals, limbic, and reptilian brain... and the part of myself that is receptive. I know the way back and forth very well, so I would say I'm one of the more balanced people that I know.

Iain: You know, it's very interesting that the whole journey we've been on in conscious.tv – I think it's six years now – we started off with many non-dual Advaita interviews which were quite fascinating. Then over the years we've become more interested in the whole embodiment: how one lives a life that we can call a free life, or embodied life, or a wise life in a day-to-day existence. And it seems that... it's almost as you hinted earlier, you know on the cushion, you can be clear and there can be non-duality...

Helen: And it lasts for a while.

Iain: ...there could be peace, but you walk out the door and in the marketplace you have all these challenges, and it does seem this embodiment is such a key.

Helen: Yes, and this is why I took the type structure in its conditioned state – the much-despised ego structure, the much-demeaned identity – that's the axis that I follow, in order to stay balanced. So I would say my activity of focusing on my patterns as they occur and applying my practise as I notice I'm going on automatic, because you can get very skilled with your eyes wide open, embodied as you would say, in a crowd: 'I'm going on automatic, I'm starting to have resistance inside'. You can recognise the cues and signs because you've gone looking for them. And that's the inner road map. You recognise them more fitfully, and by relaxing the tension, in the vocabulary of felt-sense tension, in the vocabulary of emotional tension, in the vocabulary of mental tension, like becoming compulsive, or becoming paranoid, or becoming obsessive, or whatever: 'I'm not going to do that now, I want to change *now*'.

Iain: And where does that decision come from?

Helen: It comes from the fact that you feel a whole lot better walking around embodied, if you're not clutched.

Iain: It is common sense in a way, isn't it?

Helen: The body likes it! And the physician will now tell you, "Go take a mindfulness-based stress reduction class," because your blood pressure will lower if you pay attention to your signals. Now that's just one very obvious application. It's not about non-duality, it's just about health, but it certainly speaks to embodiment.

Iain: Yes. One of the things, again, we talked about on the phone, and I think this is worth just spending two or three minutes going through, is that all the things the mind is doing and it's trying to do, almost on a constant basis, it's either coming up with memories, it's planning, it's fantasising, it's being emotional. I've probably forgotten a couple of things but our minds are all the time on a kind of journey, and it's this diligence, of coming back and seeing 'Hey, I'm off again' – past, future, emotions, whatever.

Helen: Well, that's the training that brings you into intuition because the big question is: what is the observing state of mind? If you can observe your mind being caught in memory, who's observing? Who notices this? What aspect of your consciousness perceives this? That's what you're after, and by witnessing these patterns as they unfold, the skilful means of the observing state of mind, or the witnessing state of mind, or whatever you want to call it... reflective state of mind, we have the capacity to be able to observe the mechanics of our own process. Because you and I and anybody could entertain a line of thinking, train of thought, and you could tell the train of thought that you're having, at the time that it's transpiring, and tell it to somebody else. That's what psychotherapy does. You could have an emotion as it arises and begin to describe it, and people do all the time in counselling: "Well, this is what I'm feeling inside." But what is the capacity to *witness* the arising of the structure of your own identity at the time that it occurs?

Iain: I'll repeat that. What is the capacity to witness the structure of your own identity as it occurs?

Helen: And that I feel is the wave of the future, because this capacity for inner witnessing is trainable. I know that from intuition training.

Iain: Yes. It's like a muscle, you can build it up.

Helen: Indeed, it improves with skill and practise. That's the skilful means. And I don't have to know – I think I do know but I'm not going to go into it now – what is the reflect*or*, what is the observ*er*, what is the witness*ing*, what is that function of brain that is installed in us? That is *amazing* to me – that we have this latent capacity that's the most underused function of perception on the planet and it changes everything because you're not identified with this set of thoughts. It's like 'This is what's happening and I'm separate from it. I'm separate from these different patterns in my mind'.

Iain: And you know you're separate because you can observe it.

Helen: I can tell you about what's happening inside of myself and you can do the same for me. Now, from the perspective of neuroscience this is patterns being observed by a different structure, a different perceptual mode. From the perspective of spiritual practise, *now* we're getting somewhere because you can recognise this is the fruit of it: 'I know when I'm going on automatic and I don't have to. I have a choice'.

Iain: 'I have a choice' – even though everything in me is screaming at the time to keep going.

Helen: No. It will not be screaming with sufficient emptiness, and I can't encourage you more, Iain, you don't have to be a Buddha to be able to shift your state of consciousness at will – no! That is what the tradition has informed us about because they didn't know about neuroscience, and science has come into the picture and psychology has come into the picture and we are not of the same kind of consciousness as when the Buddha was alive.

Iain: Yes, but do you know anyone that can really do that – to really catch something and not follow it even for a second or two?

Helen: Perhaps it's a second or two, so what? Just so you come back. Why make it so absolute?

Iain: No, I think it's the recognition of the pattern…

Helen: It is actually first, recognition. That is huge. The second step is shift.

Iain: I can only speak personally; the second shift for me is determination, not to go with it. That's the second point for me. I have to be sometimes very strong with myself.

Helen: Yes, I know but that's counterproductive, you see, because the will is not involved in letting go. The will lets go and then is not involved any more. If you increase concentration, it becomes will-based and that jettisons the necessary space and silence to be able to let go.

Iain: This goes back to your example earlier, with the intuition. I understand, yes.

Helen: Yes, you can't use your will. But the will, you see [sighing], the much-despised identity is a player. The identity is 'I'm determined to let go my suffering'. Because I think we'll all agree there's a generous amount of suffering in these patterns, these type-patterns. 'I am resolved not to use my will to overcome them': that's concentration – it doesn't work right here. 'I am resolved that when I notice at the time of the arising – or maybe a few seconds later, fine – that I have sufficient wherewithal, sufficient skill, to be able to love myself enough and to love my relationship enough that I don't want to be on automatic with you because I love you. I want to be receptive to you, the way I have been, the way I want to get back to the state of receptivity'. The great cry is 'Give me more intimacy'. Well, be open to it. But the second thing is 'And I can't force myself'. You see, that's a good-hearted person, Iain, that is struggling and trying to do it, but it is not effective. The letting go is everything because letting go makes space.

Iain: Yes, but you can't do the letting go; all you can do is provide the framework for letting go. You can't actually say 'I let go', can you? Or can you?

Helen: No, but as soon as you see 'I am letting go' internally reflecting on 'all right, here's my will', I'm jammed, my will is here. Just relax into it. See, it's all about progressive levels of relaxation on the horizontal plane of daily living. And *that* is holy work.

Iain: And as that takes place, then the vertical has more space. Is that correct?

Helen: What the vertical ascent is, is simply the relaxation of the type structure at a strategic moment and then you're still aware. You're still aware, like you are in deep meditation, on the pillow. You're still aware. How do you know that you're beginning to lighten up inside? How do you know and not interfere? Just accept what comes, accept what comes, letting go anything that intrudes. Accept what comes – that's the vertical ascent. And it goes into qualities of Being. I'll tell you a little secret that I've learned, if I have a couple of minutes left?

Iain: Yes, you have more than two. We like secrets on conscious.tv [*both laughing*].

Helen: There is in the Enneagram teaching a whole phase, very important phase, which I call the 'vice to virtue conversion' and I know that 'conversion' is loaded with…

Iain: Okay, let me just think… the 'vice to virtue conversion'.

Helen: It means passion, or the emotional driving pattern. In our case, fear [Type Six]. For somebody else, pride [Type Two], or envy [Type Four], or avarice [Type Five], or all of them. So you have this driving emotional pattern, which is ingrained in you by habit and reinforcement and you don't like it. But you can recognise because you've trained, you know your type and you have a modest practise, not absolute but a modest practise. When, let's say, avarice comes up, the Five would recognise 'I'm beginning to feel that constriction of avarice and I want to leave the room. I'm trying to get out of it, I don't like this'. Noticing that and relaxing into, going towards the place of suffering and contraction, instead of bailing, using the practise of relaxation into, and pretty soon it gets to be a plateau. And when it plateaus and you can't relax into any further, but you still want to leave the room, you don't leave it there, you go someplace in your body where you're not tensed up but you stay, stay in the room and you find a place in the body that is not involved at all in this avarice-contraction which is happening in a certain sector in your body. And then being fully involved in this that is already free; it might be a limb, it might be the front of your face, it might be any part of your body that isn't involved in the contraction. And then when you feel a little bit of letting go, you go back and there's more space around the contraction. You work it. Now that is a body of work, I understand it came from Peter Levine. It's a trauma reduction process.

Iain: I'm aware of this.

Helen: And it's important for us in spiritual work. Now, they didn't have this back then, in the tradition. Science has given us something. It is verifiable by machines that can measure your blood pressure now and its reduction by skilful means. The whole thing is so much faster now in its possibilities for us. It doesn't take a very long time if you have enough motive to be able to say 'I've had it with this contraction against reality'. And every type contracts in a different sector. Just touch a Two's pride and they contract. Or just touch the vanity of a Three and they contract. These contractions, in the vocabulary of felt sense in the body, can be observed, it can be witnessed. In the same way that emotional 'I've been assaulted' contraction can be felt and recognised in the vocabulary of emotion. And certainly the easiest one to see is: where is your attention drifting in the head? You see?

Iain: From the level of intuition, who's observing the observer?

Helen: I don't want to get into that. It's not of interest to me. The observer, I do believe, is a capacity to reflect reality as it actually is, rather than [as] it appears to be through type filters.

Iain: It's reflecting reality...

Helen: It only reflects. Ah... if that's your question, that's a good one. Reflection is a form of perception. It's a faculty of perception, of human perception that operates by reflection, rather than conditioned apprehension through thoughts, feelings, and sensations.

Iain: It just reminds me, I'm doing an interview with a couple of guys in two days' time and they've written a book called *Godhead*, which I've read part of, and one of the things they said, which was quite fascinating for me, was that actually consciousness needs the human race. This is what they're saying, it needs awake humans, to be aware of awareness, because without... and we've had other people on conscious.tv – scientists – that have said, "Without the observer, actually form doesn't exist." And that's a big leap from what we've talked about here, but it just came to me...

Helen: I believe that, I believe that consciousness is so...

Iain: ... conscious observation is so key, on so many levels.

Helen: Yes, and it operates by reflection. That much I'm certain of. But on a more modest level, where it's going is less important than becoming a vehicle of its use.

Iain: Okay. It's about *now*; '[a vehicle of] its use', now?

Helen: Being used. If consciousness wants to reveal itself, I better be open for it. And you see it's a very modest... it's very close to the Buddhist ideal. All we're trying to do is to get to reality as it actually is, unfiltered by all of these conditions of pattern-like way of sorting information. Getting through the veil of illusion, which is these patterns, or polishing the mirror so that the reflector is able to perceive more and more subtle events in the world. I don't care if it's in the world, or it's consciousness of God, or whatever. I don't think in those terms. I think in the relief of suffering and the ability to have clarity, and I know from my own experience that the past and the future are perceptible in the present moment. And things that are unknown to the human mind, to my mind, that are at a great distance can be described all inside of myself, by reflection. Now, somebody else can explain it. I just prefer to do it [*both laughing*].

Iain: That's a great place to stop. Thanks, Helen. Thanks very much. You were very brave at times. I asked you a couple of not easy questions and I appreciate that you responded, and thanks for coming onto conscious.tv.

Helen: I think you're doing a great service actually to the community, to build these archives so that this time of exploration, which is so fruitful, will have a voice in the future.

Iain: Absolutely. It has a voice now too. I'm going to show some of Helen's books again. The first one that I read many years ago: *The Enneagram in Love and Work* – great starting place, if you're interested. *Inner Knowing*, which Helen's talked about quite a bit. *The Enneagram Advantage*, and *The Pocket Enneagram*, which again is a really easy starting place, and she has other books as well. Thanks again, Helen.

To watch this interview please go to:
http://www.conscious.tv/consciousness/enneagram

Faisal Muqaddam
The Essential Enneagram as a spiritual path to awakening

Interview by Eleonora Gilbert

Eleonora: Today my guest is Faisal Muqaddam. Faisal is the originator of the Diamond Logos teaching. He is a psychospiritual teacher and has been teaching in the Middle East and the USA for thirty-five years and, for the last twenty-five years, in Europe, Italy, Germany, and Denmark. Faisal was born in Kuwait and is a trained Reichian and bioenergetics therapist. He has studied different systems of growth with esteemed teachers such as Tarthang Tulku Rinpoche and Dr Claudio Naranjo, as well as Middle Eastern Sufi teachers. He is currently practising and teaching in California and Europe.

Iain interviewed Faisal last year and I was personally excited about the conversations that we had afterwards so we invited him again. On conscious.tv we have a whole series on the Enneagram, and Faisal is going to be talking to me today about exploring the Essential Enneagram as a spiritual path to awakening. Tell us about the Essential Enneagram.

Faisal: Hello everybody. Thanks for the opportunity. There is a dimension of spirituality we call the 'essential domain', relating that title to different aspects of differentiated Being. We have the Being, undifferentiated, a differentiated self, and myriads of qualities. Some are major archetypes like love, beauty, clarity, power, will. Each one of them is an essential domain, an essential quality. We discovered a lot of those major qualities that we integrate in our work. And the fascinating thing was realising that these fixations, that we so much looked at from a psychological perspective, mental [perspective], led to huge limitations. And the teacher who taught it warned us not to use it this way. But [in] time, It became [a way of] ego-reduction. As [if] by continually reducing the student to their fixation, they would be able to see it and somehow magically it will break, and there will be awakening.

Eleonora: To be clear, when you talk about fixation, you also mean type?

Faisal: Yes. Enneagram type, or Enneagram fixation, yes, and the idea by the name is that part of our mind got fixated, unable to move, and unable to be resilient and maintain one job, one quest, [that] is to recreate this archetype. We didn't look so much into why is that. We understand a little bit that it was the manoeuvre the child adopted to resolve some of the difficulties in life, in childhood. And there are so many theories: that we are born in it… you name it, there is so much complexity. But there was very little saying what this type is preserving. Is this just a mental construct, a psychological construct, or does it come from an origin, and if so what is that origin? By enquiring into that, through grace, through enquiry, through revelation, the picture began to be revealed that each type is an imitation, an attempt, and a preservation of one quality of essence, or one dimension of Essence.

So then the picture started to shine: it is not just a psychological, repetitive pattern, it is really an attempt to revive and to connect [to] a certain aspect of our Being, a certain aspect of Essence. Then little by little, [over] thirteen years, the map unfolded and the dimension [that] each fixation is trying to reach or preserve became more vivid. And in our work, knowing those essential domains, it was great to weave the Ennea-type with the quality, and [with] time it opened deeper and deeper. That by undoing, or by integrating the essential domain from which the fixation has originated, it led to greater freedom, it led to discovery of the essential dimension, and that led to liberation.

Eleonora: Can you give us an example of the various different essential qualities for each type, for each fixation?

Faisal: Okay. The one that fascinates me the most, and the one that I will come to, was for me the *'guidance'*, the aspect of Essence that has to do with 'the Guide'. My love for the Guide was so great because it orchestrated this unfoldment, the psychological domain, the essential domain, and wove it in such an unbelievable intricacy, richness, and wisdom, that no ego can do. I loved this aspect. The guidance is to me the crown jewel of the essential teachings.

We call this the Guide, or we call it the objective perception or the 'diamond guidance' or objectivity. This quality is related to an aspect of Essence that has to do with knowing – the ability to know, the ability to have differentiated wisdom, guidance, all of that, and it helps so much in our unfoldment. Yet this quality is beyond knowledge. It is related so much for example to the Five on the Enneagram. The Fives, their obsession, or their drive and their inspiration, is to know. To know or not to know. To be or not to be, that is the Nine. To know or not to know is the Five. Fives, at the level of the fixation, are very fascinated with knowing. They are so knowledgeable and there is no end to that starvation for knowledge. They accumulate so much knowledge and all of that, and sometimes it is excessive. And sometimes it is wonderful to know. In this process, their preoccupation, the underground basis of their longing for knowing and for understanding, is a longing for this aspect of Being... this aspect of Being... One manifestation of it is knowledge; its Essence is 'the knower'.

Eleonora: Right.

Faisal: So Type Five on the Enneagram is pursuing this quality but taking the information, the knowledge, to be the knower. They don't know that the knower is an aspect of Essence that is made of diamond that has the ability to differentiate the Absolute into knowledge, but also into all kinds of manifestations. They get fascinated by the knowledge and forget the knower and confuse knowledge with knower.

Eleonora: And the guidance and the knower are the same aspect.

Faisal: So this aspect of Essence is perceived as a diamond and enables the mind to be clear, to be objective. [It] brings the ability to know, but it is not just about knowing, it is not bound by the realm of knowledge as intellectual knowledge, nor by enquiry – it is the source of enquiry. If you connect in your enquiry, you reach it, but then you drop enquiry and you hold the knower, and then enquiry turns into insight, into realisation. This jewel, sometimes called 'the angel of revelation', reveals to you what is in the unconscious, it reveals to you the hidden kingdom, and functions in multidimensionality. It is not just in the head and knowledge. It comes in the heart and orchestrates beauty, art, poetry, intuition. It comes in the belly and orchestrates impeccability, groundedness, the gentle warrior part, but often it gets confused with knowledge. Also they idealise this quality, take it to the head, and use it as a never-ending information of knowledge, which is beautiful but overwhelming you know. So the enquiry is about what is the Five trying to do? Realise that they are really trying to reach this quality and when they reach this knowing, this diamond dimension in our Essence, then a great deal of resolution happens in their fixation.

So, the Five is the attempt to be the knower. And when they reach it, they are not obsessed with knowledge any more, because knowledge has no end.

Eleonora: And when it comes to the other types? I know you are fascinated with Fives. Any other types that you could use as an example?

Faisal: Yes, I can go over the whole map. It was really fascinating, this discovery, that Type One in the Enneagram is obsessed or embodying and conflicted about this quality of appreciative love, unconditional appreciative love. And this appreciative love is a very sweet, fluffy kind of love. It is not a powerful kind of love, it is cotton candy, sweet, fluffy, and has to do with the quality we call pink Essence, which is a mixture of red Essence and brilliant Essence. They mix, they create softness, they create fluffiness. And Type One in the Enneagram is living all their life trying to maintain this quality, to generate it. So their fixation is not just an ego pattern. It is trying to mobilise even the system to affect certain organs, certain attitudes [in order] to keep generating this quality – and they generate a lot of it – but paradoxically they always feel they don't have enough. So the fixation is in over-work, trying to generate this quality. And since they, every now and then, get angry, they fall from the grace of unconditional acceptance, unconditional love. They constantly feel wounded and the story keeps going on.

Eleonora: Right, they feel wounded and they seek this pink love and they keep getting re-wounded, and so it is a never-ending story.

Faisal: Yes, never-ending. The moment they feel angry, they are not any more pink Essence. So they feel they have fallen from their highest ideal.

Eleonora: And to feel that pink Essence, what is a Type One to do? Because the quality is there, present in all of us, in all the various types. What is one to do?

Faisal: We all have this quality but Ones are like a nuclear fusion of pink. They have so much of it, but something within them does not see it, does not allow them to experience it enough; always making them feel hurt and a failure because they haven't healed the world from their attempt to heal it. This pain, this continuous attempt to heal this ideal quality and to actualise it… and they fall short of it. It [puts] the ego on an on-going process, like a gerbil in a wheel. It never ends – generating so much pink – but doesn't do it. In our work, the first step is to be conscious.

Eleonora: To be conscious of the pattern.

Faisal: Of the pattern, their fixation – it explains what it does, how it is doing it in terms of their mental pattern, emotional pattern, physical pattern. Then little by little, [they can] go to the essential domain. And by doing so, we also explore their childhood, what happened, what was needed in the family. Little by little, we deepen the enquiry. At the same time, by recognising the pattern around a certain quality, their consciousness begins to differentiate and [becomes aware] when the quality is there and begins to see when it is gone and the anxiety that comes when it is gone. So they begin to know their specific anxiety and their specific resistance and specific superego. It becomes more and more in focus, more and more orchestrated. And we also focus not only on the feeling of this quality, but also on the organ of the body that is ruled by it.

Eleonora: Okay, I want to stop you there for two things, so we can weave all of this in the other types. We discussed earlier that there is a family hole that occurs, and that is when the soul takes on a particular aspect that it constantly tries to come back to and reach. In this particular case, Type One is this pink

CONVERSATIONS ON THE ENNEAGRAM

love, but also there is an organ that is related to that particular typology, that particular fixation. So the family hole and the organ related to Type One – what is it?

Faisal: The family hole – shall I explain the family hole? The theory is that we as human beings are [like] Swiss cheese, full of holes – something missing – and our parents were like that too. We wish them to be these glorious gods and goddesses but they were humans, and gods and goddesses [only] to a certain extent. So at one time in the family, let's say the family was going through a conflict – which is normal – and at one time, let's say mum and dad close their heads. They don't want to understand each other, so there is impairment in the quality that can be generated by the head, [such as] clarity, precision, brilliance, overview. And another time, the parents, maybe they can understand each other, but they are hurt – they don't open their hearts to each other.

Eleonora: So in the case of the Five, for instance, the family hole would have been lack of understanding?

Faisal: Yes, it will be the 'diamond body', which brings understanding [that] was impaired. They don't want to understand.

Eleonora: And the child develops that desire to...?

Faisal: ...to solve it – but I will come to that – by saying [in] the belly 'What is lost?' And what was lost is basic sanity, basic groundedness, basic ease – and the family is anxious, insecure, ungrounded. So the belly centre has to do with groundedness, with relaxation, with ease, and that is impaired, is not functioning fully, which means that one quality or another of the belly is blocked, or of the heart, or of the head is blocked. So a soul comes to incarnate or reincarnate and it gravitates to a certain hole depending on its karma, let's say. So this soul, this baby lands in the womb. And because of the merged quality [merging with primary caretaker –FM] – let's say mum is blocking the quality of her heart and dad is blocking his heart – the baby – his heart is developing prenatally in the womb as a structure, due to merging with the environment – gets affected by the absence of this quality. That to me is what 'born in sin' [means]. We were born in a 'missing aspect'. Sin to me is a diagnostic thing, not a judgement.

Eleonora: Sure.

Faisal: It is something that is missing. Sin is a disconnect. So the soul of the baby, in developing the body and the organs, struggles so much around the heart. And the heart is closed and the heart generates gold, golden Essence, sweet love that has so much richness to it. The baby feels its golden Essence keeps depleting, [the parents] block it. Their heart is not open, but the baby is a mighty soul at that time, it is in connection with the Source. It struggles, it generates gold and merges and loses it, and then generates it again. This process makes the golden Essence the most dominant quality because its survival is happening around it. So the system generates it more and more and that child becomes so much gold, but through the attempt at releasing it, and losing it, it creates subtle membranes of resistance to that quality, so they generate it more, but feel it less. When they are born and their ego begins to develop, first year, second year, there is a preoccupation with this quality, without knowing what it is. They feel it as some kind of love, and when this love comes, mum is happy, dad is happy, their hearts soften. They begin to feel this is really the most important quality in existence. They begin to develop some aspect of ego… let's say half of the ego mechanism is based on 'to gold or not to gold'.

Little by little, the ego gets more entangled, more difficult, it separates more and more from the gold; it generates more and more of the gold. Then this domain becomes dominant in the essential level, but also in the ego. The ego then limits its perception of reality. Reality becomes limited and focuses on 'How can I generate this?' It is so important, and then that leads to an ego development that gets fixated around this quality because it is the survival for the family, the healing of the family, and it expands as a cosmic approach. Our dilemma is solved by love. But the Five in the Enneagram says 'To love or not to love is okay, but if we don't understand, what is the use of love?' So each is different: this one [fixates] on love, this one on stability. Each fixation is like a jewelled aspect of Being that got overly developed, and the ego is afraid to go and experience other domains. It is focused as a guardian. The fixation, you can think of it as a guardian, the representation of an essential domain.

Eleonora: So the 'golden domain' would be the representation of Type Two, because you talked about the heart?

Faisal: Yes, yes. The Two, for example, is so much about sweet precious love. So a Two will see pink love and say 'Yes that is sweet, but that is baby love' and another love which is pomegranate: ecstatic, passionate love. That's not enough, you know, you need most authentic love; it has to be twenty-four-carat gold. So then the Two is so occupied [with] offering the most precious love and then not only to offer this love, but also how can they manifest it? So they turn their whole system into a vehicle, an instrument that manifests preciousness and beauty, and that is another aspect of Essence. We call it the 'chandelier', the body of jewels, the body of manifestation, expression. That's when you go to a Two's house… chandeliers – my sister, she has ten chandeliers – she's a Two – it will bring the festivity, the beauty…

Eleonora: So that we don't miss out Type One, we didn't quite finish it. That was the pink love. Were there any other aspects for Type One?

Faisal: A subtle idea which is that the essential domain is made of 'dimensions' and 'vehicles'. The dimensions are like you make the whole field of awareness as a pink ocean of love. Within it, there are a variety of qualities.

You can have a sense of an individuated pink person: 'I am really appreciatively loving'. The other one says 'I not only want to be it, I also want to manifest it', so they go to pink chandelier. The other one says 'I am not only going to manifest it, but I want to know objectively what it is', so they develop pink diamond. Within the field, within that dimension, there are many qualities. That is why when you look at Ones, they are different. They are all about the same quality, but this one wants to make it personal, this one impersonal, this wants to make a celebration of it...

Eleonora: If we move on to the Threes now, since we talked about Twos, what is that?

Faisal: Threes sense that the family is missing contact and connection with each other. So they feel they really want to connect with everyone and feel their needs, find what is needed and generate it. Very close to the Twos. Type Two feels what is needed through merging. They melt with the other person and feel it – that's their affinity, and the chandelier manifests it. And the Threes, they have a quality of Essence that can connect with the other person, really tune in and be one with them and feel, and then they 'generate' it, whether for a person, or for the family, or the community. What is needed now is this... you feel it and then you set the Ferrari and you go. They are generators like that. So the quality of contact... and bonding and healthy attachment is a quality of Essence that has a feeling of resiliency. It's a conscious substance that senses. And the generator is another quality, so the combination of them [the quality of contact and bonding, and the generator -FM] is a magnificent quality of Essence that optimises the grand vehicle of the human structure in the essential domain. There is a vehicle that is the ultimate vehicle that embodies the personal Essence.

Eleonora: And what is that vehicle, can you name it?

Faisal: We name it in our work 'the stupa' – at least, I name it the stupa, the 'pearly stupa'. This quality is made of many jewels, and each jewel differentiates Being into an energetic field and it is a dynamo. Those who don't have it don't function in life. They can be couch potatoes, couch mangoes – sweet, but not dynamos, not generators. That is why it is called the 'heart of enlightenment' – the heart that generates from the field of enlightenment: love, action, contactfulness. The fixation in the Enneagram of the Three is trying to do it, which is glorious except it is doing it from the personality, which is exhausting. Their adrenals get wiped out.

Eleonora: And it is exhausting for everyone around them as well.

Faisal: [*laughing*] Yes. Let's go to the park, let's go to the park...

Eleonora: Okay, moving on to Type Four.

Faisal: Yes, the Four, when they were born, what was missing in the family was an authentic sense of self. Everybody is missing their sense of self and in their own trip. The mother may be an Eight and she wants to demolish all there is, and the father could be a Five and wants to hide from existence. Nobody is there in their real self, in a simple way, in a glorious way, in a beautiful way. So the self was missing in the family. The personal self, not the impersonal self – this light within we call the 'inner star' or the 'point of light'. So the Four suffers so much because what was missing keeps eradicating their sense of self. Nobody was looking at them as a person then, everybody was busy with their own trip. So the baby starts to struggle around maintaining this 'light' inside and [in] time, it even tries to offer it to mum and dad. You offer them the light, you offer them the spirit. Except that they [say], "Oh, thank you, you made me feel a little bit good," but they are not interested in your spirit, they are not interested in your light, they are fighting, wanting their own spirit. And the child feels 'I am failing, even my light is not good enough'. They feel wounded about their sense of self and the drama never ends, and it manifests for the Fours as this drama, this intensity of the drama. The intensity of the drama of the fixation is an attempt to make a little stone [into] sunshine. When they see that, they ease their drama, they feel the loss of the self; the self merges within as a Being of light – exquisite, gracious. This quality is the central station of what all the Enneagram [types are] seeking. The Enneagram is seeking to resolve: how to point, or not to point. [All the Ennea-types are attempting to reach the 'point of light' (the individuated true or essential self) -FM.]

Eleonora: How to point, or not to point… What do you mean?

Faisal: How to be the self, or not. So the Five in the Enneagram says 'If I solve the riddle of existence, I could rest and they could put me on my throne again'. The Three says 'If I can do all the jobs affectionately, then they will see me', and the One says 'If I can make them appreciate each other… and I appreciate the other'… All the fixations are an attempt to solve the family hole, then they can be seen and loved and provided for. Since that trip has no end, we alienate farther and farther. The Four says 'What is really needed is the self. Why are you having third world war when all you want is your own little point of light?' So the Four says 'I offer', and the Four is sacrificing all the time, but they cannot sacrifice their point, they cannot give it away, nor [does] anybody want it. You know, everybody wants their [own] point, so it is a failing task [for the Four to try to give theirs to someone else –FM]. But at least, the ultimate purpose, for me, is that we are all trying to find our self – back to this self. But some went the way of 'Where is your ear?' 'It is here' [*pointing to left ear*]. And the Four says 'It is here [*pointing to right ear*] but it is just not the right ear' – because they take the ego to be the point. Their dilemma, they constantly confuse the little ego self with the authentic self, and of course that continually feels shameful. It is a lie, so they are always hiding and all of those things, until one day they discover that yes, their ego is fake. They are not authentic, not genuine, but the fake one is holding the post for the genuine one. And there is forgiveness for the ego, there is integration of the ego instead of trying to polish it, making it something different. You appreciate this part of your soul, and then it can resolve.

Eleonora: It can relax and resolve.

Faisal: Yes, relax and just be yourself, share it. But each fixation, fascinatingly, is all about the centre of a mandala. There is another Enneagram superimposed on the Enneagram, three corners to it that reach a pinnacle of twelve, and the top of that pyramid is self, individuated self. The Enneagram is an attempt to undo the mind and the structures, resolve it in Being, in the Buddha nature, in the enlightened nature, then finding our uniqueness. So the journey starts.

Eleonora: Okay. Let's move on to Type Six now. We did Type Five.

Faisal: The Six realises that what was missing in the family was the feeling of solidity, of groundedness, safety, perseverance, will, and the courage to continue to walk the walk. They begin to struggle around that quality, which is 'brilliancy' and what we call 'the citadel'. It is a quality of Essence that when it lands, you really feel solid, relaxed. Your bones, instead of being calcified like rocks by terror, by fear, and by trying to maintain the solid quality that you are relying on, your iron will – all of that relaxes and a solid structure lands and you feel it can take care of things: 'I can have my bones breathe again. I can have my adrenals rest again'. So the Six is so much trying to be this impeccable warrior for others, and they can. They can be so loyal, so devotional, so much there [for the other]. They generate a lot of brilliancy and knowing and solidity, but when it comes to walking their own walk [clicking fingers], it is gone. They don't know how to administer this quality to themselves. Once they discover this quality is being used for others, that's the beginning of recognition and then owning it. And then they deal with the issues in the way for this quality to land for them to feel safe, secure, grounded, and [have] the courage to walk their own walk in life.

Eleonora: And to trust.

Faisal: And the 'basic trust' comes: Being will provide, the journey continues, and the universe is here for us. While in the depth of their fixation, in Sixes there is the feeling 'I am all alone and because I am all alone, I will be there for all my people, all my friends', which is beautiful, but the moment they apply it for themselves – and this applies to all fixations – their personality begins to disintegrate. The personality structure is based on the struggle around trying to generate it. Once there is no need for it, it crumbles. Once it crumbles, it can lead to the Absolute – mind free from any fixedness, but it also leads to a terror of losing one's identity. What does Descartes say? "I doubt, therefore I am."

Eleonora: I think... "I think, therefore I am."

CONVERSATIONS ON THE ENNEAGRAM

Faisal: Yes, I think. So to think, or not to think [for a Six]. For a Four, to point or not to point.

For a Nine, to be or not to be. The ego identity is based on this concept, and once I don't need to think, I am just here. The last struggle with the ego begins to emerge. Armageddon starts, and then the dissolution of Armageddon.

Eleonora: Okay, now Type Seven.

Faisal: Sevens, when they were in the womb evolving, what was missing in the family was the spaciousness and the openness to look and see all the pieces of the puzzle. Mum sees only her view. Dad sees only his view, and they only see the family view versus the world view. There is a tunnel view of a perception of reality, and that limitation of course leads to fear, leads to a lack of trust, leads to not knowing what reality is about. Reality or the perception of reality becomes limited views and belief systems. Then the baby loses the ability to see the variety of views about reality, and they are all valid, and that reality is greater than those views, so the baby aspires to know the greater plan. What is the cosmic view, what is the cosmic plan? Of course they [Seven children] open that ability, and the family restrict it. You know how dogmas are, one belief, and sometimes we even demonise other people: these are bad people, these are good people. Instead of being open and being fascinated with the richness of this culture, and of that one, with the richness of this neighbourhood and of that. This ability to be curious, spacious, is what we call the 'mind of the presence', the 'grand mind' – the openness that perceives all the pieces fitting together in the puzzle, and in our work, we call it the 'diamond dome'. For the audience who are interested in this, there is a mosque in Iran called Shah Cheragh, and they built a dome inside the mosque of tiny mirrors and between them, they have lines of coloured mirrors: stripes of red, stripes of yellow, stripes of green. At one time in my travels, I went there with a Sufi and he kept me there the whole day, around the shrine. People came to receive blessings and we sat there, and the sun came through the windows and in the morning, it hit certain combinations and the whole dome became, let's say brilliant. Then as [the sun] moved, it hit the red band and the whole dome became red. It was breathtaking really, a master architectural piece.

Eleonora: And the diamond dome is the essential vehicle, the essential quality of Type Seven?

Faisal: Yes, and I remember my guide said 'mind, the cosmic mind – not the Absolute – [but] the multi-faceted mind that can see the bigger picture'. They made it there in Shah Cheragh, an actual [structure], beautiful.

Eleonora: Wonderful. Type Eight?

Faisal: Type Eight is the animal soul, inside. This libidinal force in the baby and the energy for life... there is no force as powerful as the force for life,

CONVERSATIONS ON THE ENNEAGRAM

nothing, really. Even death is part of it, you know. It's such a powerful force – that sometimes you see those little plants coming from rocks in the mountains: 'Wow, hallelujah, how could they even come from rocks?' This force, this love of life, this ecstatic passionate love of life. When the Christ gave the bread and the wine, he said, "This is my blood, this is my flesh." What is he referring to? Christ, in my dictionary, in my culture, is a roaring lion, full of love of life, golden pomegranate lion that came to show us the glory of life and how we kill it every day by being nailed on the cross. Our cross is our personality. So the love of life, this wine of life, the Eight comes with it, which is like a tiger, full of life and power. The Eight is amazing physically, the ability and richness they have in their body is glorious. It is misused, fine, and sometimes it is well-used, fine, but you admire this phenomenon. So Type Eight is about generating this ecstatic, passionate love, different from pink love. Pink love is soft and cuddly. This one is roaring. You want to dance all night, you want to drink wine to infinity; it is like nothing is in your way. So the baby was struggling in the womb about the absence of life energy in the household. Everybody is stuck, dull and sleeping, no aliveness, so the baby roars and because it's been struggling around it, Eight has so much of this energy, they can go on and on to infinity. So this quality is a mixture of what we call 'black Essence', which erases mind [and] 'red Essence', which erases fear. So you have no mind, no fear, you have Zorba. Dancing, interacting. Zorba is the archetype of Eights, while Buddha is the archetype of Fives. This quality, of course, is so luscious because it is instinctual. Even when it is distorted… still you are amazed at the amount of energy it generates, especially in the body, because it really revives the body, strengthens it, and strengthens the heart to have the courage to walk your walk and to love the ultimate product of existence: life.

Eleonora: Wonderful… and the vehicle of this?

Faisal: This one is a dimension, the same as pink, an ocean of this pomegranate. Within it there is a *pearl*, there is a *diamond*, there is a *stupa*, there is a *chandelier*. One person has this quality, one person has that quality…

Eleonora: Okay, and Type Nine? Also I wonder – since we talked about the organs relating to each type – if we could include that? Then we will go around the symbol again.

Faisal: Yes. Nine idealises normalcy, they just want to be ordinary. The ultimate dimension is just ordinariness: 'Why are you fluffing your feathers – if you are a Three or you are a Two – that's narcissistic'. The Nine does not want to be narcissistic, so their narcissism is to be 'not-special'.

Eleonora: What was the family hole, to develop this 'not-special?'…

Faisal: First we define what is normalcy. The only thing that gives this feeling of normalcy is Being itself. Everything is special, everything has something about it, the flowers and all that, but when you feel Being, you feel normal;

it feels like I am coming from insanity to basic sanity, to ease, to relaxation. So Type Nine is constantly struggling around maintaining the Absolute – basic nature – and maintaining a quality of Essence we call 'water'. The 'water dimension' has to do with ordinariness, with ease, with relaxation. When you hold the baby's body, it is like water, liquid but mixed with little gold, so it's golden water, pink water. Babies are adorable, but their bodies are magical: you touch their skin, their suppleness and all of it is pure Being relaxing through the body. So for Nines, the whole field was dull or insane, and they are trying to maintain normalcy. Normalcy has a sense of balance and ease. When that is established, then their glory of individuation shines within it. But they were not allowed to reach that level, they got forced into [believing] 'There is nothing special about you, you are just one of the kids, we are just one of the people in the neighbourhood. So just be normal, be ordinary', which is true, but not enough.

So the Nine struggles about how not to create ripples in the household, how to calm the waters so there is basic sanity. There are ten kids in the family, mum is overwhelmed, dad is overwhelmed, all of a sudden you want gelato, then it feels like 'Who are you? We can't afford gelato, if you want [it], then the other kid wants this, and the other kid wants that'. So the Nine is asked to delete their uniqueness, to disappear, and just be normal, don't create ripples. In doing so, they have to control an organ that creates this sense of evenness and ease. So they control the pineal gland, which has the sense of calming the disservice in the system, pacifying the conflicting issues and harmonising all the energies. This happens when the pineal gland is released and begins to connect you, open the top of your head to the Absolute, and the Absolute comes and normalises you. The Absolute is very normal, enlightenment is so normal nobody wants it. Then the Nine tries to maintain this state. Somehow magically they can go to the pineal gland, do something there, block it and have it, instead of producing serotonin, melatonin, which are the products which open up in the head when the Absolute is there. These qualities bring pleasure, ease, normalcy, allow all the organs to harmonise without conflicting. Since they cannot reach it, they have to control their emotions, their instincts, their reactivity, their preferences, and they control the pineal gland. The pineal gland blocks and then it produces effects that feel like numbness in the body. So the Nine feels numb and the numbness is like fake normalcy – nothing is disturbing, it is like calm water. So that is the speciality of the Nine.

Eleonora: And Type One?

Faisal: The medulla, the stem of the brain. It controls the instincts, the animal impulses, and part of the animal impulse is like… you see the little cubs, they struggle, they fight, and all those things, but when it is asked to be perfect, to be good, and 'Good kids don't fight. Don't get angry. Don't throw a tantrum'… So they are struggling with their natural impulses. They really want to pick [up] the cat by its tail and swing it, but then you are not a good girl, or a good boy. So in order to control and suppress those impulses of the animal soul, they have to go to the controller of the impulse. Those impulses are in the pelvis, they are in the perineum, the sacrum, the solar plexus – these are the instinctual domain. In the Essential Enneagram, the instincts are located in the lower centres, the passion in the heart, and the concept in the head. So they apply this organ of the brain that controls the lower centres and shut down the rage, the anger, everything that we call improper. So they cultivate a lot of neck problems, brain [problems], and the top of the head.

Type Nine, One, and Eight suffer from a 'shrinking' of the head: migraines, headaches, dullness, limitation of spaciousness, limitation of the liquid around the sac the brain, because the controlling of the pineal gland shrinks the brain. The medulla contracts the stem of the brain, blocking the top of the head.

Type Two controls the throat and the diaphragm. [Under] the diaphragm, there is a centre and that centre affects the heart; we call it the mobius, the centre of infinity. When it opens, it becomes like a fountain of sweetness, from it runs sweet yellow gold and [it] opens the heart and makes the heart richer. The throat is the centre of expression, manifestation, the celebration of the chandelier.

Type Three controls the heart itself and the pericardium, the sac around the heart. That sac when it is relaxed is filled with amberic gold, sweetness, appreciation, value for life, for each other. And because nobody values who they are enough and what they are doing, Threes feel so much pain and they shrink the heart, they shrink their pericardium. But then they struggle, they release it and their heart is gorgeous, so beautiful. And again, the same thing, nobody sees, nobody appreciates, so they control this organ. It is good for them to really be aware of this.

Type Four is the lungs.

Eleonora: Why the lungs? That is interesting.

Faisal: The lungs have to do with aspiration and inspiration. It relates to the spirit, and the spirit is this point of light [*pointing to top of head*] and also the radiance of the Absolute.

Eleonora: Spirit, the breath… is the same.

Faisal: Yes.

Eleonora: And then we have Type Five.

Faisal: Fives control the stomach. The centre of their strength is their head and the centre of their weakness is their stomach. They have a lot of weakness physically in the stomach. Many Fives in time can't eat this and can't eat that. The organ weakens there because their ability to digest and assimilate is blocked. Their ability to differentiate expands, but they cannot take in more instinctual animalistic aspects so they try to go to knowledge and to their higher centre. Very powerful in their higher centre, very weak in the stomach. Also above the stomach is a centre we call the 'lunar plexus'. Above the lunar plexus, the solar plexus. The lunar has to do with will and the ability to surrender, and they cannot surrender because they think they haven't figured it out.

Eleonora: Right, when they figure it out, then they can surrender. Okay, Type Six?

Faisal: Type Six controls the adrenal glands and the large intestine. Sometimes they are constipated, sometimes they have diarrhoea, and the adrenals get exhausted because they are in a constant fight-or-flight mechanism. Their adrenals are so heightened: 'When is the attack going to come? Is it a safe thing?'… So it exhausts them.

Type Seven is the small intestine, the ability to assimilate – there they are starving, there is so much starvation.

Eleonora: Right, the gluttony.

Faisal: Yes, and instead of strengthening this organ, they think 'If I can find the cosmic breast – the whole global view – then I can drink from it forever!' But you can't have the akashic records – it doesn't do it. You need some milk and some nourishment.

Eleonora: And the Eight?

Faisal: Type Eight is the pituitary, the master gland that can balance the hormones. Eight is [about] extremes, they are very 'extremist' and their extremism is due to this gland. When open, there is peacefulness and empowerment, you are majestic. When closed, there is 'kill' – the kill. When the pituitary gland creates imbalance in the hormones, it creates insanity inside. Eights fear insanity so much, but they are cosmic insanity. Once they see it, they can balance this organ, relax and allow it to function.

Eleonora: Well, I think it is really fascinating to see how as spirit we come into the world with the idea of healing the hole in the family: we create this fixation [Ennea-type] and we spend our lives trying to understand or fix the fixation. In addition to that, I also find fascinating the idea that the organs are connected to each particular type. I have not come across this before. So in healing the family hole, we also heal the organs.

Faisal: Yes, and balance them. Too much heart is too much heart; too much mind is too much mind. To reach this level of equanimity, harmony, and balance… and when you know which organ, you can address it. Nowadays, we live in an incredible field of riches, with homeopathy, Chinese medicine, food, so much to strengthen and to balance the organs with.

Eleonora: Very briefly, as we have less than one minute, what kind of suggestion can you make to people to embody and be in the Essence that we all intrinsically are and that we have lost sight of?

Faisal: I think the Essential Enneagram helps define our psychological dilemma and what we are doing. By having this riddle eased and resolved, something happens, very beautifully. When I realised that my family hole was about a specific thing… and when I felt it, I could ask myself 'What am I trying to do with my ego?'… And if that is ultimately what my ego is trying to do, I check: 'Do I really want that? That has nothing to do with me!'

Eleonora: Yes, and you let go of that.

Faisal: I let go and it spontaneously started to go and that gave me a deeper connection to 'Who am I? If I am not this, then what am I?' And that led to a discovery of the self.

Eleonora: In healing yourself you are healing your family, rather than trying to heal the family.

Faisal: Exactly, you heal yourself including letting go of this quality. When you reach that dimension of openness, then the quality is balanced. You have it because you already have too much of it. And the greater space of openness, instead of the mind and the fixation blocking the Absolute, it opens to the Absolute – to the field of richness. [Freedom from the attachment or obsession to any specific dimension of Essence or quality allows the person to be in the greater space of openness and freedom, which is the Absolute. - FM] In that field, you can interact with the souls of your parents even if they are not here. You send them blessings. We all got caught in the absence of gold. [Gold is the most needed state for the baby to attain ease and relaxation and self-regulation, and that need is the root of the deepest attachment to our parents. -FM] And from what I know, no time and space is between us and our loved ones. [From the place of Being, there is no time or space, so we can directly connect with the souls of our parents and reach true healing and completion. -FM] In that level, we can function in multidimensionality.

Eleonora: Wonderful, thank you, and on that note we have to stop. And if you want to find out a little bit more about the basics of the Enneagram, we have a whole series on the Enneagram on our website. Faisal, thank you so much for coming. It has been a little bit of a marathon, but we made it.

To watch this interview please go to:
http://www.conscious.tv/consciousness/enneagram

Claudio Naranjo
Seeker After Truth

Interview by Iain McNay

We are including in this book the interview below with Claudio Naranjo. It is not strictly speaking about the Enneagram, but it covers Claudio's story. He, along with Oscar Ichazo, is probably the most important person in developing and introducing the Enneagram to contemporary society. Claudio (originally from Chile) met the Bolivian Oscar Ichazo, who had learnt the 'bare bones' of the Enneagram from sources close to the Russian mystic Gurdjieff – and then added 'flesh on the bones' to help develop what has become the Enneagram as we use it today. Claudio's life is fascinating and not always easy. His story is also a reminder that the spiritual path is not always a smooth and straightforward process and can sometimes leave you for years in the wilderness.

Iain: Our guest today is Claudio Naranjo. Claudio is someone whose name has come up consistently over the years as someone who has had a great influence on people – and has had an influence on me as well. He's written over twenty books, but first of all I should welcome you, Claudio. Welcome to conscious.tv.
Claudio: Thank you.
Iain: He's written over twenty books. For my research I've looked through some of them, *The Way of Silence* and *Healing Civilization,* and two that aren't available now: one is *The Ennea-type Structures* [about] the Enneagram, and the other *The Psychology of Meditation* which you co-wrote many years ago. We're going to talk about Claudio's life. He's had many rich experiences and met and worked with many fascinating people. Originally you trained as a doctor, didn't you?
Claudio: Yes, as a medical doctor.

Iain: Then you met somebody when I think you were in your early twenties, Totila Albert, who was very influential on you.

Claudio: Yes, he was more influential on me than medical school. I had contact with him more or less during the time I was a medical student. And if I look back, certainly it was the most important influence of my early life and perhaps of my whole life. Even though I've been a thirsty seeker, I've sought in many directions, and some teachers brought me to levels of experience that were more dramatic. But with Totila Albert, I feel as if he were a graft on my life tree, something like a spiritual father.

Iain: What attracted you to him in the first place?

Claudio: I remember Gregory Bateson saying that the greatest explanations of things are stories. It would be easier to tell the story of how our friendship came about than say in an abstract way what attracted me. But let me try to do this as you ask. Nobody asked me this question before. I would say that I knew he knew. We met on the street. We were familiar with each other because he had been in my mother's house. My mother's house was a kind of salon. Claudio Arrau, the famous pianist, who was a friend of my mother, used to say that my mother's house was like the Mendelssohn house in Germany where many musicians met, where many artists met. It was smaller of course, and Totila Albert was a face I saw among my mother's guests when I was a child. But I never approached any of these people in my mother's house who spoke of serious things.

Iain: But when you said you knew he knew, what did that mean?

Claudio: We met on the street when I was in my last year of high school and he said, "How are you, Claudio?" And not knowing how to fill the emptiness of this 'How are you?' – he asked with such a degree of interest that I couldn't just dismiss the question in a banal way – so I had to say something. I told him about something I had written in the school magazine about a new renaissance coming about that would be not just like the Italian Renaissance, bound to a geographical zone, but a world renaissance. It was going to start in Bolivia and why I wrote this, I don't know. He heard me with interest and then he remarked, "I wish I could be as optimistic as you are." I asked with some wonder, "You don't agree?" as if I was naively in love with my idea of a new renaissance coming, though I had no basis to say it. It was just an intuition and I childishly believed in my own intuition. And he said, "I think we are in great trouble. We may even destroy ourselves." And this was in the late forties probably, when I was in my last year of school. When he said this, I knew this is the person I want to learn from because he knows first-hand what he is saying.

Even though he was talking about the world being in trouble and in great danger of self-destruction, this was a new idea to me and I trusted him. I should learn something from this man.

Iain: And what form did that teaching take?

Claudio: It was more his initiative than mine. From there we went to my house – my mother was in Europe – so I felt the freedom as a teenager to invite this man to my house because we were talking about music and I had composed something for viola and harpsichord – strangely – and he wanted to hear it. So I played [it] on the piano more or less from the score and he was impressed with my musicianship, and I think that was part of the glue that brought our friendship to the next stage. But it was he who took the initiative of calling me on the phone a couple of times to ask how I was. And then at the end of my first medical school year I had typhoid fever. I had to be in bed for forty days – the famous quarantine – and he came to see me, and he brought me a book of poetry he had written in Spanish. He was not as fluent in Spanish as in German, and I felt in the form of the poetry there was something like the organic form of plants. It was not formal poetry – there was one [line] spreading out like a triangle and on the opposite side – on the next page which completed the poem – it was a symmetrical triangle. There was an interplay between sound and visual form that I trusted as the fruit of a higher inspiration. And I was reading Kabbalah in those days during that quarantine, and there was an echo between what I was half understanding about the tree of life in Kabbalah and what he wrote. It was a fuzzy understanding, but it was a kind of mutual reinforcement of these two things that were mysteries to me. So I would say this prompted me to want to know more through him and I started to pump him for wisdom. I remember when I read Plato's *Symposium*, there is a remark about Apollodorus who says he follows Socrates and tries to learn even from the way he ties his sandals, and I felt this is how I feel about my friendship with Totila. I am absorbing something and I don't know exactly what it is. I would ask him questions. I would not understand very well many of the things he responded with, but something changed in me over time – I ripened. And he had many friends in the other worlds. I would say he was a close friend of Nietzsche, he was a close friend of Beethoven, a close friend of Goethe, of people he had read, or heard, and come to feel like soul brothers to such a degree that the way he talked about them made them seem like people in his family, and they slowly seeped into my own inner world as if they were also my family. It's as if he bequeathed me an inheritance of influences and enlarged my inner world.

Iain: And obviously there was this thirst inside you because you were very receptive to him.

Claudio: He had undergone the great journey of all times, the journey of the quest without teachers. He was struck as if by lightning by the death of his father, and that prompted his transformation that started him on the way. And I had faith in the things he said to me; they had a ring of truth.

Iain: Did trust come to you easily then? Because you mentioned a couple of times you had this trust in him.

Claudio: It has not happened often in my life. I had another friend by the same time who was also a Chilean poet – or Chilean-born, like Totila. I could say of him that I also learned from him. His name was David Rosenman and he's a world-renowned poet. I had the impression that he was an enlightened being. He was connected with an esoteric school I came to know later in my life... he opened to me much later in my life. He was a little bit like a shaman. He could know things I was thinking. He could read people through their hands, or he pretended to read through their hands. So this man had an influence, but I distrusted him very much and I disliked him. And he once remarked to me, he said, "You know, you dislike me and people dislike me generally. But fortunately *things* like me. And the things I do, like me. So I can be at peace." We had intimate discussions. We were really friends. So Totila Albert was an exception, he came to be something like the grandfather I didn't have, and I could also say the same of Gurdjieff's Beelzebub – Beelzebub as he tells his grandson of his adventures... he also seeped into my life as a Being, more than the things he says in his many pages.

Iain: But did you find it very hard to read that?

Claudio: I found it very hard and I kept going like the donkey after the carrot, because he always promises that in the next page we'll get it, and the next page, and the next chapter. And I kept going on with a vague sense that – as frustrated as I was in finding the answer to what he was offering – the carrot would lead me on and on, but I was getting something: and in retrospect, I have the impression I was getting an impact of his Being, of Gurdjieff's Being projected through Beelzebub.

Iain: I know that you quite quickly got disillusioned with medicine, especially the way that medicine was taught and practised. Then you moved to Berkeley in California a few years later, and that was very much a significant time for you, wasn't it?

Claudio: Yes, well, I was disappointed with medicine and with Totila's influence. In spite of feeling he was a great Being, I felt he was not a teacher. I wanted to meet somebody like Gurdjieff. I had this image of what a teacher could be, somebody who can kick you into the next step, somebody who can tell you not to go this way, not to be this way. And Totila was always loving, I never felt there was anything wrong with me in his company. I remember saying he was like somebody who sings from the other shore, but he's not a boatman. I want a boatman, or a repair man.

Iain: Somebody who's going to direct you...

Claudio: ...and challenge me, and I met that in Fritz Perls.

Iain: I know when you first went to Berkeley you did a Zen course with Suzuki Roshi.

Claudio: That too.

Iain: Initiation to meditation, I think.

Claudio: I started meditating – Zen meditation – but in parallel I started to attend workshops, whenever it was possible, with Fritz Perls. And Fritz Perls was also like a Zen master, like the ones in the books who would not tell you just to sit, but would kick you into enlightenment, or say very challenging things or dismiss you.

Iain: I just want to go back a little bit because when I was doing my research, there was quite a fascinating story about how you met Carlos Castaneda before he wrote any of his books, before he was famous. Somebody introduced you to him and said, "You two guys should meet. You'd get on." And I think you drove to Esalen together – Carlos drove you – and you knocked at the door and the person who opened the door was Fritz Perls, which was an incredible start!

Claudio: Yes. The real start of that story is that a man called Michael Harner, the head of the Loamy Anthropology – the museum on campus – once called me and said, "I would like you to meet another shaman's apprentice here, or sorcerer's apprentice," he said, and he brought me together with Carlos Castaneda and proposed that the three of us come to Esalen and do a workshop on shamanism. And so we came as apprentices of shamanism. Carlos had not written his first book yet, and I had the challenging experience of having Fritz in my audience as I was talking about shamanism. And Fritz was a very argumentative person, polemical. But it was all filled with synchronies, and it was very remarkable that when Carlos and I after four hours driving were about to knock at the door of what's called the Big House in Esalen, the door opened by itself because Fritz was coming out at that very moment. So he introduced himself, "I'm Fritz Perls," and I'd read his book, his book from the fifties, and I had given lectures inspired by that book even in Chile. So I asked the silly question any tourist could ask, or a cocktail party question, "Have you written anything new?" He gave me a very interesting answer: he said, "I don't have much compassion for humankind." Something of that sort.

Iain: That's a strange answer, actually.

Claudio: As if implying on the one hand 'Don't think that I'm a good person or a kind person', but saying at the same time the only valid reason to write is if you have compassion: 'I don't write for show'. 'I don't write for intellectual performance'. 'I'm not part of the academic game'. It was all blended into that response, and that interested me very much.

Iain: I know at that time – or roughly that time – you were experimenting with LSD and ecstasy. They were both legal then. What kind of influence did they have on you to start with?

Claudio: Well, ecstasy I introduced later. I was the one who hit on that whole family of drugs.

Iain: You actually discovered…? I didn't realise that.

Claudio: I discovered MDA and then I explored a number of derivatives or related compounds, and it was Sasha [Alexander] Shulgin who discovered that MDMA, which is ecstasy, was available in catalogues of chemicals. So he gave me the information, and I was in Chile where there were no prohibition laws, and I worked in medical school, so I could do a lot of experimenting. I was an associate of Sasha Shulgin, who was a great chemist, who had a very great talent in synthesis, so I was the Chilean partner who did the clinical experiments, tests.

Iain: And how did you actually do those tests?

Claudio: I usually started with myself as a guinea pig in small amounts, and then went up. Then with people I knew, volunteers, and then with patients to see how it worked in healing. I tested many of them, many of which are not in the books, only in some magazines like *Nature*. They didn't come to be street drugs, but I introduced a number of drugs, also ibogaine from Africa. There was a factory in France selling it as a form of convalescence, but they didn't know that in high doses this was used in greater amounts by the natives for initiations. I suspected that ibogaine would be a hallucinogenic and I tested it on myself too.

Iain: What effect did it have on your view of consciousness when you first took ecstasy?

Claudio: When I first took ecstasy – this was much after the time we're talking about when I came to Esalen. When I came to Esalen, I had conducted experiments that became very much talked about – on the alkaloids of a plant in Brazil and Peru and Ecuador, called sometimes ayahuasca, sometimes yagé. I had been to Colombia to visit some Indian tribes and search for information about yagé and collected enough samples of the plant, started experimenting in Chile with this plant and conducted chemical analyses too. And these were very traumatic experiments because a great number of the people hallucinated snakes, or tigers, and this was not influenced by my telling them this came from the tropics, or that it was used in Indian cultures. I was only telling them – my volunteers, "This is an extract of a plant we want to experiment on." I gave no information whatsoever, but the visions that they reported were comparable to the visions of the natives in Colombia, so it was very intriguing. Is there a case of telepathy from the Indians? Or is it a demonstration of the collective unconscious? How can this be explained, that the imagery of the Indians is the imagery of my volunteers? It was certainly a demonstration that it's not a cultural artefact that Indians have these visions because they are taught, or they're told, so they expect to have them.

Iain: And what was your view at the time of what was happening?

Claudio: I was intrigued by it. I was inclined to think that there are certain experiences that are naturally translated into images and that these could be regarded as experiences of our reptilian brain, of a very primitive, instinctive brain and just like the kundalini experience, which is also symbolised naturally, or visualised sometimes in connection with the snake. So my take on it was that this is an artificial trigger of the kundalini experience.

Iain: Going back to Fritz Perls, what did you feel you really got from working with Fritz Perls?

Claudio: [*laughing*] Nobody has asked me, again, this question in a such a long life. I got more honest and I got to be more daring. I remember those years in his workshops, I was a better seeker than ever before, or after perhaps, to the extent I was willing to let go of everything but my impulse to go forward and let myself be guided by him. There was even a point where I overdid it and he said, "I am not interested in corpses." I had said to him, "I'm ready to be open like somebody who is before a surgeon," and he saw that that was a corpse-like attitude, too passive. He wanted me to take more initiative. He was a genius of therapy interaction, but the word 'therapy' gets to be too small. It's as if he knew what's missing, and like a Zen master knows when to ring the bell for you to leave because you haven't given a satisfactory answer, he would be dismissive. What I got, I might explain it by going back to my first session with him and to my fear. I had been told that he was a kind of surgeon and that it was a painful experience because he was so blunt. And I remember thinking, 'If what he says to me is true, and I'm looking for the truth, how can I be hurt if I'm getting what I came for? I should be grateful if what he says is true. And if he tells me something about myself that's hurtful because it's not true, then how can it be hurtful if it's not true?'

Iain: It's an intriguing question.

Claudio: It was an act of surrender after examining my motives, reaffirming my wish to surrender in a way to him, to his influence. So in a sense I could say I learned to make myself open to somebody with a higher authority, experience-wise. Not as an intellectual authority. Open to guidance.

Iain: This sort of burning within you for the truth, what did that feel like at the time, can you remember?

Claudio: Oh yes. I had been a seeker since I was twelve, when somebody gave me books by Vivekananda and by somebody who wrote under the name Ramacharaka, some American yogi. And these books had the influence on me of turning me into a seeker in a kind of not-active-enough way. It's as if the word 'Om' became a natural symbol of something I wished for, and because I had this thirst that was answered by 'Om' rather than answered by any worldly goal, I was in a sense protected by this awareness of seeking. Protected from becoming too ambitious and of saying 'What I want is this girl', of interpreting my search in any way less profound.

Iain: It was keeping you focused somehow.

Claudio: Yes, I was in search of something, I had an awareness of seeking. But at the time I attended my first workshop with Fritz Perls and he said, "What are you feeling now?" I said, "I feel such a yearning. It's like thirsting for... what can I say? Thirsting for Being." And he was very dismissive and said, "Tell me something more concrete. How do you feel in your body?" He wanted sensations. He wanted down-to-earth experiences and not these spiritual interpretations of experience, from his point of view. So I had a kind of rejection from him as an opening, but I do remember the feeling in answer to your question 'How did it feel?' Like a thirst. This satisfaction has an emptiness. An emptiness and a hope that this emptiness could be filled. For a long time I thought it would be filled with some kind of knowledge, and then I went to medical school thinking scientific knowledge would fill it, and I was disappointed in that. But then it was a kind of higher knowledge I was seeking and Fritz Perls would not reinforce that. He thought I needed to know something more basic about myself than know what I was standing on, or what my down-to-earth experience was.

Iain: I need to move you on because there's so much to cover and unfortunately our time is finite in this interview. I know that after a time you returned to Chile, and I think it was there you met Oscar Ichazo, who was Bolivian. Again, he was a great influence on your life, but also it was challenging in a way because you weren't sure, when you first met him, were you? I think you heard about him first, from students of yours.

Claudio: Yes, my students told me, "You must come and meet this man." And there was a sense that when people are ready a teacher appears. I left a group without a head when I came back to Berkeley. I had started a group on some work... and this emptiness came, and was filled with visits from Ichazo who was living in Bolivia at the time – he was a Bolivian. And they recommended I come down, and they said extraordinary things about him. When he first received me in the house he was occupying in Santiago he was very polite: "Come this way, Doctor, sit down please. I'm sorry I'm not wearing a tie" [*both laughing*]. I felt he was playing a role and I disdained him from the beginning – excessively polite, excessively conventional. He didn't command admiration from me and as time went on, I saw he was not reliable and he seemed to be intentionally showing me he was not reliable.

Iain: But there was something else there, wasn't there, that was very strong for you?

Claudio: There were two things. One is, he was my connection to the mysterious school behind Gurdjieff. The only person I knew who claimed to be in contact with that mother school.

Iain: Did you feel he had been to the same mother school as Gurdjieff?

Claudio: Not only did I feel, but there was some confirmation, confirmation of a different nature. Once he told me Gurdjieff was in the courts. "What do you mean, in the courts?" And he said, "Court of the Bees." And I said, "The ceremony?" [Ichazo replied,] "Ah you know about the ceremony… yes, that's where I come from." So there were moments of confirmation in private conversation. He once told me a story very much like the one told by Gurdjieff in his autobiography, *Meetings with Remarkable Men,* when he crosses a high bridge blind-folded – the same story. I didn't know whether it was true or not true, but he was letting me know he was in touch with those people, and the main argument for my thinking he was, was such a convincing body of knowledge related to the Enneagram. It was not knowledge that Gurdjieff had put out, but it was completely coherent with Gurdjieff's manner of discussing the Enneagram as a universal map that could be applied to different levels of experience. So here was the next chapter.

Iain: And where do you feel that Oscar had got this information on the Enneagram from? I've heard different stories, one that he got it in Afghanistan, another that he actually channelled it. What's your own feeling from what he told you?

Claudio: Well, he told me a number of things over time, but perhaps I should preface everything I say about him by telling you that he never described any of the character types. When people say 'a [Type] One is like this' or 'a Two is like that' or 'the pride type has such-and-such traits', that comes from my own work. And that's why only people that came through my school became teachers of the Enneagram. Everybody who's been taught the Enneagram has been taught by somebody in my original school, or some have become teachers like Sandra Maitri and like Hameed, who became Almaas. They were not in Arica, but there were a couple of people who were in Arica, like John Lilly, or my helper Rosalyn Schaffer who was in my original SAT group. She had been in Arica and she was amazed how she was hearing for the first time descriptions of the characters that Oscar had never produced, and this is what people took notes about – and transmitted to people outside our group even though there had been a commitment.

Iain: The image I'm getting is that you took a basic map that you had from Oscar and that you filled in lots of details.

Claudio: I filled it in. And as Oscar said, "I have been trained as a seed individual many times…" his function was to be a seed individual. It took many years for me to understand that what I had done was to water the seed. I had cultivated the seed and everything that emerged from my work was of that sort: fleshing in the skeletal information or the schemes he passed on.

Iain: And then, I know that you lost your son. Your son died and this was obviously personally a big blow to you, but it also opened a new stage in your life and I think – I don't know if it was at Oscar's suggestion but certainly under his guidance – that you went into the desert in Arica for forty days and forty nights.

Claudio: Yes. And the way that happened was that I told him in Santiago the year before, six months before approximately, I said, "Can I be your student? Given the fact that you seem to me to be a liar and a trickster, can I still work under you?"

Iain: You asked him this?

Claudio: Yes, "…given that I see you as a liar and a manipulator." And to me, the decisive factor in joining him was that he smiled. He smiled kindly and said, "Yes, you have been disappointed many times. I honour your distrust. But you see, our way does not require great veneration. Our way is almost scientific. All that's required is that you work and you let me work." And that was to me what made it possible to go ahead, but I was undecided still and he said, "Eventually it's by the fruit that you will know whether I am for real or not. And you won't have to wait for long because I want to make you a very special offer. I want to send you to the desert for forty days, and that's all that it will take and you will call the higher bodies and you will find everything you have been looking for. Just forty days." And how could I not accept that offer? I came to Arica because it was understood between us that this was a secret at the time, that after a couple of months there with the group at Arica, he would send me secretly to the desert. I would have to make up some excuse for disappearing from the community… and then he did strange things, like he betrayed our secret. He told the group that I had gone on my own to the desert probably thinking I was the second Jesus Christ, thinking I'm better than the group and failing in a sense of commitment and sense of community. He was very critical of me for going to the desert, but I was bound to the secret between us: that he had sent me.

Iain: And what happened to you in the desert?

Claudio: It's very hard to put into words because the basis of everything was a deep silence. It was like a fountain coming out of silence, out of nothingness. I'm reminded of a Sufi story of somebody who has to go into a kind of Aladdin's cave and find a candlestick of iron, and he finds so many pearls and emeralds and fills his tunic with all kinds of pearls and almost forgets the candlestick of iron. Afterwards everything dematerialises, everything is gone, and only the candlestick remains. It's as if everything flowed from my ability to get out of the way, to empty myself, but from this self-emptying came all kinds of visions, insights and understandings, rituals. My hands would go into movement [*waving hands in circles*] and do all kinds of things as if I was in synchrony with something that was much beyond me. It was a cosmic event and I was at the same time experiencing this as if it were the development of an embryo, as if an embryo had been born in me and I was beginning to experience its life.

CONVERSATIONS ON THE ENNEAGRAM

Iain: Were you completely alone for the forty days?

Claudio: He visited me several times. He validated for instance this insight: that some of the physical feelings of the movement of energy that are explained as energy moving between the chakras are actually embryonal feelings. I remember for instance the embryo: that this heart is formed next to the brain and then descends. And the testicles are originally formed where the kidneys are, and then descend. So I would feel these movements as if it was a flow, and I had a sense that this was something like an embryonal process. I remember telling him and he said, "Yes! You've discovered it's like Columbus' egg. I never thought of it, but that's it!" And so he would validate my experiences and tell me that I was going through something that he had gone through, and that it had been a great event in the school, as if for a Westerner to experience this somehow went beyond the previous-generation level of experience. It was a kind of prophetic feel for the way he talked about our experiences, as if this were something necessary for a new world.

Iain: You spent a year with him altogether, didn't you? And you saw him most days during that year?

Claudio: More or less, yes.

Iain: A very intense time…

Claudio: Less than a year.

Iain: Did you feel awakened afterwards? How did you feel in terms of your spiritual development after the time with him?

Claudio: It was as if I could switch into another level of my mind. I was not continuously there, but in meditation I could go into a deeper self… in contact with a deeper self than I had known before. And from there I looked upon my ordinary life as very pitiful. From my expanded awareness, I felt as if I had no arms and no legs and no voice. If I talked, it was my old self speaking. I didn't feel good about myself. It was as if having a higher self meant that my ordinary self became lower than ever. And this was a factor of growth, of purification, or stimulus.

Iain: So there was still a process in a way going on…

Claudio: No, not in the same way. There was a time when I felt I was going up and up. This proceeded for several months and then I had a kind of full birth experience. Like my experiences in the desert – many were with my eyes closed – of going into myself. And several months later when I was back in the city, when I went to my mother's house in Santiago, I was more eyes-open in the world and everything became the divine presence in the outer world too, everything became divine. I started writing an autobiography a couple of years later. I called it *Rolling down Mount Sinai* because from there onwards it was coming down, gradually. I felt it was progress, as if coming down the mountain was coming down and integrating with ordinary awareness. Integrating with other people, beginning to teach, but at the same time it was as if a seed gets to be used up when it's transformed into the growing shoots. I was becoming new life, but I was disappearing. The source, like a yolk sack, was being consumed…

Iain: Like the caterpillar and the butterfly.

Claudio: …and then I came to Berkeley and started to teach and as I taught again, it was another burst of…

Iain: Let me just stop you there… because you started a small group called SAT, Seekers After Truth, which I think Gurdjieff had also used a similar name.

Claudio: Yes, I imitated Gurdjieff's…

Iain: I know two people in that early group were Hameed Ali, whom you mentioned earlier – A.H. Almaas – and also Sandra Maitri, who've both written books about the Enneagram. Sandra was telling me that at the time, that group was very important because you were the only person who was available and bringing together spirituality with psychology.

Claudio: Yes, that was my attempt. I wanted to integrate what I learned from Mahesh and Oscar together with Buddhism and with psychotherapy. So it was a tall order – high aspiration. Buddhist meditation was part of it and psychological exercises. I tried to translate much of psychological knowledge into exercises people could practice with each other so as to become independent of a therapist.

Iain: Yes, enquiry type exercises…

Claudio: But then I was also feeling I was losing it. There was a kind of friction with the group, using up energy, and I felt as if I was using up my reserves, and I tried to compensate by meditating more. I became a kind of hermit at home. When I was not with the group, I was meditating all the time as if going back to my life in the desert, trying to not lose altitude, trying to go against this descent. But it was unavoidable. I kept going down and down and it was the entry into the so-called dark night of the soul.

Iain: What did that feel like practically? Did you have less energy? Was it a mental darkness?

Claudio: Well, grace cannot be described, but when you fall out of grace you know it. It's as if loss of inspiration, loss of creativity, loss of motivation… a kind of apathy.

Iain: Did that scare you at the time?

Claudio: I had, for many, many years, kept journals. It's the first time in life when I stopped writing. I had nothing to write about. I didn't have the motive to write, or a sense of interest in what I could say. When it came to the worst, the nadir point, the deepest, I felt like a fool. I felt embarrassment about my own foolishness and I think it's the enlargement of something I had always felt. I always felt awkward as a teenager. I always felt prone to ridicule, and this was as if this basic feeling that had been latent, or hidden behind other things, now became the foreground.

CONVERSATIONS ON THE ENNEAGRAM

Iain: The deepest conditioning was coming forward.

Claudio: Yes, it came to the surface. I was invited to teach at the University of California at Santa Cruz, and I was so embarrassed to be up there teaching the group and feeling 'I am not embodying the things I'm teaching. Who am I to teach this or that…?'

Iain: But people got a lot out of the SAT group, didn't they?

Claudio: Oh, the SAT group. That was before I had fallen.

Iain: But you did mention starting at that time…

Claudio: People got a kind of speeding up of their own process. Many people who were not seekers became seekers. Other people found their way to the next step in their life. Some people went into Tibetan Buddhism, other people went into the Bob Hoffman [process] work. Other people became therapists and tried to help others.

Iain: You were a real catalyst at the time.

Claudio: I was a very strong catalyst. And in a sense it was not something I was doing, it was more like Totila Albert said of his poetry: he never knew what he would write, but his hand moved as if by itself. Much of what is now in the Enneagram literature came to me by automatic writing. That also happened to me. But there was that quality even in my speech, as if I didn't know what would come out of my mouth during a session. I could trust that it would be of interest and people would get their tape recorders out. There was a sense of some precious material coming out.

Iain: This period lasted about fifteen years, didn't it?

Claudio: No, the rich period about three years only.

Iain: No, I mean when you were in the decline.

Claudio: Oh, the dark period. Yes, that was long.

Iain: Did you despair sometimes?

Claudio: Yes I did. Sometimes I blamed myself for having done something wrong, for having allowed my inspiration to make my ego bigger – being so near to the spiritual source became a kind of narcissistic satisfaction. I always felt I had nothing to give. Even when I trained as a psychoanalyst, I couldn't sustain the psychoanalytic role because it was like cheating people. I didn't feel I could really help such desperate people who wanted my help. I was too sensitive to that. And now I had my hands full, so I was able to give for the first time, and it was such a joyous thing that when I was empty-handed again for some time [I] interpreted [it] as if I was giving out of personal satisfaction: 'See! Finally I am somebody who has something to give!' It was an ego-contamination. Then I came to appreciate that it was also a gift, for the grace to be taken away. I was learning to be empty-handed; I was learning to become poor.

Iain: So there was somehow an acceptance that was evolving…

Claudio: It was a full training. And of course I kept reading things – and knowing that the Sufis know this process very well as a time of expansion and time of contraction, and time of contraction is a blessing. I'd read how St John of the Cross says that when we enter the dark night, it's as if it's not like breast feeding any longer. We don't feel the abundance which is like breast feeding, because we need to learn to eat solid food and chew and walk with our own legs and not be carried in our mother's arms.

Iain: Now you're teaching again. You're in London to do some teaching this coming weekend…

Claudio: Well, I've been teaching for the last twenty years or so. What I started in Berkeley, and then dropped and closed down, was re-born in Spain in the late eighties as SAT programmes in Europe. I've been doing that for a long time, and during the last ten years or so I've become especially interested in getting teachers to go through this programme because I feel that if teachers get this transformative experience, they will pass it on more to their students, to society, not just like psychologists I'd been working with before, and psychotherapists. They help a few patients, but they don't make such a dent on society. So I've become more sensitive to the world and more interested in doing something about the world, and I have a feeling that SAT is like a missing link in the process of changing education, or changing other institutions.

Iain: One thing you said to me on the phone last night when I asked you how you felt these days, was that you… "felt the taste of abundance."

Claudio: Yes.

Iain: I thought that was lovely.

Claudio: Yes, I used the phrase some minutes ago: 'I've been a thirsty seeker'. Very thirsty, always seeking, seeking, seeking, almost to the point of despair. Over-seeking and not minding earthly affairs very well because the seeking impulse has been so strong. And now I cannot say I'm a seeker, I'm a waiter [*both laughing*].

Iain: You're a waiter!

Claudio: I'm somebody who's going with the stream and knowing that the stream is taking us very near the time and place when it comes into the ocean. I can smell the ocean.

Iain: Thank you, Claudio, very much, for coming and talking to us on conscious.tv. I think you've been incredibly honest, so I really appreciate that. Your life has been very rich and you've had wonderful experiences.

To watch this interview please go to:
http://www.conscious.tv/consciousness/transformations

CONVERSATIONS ON THE ENNEAGRAM

BIBLIOGRAPHY

My life journey with the Enneagram continues to be a deeply personal experience, including the series on conscious.tv – which in many ways was miraculous. Many of my valued teachers were interviewed in the series, during which most of the books and websites on this list were mentioned. I have added a few more that were instrumental on my path, books that deepened and refined my Enneagram adventures. May these treasures enrich your life as they have enriched mine, and may they inspire you to search for more discoveries among the many wonderful resources now appearing in the world of the Enneagram.

A.H. Almaas, *Facets of Unity: The Enneagram of Holy Ideas* (2000). *The Pearl Beyond Price* (2000).

Claudio Naranjo, *Character and Neurosis* (1984). *Ennea-Type Structures* (1991). *The Way of Silence* (2006). *Healing Civilization* (2010).

David Daniels and **Virginia Price**, *The Essential Enneagram* (2009).

Don Riso and **Russ Hudson**, *Personality Types: Using the Enneagram for Self-discovery* (1996). *The Wisdom of the Enneagram: Complete Guide to Psychological and Spiritual Growth for the Nine Personality Types* (1999).

Eric Salmon, *The ABC of the Enneagram* (2003).

Ginger Lapid-Bogda, *Bringing Out the Best in Yourself at Work* (2004). *What Type of Leader Are You?* (2007). *Bringing Out the Best in Everyone You Coach* (2009).

Helen Palmer, *The Enneagram in Love and Work: Understanding Your Intimate and Business Relationships* (1995). *The Pocket Enneagram* (1995). *The Enneagram Advantage* (1997). *Inner Knowing* (1998). *The Enneagram: Understanding Yourself and the Others in Your Life* (1999).

Renee Baron and **Elizabeth Wagele**, *The Enneagram Made Easy* (1994).

Sanda Maitri, *The Spiritual Dimension of the Enneagram* (2001). *The Enneagram of Passions and Virtues* (2009).

Tom Condon, *The Dynamic Enneagram* (2007 an ebook serial).

WEBSITES

www.claudionaranjo.net
www.diamondlogos.com
www.enneagram.com and *www.enneagram-europe.com* and
www.enneagramworldwide.com
www.enneagraminstitute.com
www.ridhwan.org
www.sandramaitri.com
www.thechangeworks.com
www.theenneagraminbusiness.com

CONSCIOUS.TV

Information

conscious.tv is a UK-based TV channel broadcasting on the Internet at www.conscious.tv. Our programmes are also shown on SKY TV and FREESAT. Our aim is to stimulate debate, question, enquire, inform, enlighten, encourage, and inspire people in the areas of consciousness, science, non-duality, and spirituality.

You will also find on our website the transcripts of many of the programmes under the Transcripts section. There is also an Audio section where the audio only versions of the programmes can be streamed or downloaded.

We have two email newsletters. The first is a general newsletter that we send out every three months, and the second is our 'New Programme Alert' list where you will be notified every time a new programme is available to watch on the channel. Email us at info@conscious.tv if you would like to be included on either or both of these lists. We are always open to ideas for interesting people to interview. Do let us know if you have any suggestions.

We are run by a team of volunteers and are not a commercial business. If you would like to help us in any way, then do contact us at info@conscious.tv and let us know your skills and how you feel you could help out.

www.conscious.tv

CONSCIOUS.TV

The idea

It was approaching midnight on the 31st December 2006. My wife Renate and I were celebrating New Year's Eve on the island of La Gomera, in the Canary Islands. As usual, she was drinking Champagne and I was sipping my glass of mineral water. I had recently reached my sixtieth birthday and we were having a lively discussion about the things we hadn't yet done in our lives that we would still like to do.

"It would be great to have a TV station," I pronounced. "I could combine all my interests: consciousness, football, music, hiking – make some new programmes and broadcast some existing ones. We can get literally hundreds of channels on our TV at home and they are nearly all rubbish. I am sure I can do much better than that," I declared.

It was of course true that I had no experience in television at all, but on the other hand I had built a successful record label and music publishing company without ever knowing anything about music. I couldn't play any musical instruments and certainly couldn't read music. But I knew what I liked and I trusted my instincts. I had hired good people to work for me. I had learnt that if I couldn't do something then I had to find someone good who could complement me. "It can't be that hard to make decent, interesting television programmes," I added. I thought about it some more. "I could easily come up with plenty of programmes. I could start a satellite channel in the UK, and I am sure people would watch it." The mineral water was beginning to talk enthusiastically.

The next day we hiked into the hills behind the hotel where we were staying. Something was definitely brewing in me. The more I thought about the idea, the more I liked it. Soon after we arrived back in England, I made some enquiries and discovered that to start a proper satellite channel was going to cost getting on £500,000 a year. And that was just to rent the satellite space and the programme listing space. It didn't include the cost of making any programmes, or the overhead costs. That was definitely a step too far.

I also talked over the idea with various friends; they thought combining all my different interests wasn't going to work. "The channel would be too diverse, you would confuse people," most of them commented. "Why don't you focus on the consciousness side? No one else is doing that and there is plenty of football and music on TV already." Life went on, but the idea lingered and often surfaced in my mind. I lowered my sights a little. Maybe I could piggy-back on someone else's channel and just show a few hours of programmes a week. That seemed much more realistic. I found out that this was called a micro channel and other people were doing it. I had a few meetings, but I still felt it was working out too expensive. I was happy to spend money, but I wanted to spend it effectively.

It was now late in 2007 and Internet TV was just beginning to be established. By this time I had thought up a name: conscious.tv. I liked it, registered it, and decided to make some programmes. I rang a few TV studios and couldn't find anything under about £3,000 a day; and then, of course, there were editing costs afterwards. That was still too much. My music company had started in 1978 and was born out of the first wave of punk music. Punk was a revolution; it quickly turned a boring stagnant music industry upside down. It wasn't just about the music, it was also about the way the music was sold, promoted, and marketed. Records that cost very little to make started to sell in decent quantities. People were ready for something new. The music industry was stuck in a groove and needed a kick. I felt television was the same. People were spending fortunes making programmes that just weren't very good, in my eyes anyway. Persisting, I found a TV studio in Acton, in West London, that would do me a deal for a day: they would record the programmes as if they were live, and I could pretty much walk out with the finished programmes. This was more like it. This was what I was used to. Something that was more instant.

On 2nd November 2007 I made four programmes. I was the interviewer as I didn't have anyone else to do it. None of the programmes were very good (and I have taken them all down now). But I was determined to learn fast. Three weeks later I was back in the studio for another full day of making programmes. I had coached myself and was much better as an interviewer this time; I felt I was getting somewhere. I had also remembered a spiritual retreat that I had attended a few months earlier. We had spent four days listening to everyone else's life stories. That was seventy stories in four days. It was an extraordinarily powerful few days. I had known all those people for twelve or thirteen years, and to hear the detail of their lives was a revelation. It was very moving and touching at times. I realised that with conscious.tv I wanted to create something similar. I wanted people to learn, to be stimulated, to be encouraged, and to be touched. I was also enjoying the challenge. I liked creating something from nothing and seeing where it could go. I would book the studio for an eight-hour day, 11.00am to 7.00pm, and then invite five or six people to interview. To start with, it was mainly friends and people I already knew as I didn't feel confident enough yet to invite people I hadn't met. Conscious.tv was a free service and I wasn't in a position to pay any fees or expenses, so I was really asking people to take part in an experiment in a new form of TV: making programmes cheaply for a niche viewing audience. Having said that, I felt the programmes were technically reasonable enough. We had three cameras in a proper studio, and

CONVERSATIONS ON THE ENNEAGRAM

the director would switch from one to the other so it gave the feel of a proper programme, which of course it was. I was learning a lot, and fast.

By April 2008, I felt I had enough interviews to launch the channel on the Internet. People's response was slow to start with, but I wasn't going to do any marketing as such. The phrase 'build it and they will come' was rooted in me. I felt what I was doing was interesting and different. The word would slowly get out there. For the first few months, I didn't even check how many people were viewing the programmes. I didn't want to depress myself if the numbers were very low. I just wanted to keep going. I was enjoying the project and felt the programmes were getting better and better. And then four months or so after we started, three emails came in one week, from people I didn't know, who had found the channel and enjoyed it. Something was starting to happen....

Around this time, I was talking with an old friend, Kate Parker, who suggested, "You should make some programmes on non-duality. Talk to Julian Noyce at Non-Duality Press. He'll have some idea of who, amongst the authors that he publishes, might be willing to be interviewed."

I called Julian and explained my idea. He mused for several seconds before suggesting Jeff Foster and Richard Sylvester. And so Jeff and Richard came along to the studio in Acton one afternoon and the Non-Duality section was born. Within a few months, it became the most popular section. Renate started to help me by doing some interviews herself. People seemed to like our style. Something was now quickly building. We were soon receiving emails daily from people with suggestions of people to interview or indeed, people who wanted to be interviewed themselves. Although our interview style may look casual, we actually do a fair amount research for most of our interviews, and that takes time. We quickly learnt that we needed to be pretty selective about who appears on conscious.tv. We decided the solution was simply to interview only people we personally find interesting. People would sometimes object, "You should interview so and so; lots of people will watch it. You will find more viewers." But we weren't to be swayed. Conscious.tv is an integral part of our own personal journey, and all the interviews in this book have been important for us.

As I update this in 2015, we have made nearly 400 programmes. Apart from being available on www.conscious.tv, all the programmes are on YouTube; we now get many thousands of programmes watched each day on the Internet. We also have our micro channel on Satellite TV (via SKY and FreeSat – check www.conscious.tv for up-to-date details), with programmes broadcast daily in the UK. Our adventure is ongoing, and while we still enjoy it we will continue.

Iain McNay
iain@conscious.tv
Oxfordshire, UK 2015

ACKNOWLEDGEMENTS

This collection of transcripts was made possible by a generous group of volunteers who over the years have spent many, many hours painstakingly writing down the dialogues as recorded in these video programmes. The manuscript has gone through several editing processes with the aim, though, of presenting a book which expresses the flavour and particular characteristics of each Enneagram panel and of each interviewee. Whilst the language in parts may appear not strictly correct, it is nevertheless a representation of the verbal expression of each Enneagram type.

Grateful thanks to all our volunteers particularly Cindy King and Liz Ogilvie, who between them have transcribed many of the chapters in this book. Thanks also to volunteer transcribers Alva Eagland, Ann Kho, Gloria Oelman, Janet Nunn, Jeanet van De Riet, Joshua French, Judith Priest, Pamela D'Ambrosio, Renate Bohm and Samantha Veater.

Special thanks to Cat Anderson for her brilliant copy-editing skills and for putting so much heart into smoothing differences among transcription styles, making this book a singular pleasure to read.

The programmes would not have been possible without the contribution of all the individuals who took part in this project by generously giving of their time, openness and vulnerability.

Many thanks to: James Barlow, Anne Martin, Carlos Silva, Paul Burrows, Gill Harris, Renate McNay, Maureen Gallagher, Pat Knightley, Janette Blakemore, Rosemarie Morgan-Watson, Phil Dickinson, Angelina Bennet, Heather Brown, Kilian Gilbert, Grahame Morgan-Watson, Judith Priest, Lynne Citroen-Barratt, Chris Walton, Nina Grunfeld, Daniel Conway, Phil Wallace, Lynne Sedgmore, Christine Adames, Dottie Baynham, Cate Parker and Sam Settle.

My deepest gratitude to **Tom Condon, Ginger Lapid-Bogda, Sandra Maitri, Faisal Muqaddam, Claudio Naranjo,** and **Helen Palmer** for their willingness to be interviewed on conscious.tv and to be featured in this book. Each one of them, directly and indirectly, has contributed to my psychological and spiritual maturation.

Eleonora Gilbert, Editor
Berkshire, UK 2015

Conversations on Non-Duality
Twenty-six Awakenings

Edited by Eleonora Gilbert

Self-realisation, awakening or enlightenment has been the goal of spiritual seeking since time immemorial. Another way of putting this is simply to say that everyone is searching for happiness. What is the nature of this happiness? What is the self that is to be realised? What is meant by 'awakening' or 'enlightenment?' Can it be brought about by effort? To whom does it occur? How is it expressed in life?

Everybody seeks happiness, although it is not often noticed that seeking itself is precisely the activity that veils the very happiness that is being sought. When it is seen clearly that happiness is not to be found in any particular object, state or circumstance, a deep relaxation takes place. This relaxation leaves us at the threshold of another possibility. This possibility is felt as an invitation from an unknown and yet strangely familiar direction. It is a call to return to our true home, the source of happiness.

Conversations on Non-Duality gives twenty-six expressions of liberation which have been shaped by different life experiences, each offering a unique perspective.

David Bingham, Daniel Brown, Sundance Burke, Katie Davis, Peter Fenner, Steve Ford, Jeff Foster, Suzanne Foxton, Gangaji, Richard Lang, Roger Linden, Wayne Liquorman, Francis Lucille, Mooji, Catherine Noyce, Jac O'Keeffe, Tony Parsons, Bernie Prior, Halina Pytlasinska, Genpo Roshi, Florian Schlosser, Mandi Solk, Rupert Spira, James Swartz, Richard Sylvester and Pamela Wilson.

CHERRY RED
BOOKS

Cherry Red Books (a division of Cherry Red Records Ltd),
Power Road Studios, 114 Power Road, Chiswick, London W4 5PY